This is the first book thoroughly to explore the musical style of Henry Purcell. In this comprehensive study, Martin Adams identifies music by other composers, both within England and from abroad, which influenced Purcell's compositional decisions. Using a mix of broad stylistic observation and detailed analysis, Adams distinguishes between late-seventeenth-century English style in general and Purcell's style in particular, and chronicles the changes in the composer's approach to the main genres in which he worked, especially the newly emerging ode and English opera. As a result, Adams reveals that although Purcell went through a marked stylistic development, encompassing an unusually wide range of surface changes, special elements of his style remained constant. The book will be of interest to students and scholars of music and theatre history, and of British cultural and social history.

Henry Purcell

Henry Purcell

The origins and development of his musical style

MARTIN ADAMS

CAMBRIDGE
UNIVERSITY PRESS

Published by the Press Syndicate of the University of Cambridge
The Pitt Building, Trumpington Street, Cambridge, CB2 1RP
40 West 20th Street, New York, NY 10011–4211, USA
10 Stamford Road, Oakleigh, Melbourne 3166, Australia

First published 1995

Printed in Great Britain at the University Press, Cambridge

A *catalogue record for this book is available from the British Library*

Library of Congress cataloguing in publication data
Adams, Martin.
Henry Purcell: the origins and development of his musical style / Martin Adams.
p.   cm.
Includes bibliographical references and index.
ISBN 0 521 43159 X (hardback)
1. Purcell, Henry, 1659–1695 – Criticism and interpretation.   I. Title.
ML410.P96A32   1995
780'.92–dc20   93-48203   CIP   MN

ISBN 0 521 43159 X hardback

Contents

Preface

THIS BOOK WAS BORN out of a conviction which took root around 1974, during an analytical study of Purcell's fantasias, sonatas and a few late instrumental pieces, and at a time when some long-established views of Purcell were just beginning to be questioned. I was working on ground prepared by others, in particular by Michael Tilmouth's article on the sonatas, which demonstrated their close affinity with the fantasias, and by Margaret Laurie's demonstration, largely through a study of sources, that Purcell is unlikely to have written most of the music for *The Tempest* generally attributed to him. The results of my youthful delvings suggested there was much wrong with one prevalent view, which saw Purcell's development mainly in terms of progress towards an English version of the contemporary Italian style.

The core of my conviction, which this book seeks to validate, is that despite the extraordinary surface changes in Purcell's style between his mid teens and his death in 1695 aged around thirty-six, he was a deeply conservative composer, who had to struggle to reconcile the tide of the times – which he helped so strongly on its way, and which he identified primarily with Italian music – with the compositional priorities of his early music.

In the last twenty or so years others have expressed views more or less concordant with this position. But in the process, other misconceptions have sprung up, especially concerning possible influences on Purcell and aspects of chronology. Most of these arise from a failure to distinguish between levels and kinds of compositional development and influence, especially when seeking to identify specific pieces which might have inspired Purcell, when searching out the origin of a sudden stylistic innovation, and when considering the development of his own style.

This book attempts to draw such distinctions, and to show how complex was the web of native and foreign influence around Purcell. It is not intended as a final proof – if such a thing were desirable or even possible – nor does it attempt to present in any detail the range and chronology of his output or the minutiae of his varied private and public fortunes. Rather it seeks to define those Purcellian features common to music as diverse as the early pavans and *The Indian Queen* (Z.630), to identify or speculate upon which foreign and native music might have inspired Purcell's choices, and to see how he reconciled that which he found attractive in such music to his distinctive compositional aspirations. The evidence is drawn mainly from an examination of his changing approach to each of the main genres in which he worked.

Acknowledgements

THIS BOOK WOULD NEVER have seen the light of day without the help and encouragement of many people. Special thanks to Sir William Glock, who first suggested that I should write it, and who proved unfailingly encouraging to a very young, inexperienced and unproven academic. For help and inspiration in my earliest days of Purcell research I am indebted to Peter Evans and to Robert Hanson. Generous in his comments and encouragement was the late Michael Tilmouth, who read over portions of the text. Many others have offered support by showing an interest and engaging in conversations which have affected my own thinking – in this respect I must particularly thank Nigel Fortune, Kevin O'Connell, Curtis Price and various colleagues in Trinity College Dublin too numerous to single out. For generous responses to written and other queries over the years, thanks are due to Andrew Ashbee, Peter Holman, Rosamond McGuinness, Thomas Mitchell and Bill Vaughan. Many thanks to Michael Dervan for reading over, and commenting on, parts of the text.

Many library staff have been unfailing in their assistance, often above the call of duty. I am indebted to various staff from the Bodleian and Christ Church Libraries, Oxford; the Music Room and the Manuscript Department of the British Library, and the library of the Royal College of Music, London; the Barber Institute, University of Birmingham; and finally to many staff of the Library at Trinity College, Dublin.

In its final stages this project received financial support from Trinity College in the form of grants from the Arts and Social Sciences Benefactions Fund and from the Taylor Bequest.

Abbreviations

MB   *Musica Britannica*, London: Stainer and Bell

NPS *New Purcell Society Edition*, London: Novello (all editions after 1961, except vol. XXX – 1959)

PS   *Purcell Society Edition*, London: Novello

Note on music examples and figures

MOST MUSIC EXAMPLES have been derived from modern critical editions. In the absence of a reliable modern source, seventeenth-century sources, either manuscript or printed, have been used wherever possible. In analytical diagrams, a close onto a major chord at the end of a phrase in the minor is indicated v(V), etc. The sign ∼ is used to indicate harmonic instability. Wherever possible, time signatures are expressed in their original, seventeenth-century forms, e.g. 3I, $\frac{C}{3I}$, $\mathbb{C}$. Unless otherwise indicated, all choruses are *SATB*. All music examples were typeset by TopType Music Bureau, Dublin.

PART ONE

Stylistic development and influences

CHAPTER ONE

Early years at court and home: developments to c. 1680

THE LITTLE EVIDENCE THAT survives suggests that Henry Purcell, arguably Britain's greatest composer, was born in 1659, probably in Westminster, then a more or less separate city some three miles west of London.[1] His father was one of two brothers, Thomas and Henry Purcell, both of whom earned a living as professional musicians (the balance of evidence favours Henry as the father). Both were on the King's musical establishment in 1661, just a year after the restoration of the monarchy and, while Henry died in 1664, Thomas continued to accumulate appointments and seems at the very least to have been responsible for young Henry during the boy's youth.[2]

We know practically nothing of young Henry's childhood, beyond some dates in archives of court and church which record his teenage rise up the ladder of appointments. He became a chorister in the Chapel Royal, almost certainly not later than his tenth year. His voice broke in 1673 and in that same year he was appointed assistant to John Hingston, keeper of the King's musical instruments: effectively this made him Hingston's unpaid apprentice.[3] He must have done well in this work, for in 1675, and for several years thereafter, he tuned the organ at Westminster Abbey. In 1677, on the death of Matthew Locke at around fifty-five, the eighteen-year-old Purcell received his first major appointment. On 10 September he was admitted as one of the composers in ordinary for the violins. His duties involved writing music for the court's entertainment – Thomas Purcell had held the same post since 1671. Two years later, in 1679, young Henry's responsibilities were formally extended to church music, when he was appointed organist of Westminster Abbey.[4]

And what of composition during these years? Certainly the young Purcell was active. By 1679, and almost certainly for a few years before this, his verse anthems were in regular use in the Chapel Royal and Westminster Abbey;[5] in tandem with these unusually accomplished sacred works there was a regular output of consort music, remarkable for its technical skill and expressive profundity. As one might expect, these early pieces tend to imitate the sacred and consort music with which Purcell was most familiar; but it is still interesting to note how selective the precocious youngster was in choosing his models. Despite his later fame as a song composer, his early songs are generally less impressive than his instrumental and sacred music, though here too he made his mark early. The first reliable attribution is the five songs published in 1679, in the second book of *Choice Ayres and Songs to Sing to the Theorbo-lute or Bass-viol*. As the publication of this collection had been delayed, it is unlikely that any of them are later than 1678, and some could have been composed earlier.[6]

As a chorister Purcell received musical instruction under the supervision of the Master of the Children, Captain Henry Cooke (c. 1616–72). There is no obvious evidence in Purcell's music of the influence of Cooke's compositions; but two of Cooke's other pupils, Pelham Humfrey (1647–74) and John Blow (1649–1708) – both much better composers than their teacher and only a few years older than Purcell – were to become primary influences.[7]

On Cooke's death in 1672, Humfrey took over as Master of the Children. Although he was to hold the position for a mere two years – he died on 14 July 1674[8] – it is certain that his influence on Purcell had taken root much earlier. Humfrey had been something of a prodigy. He was taken on as a chorister in the Chapel Royal and at around seventeen years old was sent to France and Italy by Charles II to study foreign musical practices. After his return in 1667, 'an absolute Monsieur' according to Pepys, his music became a regular feature of Chapel Royal services, so Purcell must have been familiar with – indeed have sung in – a number of his anthems.[9] Also, it is possible that Humfrey taught Purcell while Cooke was Master of the Children, for senior musicians other than the Master did instruct the boys from time to time. Purcell's interest in his music is attested by the presence of five of his verse anthems in an early autograph score-book (Fitzwilliam MS 88) which, it seems likely, was assembled by Purcell between 1677 and 1682.[10]

Blow was born just two years later than Humfrey, and like him had been one of the boys in the early years of the re-founded Chapel Royal. As he took over the role of Master of the Children from Humfrey on the latter's death in 1674, he in turn became Purcell's teacher, in which role he is remembered on his memorial in Westminster Abbey as 'Master of the famous Mr H. Purcell'.[11] In Fitzwilliam 88 he is better represented than anyone other than Purcell himself, there being no less than eleven anthems of various sorts. He was a prolific, imaginative and versatile composer, whose relationship with Purcell was to prove mutually beneficial in the same sort of way as the much more famous one between Haydn and Mozart.

There is evidence that Purcell was also taught by Christopher Gibbons

(1615–76), son of the famous Orlando. Gibbons junior, who appears to have been well known to the Purcell family, was a composer, organist at both the Chapel Royal and Westminster Abbey, and court virginalist. It seems likely that he taught Purcell on those instruments;[12] but here too there is little firm evidence of influence on Purcell's compositional practice.

A rather older man, Matthew Locke (1621/2–77), was not on the staff of the Chapel Royal, but on 23 June 1660 had been appointed composer in the King's private music. He would have been known to the Purcells in that capacity; also as one of the composers for *The Siege of Rhodes*, which was first produced in 1656 with Henry Purcell senior as one of the singers, and is often described as the first English opera. But he seems also to have been a family friend: in the diary entry for 21 February 1660, Pepys mentions that he had spent time with 'Mr Lock and Pursell' singing a 'variety of brave Italian and Spanish songs' while, rather less reliably, the nineteenth-century historians Rimbault and Cummings claimed that the former owned a letter from Locke to the young Henry, inviting him to join Locke and other musicians from the court in a little domestic music making.[13] That Locke was acquainted with the family is confirmed by young Henry himself, for in the second book of *Choice Ayres* (1679) he published what might be the first of his large recitative songs, *What Hope for Us Remains?* (Z. 472), 'On the death of his worthy friend Mr Matthew Locke'.

As far as musical style was concerned, post-Restoration England was something of a melting pot. Throughout Europe, the Italian style was generally regarded as a standard bearer for innovation, to the chagrin of those who supported French practice. While Purcell was to draw extensively on French models, both he and Blow were to show a more profound interest in Italian music, by copying pieces for their own study, by imitating distinctive Italian practices and, in Purcell's case at least, by declarations in print.

It might therefore seem contradictory that both composers were also deeply affected by the work of the old-style English polyphonists. Around 1680–2 Purcell copied into his Fitzwilliam autograph three works by Orlando Gibbons (1583–1625), three by William Byrd (1542/3–1623), one by Thomas Tallis (c. 1510–85) and one by William Mundy (c. 1529–c. 1591). All had been Gentlemen of the Chapel Royal, and Purcell would have known their music, for their anthems and services were still in use there. Nevertheless, this interest at a time when his own compositional style was well developed and when he was working on his earliest successful Italianate pieces, suggests a complex musical personality.

Even Purcell's earliest surviving works show this natural complexity. *The Stairre Case Overture*, which was discovered a few years ago, minus its viola part, is a well-wrought piece unlikely to be later than the mid-1670s, and shows the imitation of established practices (in this case they seem to be those of Locke and contemporary French composers) which one might expect from a young composer eager to learn and to prove himself. The title almost certainly comes from the ascending and descending scales of the first section, which might owe something to Locke's music for the 1674 production of *The Tempest*.[14] To accompany a storm, Locke provided a Curtain Tune which begins 'soft', works up 'lowder by degrees' to rushing scales and concitato repetitions as the storm is at its height, and becomes 'soft and slow by degrees' as it passes. Then there is the First Music, the independent part writing and general style of which are similar to those of Purcell's overture (cf. Ex. 1 and Ex. 33).

Such textures and those of the second and third sections can be found in French music, which seems another likely influence on this and other early orchestral pieces. But French influences could also have been received through Humfrey, whose music displayed a French affinity in keeping with the court's tastes. The dance-like, binary form, top-line-dominated second section of Purcell's overture, is in the same style as that often used by Humfrey in his symphonies to anthems and odes, the 1672 birthday ode *When from His Throne* (BL Add. MS 33287) for example; and Humfrey in turn might have been influenced by works such as the overture to the Prologue of the 1657 ballet *L'Amour malade* by Lully (1632–87).

The Stairre Case Overture has a long-range cogency very different from Locke's striking but somewhat quirky music. Its line-driven texture is remarkably economical in motivic material and has broad harmonic paragraphs. In the second section, the top line consists mainly of repetitions of just a few motifs, counterpointed against just a few more distinctive motifs in the surviving lower parts. Such economy was to become a hall mark of Purcell's style in all genres.

The Stairre Case Overture and other early overtures might have been played by a small group, in private gatherings of the Purcell family and friends, or of the musicians of the royal establishment, or even at court. Indeed, if the portrait (of unknown provenance and whereabouts, but reproduced by Zimmerman) of a young man holding a tenor violin is in fact of Henry Purcell, it raises the prospect that he played the missing viola part himself.[15]

This overture is unusual for combining technical complexity with expressive directness. The latter quality at least seems to have been a prerequisite for any music designed for Charles II, who 'had an utter detestation of Fancys' and, apparently, of any other music to which he could not beat time.[16] It, or pieces like it, must have made an impression, for while Westrup plausibly suggests that Purcell's youthful appointment as composer for the violin owed something to 'the working of influence', it is doubtful that the honour was based entirely on preferment.[17]

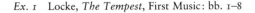

Ex. 1   Locke, *The Tempest*, First Music: bb. 1–8

Despite the young Purcell's success in a Francophile court and the fact that he later put himself forward as a champion of foreign, specifically Italian practice, he reserved his best efforts, in these early years at least, for the intimate, somewhat insular world of English consort music. He produced the final flowering of a tradition which had proved remarkably persistent and immutable – even esoteric: not only did it last through the Civil War and the Restoration into Purcell's lifetime but, in his hands and those of his immediate forbears, it also continued to use the Renaissance-based genres from which it arose, long after most of these and their equivalents had fallen out of use in France and Italy.

In 1667, in the second edition of *A Compendium of Practical Music*, which Purcell admired, Christopher Simpson (*c.* 1605–69) had recommended that aspiring composers of instrumental music 'need not seek [the example of] outlandish authors ... no nation in my opinion being equal to the English in that way'.[18] He tells us what types of piece a composer of instrumental music could use: 'the chief and most excellent for art and contrivance are fancies of 6, 5, 4 and 3 parts, intended commonly for viols. In this sort of music, the composer, being not limited to words, doth employ all his art and invention'; the next type in importance is the pavan, and this is followed by the galliard, allemande, courante, sarabande, jig, and other 'things so common'.

It is almost certain that not all Purcell's consort music has survived; but even so, the dominance in his output of the fantasia and pavan, in contrast with Simpson's list, is striking. Also, he wrote at least two In nomines, a type so conservative that Simpson did not include it (though this might have been because he regarded it as a type of fantasia – 'In nomine fantasia' was a common title).

The In nomine uses cantus firmus technique, but despite this and the long tradition of cantus firmus pieces in English consort music, there are no workings of popular melody, such as Thomas Simpson's *Ricercar* on 'Bonny sweet Robin'[19] – though Purcell was later to do this in his odes. Nor are there any division pieces for bass viol, even though these were produced in large quantities by Purcell's distinguished predecessors, Christopher Simpson and the great John Jenkins (1592–1678).[20]

The narrowness of Purcell's choices is underlined when we consider the retrospections of his contemporary Roger North, who recalled that some forty or more years before Purcell was composing his consort music

it became usuall to compose for instruments in setts; that is, after a Fantasia, [came] an aiery lesson of two straines, and a tripla by way of Galliard, which was stately, Courant, or otherwise, not unsuitable to, or rather imitatory of, the dance. Instead of the Fantazia, they often used a very grave kind of ayre, which they called a 'Padoana', or Pavan; this had 3 straines, and each being twice played went off heavyly, especially when a rich veine failed the master.[21]

The rich vein did not fail in Purcell's pavans or fantasias; and his concentration on these serious, heavy-weight genres suggests a young man who took himself and his place in the English musical tradition very seriously indeed. And why should he not? He may well have realised that with the deaths of Locke in 1677 and Jenkins in 1678 he had become that tradition's sole surviving significant representative.[22] Certainly there is something idealistic about his interest, for by the late 1670s such music had little public appeal: back in 1667 Simpson had lamented of fantasias that 'This kind of music (the more is the pity) is now much neglected by reason of the scarcity of auditors that understand it, their ears being better acquainted and more delighted with light and airy music.'[23]

Some sources of Purcell's earliest consort music could date from 1676 or earlier. Five pavans are known to have survived complete, four in three parts and one, which might be slightly later than the rest, in four. Like similar pieces by Locke and Jenkins, they were probably intended for two or three violins and continuo.

There are clear similarities between Purcell's Pavan in A minor (Z. 749) and the pavan in the C major second suite of Locke's *The Little Consort* (Ex. 34 and Ex. 2), especially the parallel movement of the upper parts and the general rhythmic character. Both share a conservative characteristic which North, writing in the 1690s, described as 'a foible ... the English Nation in their musick are comonly accused of, and that is, the movement is for the most part up and downe, and downe and up, and so jogg on in comon measure'.[24]

This tendency towards stepwise movement is partly a result of consort music's descent from *stile antico*. But even by Locke's standards, Purcell's pavan shows conservative traits: in particular, its insistent chromaticism, dissonance and false relations show an affinity with some Jacobean consort music.

As Westrup says, while such things were a feature of the time, Purcell's grip on them was unusually strong in that he was able to make captivating detail serve the purpose of the composition as a whole.[25] In this respect in particular, he was soon to go on to much better things in the fantasias.

It is likely that his earliest surviving fantasias are the three in three parts, all of which have sources dating from the mid-1670s. They too show conservative traits, such as the use throughout of time signatures of either **C** or **₵** – a good instance of North's 'jogg on in comon measure' and different from the practice of most of the later masters of English consort music such as Jenkins, whose fantasias included sections in triple time. This increasing range of contrast was partly a response to continental developments, as in ensemble sonatas by composers such as Legrenzi and Biber. But such a progressive attitude seems to have held no interest for Purcell: here and in other respects the three-part fantasias perhaps show the influence of Coprario (*c.* 1570/80–1626) and Christopher Gibbons. Consort music by both men can be seen in a manuscript which seems to have been in Purcell's possession.[26] Other possible influences are the distinguished three-part fantasias of Orlando Gibbons, and Locke's consort music, much of which was then up to thirty years old, and which shows a similar disposition of sections, plus the use of 'drag' to indicate slowing down.

Whatever debt Purcell might have had to any of these men, he here emerges as a strikingly individual voice of consistently strong character. It is often the case for characters strong in their youth, that misjudgement can be as forceful as success; but these fantasias reveal discipline, single-mindedness and ambition, qualities which were to stand the composer in good stead in his later compositional struggles and which, some twenty years after Purcell's death, were remembered by his older contemporary Thomas Tudway (*c.* 1650–1726),

Ex. 2   Locke, *The Little Consort*, Pavan from Second Suite: bb. 1–5

who 'knew him perfectly well', and declared that 'He had a most commendable ambition of exceeding everyone of his time.'[27]

The three-part fantasias tend to take the pavans' extreme economy in thematic material much further. In the first section of Fantasia No. 1 (Z. 732), for example, almost every note is derived from the opening point, for even when literal repetition of the point declines, the changes are carefully derived from it.

Even more striking proof of Purcell's inherent conservatism is to be found in the *Fantasia upon One Note* and the In nomines of six and seven parts (Z. 745–7). In 1720, Roger North wrote of the In nomine as if it were a dimly remembered antique; but even by the 1670s it was well out of date. North found the pieces he had encountered to be 'a sort of harmonious murmer, rather than musick … not unlike a confused singing of birds in a grove', and, with a fond musing on Elysian days gone by, thought them probably suitable to 'a time when people lived in tranquility and at ease'. But with rather more realism he noted that they were part of consort music's long tradition of cantus firmus writing, and that even in that context

that which was styled 'In nomine' was yet more remarkable, for it was onely descanting upon the 8 notes that which the sillables (In nomine Domini) agreed. And of this kind I have seen whole volumes, of many parts, with the severall authors names (for honour) inscribed. And if the study, contrivance, and ingenuity of these compositions, to fill the harmony, carry on fuges, and intersperse discords, may pass in the account of skill, no other sort whatsoever may pretend to more. And it is some confirmation that in two or three ages last bygone the best private musick, as was esteemed, consisted of these.[28]

North also criticises 'this kind of musick' for its lack of 'variety or what is called air', and regards it as a relic which by then had nothing to offer him or his contemporaries. But Purcell had no such reservations, and must have wished to show that in this ultimate test of skill he could match his most distinguished predecessors, including Jenkins, who wrote at least two.

Purcell's pieces lie at the most conservative end of In nomine practice, in that they show little absorption of modern instrumental styles, unlike many pieces by earlier seventeenth-century composers such as Alfonso Ferrabosco II and John Ward. It seems likely that he was responding to the methods of composers such as Bull and Jenkins, both of whom produced examples which show affinities with the genre's vocal origins. Like Bull's five-part In nomine (*MB*, vol.

Ex. 3   Locke, *The Consort of Four Parts*, Fantasia from Fifth Suite: first section

IX), Purcell's In nomine à 6 opens with a point derived from the cantus firmus, while the final closes of the Bull and of Purcell's In nomine à 7 are set up by repetitions over a dominant pedal on D of almost identical motifs which suggest closure.

More modern is Purcell's tendency to periodic organisation. The regular switching between G minor and D minor in the In nomine à 7, the point's stress on the first and second pulses of the bar and the focus towards cadence points are all reminders that these pieces are not regurgitations of Renaissance practice, but examples of true Baroque *stile antico*.

Purcell's activities in consort music culminated in the work done during the summer of 1680, when the four-part fantasias reached their final forms and were copied into BL Add. MS 30930 on the dates inscribed. Their extraordinary technical skills and their sure-footed balance of stylistic contrasts, encompassing severe *stile antico* and almost late-Baroque-style fugal subjects, suggest that Purcell would have admired comparable works by Jenkins, such as his six-part Fantasia No. 2.[29] The opening section of this remarkable piece uses an almost exact inversion of the subject, while the final section (bb. 73–92) is based on the augmented subject in both prime and inversion, with technical display superbly

Ex. 4 Locke, *The Consort of Four Parts*, Fantasia from Fifth Suite: bb. 16–19

allied to the compositional purpose of slowing the pace of movement to conclude the piece, after a relentlessly mobile section.

But Purcell's fantasias have a much more particular relationship with Locke's *The Consort of Four Parts*.[30] The opening section of the fantasia from Locke's fifth suite (Ex. 3) is a well-controlled harmonic circuit in which a largely scalic registral wedge works up from D (b. 2) and down from G (b. 7) to meet on the final A. The opening progression probably inspired Purcell when he wrote the extraordinary opening bars of the anthem *Man That Is Born of a Woman* (Z. 27), but more general similarities are evident in the openings of Fantasias Nos. 5 and 9 (Z. 736 and 740). The broad harmonic paragraph of the former includes much playing upon the possibilities of major- and minor-mode inflexions; in the latter the harmony gradually unfolds during the first two bars; all three pieces are avowedly polyphonic and tend to generate motion by twists in the part writing.

The second section of the Locke combines three main themes (Ex. 4). Purcell's response to such virtuosity reached its apogee in the second section of Fantasia No. 9 (Z. 740), where the concentration upon three ideas outdoes Locke, not least by inverting all three themes in varying temporal combinations.

The fourth, probably slow, section of the Locke (Ex. 5) highlights some of the greatest similarities between the composers, but also reveals the most significant differences – those which make Locke merely a notable composer and Purcell a great one. It states its distinction from the preceding section through the scoring for three instruments, and through the harmonic contrast with the preceding V–I close in G minor. A gradually expanding registral wedge, primarily generated from the chromatic ascent in viol I, culminates not in a high note, but in a low E on the bass, in an arresting move towards A minor, and in abandonment of the ascent (bb. 57–8). The entry of viol I on high A (b. 59) generates a balancing descent, which ends with a half close in G minor (bb. 66–7). The concept is strong and most details of part writing are well-focussed; but there is at least one case of motivic working seriously at odds with the long-range purpose.

In bb. 62–3 the descending line of viol I generates a timely inflexion, apparently suggesting iv as a preparation for some sort of cadential move in G minor – that is precisely what happens in bb. 65–7. The combination of B and

Ex. 5 Locke, *The Consort of Four Parts*, Fantasia from Fifth Suite: bb. 52–67

E♭ (b. 62) makes the $^6_5$ over F♯ function as II in C minor; so the predominant thrust of these bars is G major, as V of iv. Within this context the B–B♭ inflexion in viol II is inappropriate: although it imitates viol I's line, it achieves nothing, for the crucial pitch is not the stressed B♭, but the unstressed B♮: a local motivic gesture is in fruitless conflict with a longer-term harmonic one.

Purcell occasionally made comparable misjudgements – the first version of *Hear Me, O Lord* (Z. 13A) is in places no better than the Locke, and for similar reasons – but his fantasias are remarkably free of such aberrations and show a consistency of musical logic which was beyond Locke.[31] In this respect Fantasia No. 7 (Z. 738) in C minor is perhaps his most remarkable achievement, with compelling detail impeccably timed for expressive effect, and with finely-judged relationships between sections.

Within their perforce confined expressive palette, the four-part fantasias wear their technical prowess openly and proudly, and show Purcell relishing the resources at his disposal. They might not have the expressive weight of Bach's *Art of Fugue*, but like that peerless example of contrapuntal skill, they are the creation of a composer who is supremely confident of what he wants and of how to achieve it, and it is this confidence allied with the strength of the results which

makes the brazen technical display an experience to be relished. That at least is
unusual in one so young.

We might also consider that Purcell's grip on musical structure – on balance,
on long-term implication and realisation, on the relationship between the part
and the whole – is a manifestation of thinking no less linear than that shown by
his contrapuntal prowess. It shows a command of events in time, both local and
longer-term, which was to be crucial for the range of his later development and
for the quality of large works such as *Dido and Aeneas* and *The Fairy Queen*.

Purcell was a natural conservative, not in the sense of being old-fashioned,
but in that he seems to have been dissatisfied by modern developments which
abandoned that polyphonic and motivic rigour characteristic of those earlier
styles which interested him. Much of his unusually wide stylistic development
was involved with a struggle to adapt the priorities of these fantasias to more
modern styles – and quite a struggle it sometimes seems to have been, for the
necessary conflation of textural types and structural methods did not come
easily.

If we seek to find this clearly expressed in print we will be disappointed –
indeed, in the several prefaces in which he had at least a hand, and in his
contribution to the 1694 edition of Playford's *An Introduction to the Skill of
Musick*, he seems to proclaim the opposite. But especially in those days,
composers did not often get the chance to express sentiments other than those
which would help sell their music: Schütz's plea in the preface to the *Geistliche
Chormusik* (1648) that young composers should not lose the contrapuntal skills
central to their craft was a luxury his reputation could afford. No, the evidence
of Purcell's struggles lies in his music, particularly in the variability of his
achievements at certain periods of his life and in the care with which modes of
thinking based in his old style, and epitomised in the consort music, are adapted
to work in the new.

Purcell's consort music seems to have had little or no public recognition – the
well-informed Roger North, for example, seems to have been ignorant of it. Its
compositional priorities nevertheless informed the one area in which this
precocious young man was already widely acknowledged – church music.

After his voice broke in 1673, Purcell acquired inside knowledge of the
repertoire by the peerless method of copying parts and scores. Although what
has survived from this activity is almost certainly a small portion of what he
originally produced, we know that he made copies for his own use and that
there were commissions: in 1675 he was paid five pounds for 'pricking out two
bookes of organ parts' for Westminster Abbey; at a later date he copied out
some organ parts for the Chapel Royal.[32]

He must too have been composing anthems, for perhaps the earliest surviving
source of any Purcell anthem is a bass part-book from the Chapel Royal written

in the hand of William Tucker, which may be as early as 1677 (BL Add. MS 50860). It includes the accomplished verse anthem with strings *My Beloved Spake* (Z. 28), clearly the work of a composer already experienced in the genre (though I would be very hesitant to accept the authenticity or even the existence of the so-called *Address of the Children*, from 1670).[33]

Amongst these very early anthems is *Lord, Who Can Tell?* (Z. 26), which offers valuable evidence of Purcell's style at the time he was winning acceptance as a composer in this field. It makes an interesting comparison with Locke's *Lord, Let Me Know Mine End*, which is to be found in that part of the Fitzwilliam autograph which was definitely copied by Purcell and is well represented in other sources from the late 1670s.[34]

Both anthems set penitential texts and owe as much to the Lawes style of declamatory song as to the old verse anthem style of Orlando Gibbons and his contemporaries. Locke's piece shows a restrained version of the theatrical style for which he had by then become famous. Notice, for example, how he sets the text of Ex. 6 to chains of suspensions and repeated notes driving restlessly

Ex. 6 Locke, *Lord, Let Me Know Mine End*: bb. 90–8

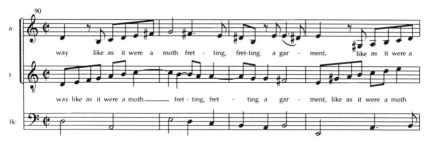

towards a close, as an apt illustration of 'fretting'. This compares closely with Purcell's methods in bb. 13–19 (Ex. 82), where the three vocal parts pile up close-harmony suspensions over the continuo bass to convey the sinner's pleadings.

The structure of *Lord, Who Can Tell?* is typical of the period in that the chorus occurs only at the end, and that boundaries of sections are marked by full closes in the tonic; but within a section harmonic circuits are more wide-ranging than in most pieces by Purcell's contemporaries, possibly because he wished to expand the expressive possibilities of this inherently conservative medium. Once the section beginning 'Keep thy servant' leaves the tonic area it barely touches on it before the concluding phrases. By contrast, *The Ways of Zion Do Mourn* by Michael Wise (*c.* 1648–87), a well-known piece in its day, has intermediate cadences as prominent as those in Purcell's piece, yet mostly in the tonic. In Blow's anthem *O Lord, I Have Sinn'd*, which dates from 1670 and which Purcell knew well, the many excursions to related keys are all short-lived.

Purcell's early church music is replete with pieces no less cheerfully derivative than *Lord, Who Can Tell?*, but full of individual power. The sombre declamatory style and structural organisation of *Who Hath Believed Our Report?* (Z. 64) are closely related to Humfrey's *Hear, O Heav'ns* and to the second setting of his *Have Mercy upon Me, O God*,[35] though again Purcell shows a wider range of harmonic motion within and between sections.

The way Humfrey extracts the cry 'Ah sinful nation' from the text of *Hear, O Heav'ns* and interjects it throughout the anthem, shows the touch of a natural dramatist, and would have appealed to Purcell, who did many similar things in his anthems and sacred partsongs. In *Have Mercy upon Me, O God* the stress patterns in 'do away mine offences' are similar to Purcell's setting of the opening line of *Who Hath Believed Our Report?* In both pieces the effectiveness of the setting depends on the urgent drive towards the close which these patterns create (Ex. 7 (i) and (ii)).

Ex. 7   (i) Humfrey, *Have Mercy upon Me, O God* (second setting): bb. 18–24

(ii) *Who Hath Believed Our Report?* (Z. 64): bb. 7–13

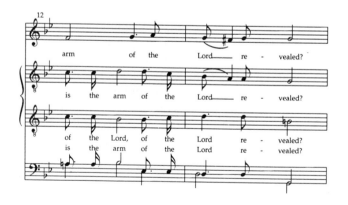

A more explicit borrowing can be seen in the early version of the funeral sentence *In the Midst of Life* (Z. 17A), which dates from the late 1670s and was revised in the early 1680s. The penitential text drew from Purcell some of his most moving early music, remarkable for combining elaborate counterpoint with fidelity to textual accentuation and motivic economy. It is in the same key as Blow's *O Lord, I Have Sinn'd*, which he copied into the Fitzwilliam MS 88 autograph sometime before 1682, and Purcell reworks one of Blow's most distinctive progressions (Ex. 8 (i) and (ii)). The effect of the Purcell is much more

Ex. 8   (i) Blow, *O Lord, I Have Sinn'd*: (bb. 12–14) (from Fitzwilliam MS 88)

(ii) *In the Midst of Life* (Z. 17A): bb. 14–16

telling, largely because its bold dissonance is aptly tied in to preceding events and resolves many of the pitch and harmonic tensions in them.[36]

It was in the anthems that Purcell's distinctive skills with scoring and with large forces first emerged. Sometimes the effects are over-contrived, as in *O Lord Our Governor* (Z. 39), where the unusual verse scoring for three trebles and two basses was inspired by the text. But there are successes astonishing for such a young composer, not least *Blow Up the Trumpet* (Z. 10), which certainly pre-dates 1679 and is scored for seven soloists and eight-part choir, plus continuo.[37]

Purcell makes a virtue of the harmonic limitations inherent in the opening fanfare figuration, creating a massive, constantly changing clamour, and spinning out the short text by repetitions varied through resourceful scoring, including *decani* and *cantoris* groupings. It makes a revealing contrast with Blow's skilful yet much more expedient approach to a similar text in *Sing We Merrily*. In Purcell's setting we see the embryonic dramatic composer using impressive simplicity to lay the ground for astonishing contrasts.

Dramatic use of resources is equally evident in *My Beloved Spake*, which in this respect and in its strongly periodic structure anticipates many future developments.[38] It seems likely that foreign influences had a hand here, if not directly, then via Purcell's older English contemporaries.

Its celebrated setting of 'And the voice of the turtle' makes an interesting comparison with Humfrey's setting of 'And an horrible dread' from *Hear My Pray'r, O God*. Both passages depend on the linear displacement of voices and on the chromatic filling in of diatonic steps within an otherwise straightforward progression. But there the comparisons end, for the renowned effectiveness of Purcell's setting depends on his superior control of context: the minor-mode chromaticisms, audaciously tagged onto a lengthy piece of major-mode jollity, are a punctuative reworking of an earlier major/minor contrast.

My Beloved Spake shows also that it was largely Blow and Humfrey who inspired Purcell in using sectional repetition and contrast to highlight the dramatic potential of the text. The recycling of material, so prominent in *My Beloved Spake*, occurs in Blow anthems from the 1670s, such as *The Lord Is My Shepherd*, while the repetition of all or part of an instrumental symphony to mark a textual division is carried to particularly subtle lengths by Humfrey, for example in *O Lord My God*.

Another early anthem with strings, *Behold, Now Praise the Lord* (Z. 3), seems indebted to the sinuous chromatic lines of Locke and, like the four-part fantasias, proudly displays its contrapuntal virtuosity. Elaboration tends to swamp the expressive clarity which the genre requires – not the last time that Purcell's technical enthusiasm dominated his better judgement – but it nevertheless seems likely that it was works such as these which helped Purcell gain a reputation in the Chapel Royal and Westminster Abbey. From around 1680, a year after his appointment as organist of the Abbey, the number of anthems surviving in part-books and other sources once in everyday use increases considerably.

It is instructive that a composer who could produce such strongly individual works when engaging in stylistic imitation should, out of the bravest imitations of all, produce one of his weakest early anthems. *Let God Arise* (Z. 23) is certainly earlier than 1679, and might even date from Purcell's choirboy days.[39] In most respects it is not typical, but as it seems to be the composer's earliest surviving imitation of Italian vocal techniques, and as so much of his compositional development is bound up with his responses to that fashionable style, it is of more than passing interest.

Purcell drew mainly on the musical imagery and textural characteristics of Italian music from the earlier part of the century. Westrup noted that it includes juxtaposed A major and C minor chords, similar to Peri's and Monteverdi's practice in *L'Euridice* and *L'Orfeo* respectively, where E major (as V of A

minor) and C minor are juxtaposed.[40] In their case it was to express the
distraction and anguish of the Messenger Scene; Purcell uses it to express
disorientation when 'The Earth shook'. The semiquaver figuration at this same
place might also owe something to the type of imagery behind Gabrieli's *Timor
et tremor* which was published in 1615[41] and features almost identical figuration.

Purcell seems to have regarded movement in parallel thirds as distinctively
Italian,[42] and this piece is full of it, to the extent that the two solo voices tend
to shadow one another rather than engage in his characteristic independent
imitation. The expertly-executed but rather obvious imagery – the descending
scales on 'scattered', the octave drop at the end of 'Like as the smoke
vanisheth', the suspensions on 'so shalt thou drive them', and the descending
sevenths at 'and the heav'ns dropped' – is almost certainly drawn from
madrigals, both English and Italian, and from the Italian dramatic motet. There
is a good chance that Purcell would have known such motets, a point reinforced
by the scoring for two tenors and continuo, rare in Purcell's anthems but
common in Monteverdi and his contemporaries.

He certainly knew Monteverdi's music, for in the same manuscript which
includes a canon by Bull there are three madrigals from the fifth book (Venice
1605). Moreover, when he was compiling his full score of his Service in B♭
(Z. 230), probably some time before October 1682, he used as a correction slip
the back of another copy of *Cruda Amarilli* which seems to be in his own
hand.[43] None of these copies includes the words, suggesting that textual
imagery was of less interest than the striking musical progressions.

The problem with *Let God Arise* is the short-breathed, disjunct construction,
due largely to a combination of the over-evident closes, and the way in which
each phrase adopts a different type of imagery; the forcefulness of the ideas
tends to project these weaknesses all the more strongly. If the number of
surviving copies is anything to go by, the piece had a certain interest in its day;
but this must have been born of its novelty: today it sounds rather like a
compendium of musical images – like a piece of expertly-executed pastiche.

The end of this early period is marked by Purcell's making what was almost
certainly his first substantial foray into composition outside home and court, the
five songs published in 1679 in *Choice Ayres ... The Second Book*. The four
strophic settings are not particularly distinguished, though their ways of
accommodating the inflexions of the poetry's stress patterns anticipate many of
the composer's later methods. *Since the Pox* (Z. 471) is perhaps the best of the
bunch.

The young Purcell tended to be at his best in those song styles which offered
the most free rein to those declamatory powers already displayed in anthems
such as *Who Hath Believed Our Report?* (Z. 64) and *My Beloved Spake* (Z. 28).
So his most important solo song from this first publication is his eloquent

lament for 'his worthy friend Mr Matthew Locke', *What Hope for Us Remains?* (Z. 472), which shows differences from the declamatory techniques of the anthems born of its different functions and generic ancestry.[44]

Features common to Humfrey's and Purcell's declamatory style have been identified by Peter Dennison,[45] and similar links can be found with Locke, who had a substantial reputation as a composer of dramatic music. In 1675 he had written the music for *Psyche*, a pioneering work in the development of English dramatic opera, and with which Purcell must have been familiar.[46] In a multi-sectional ensemble in Act I, Pan yields his command to Psyche, declaring that in her honour 'the satyrs and the Fawns / Shall nimbly trip it o'er the Lawns', these being the first two of a series of lines, the end-notes of which articulate a rising scale in a musical reflection of the rhyme scheme. In *What Hope for Us Remains?* Purcell does something similar in technique but much more plastic in detail, asserting that Locke could call 'His spirits to the fight, / And vanquish Death in his own field of Night'. Throughout, expressiveness of line depends on Purcell's ability to apply the commonplace vocabulary of the time without recourse to formula, on his capacity to vary the pacing of events so as to highlight salient parts of the text.

Then there is the command of context, which so effectively points up the text's antitheses and the other contrasts. This is inseparable from the piece's harmonic structure, which is at once the most modern and the most expansively constructed in Purcell's music of that time. We will see that the song's harmonic methods anticipate those which, in a much more developed form, were to underlie much of the best music of Purcell's later life.

CHAPTER TWO

Years of experiment: *c.* 1680 to *c.* 1685

BY 1680, THE YEAR of Purcell's majority, he was established as a rising star in music for court and church, and had a finger in several of the best musical pies of the kingdom. From then on, although records are patchy, we know when the larger part of his music was written, give or take a year or two, and can link much of it to specific events. His finest compositions of that year, the four-part fantasias, are true masterworks – works which indicate his passing into maturity, his right to act on his own – and it is no coincidence that the same year saw a number of compositional 'firsts'.

Some time between April and October 1680 Nathaniel Lee's play *Theodosius* was premiered at the Dorset Garden theatre and some of the music Purcell wrote for it was published soon afterwards. When considering how to approach what was almost certainly his first involvement in theatre music, he would not have had to look far for inspiring precedents.[1] Throughout the 1660s and 1670s the most prominent composer for the London stage had been Locke, whose occasionally eccentric, wayward style could be effective when focussed onto dramatic purpose. His largest contributions were to a much-adapted version of Shakespeare's *The Tempest* (1674), and to Shadwell's *Psyche* (1675), for which the vocal music was provided by Locke and the instrumental by G. B. Draghi (*c.* 1640–1708). Locke's contribution was published – the first dramatic score to be so honoured in England – and significantly was headed 'The English Opera', to show that this was a sally in favour of native art, as distinct from the much-favoured French and, to a lesser extent, Italian. *Psyche* is nevertheless deeply indebted to French practice, not least because of the complex political circumstances surrounding its creation; and while *Theodosius* is free of these, it does show that Purcell had at the very least encountered French music for the stage.[2]

Both the opening scene of *Theodosius* and Act II, Scene I, of *Psyche*, are religious rituals, and Purcell follows Locke's example in stringing together a number of fairly short sections. But he works on a larger scale by motivically integrating several successive items, and by creating a musical structure which encompasses the many portions of the basically strophic text.[3] The result is in some respects a little stiff, but it is authentic discourse, with textual progress aptly supported by musical events.

Within this scene and elsewhere in *Theodosius*, Purcell uses a variety of song types. In 'Can'st Thou, Marina?' (Z. 606.2), he convincingly employs the mannered, angular vocal line which he frequently used in duple or quadruple time during these years. 'Ah! Cruel, Bloody Fate' (Z. 606.9) is a 'Scotch song', a title less concerned with Scottish identity than with a generally folksy image,[4] while 'Hail to the Myrtle Shade' (Z. 606.8) is perhaps the first of those seemingly effortless, triple-time melodies epitomised in 'Fairest Isle' from *King Arthur* (Z. 628.38) and 'If Love's a Sweet Passion' from *The Fairy Queen* (Z. 629.17).

But *Theodosius* is most famous for what seems to be the English stage's first song with obbligato instruments throughout.[5] Several elements of 'Hark, Behold the Heavenly Quire' (Z. 606.4) are almost certainly derived, ultimately at least, from French music for the stage. Trio textures with a bass solo more or less duplicating the continuo line are common in French music such as Lully's first true opera, *Cadmus et Hermione*, which was premiered in 1673 and was to be performed in London in 1686. In such pieces violins are the norm whereas Purcell uses recorders. Also common to this French music and Purcell's piece are the non-imitative, parallel-thirds-dominated upper parts. Formal and ponderous as some of *Theodosius* is, it made an auspicious beginning to a peerless career as a composer for the stage.

The other notable 'first' of 1680 was the ode *Welcome, Vicegerent* (Z. 340), written for the King's return to Whitehall on 9 September and the first of Purcell's surviving odes, most of which were written for the court.[6] Perhaps the greatest challenge presented by the genre lay in creating a musically cohesive structure when dispatching a long text fairly quickly, using music that could not be over-complex. Purcell built on the methods of the restlessly innovative Blow, but from the start was even more adventurous – too much so in this case, for the grouping of individual numbers into large units is at best ambiguous.[7] It was to take him some three years to find a satisfactory solution.

Welcome, Vicegerent presents a significant disparity between the quality of its instrumental and vocal music. Some of the former is amongst his best: the first section of the opening symphony is a superbly spacious piece, partly because of the tension between the strong periodicity of the material and the independent polyphony of each line; and the ritornello which follows the chorus 'But Your Blest Presence' (Z. 340.5) is a virtuoso working of a few motifs across a rondeau structure, astonishingly resourceful in using re-harmonisations of the main theme to create a broad harmonic structure across an inherently repetitious concept.

Not so the vocal writing, which is strangely unassured; and which, where it is assured, tends either to the subtlety of a soccer supporters' song or to obvious contrivance. The extremity of the effect is not dissimilar from that produced by Beethoven at his worst, with weaknesses highlighted by the combination of poor material and forceful delivery.

In all genres at this time Purcell tended to be at his best when giving free rein to the elaborately-polyphonic thinking epitomised in the four-part fantasias; and he seems to have known it, for he applied such thinking to genres not previously associated with it – not in his practice at least.

The two-part song with instruments *See Where She Sits* (Z. 508) is an outstanding instance. The vocal style draws on many conservative rhetorical devices such as a treatment of 'Ah! mighty Love', which is almost identical to Lawes' setting of the same words in *Love's Triumph* from *Select Ayres and Dialogues ... The Second Book* of 1669 (cf. Ex. 103 and Ex. 9). In Purcell's piece

Ex. 9   Lawes, *Love's Triumph*: bb. 1–4 (*Ayres and Dialogues*, Playford 1669)

the continuo is often independent of a four-part texture as densely imitative and chromatically elaborate as many fantasias, and in which the two voices and two violins have virtually identical material.

Comparable elaboration in vocal textures can be seen in a group of verse anthems without strings on which Purcell began work around 1680 and which includes revisions of several earlier pieces, including the funeral sentences. They are distinguished by complex contrapuntal textures, an unusual degree of concentration on a limited quantity of motivic material, and sombre expression of penitential texts. They meet the challenge of uncluttered expression in complex counterpoint, by using that daring yet impeccable musical logic which justifies the best of Purcell's more harmonically adventurous passages. Writing of the dissonance in such pieces, Westrup commented that 'If the progress of the parts sometimes led to oddities, they were only temporary, and it was the idea of combined movement which would remain uppermost in the hearer's mind.'[8]

Fine, but clear musical function must underlie such passages. The setting of

'Into the bitter pains of death' from *In the Midst of Life* is a striking example, which like most such cases, depends on the linear displacement of consonant harmonic events (Ex. 87).

An even closer vocal equivalent of the fantasias is the twelve sacred partsongs, a relationship underlined by both groups of pieces appearing in the same autograph score book, BL Add. MS 30930. There was in England a long history of devotional partsongs for domestic use, but certain models for Purcell's distinctive pieces have defied precise identification,[9] possibly because they are a compendium of vocal styles and techniques derived from disparate sources.

They use, for example, the dialogue methods of the verse anthems, though with unusual force. In *Hear Me, O Lord, the Great Support* (Z. 133) the setting of 'Sin not, but fear; let quiet thoughts instruct and make you wise', is fragmented so that the singers encourage one another to this worthy endeavour – the cries of 'Ah sinful nation' in Humfrey's *Hear, O Heav'ns* are a clear precedent.[10] Indulgent breast-beating lurks round every corner, and even when dealing with more cheery subjects Purcell grasps every opportunity of making a sumptuously dismal meal, as when the psalmist is 'Assailed with grief and pain' in *Since God So Tender a Regard* (Z. 143).

Such introverted dramatic power depends partly on stylistic juxtapositions, and Z. 143 is an outstanding example. This gloomy, minor-mode trio comes between two beautifully shaped airs, the second of which, 'Nor did I cry to God in vain', is similar to Lanier's famous *No More Shall Meads* which, like the partsong, is a ground bass.[11] But perhaps the partsongs' most lasting legacy to Purcell's development lies in their recitatives, which represent a crucial stage in a carefully-cultivated development of recitative style which produced master-pieces of dramatic continuity such as the final scene of *Dido and Aeneas*.

The Fitzwilliam MS 88 manuscript contains another unique group of anthems, which have been described as 'full anthems with verse'.[12] Apart from the In nomines, they are perhaps the most profoundly *stile antico* pieces Purcell ever wrote, his nearest equivalent to the styles of those earlier English composers whose anthems he copied into the same manuscript – the virtuosic contrapuntal displays and vivid expression of Gibbons' *Hosanna to the Son of David* and Byrd's *Bow Thine Ear*, for example, obviously struck a chord with Purcell's similar propensities.

His own *Hear My Prayer, O Lord* (Z. 15), *O God, Thou Art My God* (Z. 35), and other pieces in this group, owe much also to some of the Blow anthems in the same manuscript. So Blow's *God Is Our Hope and Strength* is a virtuosic demonstration of contrapuntal skill comparable to Purcell's *O Lord God of Hosts* (Z. 37), while Blow's *O God, Wherefore Art Thou Absent?* and Purcell's *Lord, How Long Wilt Thou Be Angry?* (Z. 25) open with similar points (Ex. 10), and express similar sentiments.

Ex. 10   (i) Blow, *O God, Wherefore Art Thou Absent?*: bb. 1–5

(ii) *Lord, How Long Wilt Thou Be Angry?* (Z. 25): bb. 1–8

These anthems were finished by late 1682 – the same year Purcell was appointed one of the three organists in the Chapel Royal[13] – and mark the end of his consistent involvement with the old English polyphonic style. It was an abandonment of more than symbolic significance, for around 1681–3 his compositional interests made their first decisive shift towards a genre and style which was both modern and international.

Purcell's *Sonatas of III Parts: Two Violins and Bass: To the Organ or Harpsichord* were published by Playford in 1683, in a set of four beautifully engraved part-books.[14] It was a prestige publication and a landmark in the history of English music, being the first compositions thus called to be published in England by an English composer, and confirming significant changes in public taste. It seems likely that Purcell intended to produce a second set which never materialised, though two years after his death, the *Ten Sonatas of Four Parts* appeared.[15] (The difference in the titles reflects only whether the keyboard and string continuo are counted as one or two parts.) It is not known how long the composition of all twenty-two sonatas took, but the balance of evidence suggests that Purcell worked on them for around five years, ending in 1684–5.[16]

However fashionable Italian music might have been, it seems that the term sonata was not well known in England, for Playford's advertisements in the *London Gazette* during 1683 refer to 'new Musical Compositions called SONATA's'.[17] Purcell's pieces nevertheless had English precedents. William Lawes and Jenkins wrote consort music for two equally important upper parts and a continuo bass. Jenkins' Fantasia in F (Ex. 11) has characteristics at least as close to Italian sonatas as to English consort music, such as a tendency to move in parallel thirds and sixths, strong periodic phrasing and the use of sequences to spin out ideas and develop the scale of argument. Also, these and

Ex. 11   Jenkins, Fantasia in F: bb. 19–22 (as in Meyer, *English Chamber Music*, p. 329)

other composers tended to organise their consort music in groups, or 'setts', in a manner clearly related to early- and mid-seventeenth-century sonata practice on the continent.[18]

Purcell's interest in such music almost certainly began with those same musical gatherings which had familiarised him with English consort music. He might also have encountered Germanic and other north-European sonatas, for there are extensive manuscript survivals of such sonatas in England, and the Englishman William Young's sonatas of 1653 were published in Innsbruck – a reminder that cultural and commercial links between Britain and Germanic countries were, until the political upheavals of the twentieth century, extensive and naturally close.[19]

The *Sonatas of Three Parts* signal Purcell moving away from the esoteric world of English consort practice, towards accommodating a musical public unlikely to be conversant with such specialist requirements as continuo playing from an unfigured bass. By contrast, a figured, written-out bass was normal in Italian sonatas, and this plus commercial viability must lie behind Purcell's comments, in the address 'To the Reader', that the engraving of the thorough bass 'was a thing quite besides his first Resolutions'.

Ingenuous Reader,

Instead of an elaborate harangue on the beauty and the charms of Musick (which after all the learned Encomions that words can contrive commends itself best by the performances of a skilful hand, and an angelical voice:) I shall say but a very few things by way of Preface, concerning the following Book, and its Author: for its Author, he has faithfully endeavour'd a just imitation of the most fam'd Italian Masters; principally, to bring the seriousness and gravity of that sort of Musick into vogue, and reputation among our Country-men, whose humor, 'tis time now, should begin to loath the levity, and balladry of our neighbours: The attempt he confesses to be bold, and daring, there being Pens and Artists of more eminent abilities, much better qualify'd for the imployment than his, or himself, which he well hopes these weak endeavours, will in due time provoke, and enflame to a more acurate undertaking. He is not asham'd to own his unskilfulness in the Italian Language; but that's the unhappiness of his Education, which cannot justly be accounted his fault, however he thinks he may warrantably affirm, that he is not mistaken in the power of the Italian Notes, or elegancy of their Compositions, which he would recommend to the English Artists. There has been neither care, nor industry wanting, as well in contriving, as revising the whole Work; which had been abroad in the world much sooner, but that he has now thought fit to cause the whole Thorough Bass to be Engraven, which was a thing quite besides his first Resolutions. It remains only that the English Practitioner be enform'd, that he will find a few terms of Art perhaps unusual to him, the chief of which are these following: Adagio and Grave, which import nothing but a very slow movement: Presto Largo, Poco Largo, or Largo by it self, a middle movement: Allegro, and Vivace, a very brisk, swift, or fast movement: Piano, soft. The Author has no more to add, but his hearty wishes, that his Book may fall into no other hands but theirs who carry Musical Souls about them; for he is willing to flatter himself into a belief, that with such his labours will seem neither unpleasant, nor unprofitable.

                                                                        Vale.

Here we have the earliest open declaration by Purcell of his admiration for non-English music. However, it needs to be taken cautiously, for he might have had his eyes as much on the commercial forces of fashion as on the realities of musical style: certainly this seems to lie behind his use of Italian terms, for to the end of his life they are not a feature of his autographs. His diatribes against the music of 'our neighbours' – he must mean the French – are not borne out by his practice, for to the end of his life he regularly imitated French models: nor is his imitation of Italian music quite as 'just' as he makes out, for his attitude to Italian practice remained a complex and often contradictory one.

The identity of the 'most fam'd Italian Masters' has been much discussed, and their significance for Purcell doubted.[20] He would have known the work of a number of Italian composers, including Bassani, Cazzati and G. B. Draghi (who had lived in London for a number of years), and by 1683 he might even have encountered Corelli's sonatas. But while these and other composers are

Ex. 12   Colista(?), Sonata No. 4 in D: opening Grave

well represented in manuscript sources with possible or probable Purcellian connections, in almost all cases we find that similarities with his own sonatas do not go much further than thematic resemblances.

Not so with Lelio Colista (1629–80), 'Orpheus of the city of Rome' according to the German theorist and composer Athanasius Kircher. Colista's sonatas were extensively disseminated around Europe, and are well represented in manuscript sources in England, though it is probable that some of the pieces attributed to him outside Italy are by his younger contemporary Carlo Lonati (*c.* 1645–*c.* 1710/15).[21] Certainly there were other influences, including music by Germanic and English composers; but the fact that Italian music – and especially that originating in Rome – played a dominant role, has been clearly demonstrated in Helene Wessely-Kropik's study of Purcell's instrumental style, which shows that the ways Purcell and Colista (and possibly Lonati) conceive and handle material, and dispose movements, are far closer than can be explained by coincidence. Moreover, for the technically obsessive Purcell, the self-conscious motivic economy and contrapuntal thoroughness of these composers would have had a natural appeal.[22]

The relationship with Purcell is clearly shown in the one piece that we can be certain Purcell knew – that quoted in the 1694 edition of *An Introduction to the Skill of Musick* as an example of triple-invertible counterpoint, and which he, following the example of his sources, attributed to Colista, while the Italian evidence favours Lonati.[23] It opens (Ex. 12) with a type of movement common amongst Italian composers of the mid seventeenth century and with the somewhat younger Corelli, and significant for repeating the first phrase in a different key in order to set up a harmonic and pitch proposition. In the short first phrase the violins' suspensions and the quaver movement in the bass drive cogently for the dominant. The consequence of the half-close ending is a restatement, in the dominant, of the opening bars, but in a closed form, and this is balanced by a return to the opening phrase, but now in the closed form of bb. 6–9; the last two bars are repeated to make this tonic statement close the movement.

A few of Purcell's sonatas do likewise, such as Sonata No. 3 (1683) in D minor (Z. 792); but most which begin with this type of movement use a more sophisticated method, typified in Sonata No. 4 (1683) in F (Z. 793) where the tonic-dominant proposition is used as the starting point for an elaborate harmonic and contrapuntal discourse. In this respect at least, Purcell's methods are akin to those of Corelli's Op. 1.

There are a few examples of similar types of structure in fast movements, such as the first movement of Sonata No. 9 (1697) in F ('The Golden') (Z. 810) and the Canzona of Sonata No. 10 (1697) in D (Z. 811.1b); but the unusual nature of the practice for Purcell, and the source history, suggest that these two sonatas might be slightly later than 1683. Certainly, such structures were to become common in Purcell's late music.

Colista(?)'s Allegro (Ex. 13) begins by setting up a one-bar theme which is repeated for ten consecutive bars; the countersubject (violin I, b. 16), and a third part are complementary one-bar themes. The consequent one-bar units multiply into larger units by exploiting the harmonic possibilities inherent in the subject –answer imitation (Table 1).

The first two bars set up the norm for this expansion: subject is followed by answer, but this, being dominant-oriented, requires a balancing statement of the subject, which in turn generates yet another answer, and so on. The cycle is broken when a statement of the subject in A (b. 21) is followed by three

Table 1. Opening entries of Colista(?): Sonata No. 4 in D, Allegro

bar	15					20					
Vln I	S	CS	TP	A	CS	F	S (in A)	CS	▬	S→	F
Vln II	▬	A	CS	TP	S	CS	TP	F	S	F→	F
Bass	▬	▬	S	CS	TP	A	CS	S	CS		

S = Subject. A = Answer. CS = Countersubject. TP = Third Part. F = Free.
→ = Extended

Ex. 13   Colista(?), Sonata No. 4 in D: Allegro

statements in D (bb. 22–4), which reverse the events of bb. 15–17 by being in the order bass, violin II, violin I. The stability of the tonic plus the bar's rest in violin I, articulate the end of a unit and inaugurate an episodic passage derived from the subject.

The Italian composer's economical harmonic vocabulary is very different from the kaleidoscopic, often wide-ranging harmonic circuits of Purcell's fantasias, though it is in keeping with the latter's practice in movements such as the Canzona from Sonata No. 4 (1683) in F (Z. 793.1b) and the last movement of Sonata No. 12 (1683) in D (Z. 801.4). Purcell's sonatas also follow Colista(?) in having thematic relationships between movements and having prominent movements called 'Canzona'. The use of this term for a single movement as distinct from an independent piece was particularly associated with mid-seventeenth-century Roman composers; both they and Purcell link it with virtuosic displays of thematic concentration and contrapuntal wizardry.[24]

In *An Introduction to the Skill of Musick*, around the time that Purcell was writing the canzonas in *The Fairy Queen* (Z. 629.27b) and *The Indian Queen* (Z. 630.16b), he referred to the canzona in terms which corresponded to his practice then and in the sonatas. 'Most of these different sorts of Fugeing are used in Sonata's the chiefest Instrumental Musick now in request, where you will find Double and Treble Fugues also reverted and augmented in their Canzona's, with a great deal of Art mixed with good Air, which is the Perfection of a Master.'[25] Clearly, this is a modernisation of Simpson's definition of the fantasia.

In many respects, both sets of sonatas typify an English view of the genre as it approached the *da chiesa* form epitomised in Corelli. There are a few four-movement sonatas in the slow-fast-slow-fast format which dominates Corelli's Opp. 1 and 3 (Sonata No. 6 (1683) in C (Z. 795) and Sonata No. 1 (1697) in B minor (Z. 802) for example), but the majority have more movements, even if some of these are so short as to be preludes or postludes to, or interludes between, more weighty movements.

But what did Purcell mean when he referred in his address to 'the power of the Italian Notes' and to the 'elegancy of their Compositions'? Was this more than commercial window dressing? Was he in some way dissatisfied with the English style which he represented no less ably than Colista and Lonati did the Italian? Assessment is not helped by the difficulties such concepts hold for twentieth-century musicians, for the expressive and aesthetic immediacy they had for Purcell cannot be recovered.

Many years after Purcell wrote his sonatas, Roger North criticised the old English style and commended the Italian, mixing admiration for the expressive power of Italian music with respect for the sober traditions of his native land. He complained of Jenkins 'and others since' that the manner of movement 'was chiefly (as it were) going up and down stairs, and had less of the sault [leap] or iterations [repetitions] than the Italians have; in which respect it must be allowed the latter style is better, as more conform to men's ordinary behaviour'.[26] In the same passage North commends the Italians for their tendency to 'dash upon harsh notes...which makes their consorts more saporite [tasty]'.

The comments about stepwise movement and leaps are fairly straightforward, but that about dissonance is less so. North seems to have been ignorant of Purcell's consort music, but he knew his sonatas, plus consort music by Matthew Locke and some from the Jacobean period. To twentieth-century ears, Purcell's Fantasia No. 7 (Z. 738) or most of Orlando Gibbons' fantasias sound far more dissonant than most Italian sonatas, not least any of those by the enormously admired Corelli. The nub of the matter is that the two styles deal with dissonance and chromaticism in different contexts.

In textures such as the Colista(?), chromaticism and dissonance tend to be modifications of a consonant background well established by repetition and against which the expressive potential of dissonance is heightened. In particular, the style uses repetition to drive towards resolution in a cadence; dissonant modifications of this drive are a central means of extending the scale of a movement and of shaping tension. Indeed, Purcell regarded motion in parallel thirds, so prevalent in Colista(?)'s sonata, as an Italian characteristic, for in *An Introduction to the Skill of Musick* he altered the example of Christopher Simpson.

The first thing to treat of is Counterpoint, and in this I must differ from Mr Simpson, (whose Compendium I admire as the most Ingenious Book I e're met with upon this Subject;) but his Rule in Three parts for Counterpoint is too strict and destructive to good Air, which ought to be preferred before such nice Rules [Ex. 14 (i)].

Ex. 14   Purcell's emendation of Simpson in Playford's *An Introduction to the Skill of Musick*, 12th edn (1694)

(i)

(ii)

Now in my opinion the Alt or Second Part should move gradually Thirds with the Treble; though the other be fuller, this is the smoothest, and carries more Air and Form in it, and I'm sure 'tis the constant Practise of the Italians in all their Musick, either Vocal or Instrumental, which I presume ought to be a Guide to us; the way I would have, is thus [Ex. 14 (ii)].

The intensely wrought textures of the old English style work very differently, tending to be less concerned with airy grace, and with multiplying periodic implications across a large canvas. For us, in an age less concerned with finding universal harmony and principle, that regularity of background which was one of the expressive priorities of the late seventeenth century, has comparatively little importance.

More than any other part of his output, Purcell's sonatas embody the paradoxical tension between his modernistic and conservative aspirations. More than thirty years ago, Michael Tilmouth showed that, despite the composer's Italianate professions, many sonatas are far closer to the practice of the fantasias than to any Italian model.[27] In the opening movement of Sonata No. 6 (1683) in C (Z. 795) – a neat example of the 'up and downe staires' motion of which North complained – the theme is presented simultaneously in prime, augmentation and double augmentation, while subsequent phrases go through many other combinations. In Sonata No. 4 (1697) in D minor (Z. 805) the opening theme (Ex. 15) is, despite its chromaticism, leaps and motivic

Ex. 15 Sonata No. 4 (1697) in D minor (Z. 805): bb. 1–2

repetitions, just a broken version of the characteristic stepwise movement. The first movement of Sonata No. 1 (1683) in G minor (Z. 790) is as pure an example of *stile antico* as the In nomines; though as a reminder that Purcell had no monopoly on such textural types we might turn again to Colista(?), whose fifth sonata, as quoted by Wessely-Kropik,[28] is strikingly similar to Purcell's sonata and to Fantasia No. 4 (Z. 735).

At the other extreme are the overtly Italianate sonatas. One of the most successful is Sonata No. 9 (1697) in F ('The Golden') (Z. 810), the last movement of which is in triple invertible counterpoint, and derives much of its strength from its technical flair and its variety in contrapuntal procedure. But it might be later than the others, and its success is not typical, for the sonatas are of far less consistent quality than the fantasias.

Purcell seems to have had a penchant for the 'iterations' which appealed to North, but his application of them is often excessive, going far beyond that

which is normal in his native style. It reaches its extremity in the Largo of Sonata
No. 1 (1697) in B minor (Z. 802.2), in which triple-invertible counterpoint and
a sequentially-repeated appoggiatura figure are clearly based on Italian practice;
but the result is numbingly tedious, largely because of a lack of variation in
procedure and a superficiality in long-term processes.[29]

Similar weaknesses can be found in the Canzona of Sonata No. 6 (1683) in C
(Z. 795.1b), the Allegro of Sonata No. 8 (1683) in G (Z. 797.2b), and the
Canzona and the Allegro of Sonata No. 2 (1697) in E♭ (Z. 803.1b and 4), in all
of which short-breathed periodicity is nigglingly persistent, and the triple-
invertible counterpoint mere mechanistic juggling.

Most Italian composers, including Colista and Lonati, varied their material,
producing uneven phrase lengths and melodic variety to suit the context.
Colista(?)'s sonata shows just such a balanced approach, while in the third
movement of G. B. Vitali's sonata *La Guidoni* (Ex. 16), which survives in a

Ex. 16   G. B. Vitali, Sonata *La Guidoni*: third movement

manuscript with strong Purcellian connections,[30] the timing of imitation and the
shaping of themes are constantly varied.

North was to comment that though the sonatas were 'very artificiall and
good musick', they were 'unworthily despised' for being 'clog'd with somewhat
of an English vein'.[31] How apt! Purcell is at his best in pieces like Sonata No. 11
(1683) in F minor (Z. 800), where the periodic phrasing and harmonic clarity of
the Italian style are neatly combined with very un-Italian details of harmony and
counterpoint. Links with the fantasias are especially evident in the Adagio,
where every event is imbued with a significance derived from superb control of
motivic working and context. As always in his more successful music, Purcell
abhors the obvious in periodic organisation, producing such delights as bb.

112–20 of the last movement, where harmonic gesture has a dramatic quality anticipating the methods of the late odes and stage music.

Sometimes Purcell was at pains to display that large-scale organicism so prominent in the fantasias. Sonata No. 6 (1697) in G minor (Z. 807) is a ground on a Baroque formula bass, the working of which shows that superb skill at variation techniques and at structuring a long ground-bass composition which characterised the *Fantasia: Three Parts on a Ground* (Z. 731). It might well be an attempt to outdo an admired foreign composer, for the bass had some popularity as a ground, and was the same as that for the famous song 'Scocca pur, tutti tuoi strali', which Purcell is likely to have known.[32]

More self-consciously organic than any other sonata is Sonata No. 5 (1683) in A minor (Z. 794), which recapitulates the material of the opening movement. Purcell could have picked up the concept from a number of Italian sonatas circulating in England around that time,[33] but his methods are far more subtle and integrated than those of any possible models I have been able to trace. The return of the opening theme in the course of the final canzona contains all the essential ingredients of true drama – the setting up of a denouement by a progress which is subtle and inexorable yet never obvious; and, when it comes, the result is forceful but different from what might be expected.

Purcell was an inveterate tinkerer with his own music, and some of the *Sonatas of Four Parts* exist in two versions, the later of which precisely address the weaknesses of the earlier. The compositional struggles glimpsed through these revisions and through the unevenness of his achievement in this genre, were to persist for several years more. Moreover, when overtly Italianate textures made an occasional appearance in other genres, they often revealed the same problems – the obviousness of the transposed repetitions in the chorus with instruments 'Welcome Home', from the 1684 ode *From Those Serene and Rapturous Joys* (Z. 326.4), is a striking instance. Purcell did not acquire a consistent proficiency with Italianate textures until around 1687–8. It was first consolidated in instrumental music: the most consistent indicators of his progress in this and other respects are to be found in the opening symphonies to anthems and odes.

In the symphony to the 1682 ode *What Shall Be Done?* (Z. 341.1b) he follows the example of movements such as the Presto from Sonata No. 2 (1683) in B♭ (Z. 791.3), making a virtue out of a repetitious, periodic subject, by varying the intervals of temporal and pitch imitation. Harmonic prolongation and other modern harmonic methods are prominent, and the long-range drive these produce is intensified by restless polyphonic discourse.

The repetitive harmonic structures characteristic of this and most other symphonies begin to disappear between 1683 and 1685. The economical methods of the future are exemplified in the second sections of the symphonies to the 1685 anthem *My Heart Is Inditing* (Z. 30.1b) and the 1686 ode *Ye Tuneful Muses* (Z. 344.1b), which feature a smaller number of harmonic areas extended across a larger span through cellular motivic repetition, harmonic prolongation, melodic and harmonic sequence and a strongly periodic phrase structure.

Applying such methods to vocal music was another matter, and much of Purcell's compositional development is bound up with a search for repetition techniques which would suit the English language as well as most of the Italian music he knew suited Italian. Other English composers were moving in the same direction, but Purcell's use of the new techniques tended to be a cut above most possible models, be they English or Italian.

It seems likely, for example, that in the delightful trio 'But Heaven Has Now Dispelled Those Fears' from the late-1683 ode *Fly, Bold Rebellion* (Z. 324.9), Purcell was responding to ideas offered by Blow in his 1678 ode *Dread Sir, the Prince of Light* (BL Add. MS 33287).[34] The greater effectiveness of Purcell's setting depends largely on its use of modern methods of articulation to point up the expressive potential of harmonic gesture. Its five harmonic units span I–V–ii–IV–I and the concluding subdominant and tonic consist of transposed repetitions of the same material, the tonic having two statements. This also is the sole material for the concluding ritornello for four-part strings, which has three statements, one in the dominant and two in the tonic. All three statements are replete with sensuous harmonic detail produced by modifications of basically scalic part writing, and that no less than six consecutive statements of the same melodic material work at all, is due mainly to the harmonic circumscription they produce.

When writing for one voice, Purcell shows occasional leanings towards Italianate methods, as in the motivic repetitions in the final section of the 1683 song *Amidst the Shades* (Z. 355). Even in the notoriously conservative area of the verse anthem he made occasional forays in that direction, as in the rhetorical flair of the bass verse 'For Look, How High the Heav'n' from the *Praise the Lord, O My Soul, and All That Is Within Me* (Z. 47.6).

Songs for two voices tended to be more consistent in turning towards Italianate textures, perhaps under the influence of those Italian chamber cantatas which, if the number of surviving manuscript copies is anything to go by, were enormously popular at the time. *Go Tell Amynta* (Z. 489), which dates from around 1683–4, is an outstanding combination of melismatic, Italianate figuration and a richly imitative texture. Its pastoral rapture is very different from the stern drama of the roughly contemporary dialogue *Haste, Gentle Charon* (Z. 490), where no less Italianate imitation is used to set 'chas'd' and 'drawn'.

So what Italian vocal music did Purcell know, and did he have models as direct as those he used for his instrumental music? In his earlier days he had copied out several madrigals by Monteverdi and almost certainly knew others. Some years later, around 1688, he copied into BL MS RM 20.h.8 a fine duet, *Crucior in hâc flamâ*, by Carissimi (1605–74), but no autograph copies of later Italian music have survived. Conjecture is rather more hazardous than with instrumental music, not least due to the differences in the languages. The surest guide seems to be offered by the vocal cantatas he wrote between 1682 and 1687.

Laudate Ceciliam (Z. 329) was composed for the Cecilian celebrations on 22 November 1683 and has been discussed in detail elsewhere.[35] Scored for alto, tenor and bass soloists, two violins and continuo, it is a stylistic hotch-potch, vocally indebted to the methods of Carissimi and other Italian composers of that period, while the opening symphony is in the Anglo-French style familiar from the anthems.

It has been suggested that it was written for the Roman Catholic chapel of Charles II's wife Catherine of Braganza,[36] but a rather more likely explanation is that it was designed for the same sort of private meeting at which the Latin settings of Locke and Christopher Gibbons had been performed, perhaps at the Music School of Oxford University, with which both Locke and Gibbons were connected and which played a prominent role in fostering Italianate settings of this kind.[37] The style of notation is unique in Purcell's autographs, and was intended to indicate by visual, rather than aural means, a stylistic connection which would not have been lost on cognoscenti. Its use of 'white' note-heads thus ♩ ♪♪ ♪♩ ♪ was rare in England, though it survives in a few contemporary sources of Italianate music by English composers; but it is much more common in Italian composers such as Carissimi.[38]

Laudate Ceciliam and other obviously Italianate forays like the arresting sacred song *Awake and with Attention Hear* (Z. 181), written a year or two later, are aberrations, for Purcell's compositional development was not achieved by a series of boldly experimental thrusts. Paradoxically, there are few clearer demonstrations of just how deep-seated his style consciousness was, for while *Awake and with Attention Hear* shows that he had the technical resource to handle Italianate vocal idioms, their absorption into his personal style, to the extent that they could set English words while blending with his elaborately polyphonic thinking, was another matter altogether.

Stylistic experimentation is also evident in the various kinds of recitative Purcell wrote after 1680; most of it seems designed to intensify rhythmic energy and heighten rhetorical gesture. Compared with *What Hope for Us Remains?* (Z. 472), the sacred partsongs and pieces like 'But with As Great Devotion Meet' from the 1681 ode *Swifter Isis, Swifter Flow* (Z. 336.7) and the opening item of the 1683 ode *The Summer's Absence* (Z. 337.2), show the vocal line becoming increasingly independent of the regular movement of the continuo.

In multi-sectional secular recitatives of the early 1680s, such as *Urge Me No More* (Z. 426), *No, to What Purpose?* (Z. 468) and *Beneath a Dark and Melancholy Grove* (Z. 461), and in sacred settings like *Sleep, Adam, and Take Thy Rest* (Z. 195) and *With Sick and Famish'd Eyes* (Z. 200), these techniques are combined with a broadly-conceived structure which can provide a background both for detailed expressive gestures and for the overall sentiments of the text. So continuity of motion is maintained by an impeccable command of voice-leading which crosses sectional boundaries, to the extent that it seems to spring from the text itself.

That technical obsessiveness so evident in the sonatas emerges in these pieces too, and the result is sometimes a little too experimental. The tuneful middle section of *No, to What Purpose?* (Z. 468) constantly mixes hemiola and regular triple-time rhythms, apparently in an attempt to avoid regular phrasing. Purcell may have got the idea from Blow, who did the same in the pre-1681 ode *Awake, Awake My Lyre*;[39] and while in both pieces the result is too self-conscious, it does mark a step towards a freer and more distinctive style within the triple-time air.[40]

Similar priorities emerge in Purcell's ground bass pieces. As Westrup says, ground bass was a conundrum of the time,[41] but so enthusiastic was Purcell in solving its distinctive challenges that North declared

There are indeed some diversifications upon grounds, especially of Mr Purcell[,] which shew the many ways a base may be handled or rather tormented and which as artfull example[s] may be useful. But there is one excess seldom wanted in them, which is a wiredrawing of various keys and cadences out of the ground which the air of it doth not in any manner lead.[42]

North was showing the same aesthetic priorities which led Burney implicitly to damn the whole technique as 'Gothic'.[43] But for Purcell, especially in his younger days, such niceties had little appeal compared with rugged inventiveness, and while some grounds are overly experimental, far more show a grip on form even more remarkable than their contrapuntal and harmonic wizardry. The famous string *Chacony* (Z. 730), for example, which dates from around this period and owes much to French pieces of this kind, impeccably sustains variations which culminate in a superbly-timed recapitulation of the opening. Text setting, however, is a different matter and, as with so many areas of vocal music, Purcell had to work at it.

The sacred partsong *Since God So Tender a Regard* (Z. 143) is unique in that the six sections in contrasting styles and tempo see no change in the simple four-bar ground. But that somewhat highbrow approach was not suitable for most genres and, in the ode in particular, Blow seems to have led the way with brave techniques which Purcell copied, often with better results.

Transposing the ground to another key was to prove one of the most fruitful developments. Blow probably learned this from Italian music and in the 1681 New Year ode *Great Sir, the Joy of All Our Hearts* set an example which Purcell was to follow in 'The Sparrow and the Gentle Dove' from the 1683 court ode *From Hardy Climes* (Z. 325.8). The experimental nature of both composers' efforts shows itself in the bumpy, even crude transitions, but their common purpose is revealed in that the running-quaver ground bass became a more or less obligatory feature of at least one solo in every subsequent ode.

The odes also show Purcell's growing capacity to range freely across a variety of styles. In textures as diverse as the rugged yet basically Italianate 'With Trumpets and Shouts' from the 1684 ode *From Those Serene and Rapturous Joys* (Z. 326.11), and the astonishingly elaborate instrumental reworking of 'But Kings Like the Sun' from *Fly, Bold Rebellion* (Z. 324.8b), there is a marked improvement in the appropriateness of his choices and in his capacity to deliver what the boldness of his imagination seems to have been after. The verse anthems with strings also benefit from these developments: one of the best is *I Was Glad* (Z. 19), from 1683–4.

By 1684 the basic structural concept of the ode – a series of units each of which increases in density – had become a vehicle for truly dramatic contrasts, and this affected anthems too. In the ode *What Shall Be Done?* (Z. 341), from 1682, Purcell had made a shot at contrasting flutes and strings, apparently his first use of a technique extensive in the late dramatic music, though the result is rather mechanical. A much more highly-charged result is achieved in the anthem *Praise the Lord, O My Soul, and All That Is Within Me* (Z. 47) which dates from around 1684 and uses strings and voices alone to produce some of the most elaborate and fast-moving exchanges of this sort in Purcell's output – a superb instance of the clamour of the crowd harnessed for dramatic effect. It is particularly striking for the way discourses between small groups are used to build tension, each cycle of which culminates in a chorus or a string piece. Purcell might have got the idea for such elaborate textures from Blow, though both his and Purcell's efforts are reminiscent of concertato motets by composers such as Carissimi and Stradella; nor should Germanic music be excluded from the possible range of influence either.

The simpler harmonic structures which were emerging around 1683–6 tend to underline the effectiveness of such contrasts, and to increase dramatic tensions by improving large-scale focus, even in less elaborate textures such as the vocal dialogues. *Haste, Gentle Charon* (Z. 490) is an outstanding example: inflexions to the minor mode express notions such as 'The pains that parted lovers undergo' and 'these gloomy regions of despair', and their expressive clout owes much to their occurring during harmonic prolongations, the singularity of which heightens the effect of 'bending' the harmonic motion.

Such skill was increasingly recognised by Purcell's contemporaries. Publication of the *Sonatas of Three Parts* was a statement of faith in the composer, and even though they seem not to have achieved the anticipated commercial success, his stream of publications, especially of songs and catches, increased markedly after 1682.[44] Perhaps the ultimate accolade came hard on the heels of the sonatas, when in 1683 his fellow musicians asked him to produce the first of the St Cecilia odes. *Welcome to All the Pleasures* (Z. 339) is a fine piece and set a high standard for his contemporaries to follow in later years.

CHAPTER THREE

Consolidation: *c*. 1685 to *c*. 1688

FOR PURCELL AND OTHER court musicians, 1685 must have been memorable chiefly for the consequences of the death of Charles II on 6 February and the ascendancy of James II, who together with Mary of Modena was crowned in Westminster Abbey on 23 April. The obsequies and the coronation would have kept the musicians busy. Indeed, many of them would not be so busy again with court affairs, for the new king and queen were less interested in artistic patronage than their predecessors, and were Roman Catholics. The detailed reasons for the changes they instituted are beyond our scope here, but we might note that the Chapel Royal lost some of its status, and that the Roman Catholic chapel which opened at the end of 1686 proved an even stronger platform for specially imported foreign musicians than Catherine of Braganza's chapel had done, with the result that natives faced more competition than before.[1]

During the short and tempestuous reign of James II, Purcell produced some of his finest anthems; but in comparison with any earlier four- or five-year period the quantity of sacred music declined. Also, perhaps because of new artistic policies at the court – or a lack of policy – and certainly because of the period's political uncertainties, there are fewer court odes from these years: Purcell's involvement was confined to the birthday celebrations of 1685, 1686 and 1687.[2]

By contrast, there is a marked increase in the amount of music by Purcell intended for a wider public. His growing contributions to vocal anthologies culminated in 1688 with the publication of the first book of *Harmonia sacra*, a compilation of music by himself and other English composers, and which he edited. In court records from 1685 he is listed as a harpsichordist,[3] and it seems that much of his later reputation on that instrument (he was already known as an organist, of course) was built on his activities during these years. We know that by 1686 musicians were coming to him for lessons, and that by the 1690s at least he was recognised as a notable keyboard teacher.[4] 1687 saw his first didactic publication, when a four-part canon (Z. 109) appeared in the eleventh edition of Playford's *An Introduction to the Skill of Musick*, a small beginning perhaps, but presaging much greater things.[5] Then in 1689 he contributed the Suite in C (Z. 665) and numerous small pieces to the second part of *Musick's Handmaid*, described as 'the newest Lessons ... for the virginals, harpsichord and spinet'. Much more of his keyboard music than this almost certainly dates from these years.

The changed circumstances at court might have been difficult for English musicians, but for Purcell they were in many respects opportune. Freed of Charles II's Francophilia, he could develop much more intensively the stylistic conflations on which he had been working since around 1682.

In instrumental music he moved towards the methods of Italian composers nearer his own generation than was Colista. The symphony to the coronation anthem *My Heart Is Inditing* (Z. 30) is something of a landmark, for it is the first of Purcell's anthem symphonies to combine in its second section the dance-like character which had been the norm in earlier anthems, with the fugal writing and extended sequential patterning which was becoming the norm in the ode. Both sections consist almost entirely of reworkings and transpositions of material developed directly from the opening bars. The I–vi–ii–IV–I harmonic design of the second section might seem conservative, but the context makes the structure as economical and organic as a more obviously modern design, in that it reworks the distinctive harmonic emphases of the symphony's opening, as does the rest of the anthem.

An increasingly mature approach is especially evident in Purcell's willingness, in this and other instrumental works, to abandon the literal motivic repetition so prominent up to and including the sonatas. The significance of this should not be underestimated, for it produces Purcell's first reconciliation, on equal terms, between modern structural and textural methods, and the compositional priorities which had absorbed him from his earliest days.

In the second section of the symphony to the 1686 ode *Ye Tuneful Muses* (Z. 344), the fugal texture is based on a two-part, fully invertible subject consisting of a number of repetitions of three one-bar motifs. The section puts the material through every conceivable combinatorial possibility, and freely adapts motifs according to context. The economical harmonic structure includes a number of extensive prolongations, and each harmonic area deals with a specific type of combinatorial possibility.

This was to prove the way forward for Purcell's style as a whole, and a particularly potent indicator of this is the extent to which, from the end of 1687, Italianate textures with these characteristics start to appear in that most conservative of genres, the verse anthem with strings. The earliest appears to be *Behold, I Bring You Glad Tidings* (Z. 2), written for Christmas Day 1687.

Its first section abandons Anglo-French textures in favour of a seemingly more homophonic fanfare style reminiscent of the Italian sonata. By 1687 Purcell must have encountered such pieces by Italian composers and by English composers with Italianate interests. As in other areas, Blow seems to have been in on the act first; his 1686 ode *Hail, Monarch, Sprung of Race Divine*, for example, begins with a fanfare-like figure treated imitatively and with many Italianate textural features (Ex. 17).

Ex. 17   Blow, *Hail, Monarch, Sprung of Race Divine*, opening symphony (from BL Add. MS 33287)

A closer relationship can be found with a piece Purcell must have encountered just a few weeks before the first performance of his Christmas anthem. For the 1687 Cecilian celebrations, Dryden's text *From Harmony, from Heav'nly Harmony* was set by the Italian Draghi, who had been resident in England for more than twenty years. Draghi's style was deeply influenced by English practice, but to his English contemporaries his setting must have seemed assertively Italian. The opening of the symphony (Ex. 18) has textures similar to

Ex. 18   Draghi, *From Harmony*, opening symphony (from BL Add. MS 33287)

those of Purcell's anthem, and even more so to those of the symphony from *My Song Shall Be Alway* (Z. 31), written a year or so later. The second section of the symphony to *Behold, I Bring You Glad Tidings* is Purcell's most obviously Italianate since that to *What Shall Be Done?* (Z. 341) back in 1682. Like that earlier landmark, it is dominated by harmonic prolongations and by extensive cellular repetitions derived from the subject; but it is markedly different in detail, concentrating on two two-part, contrasted ideas, fully invertible and readily extensible by fragmentary repetition. The strongly periodic phrasing sets up long-term harmonic functions of a decidedly modern character, though spiced with details drawn from Purcell's earlier style, not least in the use of entries which overlap structural boundaries.

In the rest of the anthem Purcell follows well-established continental practice in using dramatically contrasted groupings of soloists, chorus and instruments to portray one or several angels, the earth-bound shepherds and the heavenly hosts. The vocal writing too tends to be more Italianate than most earlier anthems.

Just a year or so later Purcell was to go on to much better things than this technically skilled but rather obvious piece, notably in *O Sing unto the Lord* (Z. 44), in which a return to literal repetition in Italianate textures marks a resolution of several areas of his stylistic struggles. Nevertheless, the timing of *Behold, I Bring You Glad Tidings* (Z. 2) is significant, coming as it does so soon after Draghi's Cecilian ode and Purcell's own *Sound the Trumpet* (Z. 335) – much his most Italianate ode to date – and just before his first really successful set of Italianate songs, his contribution to D'Urfey's play *A Fool's Preferment*.

Since 1685 Purcell had been achieving rather less consistent results in producing a comparable stylistic conflation in vocal music. Again, the odes provide the most consistent evidence, with Purcell and Blow keeping close company in forging new methods. In the verse and chorus 'Look Up, and to Our Isle Returning See' from Purcell's first ode for James II, *Why, Why Are All the Muses Mute?* (Z. 343.6) he begins to move away from the choral textures of the earlier odes and anthems, towards fragmentary repetition as a primary means of expansion. Blow's 1685 New Year ode *My Trembling Song Awake* includes similar types of texture, notably in the *atbb* verse 'Call Loud for Songs'.

That the amalgamation of complex polyphony and modern structural methods was in an essentially transitional stage during these years, at least in Purcell's vocal music, is shown by some of the means he adopted to keep motivic proliferation in check while dealing with the detailed progress of the text. In *Why, Why Are All the Muses Mute?* the solo with violins, 'Accursed Rebellion' (Z. 343.7), adopts the scoring of bass solo and instrumental trio which was common in French opera. The dense imitation between soloist and violins is supported by an often independent, largely unornamented continuo line, which outlines regular harmonic progressions and helps to articulate the prolongations which form such a large proportion of the piece.

Harmonic function is nevertheless much less focussed than in many contemporary instrumental works, partly because of the tendency to keep referring incidentally to other harmonic areas and partly because the violin writing is more concerned with exact imitation than with reinforcing the harmonic functions outlined by the bass. Comparison with 'While Caesar, Like the Morning Star' (Z. 335.8), the equivalent piece from the 1687 ode *Sound the Trumpet*, is revealing.

No less transitional are the rather different techniques seen in this ode's concluding item, the solo, ritornello, verse and chorus 'O, How Blest Is the Isle' (Z. 343.13). The chorus is a reworking of the solo, and achieves appropriate length by extending carefully chosen moments of the solo. The result offers a secure foundation for the chromatic excursions developed by concentrated imitation, though the technique has limitations in that it produces a series of prolongations which are inserted into a pre-existing structure, rather than being an integral element.

Nevertheless, the increasing expressive power of Purcell's vocal music is inseparable from his growing command of harmonic structure. In the 1686 ode *Ye Tuneful Muses*, the trio with flutes 'To Music's Softer But Yet Kind and Pleasing Melody' (Z. 344.10) is a series of short, superbly expressive vocal phrases separated by instrumental reworkings, each phrase being either a prolongation of a single harmony or a progression from one harmonic area to another. The result is far more effective than his earlier use of similar resources in *What Shall Be Done?*, largely because the dialogue between groups is part of the basic process of the piece, rather than being repetitions inserted into a shorter structure.

Purcell's striving towards explicit expression and consequent dramatic potential, so clearly implied in the preface to the *Sonatas of Three Parts*, is nowhere better seen than in the songs he produced during these years. Here he is in many respects at his most experimental – an approach shown not least in the marked stylistic differences between, and inconsistent achievements in, the 'Sighs for our late sovereign King Charles the Second' *If Pray'rs and Tears* (Z. 380), a full armoury of English rhetorical devices, and *Awake and with Attention Hear* (Z. 181), written not long after, and a forceful attempt to draw on more Italianate methods.

These songs epitomise a general propensity to associate certain expressive areas with specific stylistic methods. Up to and including 1685, Purcell's highest powers in vocal music tended to be brought out by penitential or other less-than-happy texts, and he had been in his métier in avowedly English recitatives such as *With Sick and Famish'd Eyes* (Z. 200). While *If Pray'rs and Tears* is

Ex. 19 Carissimi, *Lucifer, cœlestis olim hierarchiæ princeps*: bb. 1–11 (from BL Add.
MS 33234)

much less successful, its expressive world is essentially the same – an appropriate style for a lament for an English monarch.

For more forceful, dramatic expression, Purcell turned to the Italian style. *Let
God Arise* (Z. 23) is a striking, very early example, but one should also consider
early recitative songs such as 'Blow, Boreas, Blow' from *Sir Barnaby Whigg* (Z.
589) and *From Silent Shades* (Z. 370), which achieve their unusual expressive
scope partly through internal stylistic contrasts which include the use of frankly
Italianate figuration.

Awake and with Attention Hear is by far Purcell's boldest essay in this
direction to date, for whatever pious thoughts might have motivated the poet
Abraham Cowley, we can be fairly sure that it was the text's vivid pictorial
imagery and dramatic contrasts which appealed most to Purcell. He was
perhaps attempting a modern equivalent of Lanier's *Hero and Leander*, then
well known for its bold expression of 'passion, hope, fear and despair, as strong
as words and sounds can bear'.[6] But Purcell breaks new ground in combining
such emphases with a consistent concern for large-scale musical design and
continuity.

Awake and with Attention Hear draws deeply on Italian music known to

Ex. 20   Awake and with Attention Hear (Z. 181): bb. 1–8

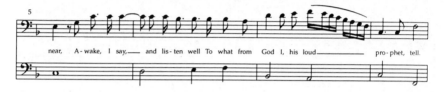

Ex. 21   Carissimi, Crucior in hâc flamâ (from BL MS RM 20.h.8)

have been in circulation in England during Purcell's lifetime. It was probably two or more years later that he copied into BL MS RM 20.h.8 Carissimi's duet *Crucior in hâc flamâ*, one of only two works by other composers to be included in the manuscript (the other is Blow's *O Pray for the Peace*), and the most explicit example of an interest in that composer which can be identified much earlier.

If the number of manuscript and published copies is anything to go by, Carissimi's *Lucifer, cœlestis olim hierarchiæ princeps* was one of that composer's best-known works in England. It was printed in a corrupt form in the second book of *Harmonia sacra*, where it kept company with several of Purcell's sacred songs. Its opening bars (Ex. 19) have much in common with those of *Awake and with Attention Hear* (Ex. 20) and, indeed, with other Latin settings by Purcell.[7]

Both pieces combine a rapid dispatch of the text with fine attention to its stress patterns and to representative detail. Both composers use the flattened seventh for similar expressive purposes, Purcell on 'drowsy' and Carissimi on 'fatue'. A harmonic circuit within the tonic is punctuated about halfway through by a prominent progression stressing an important word – Carissimi goes to IV on 'elatus' and Purcell has V on 'near'. Both composers precede the final closes with a flourish, Carissimi with a particularly elaborate one.

Such methods recur in the opening bars of *Crucior in hâc flamâ*, shown in Ex. 21 in the form in which it appears in Purcell's hand. Other stylistic connections are Purcell's roulade on 'round' and Carissimi's on 'coronaberis' (Ex. 22 (i) and (ii)), and the way Purcell gets through text on rapidly repeated notes for 'The

Ex. 22   (i) Carissimi, from *Crucior in hâc flamâ* (from BL MS RM 20.h.8.)

(ii) *Awake and with Attention Hear* (Z. 181): bb. 22–4

wide-stretched scroll of heav'n', similar to Carissimi in 'Ite pugnate' from *Lucifer, cœlestis olim hierarchiæ princeps*.

It must be admitted that *Awake and with Attention Hear* promises more than it can deliver: neither Purcell's control of rhetorical devices nor his command of large-scale musical process are yet up to this scale of operation. Expressive potential is seriously weakened by a context which replaces continuity of motivic operation with surface flamboyance, and which attempts to spin out the scale of operation by extending and repeating harmonic techniques essentially suited to earlier songs.

His solution to these difficulties involved a particularly subtle adaptation of repetition techniques derived from Italian music. For English composers of this time, repetition and melisma were defining features of the Italian style and are prominent in Playford's 1679 compilation *Scelta di canzonette Italiane*, which included a number of songs by composers older than Purcell, such as Cesti (1623–69), Luigi Rossi (*c.* 1597–1653) and Carissimi (1605–74), plus closer contemporaries such as Stradella (1642–82). One of Stradella's songs shows motivic repetition to a changing text (Ex. 23) and a cogency of harmonic

Ex. 23 Stradella, *O ben che mi saetano*: bb. 1–7 (from *Scelta di canzonette Italiane*, Playford, 1679)

direction comparable to Purcell.[8] In the same volume, a multi-sectional song by the Italian composer and violinist Nicola Matteis (fl. *c.* 1670–*c.* 1702), who was resident in England, shows a larger-scale application of repetition (Ex. 24). Again, the same motifs are used for different words, and the cellular repetitions articulate a gradual pitch progression.

Purcell's equivalent of such methods emerges around 1687–8, in the later songs in *Harmonia sacra* such as *Begin the Song* (Z. 183) and *Now That the Sun Hath Veiled His Light* (Z. 193). The former uses a wide range of rhetorical contrasts underpinned by strongly-articulated prolongations, changes of harmonic function progressing at more or less the same pace as the textual images. The latter is a ground bass and uses a few short motifs as the basis for the repetition, on different harmonic and pitch levels, of a fairly large portion of the text. In songs as stylistically diverse as these and the impeccable strophic miniature *Sylvia, Now Your Scorn Give Over* (Z. 420), Purcell had accomplished in vocal music an approach to repetition well suited to the English language and as effective as that which he had already mastered in instrumental music a year or two earlier.

Armed with such experience he turned, from around 1687, to an increasing stylistic synthesis and often used it in an inherently dramatic way. Many movements of the 1687 birthday ode *Sound the Trumpet* (Z. 335) are profoundly indebted to French models, and there was to be plenty more such modelling in

Ex. 24   Matteis, from *Il dolce contento* (from *Scelta di canzonette Italiane*, Playford, 1679)

his stage works; but even in the most distinctively French piece of all, the massive F major Chaconne (Z. 335.7), the strongly delineated contrasts are more closely related to Italian practice than to French, while its details of execution show that combination of Italian and English practice which Purcell had now made his own.

A similar conflation of French and Italian practice can be seen in the final verse and chorus 'To Urania and Caesar' (Z. 335.9), a rondeau featuring the sort of scoring contrasts which can be found in many such pieces in Lully's operas. But it is replete with products of Purcell's Italianate leanings, such as strongly periodic phrasing and a broadly-shaped harmonic structure built around harmonic prolongation. Still more obviously Italianate are the ode's opening verse and chorus with instruments, and the subsequent ground bass duet 'Let Caesar and Urania Live' (Z. 335.5); the latter's leaping quaver bass and concentrated motivic repetitions are plainly indebted to the vocal methods of Italian composers of the generations of Stradella and Alessandro Scarlatti (1660–1725).

It cannot be coincidental that such an explicitly French piece as the Chaconne should occur just two years after the premiere of Grabu's *Albion and Albanius* and a year after the London premiere of Lully's *Cadmus et Hermione*.[9] Both operas feature a large chaconne which includes wind forces – Purcell was not to imitate that feature until *Dioclesian*, some three years later. All three pieces use stock-in-trade chaconne basses, but Purcell's shows a distinctive approach to technique and structure.

Lully's chaconne is by far the best of the French pieces. It tends to preserve the main elements of the harmonic progression set up by the initial statement, but readily alters the melodic shape of the bass and includes episodes which depart more radically from the main material. Purcell's priorities are different: he characteristically preserves the melodic shape of the bass and depends on contrapuntal manipulation, including part and melodic inversion, to derive variations which change the harmonic progressions.

But the most important differences from Lully do not involve techniques – most of those in Purcell's chaconne can be found in *Roland* (1685) – as much as expression. Lully's constant, subtle shifts of colour and scoring, allied to repetitive continuity, make it a superb piece for protracted dancing; and it is considerably longer than the Purcell. There can be little doubt that a dance took place during Purcell's chaconne; but there also is a purely musical drama, much more forcefully projected than in Lully's. Purcell's concentration on the chaconne theme acts as a platform for a series of bold groupings of variations, sharply contrasted in textural type, harmonic colouring and rhythmic character, while the dance itself is the culmination of a musical tension accumulated over the preceding numbers.

Another possible connection with *Cadmus et Hermione* is 'From the Rattling of Drums', from the 1686 ode *Ye Tuneful Muses* (Z. 344.9). This is a massive and elaborate rondeau, and is Purcell's earliest large-scale use of a structural type which was to be of paramount importance in the stage works, notably *King Arthur*. Its militaristic tone is represented in the drum-like tonic and dominant alternations in the bass during the refrain. In this respect at least it is similar to the sixth scene in Act III of *Cadmus* which also uses rondeau methods (though rather more freely than Purcell) and which includes within this structure a short rondeau for trumpets, drums and strings with a refrain similar to Purcell's (Ex. 25).

Without such stylistic progress, the songs Purcell wrote in 1688 for *A Fool's Preferment* (Z. 571) are inconceivable. The increases in local repetition which 'I'll Sail Upon the Dog Star' (Z. 571.6) so convincingly employs, make it possible to give short texts a pithily-concentrated or an extended setting, to spin out any setting be the text short or long, and to intensify the expressive substance of parts of a text. As in Purcell's most successful Italianate instrumental music, the repetition is often disguised: the setting of 'I'll climb the lofty mountain' and 'I'll chase the moon' are particularly striking instances of

Ex. 25 (i) Lully, *Cadmus et Hermione*, Act III, Scene VI: rondeau refrain

(ii) Ye *Tuneful Muses*, 'From the Rattling of Drums' (Z. 344.9): rondeau refrain

traditional contrapuntal techniques applied in a non-doctrinaire way. No less characteristic of this composer's predilections are the recurrence of a distinctive cadential figure and the close motivic relationships between superficially different material. Its motivic concentration stands in marked contrast to earlier Italianate essays, such as *Awake and with Attention Hear*, and the opening verse of *From Those Serene and Rapturous Joys*.

A very different stylistic origin is seen in the melody of the delightful duet 'Jenny 'gin You Can Love' (Z. 571.7). It is described as 'A Scotch song' and, like many so-called, could pass as a folk song or dance.[10] A glance through the pages of *The Dancing Master* or any other late-seventeenth- or early-eighteenth-century dance anthology raises the suspicion that Purcell adapted rather more popular tunes than have been identified. Whether or not this is one, the stylistic debt is undeniable; but even so, we find a piece replete with characteristic motivic imitation and repetition. Such songs were to become increasingly common, and their seemingly-simple expressiveness is as important to Purcell's expanding stylistic range as the more obviously artful settings such as *Gentle Shepherds* (Z. 464) and the songs for *Harmonia sacra*.

CHAPTER FOUR

Public recognition: *c.* 1689 to *c.* 1691

THE POLITICAL INSTABILITIES OF James II's reign culminated in the King and Queen leaving England at the end of 1688, to be replaced by William of Orange and his consort Mary. The new political climate and the new court's attitude to music brought to the lives of professional court musicians changes greater even than those which had occurred in 1685.[1] As far as Purcell's compositional activities were concerned, the biggest change was in church music. He was involved in the coronation at Westminster Abbey – indeed, he became embroiled with the Abbey authorities over monies collected from those granted places in the organ-loft during the ceremony – and he almost certainly wrote the fine anthem *Praise the Lord, O Jerusalem* (Z. 46) for that occasion.[2] Thereafter, however, there is a drastic decline in the quantity of church music and, for the most part, in its quality too. That the monarchy was less interested in church music was doubtless due in part to William's character, but shifting views on the monarch's role must also have played a part. Certainly, with the relinquishing of the divine right of kings there was less need to use religious ceremony to bolster divinely bestowed authority, so the Chapel Royal and its music suffered a further decline in prestige.

Purcell continued to compose music for the court, most importantly for the Queen's birthday, while Blow continued to provide the New Year odes, as he had done for around ten years. But there was a decline in the strength of the royal musical establishment, and on the whole Purcell seems to have been rather less involved with the court than before – he may even have been out of favour.[3]

Whatever the truth of the matter, he was now freer to concentrate on music for the general public, primarily for the stage. His change of emphasis had been signalled by the songs for *A Fool's Preferment* (Z. 571) back in April 1688, and was confirmed by *Dido and Aeneas* (Z. 626) which, although it was not performed in a public theatre, seems to have played some role in his being

commissioned the following year to compose the music for *Dioclesian*, his first
large stage work for a paying public.

It has recently been suggested that *Dido and Aeneas* was composed some
years earlier than the commonly accepted date in the first half of 1689. It is
indeed possible that the concept and perhaps some of the work on text and
music dates back to 1684–5. But the repetition techniques of songs such as
'Pursue Thy Conquest, Love' (Z. 626.11), and the large-scale organisation of
most scenes, are dependent on later methods, making 1687–8 the earliest
possible period for the completion of the score.[4]

It has also been suggested that both *Dido and Aeneas* and Blow's *Venus and
Adonis* – a neat combination of English masque traditions and quasi-operatic
musical continuity, mounted as a private court entertainment around 1682, and
revived in 1684 for a performance in Josiah Priest's school, where *Dido and
Aeneas* also received its premiere[5] – might have originated in an attempt to
establish a truly English form of wholly sung opera.[6] This is possible; and that
Venus and Adonis is *Dido*'s closest relation by far is beyond dispute. Nahum
Tate's libretto seems to have been designed with parts of *Venus and Adonis* in
mind: a few musical passages in the earlier work reappear in an altered form in
the later (Ex. 26 (i) and (ii)), and there are direct parallels between items such as

Ex. 26   (i) Blow, *Venus and Adonis*

(ii) *Dido and Aeneas* (Z. 626.4)

the closing lamenting choruses, and between Blow's D minor dance in the style
of a chaconne and Purcell's 'Triumphing Dance' (Z. 626.13).[7] The relationship
between the two pieces remains on that level, however, for if Purcell's music
offers any general stylistic parallels with *Venus and Adonis*, they are in the
chamber cantatas roughly contemporary with it, such as *Hark How the Wild
Musicians Sing* (Z. 542) and *If Ever I More Riches Did Desire* (Z. 544).

Dido and Aeneas is without obvious precedent in Purcell's career: even in the incomplete form in which it is known today, it would have been by far the longest text he had grappled with; and it is replete with dramatic contexts and musico-dramatic challenges which were new to him. In that light, it is not surprising that Purcell should draw on generic concepts familiar to him – on song and chorus types essayed in the odes, and, of course, on *Venus and Adonis*.

That *Dido and Aeneas* has a greater expressive impact than *Venus and Adonis* cannot be explained by its plot alone, nor by the quality of single items. It is Purcell's grip on musico-dramatic context which sets his work apart: it is significant, for example, that even the three ground bass airs do not survive performance outside the opera as well as many pieces from Purcell's later stage works; and the impact of the many short numbers depends greatly on the skill with which Purcell deploys stylistic contrast as an element of large-scale tension.

Baroque opera was always something of a stylistic pot-pourri, and *Dido and Aeneas* is no exception. For individual items Purcell drew on Italian, French and English precedents, many of which he had already grappled with in his odes, stage music and verse anthems with strings. Westrup asserted the Italianate nature of some of the instrumental music, noting similarities between the main themes of the prelude to Act III (Z. 626.29a), and pieces by Blow (*Venus and Adonis*) and Ziani (*La schiava fortunata*).[8]

Some foreign models are more specific: the most famous must be the lament 'When I Am Laid in Earth' (Z. 626.38). By 1689 Italian opera had a long history, at least as far back as Monteverdi, of featuring a lament at the opera's expressive climax. Purcell's use of four-part strings, triple time and a chromatically-descending ground are all drawn from Cavalli (1602–76), some of whose operas were known in England at the time, and whose laments seem to have started a trend which was to persist for over a hundred years.[9] An Italianate background seems certain also for 'Pursue Thy Conquest, Love' and 'Haste, Haste to Town' (Z. 626.11 and 27), both from the same stable as 'I'll Sail upon the Dog Star' (Z. 571.6), and for the sequential roulades and suspensions of the duet 'But Ere We This Perform' (Z. 626.20).

There is French blood too, most evidently in the rondeau duet and chorus 'Fear No Danger' (Z. 626.7), many parallels to which can be found in Lully's operas. By 1689 Purcell would almost certainly have encountered, for example, 'Heureux qui peut plaire' from Scene V of the Prologue to *Cadmus et Hermione*, though this was to have a much more explicit influence in 'How Happy the Lover' from *King Arthur* (Z. 628.30).

The dances in *Dido and Aeneas* – Purcell's first extensive collection of dances known to have to been written for the stage – have precedents in Locke. Contrasting sections, as in the 'Witches' Dance' (Z. 626.34), can be seen in a rather less cohesive form in Locke's Act I Curtain Tune and 'Dance of

Fantastick Spirits' from *The Tempest*, and in 'The Statues' Dance' from *Psyche*; and the 'Sailors' Dance' (Z. 626.30) comes from the same Anglo-French stable as much of *The Rare Theatrical*.

Almost every number in *Dido* has precedents in Purcell's earlier practice. The skill the opera shows in sustaining extended recitatives had been honed partly in the odes and independent songs, but more especially in the pastoral dialogues. None of these can match the dramatic potency of the final scene, but nevertheless, works written over the previous two or so years such as *Has Yet Your Breast?* (Z. 491) and *Hence, Fond Deceiver* (Z. 492), show a comparably sure command in timing events and deploying musical imagery.

Most other precedents are equally straightforward: compare the ground bass song 'Oft She Visits' (Z. 626.25) with 'The Sparrow and the Gentle Dove' in *From Hardy Climes* (Z. 325.8) and 'These Had by Their Ill Usage Drove' from *The Summer's Absence* (Z. 337.10); the opening air 'Shake the Cloud from Off Your Brow' (Z. 626.2a) is related to the expressive melodic style seen in 'What makes the spring retire' from the multi-sectional song *Young Thirsis' Fate* (Z. 473) and, more dramatically, in *This Poet Sings* (Z. 423). The echo chorus 'In Our Deep, Vaulted Cell' (Z. 626.21) has no direct precedent in Purcell, though if the echoes are removed, the lop-sided remnant (Ex. 127) has features in common with some choruses from the odes, such as 'Whilst in Music and Verse' from *Ye Tuneful Muses* (Z. 344.13). However, its use of double echoes is clearly based on Locke's engaging 'Song of Ecchoe's Planted at Distances within the Scenes' from *Psyche*; but Purcell characteristically makes the echoes part of the main structure rather than grafted repetitions.

For structural organisation Purcell turned to methods common in French opera and the English masque[10] – methods of accumulating and releasing tension which he had already applied with great success to the court ode. The details differ greatly from those of French opera, but the last act of *Cadmus et Hermione* shows that there is a basic dynamic similarity. Lully's first scene comprises a fine, lamenting *air en rondeau* for Cadmus, beginning in E minor, and ending in A minor with the first part of the opening phrase, summing up Cadmus' thoughts at losing Hermione just before their wedding. In the second scene Pallas, in a short piece of recitative in A minor, sets the stage for the *deus ex machina* solution of the large third scene, which is dominated by a huge rondeau for chorus and orchestra, with solo parts for various supernatural beings. Throughout it Lully maintains a captivating momentum, partly by ensuring that each solo phrase and repetition of the refrain is open-ended, either by concluding with something other than a full close in A minor, or by having lighter scoring, or various combinations of both. An air for L'Hymen begins in A minor and ends in C, and the opera is brought to a close by a series of celebratory dances ending in A minor.

Purcell's scene for the witches is likewise sustained by contrasts between solo and ensemble sections, and it ends with a dance. But there is also the pitch process which encompasses most of the scene and which gives the passage of events a purposefulness well suited to the dramatic context. Not all the opera is as tautly structured; but even the comparative looseness of the grove scene has purpose, articulating a dramatic relaxation, which in turn heightens the tension of subsequent events.

The sustained compression of *Dido and Aeneas* was possible only because of recent developments in repetition techniques and harmonic practice. The economy of the da capo air 'Pursue Thy Conquest, Love' (Z. 626.11), for example, depends on its uncluttered I–V–I harmonic structure, and its taut motivic working. The instrumental parts of 'When I Am Laid in Earth' (Z. 626–38) are dominated by repetitions of the descending scale step, while the moves away from and back to this central motif are a core feature of Dido's vocal gyrations. Such concentration continues in the concluding chorus, which reworks the so-called 'grief' motif.[11]

The wide-ranging nature of these motivic relationships underlines the fact that *Dido and Aeneas* is remarkable more for eclectic fusion than for stylistic imitation. For all the Italian history of laments, the dense texture of 'When I Am Laid in Earth', with its line-driven, contrapuntally-animated detail, is quintessentially English. While Italian and French opera can offer parallels for accompanied recitative such as the Witches' opening scene, it is full of that polyphonic detail, superbly calculated in expressive effect, at which Purcell had no equal. Memorable examples are the settings of 'hate' and 'sunset'.

For reasons which are not clear, *Dido and Aeneas* was not performed again in Purcell's lifetime; nor was he to write another true opera. But the musico-dramatic ideals it so convincingly displays were to inform much of his later music for the stage and it is the most consistently organic large piece he ever wrote.

At around the same time as *Dido and Aeneas*, Purcell was involved with another important 'first', his first ode for the new monarchs and the first of six he was to write for Queen Mary's birthday. *Now Does the Glorious Day Appear* (Z. 332) is scored for five-part strings, and more than any other of his large compositions to date, shows that the composer's interest in Italian practice had gone beyond that which can be specifically associated with the generation of Colista and Carissimi. It is the first of his odes to move decisively away from the Anglo-French style of opening symphony, and the first to follow the example of the verse anthems *Behold, I Bring You Glad Tidings* and *O Sing Unto the Lord* (Z. 2 and 44) in having an opening in the style of an Italian orchestral sonata.

The thematic material would not be out of place in Purcell's trio sonatas, especially the more assertively Italianate ones like Sonatas Nos. 9 and 10 (1697) in F and D (Z. 810 and 811), but the treatment has changed. Purcell has learned how to use a simple harmonic background more effectively and on a larger scale, and how to deploy across it, with the utmost elaboration, Italianate material which is apparently unpromising for polyphonic discourse, a combination which, more than any other feature, gives this music its energy and expressive directness.

The first chorus is perhaps the most overtly Italianate of all the vocal items. It expands by repetition, but is far more motivically economical than any Italian equivalents I have found. As usual, Purcell wears his skill on his sleeve. That just two lines of text, set to two contrasted fugal points, can generate a chorus and ritornello of thirty-two bars – very much longer than any earlier setting of two lines – indicates how well developed such techniques had become.

The directness of this music appears to be part of a general change which was to have enormous effects in all genres. The diatonic simplicity set up by the symphony and opening chorus underpins, and acts as a binding agent to, a wide range of surface differences between later movements; and these differences are used to articulate structure, as where the bass solo 'It Was a Work' (Z. 332.6), in vocally florid but harmonically direct recitative, marks the move out of the sequence of numbers closed off by the repetition of the opening chorus. It is the first ode in a progress away from using a conglomeration of small items for climactic effect, towards the use of stylistically contrasted, larger movements.

Enterprise is even more pervasive in 'The Yorkshire Feast Song' *Of Old, When Heroes Thought It Base* (Z. 333), which Purcell must have started by the end of 1689, and which was premiered on 27 March 1690, a postponement by several weeks from the originally intended date. This was not the first time he had been commissioned to provide an ode outside the court, but his music is much his most ambitious for any ode to date, not least in being the first piece by an English composer to use the full range of late-Baroque orchestral forces – four-part strings, trumpets, flutes and oboes.

The opening symphony is the first certain instance of Purcell writing fully independent parts for trumpets, though, as the keyboard version of *The Cibell* (Z. T678) was published in 1699, it likely that the orchestral version (*NPS*, vol. XXXII, p. 95) is earlier. Purcell's parody of the 'Descente de Cybelle' from Lully's *Atys* (1676) was famous in its day,[12] but its style is not typical of most of his pieces for trumpet and orchestra, which are more likely to have been inspired by a complex amalgam of developments originating in many parts of Europe, including England. The trumpet sonatas of Bolognese composers such as Torelli must have been around by 1690, a connection suggested particularly by the second section of Purcell's symphony, his first to feature the fugal textures in $\frac{3}{8}$ time which were prominent in both his own and Italian trio sonatas, and in

Bolognese trumpet sonatas.[13] Then there were the several Germanic players and composers active in London at that time, including Gottfried Finger, whose sonatas for ensembles including trumpet were quite well known.

It has been suggested that over the previous few years the skills of English trumpeters had developed greatly and that trumpets had been used in earlier court odes and even anthems, on an ad hoc basis, depending on the style of composition concerned. Whatever the details of this matter, while Purcell's symphony is not the first piece of English art music to use trumpets it did tread new ground in several respects. Also, there is little doubt that the superlative playing of the Shore family of trumpeters would have encouraged Purcell to believe that justice could be done to his innovations, making this piece perhaps the first result of a fruitful collaboration cut short by Purcell's death.[14]

The trumpets use the same thematic material as the strings – making effectively, a six-part texture far more contrapuntal and elaborate than continental equivalents. Purcell's skill at grappling with the new medium is extraordinary, combining as it does a feel for sonorous effect, with characteristically deft counterpoint: unlike his continental models, he readily allows the second trumpet to rise above the first to preserve motivic exactness, and in both sections of the symphony no opportunity is lost to display the invertibility of themes.[15]

Of Old, When Heroes Thought It Base draws on an unprecedented range of formal and other contrasts, and features Purcell's first extensive use of instrumental preludes to songs. So it includes, for example, an accompanied recitative ('Of Old, When Heroes Thought It Base'), an elaborately accompanied, binary-form solo plus choral reworking ('The Bashful Thames'), an alto duet with independent trumpet parts ('And Now When the Renown'd Nassau') and an accompanied, binary-form ground bass song with a prelude for strings ('So When the Glitt'ring Queen of Night'). Such variety achieves expressive coherence partly by an impressive range of rhetorical devices, such as martial motivic repetitions on strings to depict the battlings between 'The Pale and the Purple Rose', and the use of double augmentation in the bass of the chorus 'Let Music Join in a Chorus Divine' – an embodiment of skill so high that it must be inspired by God himself.

Although the result has a technically self-conscious, highbrow quality, such methods have inherent dramatic possibilities, and it is no coincidence that they emerge just as Purcell was embarking on a peerless career as a composer for the public stage. They reappear in his second birthday ode for Queen Mary, *Arise, My Muse* (Z. 320), especially in 'But Ah, I See Eusebia Drown'd in Tears' (Z. 320.9). By then, however, he would have been working on a much more important project, for just two months after that birthday came the premiere of his collaboration with Thomas Betterton, *The Prophetess, or The History of*

Dioclesian. This was by far his most ambitious and prestigious composition to date, his first contribution to that uniquely English concept, dramatic opera. Its very existence testifies to his rising public reputation.

Lofty intentions are expressed in almost every line of the preface to the published score, which appeared the following year and was dedicated to the Duke of Somerset. This preface was almost certainly written by John Dryden, the senior English dramatist of the day, who back in 1685, in the preface to *Albion and Albanius*, had praised Louis Grabu, and had justified his choice of a foreign composer to set his text by declaring that 'When any of our Countrymen excel him, I shall be glad, for the sake of old England, to be shown my error.' Having encountered *Dioclesian* and, it seems certain, *Dido and Aeneas*, he thought the time had come. When his own *Amphitryon*, premiered in April 1690, was published, he paid fulsome tribute to the younger man:

What has been wanting on my part, has been abundantly supplied by the Excellent Composition of Mr Purcell; in whose person we have at length found an English-man, equal with the best abroad. At least my opinion of him has been such, since his happy and judicious Performances in the late Opera [*Dioclesian*]; and the Experience I have had of him in the setting of my Three Songs for this *Amphitryon*.

There seems little reason to doubt that the preface to *Dioclesian* is a faithful reflection of the composer's thoughts. No less emphatically than that to the *Sonatas of Three Parts*, it declares an interest in foreign styles:[16]

Musick and Poetry have ever been acknowledg'd Sisters, which walking hand in hand, support each other; As Poetry is the harmony of Words, so Musick is that of Notes: and as Poetry is a Rise above Prose and Oratory, so is Musick the exaltation of Poetry. Both of them may excel apart, but sure they are most excellent when they are joyn'd, because nothing is then wanting to either of their Perfections: for thus they appear like Wit and Beauty in the same Person. Poetry and Painting have arrived to their perfection in our own Country: Musick is yet in its Nonage, a forward Child, which gives hope of what it may be hereafter in *England*, when the Masters of it shall find more Encouragement. 'Tis now learning *Italian*, which is its best Master, and studying a little of the *French* Air, to give it somewhat more of Gayety and Fashion. Thus being farther from the Sun, we are of later Growth than our Neighbour Countries, and must be content to shake off our Barbarity by degrees. The present Age seems already dispos'd to be refin'd, and to distinguish betwixt wild Fancy, and a just, numerous Composition ... The Town, which has been so indulgent to my first Endeavours in this kind, has encourag'd me to proceed in the same Attempt; and Your Favour to this Trifle will be good omen not only to the Success of the Next, but also to all future Performances of

> Your Grace's most Obedient
> and most Obliged Servant,
> Henry Purcell.

We can safely assume that in 1690, no less than 1683, Purcell had his eye partly on the forces of fashion; but the references to a blend of stylistic practice are indeed reflected in the music, even though, more than any other of his stage works, *Dioclesian* is indebted in concept and detail to a few definable models, notably Grabu's *Albion and Albanius* from 1686. Many of its shortcomings are directly attributable to such modelling, but it is significant that it includes not one piece which has the pastiche-like weaknesses of some of the trio sonatas.

On the contrary, it includes several items which, by any standard, are gems. The duet 'Oh the Sweet Delights of Love' (Z. 627.30) is a captivating rondeau which creates expressive highlights by capitalising on the unpredictability surrounding a flexible approach to phrase lengths and harmonic functions – an intensification of techniques already seen in 'To Urania and Caesar' from the 1687 ode *Sound the Trumpet* (Z. 335.9).

Dioclesian's most consistent achievements are in the instrumental music, perhaps most obviously in the 'character-piece' dances. If Purcell needed any encouragement for the imaginative boldness of the 'Dance of Furies' and the 'Butterfly Dance' (Z. 627.14 and 20), he needed to look no further than his old mentor Matthew Locke; but, as in other genres, we find that Purcell has the stronger grip on context. The 'Dance of Furies' (Z. 627.14), for example, presses stylistic diversity much further than did the 'Witches' Dance' from *Dido and Aeneas* (Z. 626.34), deftly balancing textures as contrasted as *stile antico* consort music and a Corellian trio sonata, against a background consistency based on a subtle mix of motivic links across the sections, and on a distinctive melodic and harmonic process which recurs in each section.

The expressive directness of these dances owes much to their modern features – to their harmonic and periodic clarity and to the impeccable shaping of the outer parts – but much of their character depends on their ruggedly-independent inner parts, the concentrated detail of which suggests a continuation of the compositional priorities displayed in the fantasias and other early instrumental music.

Dioclesian was popular in its day, but taken as a whole it lacks the direct communication which makes *Dido and Aeneas* such a success. This flaw is discussed in detail in Chapter 14, but we might note here that it stems largely from fundamental weaknesses in the relationship between music and drama, and from a wide-ranging succession of musical styles, not bound together by that organic musical thinking which helped make *Dido* such a convincing musico-dramatic entity. True, a number of writers have referred to the orderly key-schemes around which groups of pieces are arranged.[17] Orderly they are: but a key scheme does not make structure.

These problems are epitomised in the first musical scene. Despite brilliantly imaginative touches, such as the setting of the quatrain beginning 'Sound all your instruments', the successive numbers have little musical connection with one another; and unlike *Dido and Aeneas'* virtually impeccable relationship between tensions dramatic and musical, *Dioclesian*'s musical high spots have little to do with dramatic equivalents. Indeed, the weaknesses inherent in the whole concept, which treats music as a series of essentially non-dramatic, static set-pieces, mean that such a relationship is almost certainly impossible.[18]

The compression of *Dido and Aeneas* was not appropriate to the expansive heroics required in *Dioclesian*. Instead, Purcell relied on the complex contrapuntal elaboration at which he was peerless, and the results tend to be over-elaborate for their purpose. There seems little doubt that Dent is correct in linking this tendency to the relationship with *Albion and Albanius*: it is as if the precision of the intention has produced an over-studied musical style. The final consequence is that *Dioclesian* is the least satisfactory of Purcell's large stage works.[19]

That said, there is no denying the forcefulness of much of *Dioclesian*'s vocal music, even if it does not always seem well-suited to the stage. This is especially true of the choral music, the sheer impressiveness of which is due partly to the unusually large canvas on which it operates, via practices Purcell had consolidated mainly in the odes and anthems. In the prelude and chorus 'Behold, O Mighty'st of Gods' (Z. 627.28) each phrase has a distinct harmonic function (bb. 65–8 prolong the B♭ harmony tonicised by the preceding phrase, for example), each is dominated by just one or two motifs, cadential articulation is forceful, and motivic economy is produced by the repetition of periodically-organised motifs and phrases.

Modelling on French practice is especially evident in 'Triumph, Victorious Love' (Z. 627.38), which closes the concluding masque, and makes an interesting comparison with Grabu's chaconne in the same key from *Albion and Albanius*. A close relationship to French practice can be seen also in the accompanied bass song 'Great Diocles the Boar Has Kill'd' (Z. 627.5), though Lully's equivalents avoid the over-elaboration which hinders Purcell's piece. The web of stylistic influence is complex, for the descending thirds of 'Down the bloody villain falls' are related to settings of similar lines by both Locke and Blow, who in turn might have been indebted to Carissimi's then well-known *Lucifer, cœlestis olim hierarchiæ princeps* (Ex. 27).

A number of other items are less interesting in themselves than as forerunners of later works. The ground bass song 'Sound Fame, Thy Brazen Trumpet Sound' (Z. 627.22) is one of Purcell's earliest pieces to show an attempt to move away from strict repetition of the ground and towards free ostinato; although the seams between plain repetition and other figurations tend to show, it points clearly towards those practices consolidated in *The Fairy Queen*. 'Triumph, Victorious Love' (Z. 627.38) is Purcell's first chaconne to feature groupings of

Ex. 27   Carissimi, *Lucifer, cœlestis olim hierarchiæ princeps* (from *Harmonia sacra*, Book II)

strings, oboes and trumpets; but it is less impressive than 'How Happy the Lover' (Z. 628.30) from the next season's work *King Arthur*. 'Tell Me Why' (Z. 627.35) is a pastoral dialogue, several of which by Purcell had been printed in song collections since 1685. Unlike any of these, or those by Blow and others in the same collections, this one attempts motivic consistency by beginning most sections with a 'head-motif', the rising or falling fourth of which also is a prominent feature of many intermediate phrases. While it is not a particularly compelling piece, it is an interesting precursor of 'You Say 'tis Love' from *King Arthur* (Z. 628.35). The ceremonial music is indebted to the anthem and the ode and was to be considerably bettered in *King Arthur*. The bacchanalian scene, with its drinking glasses clashing, comes from the same stable as the catch and drinking songs like Blow's 'When I Drink My Heart Is Possest',[20] and anticipates the methods of the drunken poet scene from *The Fairy Queen*.

Between *Dioclesian* and the premiere of Purcell's next large stage work, *King Arthur*, in 1691, Purcell consolidated his methods to the extent that one of the most significant stylistic differences between the two works is the latter's use of harmonic prolongation to achieve scale. The path he took to this can be glimpsed in many pieces written during 1690–1, such as the opening prelude and chorus in *Circe* (Z. 575), and above all in the overture to *The Gordian Knot* (Z. 597).

In no piece before this overture had Purcell concentrated so singularly on this technique. He was not to do anything quite like it again. It is nevertheless a landmark in his stylistic development – an astonishing tour-de-force of technique and compositional imagination, as remarkable for *c*. 1690 as the symphony for *What Shall Be Done?* (Z. 341) was for 1682.

The second section consists almost entirely of long prolongations, each concerned with a specific combinatorial possibility of the subject and one or two secondary motifs. The concentration on a few motifs highlights the various large-scale harmonic progressions, and these are driven home by specific-pitch connections, each of which encompasses a single harmonic function. Those in bb. 42–6 and 58–70 are perhaps the most highly developed, the latter particularly interesting in that it prolongs functions other than the dominant – the earliest such instance I have so far identified in Purcell's work.

Techniques such as these were to become the commonplace currency of the late Baroque. But Purcell's usage is nevertheless unique, largely because of the independence of his part writing which, if we can ever regard it as an element within a Western-European lingua franca, is rather closer to the line-driven textures of some Germanic composers than to Italian practice. This relationship is underlined by the similarity between this last passage and part of the overture from the Fifth Suite of J. K. F. Fischer's (1670?–1746) *Journal du printemps*, published in Augsburg in 1695 (Ex. 28. cf. Exx. 68 and 69).

One event which must have added to Purcell's burdens at this time was the King's visit to Holland early in 1691. In the lists of forty or so musicians who travelled Purcell is described as a harpsichordist and as a composer. Unfortunately we know very little about when or where the English musicians performed.[21]

They did not return until early April 1691, just in time to prepare for the Queen's birthday ode *Welcome, Welcome, Glorious Morn* (Z. 338). Just as the larger works of early 1690 showed specific structural preoccupations so do *Welcome, Welcome, Glorious Morn* and *King Arthur*, with parallels which predicate one of the closest cross-genre relationships in Purcell's output. Like *King Arthur*, the ode features extensive sectional repetition as a means of articulating structure; and this repetition is not grafted on, but results from the musical process itself.

Rather more than anything in *King Arthur*, some of the items in *Welcome, Welcome, Glorious Morn* show that tendency to merge the methods of ground bass and free ostinato which had been anticipated by 'Sound Fame, Thy Brazen Trumpet Sound' in *Dioclesian* (Z. 627.22). Technically and expressively, the solos 'To Lofty Strains' and 'I See the Round Years' (Z. 338.9b and 10b) are far more accomplished than the previous year's effort, though Purcell's desire to maintain the ostinato produces the odd lump in voice-leading, and the repetition of rhythmic patterns and phrase lengths becomes a little too constant, especially in 'To Lofty Strains'. It was to take another year or so for Purcell to strike a more happy balance between exact repetition and free variation.

It is almost certainly a sign of Purcell's greater confidence in stylistic matters that, despite these forward-looking developments and the apparently Italianate recitative-air pairings, this ode shares with a number of other pieces written in and after 1691, a re-creation of aspects of his earlier style. This is especially evident in the chorus 'Then Our Sad Albion' (Z. 338.10c) which, like a number of pieces from this period, uses progressions which had become rare during the late 1680s. The $^6_3$ on the dominant, for example, is common throughout this ode and *King Arthur* and, as it often coincides with cross relations, carries a distinctly antique flavour.

For Purcell, *King Arthur* (Z. 628), which received its premiere in May or June

Ex. 28 J. K. F. Fischer, *Le Journal du printemps*, overture from Fifth Suite, second section (from *Denkmäler Deutscher Tonkunst*)

of 1691, was even more prestigious than *Dioclesian*. The project had a complex history stretching back into the early 1680s.[22] The text was by Dryden, who, in choosing Purcell as the composer, was giving substance to the praise he had offered in the preface to *Amphitryon* (Z. 572).

King Arthur was to become one of the most frequently performed of all Purcell's stage works, and it is somewhat ironic that its very popularity led to so much adaptation that no finally authoritative musical text has survived. Nevertheless, what we have is sufficient to show that, while *King Arthur* never approaches the personal intimacy of *Dido and Aeneas*, the music is nevertheless in far closer contact with the expressive core of the drama than in *Dioclesian*, and makes up for its lack of intimacy with boldness of imagination and with a musical scale in keeping with that of the drama.

Most scenes are far more musically organic than anything in *Dioclesian*, though not in the same way as *Dido and Aeneas*. In Act I, for example, motivic patterns are concerned with various ways of filling out thirds, a technique close to that of the verse anthem, and inspired perhaps by the ritualistic function of the scene – indeed, one eighteenth-century observer noted that the music in *King Arthur* was 'church music'[23] – but the stylistic contrasts within any single scene are far wider than those of any verse anthem. In the famous Frost Scene, motivic variations derived from the orchestral prelude are timed and characterised to reflect dramatic progress across a series of highly contrasted movements, to articulate connections between events and characters, and to reflect the characters' changing postures, most strikingly in the case of the Cold Genius and his people. This equivalence of musical gesture and dramatic progress is at its peak in the large musical scene in Act II, the first in English dramatic opera to carry some of the main action.

Most of *King Arthur*'s large-scale organicism rests on enormous rondeau-like structures. No other stage work by Purcell, *Dido and Aeneas* excepted, is so dominated by a single structural concept. As before, the concept seems to be based on French rather than Italian practice. In *Cadmus et Hermione* complex ensemble scenes tend to use combinations of rondeau and ritornello methods: the second and fifth scenes of the Prologue and the sixth and seventh scenes of Act III are perhaps the most elaborate examples, and the two latter scenes are particularly close to Purcell's practice. They keep reworking the short choral refrain 'O Mars O Mars', sometimes to close sections by a full close with the tonic uppermost, and sometimes to herald new material, typically by ending with a half close or with a full close with the third uppermost. Moreover, embedded within this large structure is a rondeau, a sturdy piece for strings, trumpets and drums (Ex. 25 (i)); the relationship between 'Sound a Parley' (Z. 628.26) and the Frost Scene is similar.

A more famous French connection is a possible relationship between the music for the Frost Scene and the 'shivering chorus' from Lully's *Isis*. The massive passacaglia 'How Happy the Lover' (Z. 628.30g) is also certainly indebted to French models and includes a particularly close similarity between the trio 'In vain are our graces' (Z. 628.30g) and the strophic trio 'Heureux qui peut plaire' from Scene V of the Prologue to *Cadmus et Hermione*, both pieces having a similar text (Ex. 29 (i) and (ii)). On the Italian side there are the trumpet overture (Z. 628.4), originally from the previous year's ode *Arise, My Muse* (Z. 320), and the Act I chorus 'Brave Souls' (Z. 628.7b), which is almost certainly inspired by the oratorio style of Carissimi and perhaps of Alessandro Scarlatti or his contemporaries. No less explicit in stylistic background is the 'buffo' tenor solo 'Your Hay It Is Mowed' (Z. 628.37), in that artified, popular style which Purcell had mastered during the previous three years or so.

As always, influences are constantly mingled, and execution is unfailingly Purcellian. The trumpet tunes, for example, have universal models; but Purcell's practice in the one (Z. 628.31) before 'Ye Blust'ring Brethren' (Z. 628.32), is strikingly individual in its lively, independent part writing and in its avoidance of the rather static tonic-dominant repetitions so common in this style. Compare it, for example, with the D major First Act Tune from *Timon of Athens*, which is now known not to be by Purcell (Z. 632.2).[24]

The symphony (Z. 628.33) after 'Ye Blust'ring Brethren', almost certainly for

Ex. 29   (i) Lully, *Cadmus et Hermione*, from Prologue, Scene V

(ii) *King Arthur*, 'How Happy the Lover' (Z. 628.30g): bb. 197–201

two violins and trumpet, has a rather more complex stylistic background. The elaborate figuration is unusual for Purcell, and seems to owe something to earlier seventeenth-century Italian music. It may also be related to the elaborate passage work found commonly in mid- and late-seventeenth-century Germanic music, including ensemble sonatas by composers associated with the trumpet such as Biber and Schmelzer and, almost certainly, Finger. The latter's sonata for trumpet, oboe, violin and continuo survives in BL Add. MS 49599, a manuscript with known connections with the circles in which Purcell moved.

The subject of Purcell's symphony seems unpromising for imitation, yet he puts exact repetitions through combinatorial possibilities unheard of in the music of his Italian and Germanic contemporaries.[25] Even more remarkable is the extent to which he manages to keep the trumpet line an equal partner in a piece in which almost every note is derived directly from the subject, and which includes closes into the relative minor and the minor mode of the dominant.

A no less individual treatment can be seen in the Act V trio 'For Folded Flocks' (Z. 628.36), which Westrup describes as 'a pastoral trio in the Italian style'.[26] So it may be, but it surely owes at least as much to the many English works of this sort, such as the trio for two nymphs and the God of the River which Locke wrote for *Psyche* (1675).

The idea of an instrumental piece representing the rise and fall of a storm would have been familiar to Purcell from a number of sources, which make a revealing comparison with his bass solo with strings, 'Ye Blust'ring Brethren' (Z. 628.32). Nearest to home would have been Locke's Curtain Tune to Act I of

The Tempest, written for Dryden's and Davenant's adaptation of 1674 and which, it is likely, had already influenced the very early *Stairre Case Overture*. Locke's music accompanies 'spirits in horrid shapes' flying above a sea 'in perpetual Agitation' and uses directly representative techniques such as a 'soft' beginning in long note values, an increase in pace and volume culminating in *stile concitato* repeated chords, and a dying away as the music becomes 'soft and slow by degrees'.

Locke's piece is something of a tour de force, the effectiveness of which depends mainly on the forceful obviousness of its progress, its bizarre juxtapositions notwithstanding. Purcell's methods are different and characteristically integrated, and include a vocal line which does far more than merely embroider the string texture. The fugal-type subject in the strings is straightforward enough: it is the decisive irregularity of the treatment, allied with a clear long-range shape, especially in the voice, which gives to the predominant sense of bustle a meaning greater than mere depiction, for when the winds 'retire' at Aeolus' command, the gradual slowing is part of a process set up earlier in the scene. In the opening bars the motion is so rapid that it approaches the limits of our capacity to absorb musical events. No wonder we feel buffeted.[27]

The somewhat learned, even highbrow qualities of *Dioclesian* are hardly ever present in *King Arthur*, and nowhere is this more obvious than in the large ritual scenes which open the first acts of both works. In 'Woden, First to Thee' (Z. 628.5) the accompanimental figuration is no less closely derived from the vocal material than it was in 'Great Diocles the Boar Has Kill'd' (Z. 627.5); but rather than being based on contrapuntal elaboration, it mainly involves a succession of taut, even sparse, motivic responses to the choral exclamations. The result is a clearer, simpler texture, in which presentation of the text has priority.

King Arthur also has a much simpler harmonic style, and this is crucial to its capacity to combine detailed expression with direct communication. The Cold Genius' aria 'What Power Art Thou?' (Z. 628.20) is a good example, for its chromatic manipulations of slow melodic and harmonic sequences depend for their clarity upon clear underlying functions against which the chromaticism can press.

This brings us to the core issue in tracing foreign influence on Purcell's compositional development. For all his drawing upon French models for individual items and for structural outlines, the musical processes of most movements of *King Arthur* are far closer to Italian practice than to any other foreign style. In the miniature cantata 'You Say 'tis Love' (Z. 628.35) they are clearly related to those observable in Italian songs Purcell would have known, even though the details of the relationship between text and music inevitably differ.

One such song is *Velut Palma* by Bonifazio Graziani (1604/5–64), which was published in 1679 in *Scelta di canzonette Italiane*, is well-represented in English manuscript sources, and appears in the second book of *Harmonia sacra*, published in 1693. (The 1688 edition includes no foreign music.) It has a longer text than Purcell's duet, and therefore uses far less textual repetition; but both songs expand by the same means, the first five bars of Graziani (Ex. 30 (i)) by

Ex. 30 (i) Graziani, *Velut Palma*: bb. 1–4 (from *Harmonia sacra*, Book II)

(ii) *King Arthur*, 'You Say 'tis Love' (Z. 628.35): bb. 47–50

variations on the first bar's distinctive rhythmic and melodic profiles on 'Velut' and 'Palma', and Purcell's (Ex. 30 (ii)) by apt repetitions of 'thousand'. Later in the same section, the setting of 'But absence soon' is even closer to the Italian's practice in that Purcell sets different words to repetitions of the same motif (Ex. 31).

Ex. 31 (i) Graziani, *Velut Palma* (from *Harmonia sacra*, Book II)

(ii) *King Arthur*, 'You Say 'tis Love' (Z. 628.35): bb. 67–70

The harmonic styles of the two songs are also closely related; in particular, repetition of all or part of a phrase on a different harmonic level is far more prominent than in most contemporary French songs. The way Graziani reaches firmly for the relative major in the first few bars finds a direct parallel in Purcell's setting of ''Tis not my passion'. The first section of the Italian song ends with a varied repetition on G minor of a phrase which had just been heard in B♭; Purcell does the same, ending his first section with a transposition into G minor of a phrase which has just reached for F.

Any doubts that it was Italian music which formed the dominant foreign influence on Purcell's practice can be readily dispelled by the music written during the year or so after *King Arthur*, which will be examined in Chapter 5.

CHAPTER FIVE

'Meaning motion fans fresh our wits with wonder'[1]: *c.* 1692 to 1695

THE LAST FIVE OR SO YEARS OF Purcell's life are so dominated by his enormous output of music for the stage that it can become impossible to distinguish his general stylistic development from his practice in what was, by 1691, by far his largest area of compositional activity. That his emphasis on the stage was due to more than circumstantial convenience is demonstrated by the declining quantity and quality of his church music, which had been one of the the two fields in which he first acquired proficiency.

The anthem composed in 1695 for Queen Mary's funeral, *Thou Knowest, Lord* (Z. 58C), with its specific and personal expression and its calculated use of *stile antico*, is a significant exception to the generally unremarkable quality of Purcell's late church music. More characteristic are *O Give Thanks* (Z. 33) and *The Way of God Is An Undefiled Way* (Z. 56), respectively from *c.* 1693 and 1694. These anthems were popular in their day, but tend to use modern rhetorical gestures and the structural disposition of the verse anthem in a formula-ridden way, with a consequently limited expressive power. Perhaps the only exception to this amongst large pieces is the Te Deum and Jubilate in D (Z. 232) of 1694, though even this, with its calculated sequence of stylistic and technical devices, has lost much of its former impact.[2] That sense for the dramatic, which had been shown in verse anthems as diverse in date and style as *My Beloved Spake* (Z. 28), *My Heart Is Inditing* (Z. 30) and *O Sing unto the Lord* (Z. 44) was still there, but was now finding an outlet in stage music, an area inherently suited to it and replete with possibilities for initiative.

The stage music from these last years presents a vast catalogue of innovation and success. Central to this are the considerable increases of scale which *The Fairy Queen* (Z. 629) of 1692 – and its contemporary birthday ode *Love's Goddess Sure* (Z. 331) – show over earlier works. True, these are dependent on repetition techniques which can be traced as far back as 1688. But *The Fairy*

Ex. 32   The Fairy Queen, 'See, I Obey' (Z. 629.50b): bb. 1–8

Queen shows applications of them far more highly developed than in *King Arthur*; moreover, in this respect, the differences between these two works are far greater than those between *King Arthur* and *Dioclesian*, and are a primary reason for *The Fairy Queen*'s greater directness.

From our standpoint Purcell's achievements might seem inspired by extensive familiarity with modern Italian music. There is nothing essentially wrong in that view, but surely Westrup was right in asserting that developments of this sort did not come naturally to Purcell, but were born of hard labour.[3] For example, a comparison between the bass song for Hymen 'See, I Obey' from *The Fairy Queen* (Z. 629.50b) and equivalent items in *Dioclesian* and odes from the early 1690s, reveals changes calculated to achieve just that sort of homogeneous stylistic and technical conflation which eluded the composer in so many of his earlier essays, be they in Italianate techniques or in achieving a simple and direct style.

Hymen's solo is a much more convincing achievement than either the over-worked texture in 'Great Diocles' from *Dioclesian* (Z. 627.5) or the routine imitative working between the two violins and the bass singer in the opening section in 'And Since the Time's Distress' from the 1690 ode *Arise, My Muse* (Z. 320.7), the zest of the latter's vocal line notwithstanding. In 'See, I Obey' (Z. 629.50) Purcell deftly combines direct vocal expression with the irregularities, motivic concentration and independent part writing central to his style. Most of the time the voice is paired in tenths with the second violin, while the first violin imitates the rhythmic and melodic patterns of the pair (Ex. 32). The vocal rhythm stresses the second syllable of 'obey', and repeats every one and a half bars; so the sequence of events in the pair and in the first violin constantly overlap, combining motivic repetition and clear articulation in an essentially polyphonic manner. Such forceful simplicity is underlined by the straightforwardness of the harmonic progressions which, especially at the setting of 'long', might have stepped out of a Corelli trio sonata.

In 'Hark, How All Things' (Z. 629.47), *The Fairy Queen* steps into new territory in blending concentrated free repetition, expansive scale and direct communication. It is an ABA structure, in which the recurrence of A is not called for by the text, but makes perfect musical and poetic sense, especially as the first A, which is repeated, ends with a close into the dominant, and the last one is reworked to close in the tonic. To achieve its considerable length the song sets up long-term harmonic goals, uses motivic repetition to manipulate the journeys to them, and links the goals to the main punctuation points of just two lines of text.

Similar harmonic methods are applied to a very different type of texture in 'See, Even Night' (Z. 629.11). The text is longer, so Purcell gives the repetition to the instruments, which constantly rework two main motifs while the voice slowly wends its way through the text using elaborations of these and other ideas, in a remarkable combination of motivic concentration and harmonically-propositional methods.

Such textures are as intensely line-driven as any of Purcell's fantasias, and in *The Fairy Queen* we see Purcell beginning to take advantage of this to produce striking effects in genres where such textures are unprecedented. The strophic song and chorus 'If Love's a Sweet Passion' (Z. 629.17) squeezes the melody into a remarkable range of dissonant harmonisations which have their nearest relations in some music written around 1683–4, such as 'But Heaven Has Now Dispelled Those Fears' from the ode *Fly, Bold Rebellion* (Z. 324.9) and the G minor symphony from the anthem *I Was Glad* (Z. 19.4). But in 1692 Purcell produces a much more cogent expressive effect by fitting the harmonic spicing to specific details of the text.

The organisation of the several masques which constitute most of the music in *The Fairy Queen* is on a much more sophisticated level than *King Arthur's* elaboration of rondeau techniques. This is particularly true of Act IV, which uses a far wider range of styles, textures and techniques than any earlier grouping of comparable size, be it in the odes or on the stage. While each item is detachable from the masque (many were published separately during the next thirty or so years), in most of them movement into another section is suggested by implications either textual, or musical, or both. Some pieces involve unusually large-scale harmonic progression, most obviously the chorus 'Hail!

Great Parent', while the Seasons' arias articulate a systematic progress of tonics which descend in thirds from D to E minor. This is, of course, similar to the organisational pattern seen in the *Sonatas of Three Parts*; but now it is far more than an orderly succession of keys, as Purcell highlights the harmonic differences involved and their relationship to the main tonic, D major.

This masque in particular shows that in developing musico-dramatic structures for dramatic opera, Purcell was out on his own, for it goes far beyond anything he or anyone else had done. Nevertheless, specific pieces in *The Fairy Queen* have evident debts to his English predecessors. For the conclusion of *The Tempest* (1677) Locke had provided a dance marked 'A canon 4 in 2', a triple-time piece in G minor featuring solid and effective canonic writing which neatly uses the consequent drive of parts occasionally to 'bend' the harmony. Purcell's 'Dance for the Followers of Night' (Z. 629.15) also is a 4 in 2 canon, but is much less straightforward than Locke's piece, and uses the harmonic implications of the opening canonic entries to generate a subtle yet distinctive series of harmonic twists which animate the whole piece.

The Fairy Queen is replete with pieces which, on the surface at least, are indebted to foreign music. There are plenty of Purcellian versions of French types, most obviously the chaconne commonly called 'Dance for Chinese Man and Woman' (Z. 629.51),[4] perhaps Purcell's most energetic piece of its kind to date, and the B♭ Rondeau from the Second Music (Z. 629.2b), one of the most perfectly formed instrumental pieces he ever wrote. But this and all other references to foreign practice are put into the shade by the massive 'Sonata While the Sun Rises' (Z. 629.27) from Act IV.

It is surely significant that for this, an accompaniment to what must have been one of the most spectacular pieces of stage craft ever seen in London, Purcell should choose an Italianate orchestral sonata for strings, trumpets and drums. Much of the piece's impact depends on sheer massiveness of sound, but there also was plenty to appeal to the cognoscenti, not least the contrapuntal virtuosity of the final Allegro, which gets astonishing combinatorial variety out of the tonic and dominant arpeggios to which the trumpets are perforce largely restricted, and of the second movement, a brilliant piece on two subjects and headed 'Canzona'.

This appears to be Purcell's first use of the term for some eight to ten years, and he was to use it at least twice more, always with the same stylistic and technical connotations. But his compositional methods show significant differences from those in the equivalent movements of the sonatas. The punchy effect is attributable partly to the impressive forces, but more particularly to Purcell's flawless control of proportion, now liberated from that comparatively uncritical parading of combinatorial possibilities which affected some sonatas. The sharply-differentiated character and, at first, instrumentation of the two subjects, give a clear headline to each section of the canzona, and the subjects' strong periodicity is a central animating force, struggling through a contrapuntal kaleidoscope during the two main expositions and emerging during the episodes and at the approach to main closes.

As a celebration of contrapuntal skill this canzona has a value both inherent and symbolic, for it highlights the fact that, in *The Fairy Queen*, Purcell had achieved a significantly new level of stylistic conflation. It is Purcell's first quasi-fugal piece for many years to reach the level of exact imitation seen in his early music, for even the overture to *The Gordian Knot* (Z. 597), from a year or two before, is freer in its derivation of secondary material.

The changes are so comprehensive that they might be taken to suggest some foreign intervention, comparable to the way the 'most fam'd Italian masters' influenced the sonatas. But whereas the more Italianate pieces in the sonatas are a radical departure, there is no stylistic feature of *The Fairy Queen* that cannot be linked to preceding developments. Thus, if we regard the sonatas as inaugurating a process of stylistic assimilation, we might regard *The Fairy Queen* as marking its completion. In all genres, there is a clear dividing line between pre- and post-*Fairy Queen* music: in many respects it is the clearest stylistic boundary of Purcell's career.

The single-mindedness with which Purcell pursued this assimilation, determined to do justice to both sides of the stylistic conundrum, is extraordinary. The result is vital, and shows the composer's ability to draw at will on his early style or the most modern Italian instrumental textures. The 1692 ode *Love's Goddess Sure* (Z. 331) is a good instance, for despite its sophisticated free repetition techniques and the length of most items, it is full of conservatisms. It is, for example, the only late ode to begin with a symphony following the French-derived slow-fast-slow pattern. Such symphonies were common in the late dramatic music, but even in comparison with these, the piece's conservatism is striking, being evident as it is heard, by textural characteristics, as much as by subsequently perceived formal arrangements.

Although there is much parallel movement of parts, and although the larger-scale structural aspects are of their time, the texture has a complexity typical of earlier music. The first section is based on two sharply contrasting themes, concentration on which results in many differing, complex rhythmic patterns. In the second section the sequentially repeated rhythms and the methodical way in which the material is put through its combinatorial paces, are similar to some of the more Italianate sonata movements, though the non-repetitive harmonic structure and the phrase structure show that expansiveness typical of *c.* 1692.

The verse section 'As Much As We Below' (Z. 331.9a) bears close comparison with the early funeral sentence *In the Midst of Life* (Z. 17A) and with Fantasia No. 7 (Z. 738). All three pieces have distinctive sonorities in common, produced by motivic concentration within an intensely line-driven texture. The most important differences lie in the types of musical process: in the later piece harmonic tension has a much more prominent long-term role, deeply dependent on local repetition to articulate harmonic prolongation and specific-pitch connection.

Another stylistically eclectic piece is the Prelude from the First Music of *The Fairy Queen* (Z. 629.1a). With Purcell at least, this title was commonly associated with keyboard music and in this large, binary-form piece, the style of the melodic material, particularly the running, scalic figures, is indeed reminiscent of keyboard style, including Purcell's own. But both in character and length they also are reminiscent of some of his earliest instrumental music, such as the Overture à 5 in G minor (Z. 772), even though the harmonic design is bang up to date.

For this technically obsessive composer, the road to the mature judgement which made such pieces possible is perhaps epitomised in his approach to the ground bass. Back in 1689, in 'This Does Our Fertile Isle' from *Now Does the Glorious Day Appear* (Z. 332.4), he had blurred the boundaries between ground bass and free ostinato through persistent transposed repetitions of a two-note figure. In 1691 in the soprano song 'I See the Round Years' from *Welcome, Welcome, Glorious Morn* (Z. 338.10b) he took this technique significantly further with incessant repetition of a malleable, one-bar bass, shifting onto different harmonic and pitch levels. In *The Fairy Queen* such techniques become much more common, notably in 'Come All Ye Songsters' (Z. 629.7) where, after five complete statements of the two-bar ground, movement through related keys is achieved through fragmentation, and harmonic areas are defined by complete statements.

This increasingly free approach should not be attributed to a loss of interest by Purcell in the rigour of traditional ground-bass technique, for to the end of his life he wrote pieces which revel in the challenge offered by sticking to the original pattern as closely as possible. Moreover, these occur across a wide generic and stylistic range, and the total number of such pieces is not significantly different from in his earlier years.

No, the development of free ostinato is better seen as part of a general aspiration towards motivic economy. Even in short binary airs, simplicity cloaks high art; so the first half of 'When I Have Often Heard' from *The Fairy Queen* (Z. 629.23) is dominated by varied reworkings of a single vocal motif, and the first three bars of the bass consist of three statements of a one-bar pattern (Ex. 129 (ii)).

Instrumental music shares in these developments. The preludes from the Frost Scene of *King Arthur* and the second act of *The Fairy Queen* are both based on ostinato patterns. But whereas *King Arthur* has all four strings repeating together a single up-beat semiquaver pattern, *The Fairy Queen* applies similar patterns to varied groupings of instruments so as to create stratified layers of metrical counterpoint. The resultant texture is in many ways an ultimate example of Purcell's aspiration towards 'art mixed with good air, which is the perfection of a master',[5] combining as it does the ready accessibility of the modern style with a metrical polyphony as intricate as any early fantasia.

As far as music from 1692 is concerned, the pinnacle of achievement in free ostinato is the prelude to Juno's song 'Thrice Happy Lovers' from Act V of *The Fairy Queen* (Z. 629.39a), which hides under a 'character-piece' surface a motivic concentration as tight as anything Purcell had ever done. The continuo consists almost entirely of repetitions of a one-bar figure, transposed to differing harmonic levels to underpin progression within the tonic and to other keys. The three upper parts have their own distinctive figuration, in rhythmic unison, but with dissonances produced by modifications of the basically scalic lines. It makes a revealing comparison with, for example, the Air from *Distressed Innocence* (Z. 577.4) of 1690, which with its running-quaver bass and repeated ♩ | ♩ ♪ ♩ | rhythm in the upper parts, has a texture as consistent as that of the prelude, but without its motivic economy.

The concept of an instrumental character piece was not new to English theatre music: that large collection of Locke's music, *The Rare Theatrical*, includes many examples; and Purcell's dances for *Dido and Aeneas* and *Dioclesian* are very much in that vein. But the expression of his later essays has a distinctively concentrated focus and vitality, deriving partly from their textural consistency and partly from their strong periodicity and simple harmonic structures.

This emerges comprehensively in 1693, in the drunken poet scene which Purcell provided for that year's revival of *The Fairy Queen*.[6] In the prelude to 'Come, Let Us Leave the Town' (Z. 629.4) he uses the two motifs which will begin the vocal setting in such a way that from the outset they trip over one another in their attempts to establish a clear metre. The vocal setting is more regular, but the prelude has set the scene for the 'harmless sports' which dominate the masque, all of which is a paragon of comparable motivic economy.

In that same year Purcell contributed large sets of instrumental music for the plays *The Old Bachelor* (Z. 607) and *The Double Dealer* (Z. 592), which include similarly concentrated character pieces. From the former we have the Rondeau (Z. 607.5), unusual for being in ₵ time and dominated by double-dotted rhythms; but perhaps more unusual is the March (Z. 607.8), in triple-time, with the opening repeated-note figure treated imitatively across the whole texture and with motivic repetition generating some engagingly wrong-footed phrasing. From the latter there is the final B♭ Air (Z. 592.9), full of detailed imitation yet in its phrasing as clear as any minuet.

Purcell's composition of instrumental sets reaches something of a climax in 1694, with the music for Crowne's comedy *The Married Beau* (Z. 603). Purcell's nine pieces are the nearest he got to writing a musically integrated suite, for most of them have extended references to motifs and progressions set up by the superb overture. Most memorable, perhaps, is the 'Hornpipe on a Ground' (Z. 603.9), which makes a point of giving each line something distinctive yet repetitious, while the bass jogs along with its utterly regular, repeated four bars of minims.[7]

Some music seems to go out of its way to include whimsical detail. Amongst the music written in 1692–3, the A minor Hornpipe from *The Double Dealer* (Z. 592.5) is a good instance. In the second section the second violin sometimes spices up the basically trio texture with accented passing notes; but it is the viola line, wending its own sweet but well-shaped way, which is definitely an 'extra' and gives the piece much of its interest.

Control of such textures can be a knife-edged business, and sometimes Purcell overdoes it. In finding 'acute' the part writing irregularities of the first half of the A minor Hornpipe from *The Double Dealer* (Z. 592.5), Price is identifying a case where Purcell's enthusiasm for such things runs away with him, for the inner parts are so overloaded that they tend to obscure the clarity of the functions outlined by the first violin and continuo.[8] The A minor Air from the same suite (Z. 592.4) has similar problems, but on the whole Purcell's mastery of such stylistic conflation is, by 1692, complete. The Second Act Tune from *The Fairy Queen* (Z. 629.16) is a superlative confirmation of this, with the breezy confidence of its outer parts neatly complemented by the elaborate imitative detail of the inner.

For the final word on this subject we can move to 1695, to *The Indian Queen*'s Third Act Tune (Z. 630.18), a flawlessly shaped rondeau with all its main structural elements in the violins and the bass (it also exists in a version for keyboard – Z. T677 – using only the outer parts, and works well in that form). But the viola part is an astonishing display of self-conscious independence, often motivically unrelated to its surroundings yet, with its timing of dissonance and rapid motion, unfailingly complementary to the functions of the outer parts – so much so that it defines much of the piece's character. Were its detail not so calculated one might suppose it to be a written-out improvisation, like several surviving continuo parts from the time; the supposed portrait of the young Purcell holding a tenor violin raises the engaging prospect that the part has its origin in just such a flight of fancy.[9]

It was fitting that just a few months after the premiere of *The Fairy Queen*, Purcell should have had the honour of parading his newly-refined talents before his fellow musicians. Over the previous few years several of his contemporaries, notably Draghi and Blow, had written odes for the Cecilian celebrations held more or less annually on 22 November; on his turn in 1692, Purcell produced *Hail, Bright Cecilia* (Z. 328), the culmination of an association with the celebrations which went back at least as far as 1683 and which eventually produced five substantial pieces – the others are *Welcome to All the Pleasures, Laudate Ceciliam, Raise, Raise the Voice* (Z. 339, 329, 334) and the *Te Deum and Jubilate in D* (Z. 232), written two years later in 1694.

Nicholas Brady produced a text packed with musical imagery and rhetorical gesture; and in response Purcell drew upon a battery of techniques and styles which reached most corners of contemporary English practice and essayed much new ground. He was free to draw upon the full resources of the late Baroque orchestra, including flutes, oboes, trumpets and drums, and he wrote no other piece of comparable length – some 50 minutes – so consistent in quality and so resourceful in its imagination.

Some items are a response to his English contemporaries. 'In Vain the Am'rous Flute' (Z. 328.10) has much in common with Blow's 'Ah Heav'n', which was published in *Amphion Anglicus* and was taken from his 1691 Cecilian ode *The Glorious Day Is Come*. In 'The Fife and All the Harmony of War' (Z. 328.11) the minor-mode twists in the trumpet part at 'compose and charm' use notes outside the trumpet's natural scale, inspired perhaps by the feats of the trumpeter John Shore during the previous year's celebration, when he played Gottfried Finger's 'flat tunes', to the amazement of his audience.[10]

Other pieces are in a lineage in which Purcell himself had played a part at least as significant as anyone else. 'Let These Among Themselves Contest' (Z. 328.12) follows on from other duets for two basses such as 'They Did No Storms' (Z. 333.10) and 'He to the Field' (Z. 338.11), and the prevalence of such pieces after *c.* 1690 suggests that more than one pairing of the basses available at that time was a happy combination (three names are mentioned in Purcell's manuscript of *Hail, Bright Cecilia*).[11] But chief amongst such Purcellian styles must be ''Tis Nature's Voice' (Z. 328.4), an astonishing piece of elaborately-ornamented recitative which might have been sung by the composer. In *The Fairy Queen* Purcell had produced some elaborate recitative, notably the first sections of 'Ye Gentle Spirits of the Air' and 'Thrice Happy Lovers' (Z. 629.21 and 39); but never had he done anything quite like this confection, as 'captivating' as his setting of that word in Brady's text, and which anticipates aspects of his late recitative songs such as *Tell Me, Some Pitying Angel* and *Incassum, Lesbia* (Z. 196 and 383).

This song also underlines just how complex Purcell's relationship with non-English music had become, for while it and many other pieces in *Hail, Bright Cecilia* can be linked generically to foreign example, specific foreign models become difficult to identify, especially in vocal music, as he consolidates modern methods with that thoroughgoing polyphony which was so important to him.

Nevertheless, if anyone in the audience was looking for music in Italianate dress, some at least of their hopes would have been satisfied by 'The Airy Violin' (Z. 328.9) and by the forceful periodic phrasing and long roulades of 'The Fife and All the Harmony of War' (Z. 328.11). Then there is the massive closing chorus, plainly indebted to the oratorio manner of Stradella and, perhaps, Scarlatti, and which at the setting of 'Who whilst among the choir above, / Thou dost thy former skill improve' does just that by reworking one of the themes from the opening canzona and presenting it in double augmentation in the bass.

Again it is opportune to recall that public declarations of affinity with Italian music must be taken cautiously. A good case is the song 'Ah Me! To Many Deaths Decreed' (Z. 586), written for the premiere of John Crowne's play *Regulus* in June 1692, immediately after *The Fairy Queen*, and the only song by Purcell known to have been regarded by a contemporary as Italianate. It was first printed in *The Gentleman's Journal* the following August, when Motteux described it as being 'set by Mr Purcell the Italian way'.

The crucial issue is not so much whether the song resembles Italian vocal music – which it certainly does not – as what features in it Motteux found Italian. Price argues against extensive Italian influence on Purcell's late music and compares this song to 'Ingrateful Love' from *The Wives' Excuse* (Z. 612.1), written just a few months earlier. He notes that both songs have extensive recitative, and like Zimmerman, justly emphasises the individuality of Purcell's achievement.[12] But there is more to it than this.

As Price observes, the play presents 'Ingrateful Love' as an example of an English song. Its mix of English declamatory phrases and the occasional modernistic melisma is something of a stylistic hotch-potch,[13] but its structure is of the kind associated with English ballad-type songs, most obviously in its regular harmonic rhythm and in its binary-form design.

By contrast, in the later song, melisma and other types of repetition are pervasive, and ornamentation is far more elaborate; and even though it is a strophic setting, the recitative-like ornamentation fits the text each time, a subtle and much more successful example of methods Purcell had hitherto essayed only in 'Retir'd from Any Mortal's Sight' from *King Richard II* (Z. 581), back in 1680.[14] Moreover, although the phrasing of 'Ah Me! To Many Deaths Decreed' becomes periodic towards the end, the harmonic structure is in most respects typical of the recitative proper – irregular and generally slower than that of ballad-type songs, with strong intermediate cadences articulating a series of large units corresponding more or less to the main textual divisions; also, it is dominated by prolongations, and there are harmonically-propositional contrasts between lines, as when the first line ends with a close on the dominant and the second sets off in the relative major. It seems likely that on their own none of these characteristics would have led Motteux to describe the song as

Italianate, but together they produce a much more modern feel than 'Ingrateful Love'.

The importance of harmonic prolongations in this and other pieces can scarcely be underestimated, for while the overture to *The Gordian Knot* (Z. 597.1) signalled a decisive stage in Purcell's use of them, they did not become pervasive until 1693, as is exemplified by their prominence throughout the ode *Celebrate This Festival* (Z. 321) and in the chorus from the 1693 music for *The Fairy Queen* 'Drive 'em Hence' (Z. 629.5l).

This F major chorus shows that such prolongatory techniques were an essential adjunct of that cross-textural motivic economy towards which Purcell was working, for it consists of just three prolongations and a mobile sequence, while the two contrasted subjects are readily fragmented. Despite such simplicity the chorus is peppered with elaborate detail derived from older music, and Purcell justifies such stylistic eclecticism through rigorous motivic and con-textual economy. So the aptness of the ending – the famous setting of 'Let 'em sleep till break of day' – is produced by using prominent E♭s suited to the text and which pick up unfulfilled subdominant implications from earlier in the chorus.

By 1693 Purcell was at the height of his musical powers and public reputation, and was the main contributor to a number of prestigious publishing projects. That year a second book of *Harmonia sacra* was produced, featuring Italian songs and new music by both Blow and Purcell, including the latter's remarkable scena *In Guilty Night* (Z. 134) and the long recitative song *Tell Me, Some Pitying Angel* (Z. 196). Significantly, it included a laudatory poem by Thomas Brown which attributes to Purcell the rescue of British music from 'dark ignorance'. Presumably this was thought to have been achieved since the publication, in 1688, of the first book, which contained no such commen-dation.[15]

The poem is full of the usual extravagant analogies between legendary figures and present achievement. Purcell is compared to King David, the great psalmist and harper, a natural parallel perhaps, in view of the sacred texts; but as a statement of contemporary taste the comparisons with living musicians are more revealing. Italy is the 'mother of each art' (words and music), who could not herself supply a 'juster ... son' for,

> In thy performance we with wonder find
> Bassani's genius with Corelli's joyn'd.
> Sweetness combin'd with majesty, prepares
> To raise devotion with inspiring airs.

Both Italians are quite well represented in English manuscripts of the time and were famous as composers and performers of secular instrumental music, though Bassani's oratorios and other sacred music also had a considerable reputation.

Purcell himself was just as eager to praise Italian music. Playford chose him to update the well-known teaching manual *An Introduction to the Skill of Musick*, which in 1694 duly appeared (the twelfth edition) with extensive alterations, in particular a new section on composition.[16] Even when discussing 'fuguing', at which he was second to none, Purcell draws on an example attributed to Colista. The sections on figured bass include several progressions praised for being after the manner of 'Italian masters', especially certain types of chromatic formula such as the diminished seventh, the 'Neapolitan' sixth ('a favourite note with the Italians') and 'the third and fourth together to introduce a close'.[17]

From 1693 such sounds become increasingly common in Purcell's own music. He was also drawing increasingly on antique effects at this time, though the increasing number of these sonorities would not be so striking without the more profound textural changes, especially the seeming increases in simplicity, periodicity and general diatonicism. It is surely significant that this trend reaches its peak in one of his very last pieces, *The Indian Queen*. The setting of 'From thy sleeping mansion rise' in 'Ye Twice Ten Hundred Deities' (Z. 630.13) is a striking instance, beginning with imitations on a rising chromatic line similar to those which, in the early setting of *In the Midst of Life* (Z. 17A), had accompanied 'into the bitter pains of death', and ending with a superbly-timed augmented sixth, as 'Italian' a chord as any seventeenth-century composer could wish to find.

Given the benefit of hindsight, there is a certain poetry in Purcell's fondness, during the last year or so of his life, for reworking or otherwise resurrecting older pieces and styles. The canzona from the great Trumpet Overture from *The Indian Queen* (Z. 630.16) is based on a variant of the subject from the canzona in Sonata No. 7 (1697) in C (Z. 808.3b), a movement which he had already reworked at some earlier stage of its life. Then there is the string prelude to 'While Thus We Bow' (Z. 630.21a), an entirely modern piece in its harmonic style yet in its 'up and down stairs' movement 'and so jogg on in comon measure', a distinct recollection of the very early Pavan in A minor (Z. 749).[18] On the death of Queen Mary in December 1694 he wrote the anthem *Thou Knowest, Lord* (Z. 58C) – pure *stile antico*, a lament for things lost, which seems to have made a profound impression at the funeral.[19]

The seeming simplicity of most late Purcellian textures and forms hides both the profundity of his stylistic assimilation and the subtlety of his compositional thinking. ABA structures are predominant in *The Indian Queen*, but the ways in which Purcell makes the repetition of the A section a truly organic event – in 'What Flatt'ring Noise Is This?' (Z. 630.7), for example – result from that same concern with integration which he displayed in early multi-sectional pieces such as the fantasias. The strongly periodic phrasing and high levels of undisguised repetition in songs such as 'Wake, Quevira' (Z. 630.4b) (also from *The Indian Queen*), the opening song of the ode *Who Can from Joy Refrain?* (Z. 342), and 'Sound the Trumpet, Beat the Warlike Drum' (Z. 342.6) from the same ode, are likewise much less straightforward than they seem. In this last song Purcell plays around with the expectations generated by the imitation between the trumpet and the alto solo, producing a constant variety which more than compensates for the mechanical nature of the concept. But in these and other respects, neither this song nor very much else from this last year can match the second setting of *If Music Be the Food of Love* (Z. 379C), a fully modern, triumphant celebration of music's power and of compositional flair, which sees Purcell exercising flawless control over vastly extended motivic and phrase repetitions.

One of the most important events in the last year of Purcell's life was the crisis in the theatre world, which culminated in the larger part of the United Company defecting to the newly-refurbished theatre in Lincoln's Inn Fields. Purcell did not go with them and, in his final works for the London stage, such as *Bonduca*, *Timon of Athens* and *The Indian Queen* (Z. 574, 632 and 630), was catering for a trimmed-down operation. It is hard to know the extent to which this affected his purely compositional decisions, but it is noticeable that in *The Indian Queen* there is proportionally less instrumental music than in any of the earlier large works, and that most of the stage songs from this time are vocally less virtuosic, perhaps to cater for the less experienced singers he had at his disposal.[20]

Several pieces have been claimed as Purcell's last composition, including *Lovely Albina* (Z. 394) and 'From Rosy Bow'rs' (Z. 578.9) from the third part of *Don Quixote*.[21] Which it was does not make much difference, unless perhaps one persists, against all the stylistic and documentary evidence, in the belief that Purcell composed all or most of the music for *The Tempest*. Clearly, his music shows what might be termed a 'late' style but, as with Mozart and Schubert, our perceptions of it are coloured by our knowledge of his untimely death (in 1695 on, ironically enough, the eve of St Cecilia's Day) and run the risk of attributing to him an unprovable prescience.

What is provable and seems to have been recognised by at least some of his contemporaries, is the consistency with which he pursued modern continental styles, predominantly Italian, without doing violence either to the English language or to native identity. The many eulogies published after his death are particularly revealing.[22] 'A lover of music' described him as 'the glory of our Age, / The pride and darling of the stage.' Henry Hall, a fellow pupil of Blow, produced verses which, while dreadful poetry, reveal a professional musician's perspective.[23] As before, the names of Corelli and Bassani are coupled for comparison with Purcell; music 'Confin'd to Italy did ages dwell' and came 'at length to France'; she was

> As yet a stranger to the British shore,
> Till Locke, and Blow, deep learn'd in all her lore,
> And happy artful Gibbons, forc'd her o'er.
> Where with young Humphries she acquainted grew,
> (Our first reforming music's Richelieu)
> Who dying left the goddess all to you.

Rather more tantalising is the Pindaric Ode on Blow by Mr Herbert. Published in the third edition of *Orpheus britannicus*, it claims that Purcell's 'fam'd Te Deum, all the world admires, / Perform'd in those renown'd Italian choirs'. Was Purcell really that well-known abroad? Perhaps this too does not matter much, but yet again we have a dwelling on the Italian connection.

No less frequent are references to his skill in setting language. These include a comparison with 'old Morley', Thomas Morley who in 1597 had set out precepts for composition and word setting which guided most seventeenth-century English composers,[24] but which, according to Henry Hall, were done true justice to by Purcell alone.

Amongst the platitudes and enthusiasms, one comment stands out. It comes from three years after Purcell's death, in the memorial volume *Orpheus britannicus* (1698), and from the mature recollection of Henry Playford, whose family had been deeply involved in the publication of Purcell's music. In the address 'Publisher to the Reader' he declares that Purcell had 'a peculiar genius to express the energy of English words, whereby he mov'd the passions of all his auditors'.

He could bring to life the quintessence of the poetic idea, and that 'energy' which emerged so strongly in text setting defines his better music; for both the idea and the enthusiastic execution compel. And his struggle for perfect execution is embodied in his extensive revisions, in his technical self-consciousness, in his single-minded pursuit of stylistic assimilation, and in his sustenance of those wiry contrapuntal details which animated his early consort music.

> His vigorous notes with meaning teem,
> With fire, with force explain the theme,
> And sing the subject into life.

So wrote Christopher Smart, some fifty years after Purcell's death,[25] capturing something of the relationship between Purcell's public face – 'The pride and darling of the stage' – and the more private Purcell, the composer who, when young, had revelled in arcane technical display, and who in his music for the stage managed to enthral his public while displaying his matchless technical skills for the delectation of the cognoscenti.

PART TWO

Analytical and generic studies

'Clog'd with somewhat of an English vein'[1]: early instrumental music, the fantasias and sonatas

POSSIBLY THE EARLIEST PIECE by Purcell to have survived in anything approaching complete form is *The Stairre Case Overture*, which was written almost certainly no later than 1675, when Purcell was around sixteen. It was discovered a few years ago, minus its viola part, in an eighteenth-century manuscript, while the bass part is extant in what appears to be a few pages of Purcell autograph.[2] Both title and material show a fascination with conceptual and technical challenge, while the execution shows an unerring grip on the relationship between fundamental and orna-mental movement, and on the use of a limited range of motifs across a wide range of contexts. For such a young composer it is a considerable achievement.

The first section (Ex. 33) concentrates on two motifs, each with a distinct function. Reworkings of the scalic line *a* produce a long-range pitch and harmonic movement from B♭ major towards F (b. 5), later turned (bb. 7–8) to the minor mode. Much of the opening bars' tension comes from pitch manipulations produced by the overlapping of the two violin lines. In bb. 2–3, instead of bringing the D–C progression of the line *x* down to B♭, they sweep up an octave, and the consequent registral tension helps drive the move into the dominant, which is also intensified by the purposeful line *y* in the continuo bass. But the implications of *x*, with its prominent B♮ and G (bb. 3 and 4), produce stress on A rather than the potentially more stable F, and together with the violin motion, this drives on through the V–I of b. 5 and into the minor mode inflexion of bb. 6–10.

Motif *b* is defined by its rhythm and is used to articulate the approach to an important harmony. It therefore becomes associated with harmonic assertion, as the registral sweeps pass to the bass and produce the complementary lines *m* and *n*. Together, these emphasise E♮ in b. 7 and go on to set up the inflexion to

Ex. 33   The Stairre Case Overture: first section

Ex. 33   Continues on facing page.

the minor mode of the dominant, which is fully effected by violin I's E♮ in b. 7 and by the following D♭ in the bass.

The second and third sections of the piece show thinking entirely consistent with such strong voice-leading, though neither is as effective. It is significant that the third section is by far the weakest, largely because of its failure motivically to drive the harmonic excursions around the tonic minor. In this respect it

makes an instructive comparison with the slightly later overtures in D minor and G minor (Z. 771 and 772).

Impressive as this piece is, it is not in the same league as the best of Purcell's consort music, of which almost all the surviving pieces are in a large manuscript volume, BL Add. MS 30930, which he seems to have assembled around 1680 and which was almost certainly intended to be the beginning of a grand scheme to compile into one volume his fantasias in three, four, five, six, seven and eight parts, plus domestic vocal music. But he never completed it; and calculating his intentions and the chronology of the consort music is made all the more hazardous by a later, careless rebinding inflicted on the volume, probably in the late nineteenth century. Onto all the completed four-part fantasias, Purcell wrote dates in June and August of 1680: the rest – the *Fantasia upon One Note*, the In nomine à 6, the In nomine à 7 (Z. 745–7) and the three-part fantasias (Z. 732–4) – are undated and, judging by this fact and stylistic grounds, are likely to be earlier. It has long been supposed that these dates refer to composition. However, an important secondary source suggests that the four-part fantasias might have been in circulation before they were written into BL Add. MS 30930.[3]

BL Add. MS 30930 includes one pavan (Z. 752), but Purcell almost certainly composed at least six more, only four of which are complete. Like similar three-part pieces by Locke and Jenkins, these four might have been intended for two violins, bass viol and continuo.[4]

The pavans in three parts are probably contemporary with, or were written soon after, *The Stairre Case Overture*. Even more than *The Stairre Case Overture*, they tend towards extreme motivic economy, and in this respect the Pavan in A minor (Z. 749) is perhaps the most remarkable (Ex. 34).

Repetitions of the basic motif *a*, in prime and inversion, generate a series of overlapping voices which effect a gradual alteration in the function of the note E (*b*): it begins as a fifth above the tonic A, and ends as a locally-reinforced tonic. The chromaticism driven by the line *m* is deflected by the intermittent

Ex. 34 Pavan in A minor (Z. 749): first strain

return to A minor in bb. 8–10, but is pressed further by *n*, culminating in the key of E being reinforced by its own leading note. The bass describes a gradual descent from high register (bb. 2–4); the crucial harmonic event occurs when A rises to a stressed B (b. 12), setting up E as the goal of line *p*.

The opening motif of the second strain (Ex. 35 (i)) begins by elaborating on the functions of E and C. Exact imitation on this leaping motif produces pungent dissonance (Ex. 35 (ii)), while the rest of the piece uses further derivations (Ex. 35 (iii) and (iv)).

The other three-part pavans show equally strong manipulation of counterpoint for calculated expressive results. In this respect, perhaps the most compelling is the Pavan in B♭ (Z. 750), a suavely beautiful exploration of differing types of motion. In the first strain the violins elegantly work suspensions primarily involving F, E♭ and D (Ex. 36), while the bass provides simple harmonic support. In the second section all three instruments are involved in a discourse which begins with an arpeggio motif, but in which underlying scalic movement comes again to the fore. The third section sees a neat combination of scalic and arpeggio movement involving all three instruments on an equal basis; towards the end it concentrates on the distinctive register which dominated the first bars of the piece.

In most of the pavans these contrapuntally-driven processes involve changes in pitch emphasis in which harmonic movement plays a largely local role. This

Ex. 35 Pavan in A minor (Z. 749): motifs from second and third strains

Ex. 36 Pavan in B♭ (Z. 750): first strain

old-fashioned approach to harmonic practice plays a large part in producing these pieces' antique flavour. In the Pavan in A minor (Z. 749) the move from A minor to E minor takes place only at the very end of the first strain (Ex. 34). In the Pavan à 3 in G minor (Z. 751) there is a strong close into F minor just six bars before the end, which is cancelled by a move through C minor to G minor, but with no compensating move to the 'sharp' side of G minor, such as D minor or F; consequently the final close tends to sound like the dominant of C minor. In the Pavan in A (Z. 748) violin I begins in a Mixolydian-oriented A major, with just three G♯s before b. 11, by which point the flatwards orientation is well established through the C♮ in b. 6; the first strain's conclusion in A minor is therefore entirely consistent.

Even this level of conservatism is considerably surpassed by the two In nomines, both of which almost certainly date from the late 1670s. The In nomine à 7 (Z. 747) deftly balances long-range structural articulation – achieved mostly by the cadences which define the end of each of the seven sections – with that constant polyphonic generation which is such a feature of those *stile antico* In nomines which seem to have inspired Purcell. It is based around a quasi-Dorian G minor, set up by the first section's alternations of G minor and D minor harmony. Changes in harmonic centre are effected mainly by distinctive entries: the inverted subject beginning on C (bb. 7–8), produces inflexions to B♭ and F, for example. While the cantus firmus wends its sweet and simple way, the other parts concentrate on their thematic material to the extent that there are very few notes which are not in some way derived from the main points.

Most sections are cumulative, but the agent of cumulation is different in each, and structure is to a large extent embodied in the successive tensional waves produced by these sections and by the contrasts between their distinctive harmonic areas, registral emphases and types of motion. The pivotal point in this process is the repeated chords of bb. 27–9, which present in their most stark form a wide register, and the G minor/D minor juxtapositions of the first phrase (see Table 2).

The first two sections set up several notions which are maintained for the rest of the piece: Dorian G minor is the 'home' harmonic area; harmonic and motivic generation tends to begin in F or in D minor and to dissolve in a close when the texture is at a registral extremity; scalic motion is the norm; the main imitative point for any section enters before the previous section has closed; main cadences end a section through the coincidence in most parts of stress patterns in a single harmonic area, but they tend to maintain motion by not being in the harmonic areas which dominated the section.

Subsequent sections build on these premises, each in a different way. So the prominence of arpeggio movement in section 3 produces another wave of

Table 2. Structure of In nomine à 7 (Z. 747)

Section	Bars	Main harmonic areas	Last close	Main type of motion
1	1–13	Gm and Dm	Full in Dm	Scalic
2	13–22	Dm and F	Full in Cm	Scalic
3	22–27	F	Full in Gm	Arpeggio
4	27–29	Gm and Dm	½ in Dm	Chords
5	29–43	Dm and F	Full in B♭	Scalic then arpeggio
6	43–49	B♭m, Fm, F, Dm	Full in Dm (♯3)	Scalic and arpeggio
7	49–54	Gm	Full in Gm	Scalic

registral expansion, reaching a peak in a close into G minor. This return to the home harmonic area, but using a textural type far removed from the opening, sets up the extreme textural variation of the repeated chords in bb. 27–9. Thereafter arpeggaic and scalic motion are more readily mixed, culminating in section 6 where, for the first time two points are combined, one scalic and one arpeggaic. The latter is particularly important, for its repeated oscillations between the tonic and dominant of the harmonic areas concerned – first B♭ minor then F minor – seem to be setting up some sort of closure, albeit in the piece's harmonic extremities. This carefully judged balance of closural suggestion and harmonic distance is neatly responded to by the last section, where harmonic stability within G minor and scalic motion are at their most consistent, and where closure onto G minor is achieved via a scalic descent from the high register, which formerly was associated with maximum tension.

The In nomine à 6 (Z. 746) is no less complex contrapuntally than that in seven parts: the cantus firmus moves more quickly – the total piece lasts only thirty bars, barely more than half the length of its companion – and all three points (one per section) are derived from the cantus firmus. It is a scarcely less remarkable demonstration of technical skill and compositional judgement and, given its extreme overlapping with cadences and textural consistency, is perhaps even more conservative.

The compositional priorities of the pavans and In nomines are continued in the three-part fantasias. But the fantasias are more stylistically varied, and have a consequently wider expressive range, being multi-sectional (though each has just one time signature), with between two and five sections, and with speed changes sometimes indicated. The In nomines apart, Fantasia No. 3 (Z. 734) – with just two sections, both remarkable for their contrapuntal virtuosity – is perhaps Purcell's most severely *stile antico* piece. As originally conceived, Fantasia No. 2 (Z. 733) was also in two sections, but Purcell added a third, and continued tinkering with the piece to such an extent that he never completed the last two or so bars.[5]

By contrast, Fantasia No. 1 (Z. 732) is in five sections, and is remarkable for combining technically-studied operation with spontaneous-sounding inventiveness. The first section (Ex. 37) is built entirely from the subject *a* and motif *x*, which emerges from *b*, itself a derivation from *a*. The section's internal processes are defined by a combination of events both contrapuntal and harmonic. The entries of the subject and answer occur in varied order and at irregular temporal intervals, producing kaleidoscopic alternations between D minor and A minor.

In this context, viol I's G minor entry in b. 11 produces a marked change, to some extent set up by alterations in the thematic material during the preceding bars. From b. 8 the scalic element of *a* increasingly dominates the texture; in b. 9 this is broken by octave displacement, the consequential leaps initiating the more substantial change *y* in bb. 9–10. Three successive entries on G, all at one and a half bars, produce a brief but distinct G minor 'plateau' lasting nearly four bars. This incursion is firmly parried, hard on the heels of the G minor entry in the bass, by the first entry on A to use the pitches of D minor; the harmonic switch is bolstered by the entry on D half a bar later. The close of the section is entirely consistent with these processes, being set up by the return of harmonic stability and unalloyed descending scales over a dominant pedal.

Perhaps the most impressive feature of this fantasia is its impeccable control of fast-moving events, be they within a section or in the rapid moves from one section to another. Each section concentrates on a specific type of texture: the first on constantly shifting patterns of register and harmony produced by the octave-wide sweep of *a* and the entries on different levels in different parts; the second on closely-spaced imitations of a point which uses syncopations to span perversely the octave or so covered by *a*; the third on a more rhythmically smooth texture and a sweeping harmonic circuit touching on F minor and B♭ minor before closing in D minor; the fourth on a frantically imitative texture dominated by semiquavers, which extricates itself by ending with tidy quaver imitations between paired parts; and the fifth on a slow chromatic exploration, featuring mode inflexion and descending chromatic lines in seamless imitation.

The last section of Fantasia No. 2 (Z. 733) (Ex. 38) – a late addition, dating perhaps from the late 1670s[6] – is one of the most striking passages in Purcell's early music, and reveals much about how he maintained musical coherence within chromatically-extravagant textures. It grows out of the extension generated by the juxtaposition of bb. 52 and 53, which includes, in addition to the F major/E major harmonic contrast, a melodic juxtaposition from high F to B♮. This use of the tritone as an agent of disjunction is important later in the section.

Within the first four bars of the section, the two main motivic elements are presented: the leap *a* in viol I and the scalic descent *b*, which can appear in

Ex. 37   Fantasia No. 1 (Z. 732): first section

crotchets or minims. The leap emphasises the first step (B–A) in a long descent, and through its inherent registral contrasts sets up the octave displacement of F♯ in b. 56. Related leaps recur at the two points where the beginnings and ends of melodic processes are stressed – the beginning of the long bass descent from b. 60 to the end, and in bb. 65–6, where the stress produced by the B♭–C leap articulates the finality of the C.

Ex. 38   Fantasia No. 2 (Z. 733): 'Slow' section

The scalic motion undergoes transformations which combine underlying consistency with contrasted surface appearances: so the scalic motion in the bass (bb. 56–9) works in contrary motion to the upper parts; in bb. 58–9 (viol I) appears the first chromatic filling out of what had mostly been diatonic steps. These transformations are themselves responses to alterations in the texture: the bass ascent (b. 56) occurs after the entry of the high F♯ in viol I; the chromatic filling out occurs as a response to viol II's imitative entry in b. 58. The most subtle development is in the bass in bb. 62–6, where the semitonal descent is broken. This is a response to the motif *x* in viol II, b. 61. By analogy the imitation *y* on viol I should end on E, but this is picked up instead by the bass, a reworking of the registral switches which were prominent in bb. 52–6; significantly the breaking of the chromatic line after B♭ is effected by a tritone leap (cf. bb. 52–3).

This section's tightly-drawn motivic working is closely related to the similar qualities seen in the four-part fantasias, most of which reached their final forms in the summer of 1680, when Purcell copied them into BL Add. MS 30930. Technical virtuosity was expected in the genre, and to demonstrate Purcell's skill, an account of a single typical passage is preferable to a more wide-ranging yet dreary catalogue of contrapuntal devices, which can tell us little about the music itself.

The first section of Fantasia No. 4 (Z. 735) is outstanding even in such a distinguished group. Statements of the opening point go through an enormous variety of possible pitch and temporal combinations, including stretti, diminution and inversion. Bar 5 sees the emergence, in viol III, of a secondary figure – quavers scalically rising a fourth – which neatly balance the preponderantly falling scalic lines. In b. 9 an augmentation of the subject begins, proudly displaying itself by entering a fourth higher than any previous pitch in the piece; an augmented inversion follows in the bass (bb. 11–13). Finally, tenor II begins a double augmentation in b. 14, during and after which the secondary figure dominates the texture, although references to the subject are constant.

Technical virtuosity is superbly allied to structural concept. The section is driven partly by a progressive intensification of metrical imbalances posited by the first two entries, which come respectively on the first and fourth beats of the bar. Viol I's augmented entry in b. 9 has a stabilising influence, but the clearest metrical implications are in the secondary figure, and as it increasingly dominates the texture, it produces a clarity which neatly sets up closure of the section.

The self-consciousness of the four-part fantasias' technical display is also underlined by the intensity with which any single section concentrates on a specific range of techniques. The first sections of Fantasia No. 8 and Fantasia No. 11 (Z. 739.1 and Z. 742.1) each use one subject, from the outset presented in prime and inversion, and which later appears in augmentation. The second section of Fantasia No. 9 (Z. 740.2) presents simultaneously three highly contrasted, fully invertible subjects, and puts them through an astonishingly harum-scarum series of combinations, including inversions of all three. The second section of Fantasia No. 12 (Z. 743.2) gradually increases the augmentation of the subject until at its end what were crotchets have become breves, surrounded by elaborations on the original figuration, more or less in cantus firmus style.

The less obviously contrapuntal sections are no less profoundly polyphonic. Linear thinking like that in the final section of the three-part Fantasia No. 2 (Z. 733.3) lies behind the superbly sonorous textures of the first section of Fantasia No. 5 (Z. 736), the chromatic excursions of the 'drag' section of Fantasia No. 11 (Z. 742.2), and the seamless flow of the second section of Fantasia No. 6 (Z. 737.2).

It is only in this polyphonic context that the harmonic excursions of many of these pieces can be properly understood. The first section of Fantasia No. 6 (Z. 737) is a particularly revealing case, expressively far removed from the sombre, breast-beating spirit often associated with Purcell's extreme chromaticism. The pitches common to the beginnings of its two subjects (*a* and *b* of Ex. 39) facilitate an almost seamless flow of combinations. These first bars include a secondary gesture – the E♮ in viol II, b. 4 – which becomes increasingly strong as the imitation starts to leave the immediate F major/C major orbit, and which thereby leads into a series of restless harmonic explorations which reach as far from F as B♭ minor and E minor.

The E♮ is produced by filling out a diatonic step and the momentary inflexion to C minor is quickly cancelled; but the gesture is prominent enough to set up an association between imitation on the subject and flexibility of mode. Everything remains firmly in the F and C areas until b. 13, when E♮ again appears, but now immediately after C major harmony, strongly prepared for by the preceding progression. This produces a move not towards the minor mode of the dominant but to the subdominant, confirmed by the entry of *a* fully in B♭ in b. 15. A chain of subdominants is then pressed home by a series of similar inflexions using E♮, A♮ and D♮ in bb. 17 and 18, and culminating in bb. 20–1 with a V–i(I) in B♭ minor, the most prominent closural gesture of the section. Purcell neatly foils this gradual move towards the minor mode of the subdominant with a major third on the stressed beat and an entry of the subject in the bass, in B♭.

Subject *a* has always been treated as if it begins on either the tonic or the dominant of the relevant harmonic area, and Purcell now uses this association to drive a series of entries which pushes in the opposite direction, sharpwards from F, towards A minor and E minor, the latter being reached in bb. 30–2. By now harmonic mobility is more prominent than imitation, and for the rest of the section there are no more presentations of *a*; instead, close derivations of *b* press on with a harmonic circuit which continues the already established patterns of mode flexibility and which touches areas as distant as E minor and B minor (bb. 37–8) before closing in C.

It is common to refer to the thematic concentration and technical virtuosity of the fantasias as a unifying agent. This is a dangerously limited view: firstly it suggests that by increasing thematic concentration a piece is inevitably more unified; secondly, and perhaps more disturbingly, it suggests that this is the most significant level of unity. Its inadequacy is clearly shown by Fantasia No. 7 (Z. 738), in which thematic concentration is secondary to the tensional patterns generated around pungent false relations produced by linear thinking and developed out of the opening idea.

The two main themes in the first section (Ex. 40) are distinct yet complementary: the opening of *b* inverts the direction of *a*; both are built

Ex. 39 Fantasia No. 6 (Z. 737): bb. 1–16

around the C minor triad and have the elements *x* and *y* in common; both move largely by step yet have important leaps, the most prominent being the descending fourth and upward seventh in *a*.

The harmonic context of the two lower parts in bb. 1–2 suggests that the stressed D/G in the second half of b. 2 functions as V of C minor, but it coincides with the registral peak on B♭ produced by imitation on *b*. The consequent B♮/B♭ contrast seminally articulates the proposition that the harmonic implications of one part can conflict with the rest of the texture to

Ex. 40   Fantasia No. 7 (Z. 738): bb. 1–9

Ex. 41   Fantasia No. 7 (Z. 738): bb. 24–7

drive subsequent events. So the bass replies to viol II's G minor entry by presenting *a* in G minor, thus positing a finely balanced tension between the implications of the outer parts on the downbeat of b. 3: either can be regarded as dissonant – if the F♯ is dissonant the harmony is G minor; if the B♭ is dissonant the harmony is V of G minor.

Any attempt rigidly to categorise harmonic function misses the point: tension is generated partly by the combination of thematic exactitude and harmonic obliquity; context establishes meaning. The imitation tends to work in overlapping two-bar cycles: so, as the C minor statement (b. 1) was answered on G minor (b. 2), the G minor version of *a* (b. 3) is answered on D minor (b.

4); however, beneath this the lower parts present the dominant of G, and it is this function that wins through in going to G major as V of C minor (b. 5). The possibilities hinted at by the B♮/B♭ contrast are now realised in a particularly striking way, and thereby one of the most important features of the piece unfolds: the expressive effect of the contrast and related dissonance derives partly from conflict with the main harmonic functions, which are articulated by being consonant. So, immediately after the strongest dissonance thus far, the downbeat and the third minim of b. 5 are consonant and, with the sustained G in the bass, articulate the primacy of this G major harmony. On the first beat of b. 5 the chord has no fifth and, in keeping with the preceding dissonant strong beats, an E♭ is placed on the second crotchet, consonant with the bass yet dissonant within the texture as a whole.

Although bb. 1–5 are articulated as a unit, they are open-ended. The regular two-bar sequence of *a* followed by *b* could be maintained in bb. 5–6, but instead a derivation of the opening ascending line of *b* (*m*) comes at the end of b. 6. Purcell puns on the common use of *y* to turn this into a statement of *a* in b. 7; and now it is *a* which exploits *y* to produce the false relations that formerly were generated by *b*.

In b. 5 there is a palpable change of character, partly due to the greater harmonic stability produced as the bass abandons exact imitation in favour of sustained harmonic support, and also due to the first sustained motion in parallel thirds. This inaugurates a harmonic progress away from the tortuously-articulated C minor/G minor area, one in which no single harmonic area is of comparable importance: within just twenty bars the piece goes as far as A minor. The more significant harmonic areas are established by cadences, though these are invariably deflected, either by an entry on the downbeat as in b. 17, or by an overlapping entry as in bb. 9–10; moreover, the tension generated by the false relations before most of these would-be cadences is so strong that it compels further movement – such was the pattern in bb. 1–5. So, as in the pavans, harmony has a essentially local function.

By contrast, specific pitches are projected over considerable spans, even if their articulation is somewhat muted. In viol I, for example, there is a series of successive registral peaks articulated by various combinations of dissonance and stress. These are projected not by being unresolved in their local context, but by their prominence. They reach their maximum in register and dissonance in b. 23 on V of C minor, and thus neatly set up the close of the section.

The kaleidoscopic harmonic juxtapositions of the second section (bb. 27–34, probably in a faster tempo) are an expansive response to the open-ended last bars of the first (Ex. 41). The pell-mell imitation is dominated by *c* and *d*, which reverse the harmonic progress of the altered *b* in bb. 24–6 by their clear presentation of V and i. Yet as they do so, viol II presents *d* on G minor. The

Ex. 42   Fantasia No. 7 (Z. 738): bb. 34–5

Ex. 43   Fantasia No. 7 (Z. 738): melodic relationships between sections 3–5

consequent energy relaxes only when the pattern of events changes: for much of
bb. 30–4 the bass ceases contrapuntal discourse and supports more clearly-
defined harmonies which, in bb. 30–1, prolong V of E♭. Although the closure in
C minor (b. 34) is strong, the tension produced by the textural contrast between
the sections, and by the energy of the second section, is far from spent.

Across the rest of the piece closure is achieved by gradually returning to the character and substance of the opening section. The third section articulates increasingly explicit links. In its opening bars (Ex. 42) motif f is related to b as shown in Ex. 43 (i). The treble replies with g (Ex. 43 (ii)), the bass of f and which in rhythm and shape is related to a. Also, the section paraphrases the harmonic patterns of the first: in particular it goes as far as A minor (b. 38) before returning fairly rapidly to C minor, as it did in bb. 19–23. As it returns to C minor it uses thematic fragments derived even more directly from a and b, and chromatic inflexions reminiscent of the harmonic style of the first section.

The first section ended with a half close, and this was answered (bb. 27–8) by a return to the tonic; similarly the half close in F minor in b. 42 is answered by the strong subdominant orientation of the fourth section (bb. 43–5). The section is based almost entirely on motif h, which has links with g (Ex. 43 (iii)).

The final section (bb. 47–51) reworks material (j of Ex. 43 (iv)) mainly from the end of the third section, but firmly in C minor. Given the brevity of the fourth section, it is this relationship between the third and the fifth which dominates, and which articulates the cyclic return to material derived directly from a.

Taken as a group, the four-part fantasias display a stylistic range considerably wider than those in three parts. Conservative they certainly are, but the extremity of Fantasia No. 12 (Z. 743), with its chromaticism in the style of a Jacobean 'hexachord' fantasia is not typical. More representative are the *ricercare*-like textures found in the first sections of Fantasias Nos. 8 and 11 (Z. 739 and 742), which combine austere fugal writing with a generally diatonic, typically mid-seventeenth-century harmonic style. Indeed, the leaping figures of the last section of Fantasia No. 4 (Z. 735) (bb. 35–47) would not be out of place in a sonata by Legrenzi (1626–90), while the subject of the second section of Fantasia No. 5 (Z. 736.2) could almost pass muster in a late-Baroque fugue. Some of the most striking sections are those slow ones, such as the 'Drag' in Fantasia No. 11 (Z. 742.2) and the 'Slow' of Fantasia No. 4 (Z. 735.2), which treat chromatic progression in a overtly sensuous way, and which perforce have a strong grip on harmonic function.

But perhaps more remarkable than the stylistic range of the collection is the skill with which Purcell uses contrast within any one piece. Not all the four-part fantasias are as integrated as Fantasia No. 7, but stylistic juxtaposition is one of Purcell's main expressive tools, and a clear indicator of his sense for a purely musical drama.

Both in quantity and quality the four-part fantasias dominate Purcell's early instrumental music. The compositional priorities they so forcefully represent can be found in many other early works such as the Overture in D minor (Z. 771) which, unlike its generic predecessor *The Stairre Case Overture*, has a fully worked, fugal second section. Then there are the two other fantasias, the

Fantasia upon One Note (Z. 745) and the *Fantasia: Three Parts on a Ground* (Z. 731). The former is an extraordinary feat of technical virtuosity, but the latter is the better-integrated composition. It is perhaps the earliest survivor of Purcell's ground bass compositions, and the ordering of variations shows that sure judgement which makes his later instrumental grounds so compelling; it also has an astonishing range of traditional contrapuntal techniques, many of which are proudly written on the autograph score – 'recte et recto and arsin per thesin' and canons '3 parts in one'.

Amongst the finest of these early pieces is the Overture à 5 in G minor (Z. 772), which probably dates from around 1679–80, the very period when Purcell was working on the fantasias. It has a richly dissonant, contrapuntally driven first section, but it is in the second, based on two distinctive, scalic subjects, that the relationship with the fantasias emerges most clearly. These subjects are put through almost every conceivable contrapuntal combination, producing an extraordinarily restless energy, intensified by 'sudden death' closes such as that into C minor in b. 39, produced by a transposed repetition of the approach to the immediately preceding close into F minor.

Purcell seems to have been an unusually methodical composer, his interest in any one genre or technique often being concentrated into a specific period. That this was so for consort music is somewhat ironically confirmed by the incomplete state in BL Add. MS 30930 of the fantasia (Z. 744) dated 24 February 1683, the only date after 1680 in that manuscript.

This same manuscript includes early versions of eight trio sonatas, and it is partly this which suggests that all twenty-two known sonatas were written across a period not longer than the late 1670s to 1684 or 1685, and could well be much more concentrated in the early 1680s. The posthumous 1697 publication, the *Sonatas of Four Parts*, includes some of the most conservative as well as some of the most modern pieces, and the differences between it and the 1683 publication, the *Sonatas of Three Parts* (the differing titles denote only whether the continuo parts are counted as one or two), are not sufficiently marked for any firm conclusions to be drawn about compositional chronology. The source history of both sets is perhaps the most complex and vexing in Purcell's output, and has been brilliantly analysed by Michael Tilmouth, by way of arriving at a viable text for the *Sonatas of Four Parts*.[7]

The importance of the sonatas as an indicator of Purcell's changing interests can scarcely be underestimated, especially as they are his first publications of instrumental music, and his first explicit imitations of Italian instrumental practice. Moreover, they are his earliest pieces extensively to achieve scale by harmonic proposition. The most obvious and frequent examples are in slow first movements, as in Sonata No. 4 (1683) in F (Z. 793) (Ex. 44).

The repetition of the first phrase in the dominant throws the differences of

Ex. 44   Sonata No. 4 (1683) in F (Z. 793) : first movement

Ex. 45　Sonata No. 4 (1683) in F (Z. 793): motivic links between movements

pitch and harmony into relief, and the function of the consequent proposition is intensified by a subtle difference between the first two phrases: the octave drop in the bass (b. 2) is not repeated in b. 6, so that tenor C, which in b. 3 was associated with the move towards tonic harmony after the subdominant inflexion, does not occur again until the opening of the third section, when it again points back to tonic harmony, but through a different route.

In bb. 1–4 the violins establish two types of movement – rapid ascent in small note values, and a more protracted descent. The third phrase combines the two types of motion in invertible counterpoint. The descent of a sixth in violin I (bb. 1–4 and 5–8) is reflected in the quavers' ascent in bb. 8–9, counterpointed against a more slowly moving bass. The rest of the section consists of expansions and contractions of this pattern (cf. bb. 17–22 and 15–17). To balance the weight of this excursion, tonic harmony is prolonged in bb. 20–1, before the final full close.

This sonata's links between movements typify Purcell at his best, and bear comparison with the methods of Fantasia No. 7 (Z. 738). The Canzona uses a double subject which picks up the first movement's contrast of motion in crotchets and quavers (Ex. 45 (i)). It translates the C–F move which opened that movement, so that it moves towards, instead of away from stability, through the end of the subject having an emphatic close into the tonic, while the upper register's comparative stability is reflected in the movement closing in that register.

The third movement's less direct relationship to the first includes the C–F move, plus ascent followed by descent (Ex. 45 (ii)), while its tendency to mainly melodic relationships and little contrapuntal elaboration is in keeping with its dance-like character. Here too Purcell transposes statements of the opening material to various levels, though they include chromatic alterations which render them harmonically mobile rather than propositional (b. 76).

The main theme of the Allegro fourth movement (Ex. 45 (iii)) seems to have little relation to the first movement, except perhaps that it describes a general descent towards F. But after about eight bars a secondary figure in minims appears in the second violin (bb. 104–6, Ex. 45 (iv)) and eventually emerges in the first violins as a paraphrase of the sonata's opening melodic contour (bb. 110–14, Ex. 45 (v)). Thereafter there are further references, though increasingly the texture is dominated by irregular descending patterns (Ex. 45 (vi)).

The last movement repeats motif q sequentially to produce a larger-scale and more regular descent (Ex. 45 (vi)). The opening bars' subdominant inflexions (cf. bb. 135–6) are the starting point for a long series of imitations which press towards the minor modes of the tonic and dominant and include many contrapuntally generated false relations. Chromaticism reaches a peak with a sequential series of harmonic moves passing rapidly through ii (bb. 149–50), vi (bb. 150–1) and V (bb. 153–4), this last affirmed by a strongly-prepared V–I in that key.

To break out of this massive momentum Purcell uses an antithetical gesture of bold simplicity. The comparative harmonic stability of the dominant is taken as a cue for a nobly-plain series of descending $^6_3$ chords which inaugurate a return to diatonic imitations on q, all within tonic-oriented harmony. Harmonic stability is affirmed by the bass using diatonic, scalic minims, though characteristically, these are inverted augmentations of q, covering the ascending fourth of the sonata's first bar. The augmentations and inversions become increasingly prominent, and lead into the final close.

Such large-scale integration can be found in many other sonatas, but Sonata No. 5 (1683) in A minor (Z. 794) is unique in using a particularly subtle form of recapitulation. Its texture is quite Italianate, very periodic, replete with fragmentary repetition and with much parallel movement in thirds and sixths. Purcell might well have encountered comparable returns of the opening material in Italian sonatas which were around in England at the time.[8] But his effort is entirely distinctive, and hinges upon the use of harmonic relationships which dominated earlier movements, to trigger the return of the first movement's main theme. Throughout the sonata the subdominant and minor dominant harmonic areas occur frequently and the relative major rarely. This is set up by the opening bars (Ex. 46), which include a tonal answer with a particularly prominent G♮, and which in the bass use the F–E of the subject as the first component in a prominent iv⁶–V–i progression. Comparable prominent predominants occur several times during the movement, in the tonic (bb. 14–15, 22–3) and other areas.

The second movement's main motif makes capital out of an inversion of the first movement's semitonal F–E moves, such as the B–C–B of bb. 24–5. These too are often associated with iv–v and iv–v–i moves, as in bb. 25–6.

In the third movement these relationships are worked out even more expansively; but the subdominant-related areas are now so heavily weighted that the concluding tonic sounds like v of iv, an emphasis considerably increased by the following eleven-bar Grave movement.

The concluding Canzona begins with brilliant, distinctive figuration largely in A minor; but the area has yet to be fully tonicised, especially as the subject follows the first movement in persistently presenting G♮ rather than G♯. After

Ex. 46   Sonata No. 5 (1683) in A minor (Z. 794): bb. 1–5

some six bars of exposition in and around A minor the subdominant (b. 118) is projected by using a distinctively leaping new theme for a series of entries in and around D minor and by a B♭–C–C♯–D bass-line (bb. 121–2). The purpose behind the earlier non-tonicisation of A minor now emerges as subdominant harmony goes to dominant harmony – the first such move for a long while – and the opening theme simultaneously returns in the bass. It is this return which fully tonicises A minor. For the rest of the movement, the opening theme gradually takes over until the adagio coda uses it alone to summarise many of the earlier thematic and harmonic relationships, but within an A minor context.

The concentrated motivic repetition seen in this and some other Italianate sonatas is not always so successful.[9] The Largo (bb. 45–96) of Sonata No. 1 (1697) in B minor (Z. 802.2), for example, has two main motifs, *a* in the violin and *b* in the bass (Ex. 47 (i)). The former is not greatly altered during the course of the movement; the latter emerges as a distinct theme in b. 60 (Ex. 47 (ii)), on

Ex. 47   Sonata No. 1 (1697) in B minor (Z. 802)

(i) bb. 45–52

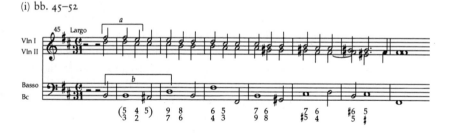

(ii) bb. 59–65

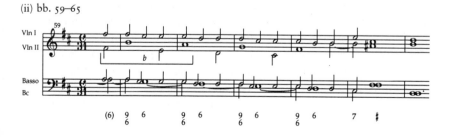

Table 3. *Largo from Sonata No. 1 (1697) in B minor (Z. 802): motivic permutations*

Vln I	Vln II	Bass	Bars
a	a	b	45–52, 53–9, 77–80
a	b	a	60–5
b	b	a	72–6, 81–4
b	a	b	66–71, 85–90
a	b	b	91–6

its first appearance in one of the upper parts. In each phrase one of the themes appears in two parts, the other in the third. All six possible permutations appear except the pairing of *a* in the bass and violin II (see Table 3).

The successive phrase lengths and their concluding cadences are:

$$7 + 7 + \quad 6 + 6 + 5 + 4 + \quad 4 + 6 + 6$$
$$i - \quad v - \quad VII - \quad i - \quad i - \quad v - \quad III - \quad i - \quad i - \quad i$$

All things being equal, the progressive reduction in phrase length could generate a large-scale momentum by quickening the pacing of successive cadential punctuations: but if all things really are equal, then they are equally bad. The rhythmic periodicity, based on repeated one-bar units, and the motivic economy, emphasise repetition beyond the point of redemption, and this is not helped by the repetitive harmonic structure. Moreover, all the cadences are of comparable strength and have the same figuration. There is little or no connective process on a scale larger than the phrase, so the various melodic combinations are mere mechanistic juggling. It is an extreme case of technique triumphing over process.

Other movements in the sonata work better, though most have faults similar to, though less extreme than, the Largo. That these difficulties are not confined to this sonata or to the *Sonatas of Four Parts* is shown by bb. 48–60 of the Canzona of Sonata No. 6 (1683) in C (Z. 795.1b). Each two-bar statement ends with a V–I in the dominant if the subject, or in the tonic if the answer. Although these bars do not present all possible combinations of the subject and the two countersubjects, all three themes appear in each part at least once, and the subject and answer appear above and below the first countersubject. The result has an over-obvious four-squareness in the constant repetition of two-bar phrase lengths, in the tonic-dominant interchanges of the subject and answer, and in the recurrence of the same high G in almost every bar.

Purcell's revisions of some of the *Sonatas of Four Parts* suggest that he was aware of these weaknesses. The autograph version of the Largo of Sonata No. 7 (1697) in C (Z. 808.2), for example, is almost certainly the earlier of the two.[10] Its thirty-five bars begin with a ten-bar phrase in A minor and a harmonically propositional repetition in E minor. The third section touches on C before re-establishing A minor and is dominated by a single motif derived from the first phrase. An eight-bar Grave ends in C and the Canzona follows immediately. The published version's forty-one bars are achieved by a much more expressive treatment which hangs upon a constantly changing view of the material's possibilities. The second phrase sets out as an exact repetition of the first, but the motifs which closed the first phrase now enter much earlier, and sequential repetitions of them produce a 'bending' to a wide range of harmonic areas, including inflexions of major mode keys to the minor.

In the autograph the short Grave movement functions partly as a transition from A minor to C major. Although the published version incorporates ornamentation which is more Italianate, its main pitches are almost identical. However, because the context has changed, its functions are different. The C major ending of the published Largo means that the A minor orientation at the beginning of the Grave immediately hints at the opening of the preceding movement, a connection maintained by the subsequent minor-oriented inflexions.

The following Canzona might have been a favourite of Purcell's: at least he found the material sufficiently interesting to rework it in 1695, in the Trumpet Overture from Act III of *The Indian Queen* (Z. 630.16b). In the sonatas the autograph is forty bars long and the published version thirty-eight bars – clearly, the revision is not concerned with expanding scale. But what it is concerned with is the projection of structure and a more flexible use of the main material; and this is achieved partly by a much clearer division into episodes and statements, each of which has a distinct harmonic focus. So the theme is inverted for the first time after a four-bar episodic passage leading to a close in D minor. Moreover, this entry is an 'answer' on G major, and generates an inverted subject (b. 98) which enters half a bar early. The greater freedom of phrase length and the avoidance of closure in the tonic or dominant give the published version a much more purposeful thrust. It concludes with brilliant Italianate flourishes derived directly from motifs heard during the movement.

Of the twenty-two published sonatas by far the most famous, indeed the only one to have been available in print with any regularity ever since the late seventeenth century, is Sonata No. 9 (1697) in F ('The Golden') (Z. 810). Its popularity at a time when the Handelian style was pre-eminent must owe much to the success with which it combines an Italianate idiom with the polyphonic independence characteristic of the more obviously English sonatas, using revealing methods of synthesis.

The first movement is based on just two ideas (Ex. 48), both of which can be presented as a single line or in parallel thirds. It is driven partly by the counterpoint of their different stress patterns, both *a* and *b* being essentially in

Ex. 48   Sonata No. 9 (1697) in F ('The Golden') (Z. 810): bb. 1–10

duple time, but with their stresses one crotchet apart. The consequent tension is highlighted by the way the continuo leads off with a strong downbeat but, because of the presentation of *b*, does not do so the second time (b. 2) around. Motif *a* therefore becomes the metrically stable factor, a connection forcibly made by the return of a continuo downbeat on b. 4 to set off the inverted presentation of the two motifs. Escape from this deliciously knotty metrical counterpoint is achieved by condensing *b* to varied repetitions of its first two notes *c*, and these are capped off by a shifting of *b* to the 'correct' position (*d*) to produce a neat wedging onto a stressed dominant (bb. 7–8).

   The opening is repeated in the dominant, but the *c* derivation soon takes over, and after just four and a half bars the phrase ends with another close in C (b. 12). Now inversions of both *a* and *b* appear, presented quasi-canonically, with results even more metrically elaborate than the two earlier phrases. There is a close in vi, after which repetitions of *a* are counterpointed against *c* inverted and *b* in prime. A prolongation of V (b. 21) using derivations of *a*, *b* and *c*, leads to a close in the tonic.

Ex. 49   Sonata No. 11 (1683) in F minor (Z. 800): bb. 69–72

This willingness to alter the material so that it can be used in a larger range of contexts, is a large element in the sonata's success. The Largo second movement uses material almost identical to that in the Largo of Sonata No. 1 (1697) in B minor (Z. 802.2) discussed above, but with incomparably better results, for its priority is not the parading of combinatorial variation, but the exploration of the harmonic tensions implicit in the double appoggiatura.

This sonata's source background, its superb blending of Italianate textures and its free approach to motivic elaboration all suggest that it might be slightly later than those published in the *Sonatas of Three Parts*. Within the 1683 set itself, the better pieces tend to be less obviously Italianate. A particularly fine example is Sonata No. 11 (1683) in F minor (Z. 800).

The stylistic differences between movements are underpinned by subtle motivic links. So the Adagio explores with great intensity various ways of filling in the area between the high C–E♭ register and the low F which is the point of cadential repose in all movements; in the process it incorporates the chromatic pivoting around D♭/D♮ and A♭/A♮ which were the two most prominent focusses of chromatic tension since the first movement.

The diatonic lucidity of the final Largo is a perfect foil to the Adagio's tortuous chromaticism. Each area of the non-repetitive harmonic scheme:

i –	v –	VII –	III –	iv –	i
(80)	(88)	(107)	(112)	(128)	

is articulated by a cadence, except that in v, which is propositionally juxtaposed to i in a manner similar to the first movement. Each area is based almost exclusively on the subject and on the scalic derivation *n* (b. 71, Ex. 49), and features distinctive combinations of temporal and pitch imitation.

The subject and answer (bb. 69–72) establish a basic phrase length of two bars. The distinct functions of each bar help project the unit as the basis against which variations, such as the early entry of violin II in b. 83, operate. The first bar (*l*) is a protracted ornamentation of one note and is therefore more static than the forward-driving rhythm and consistent direction of the second (*m*). This functional connection means that as the movement progresses, *l* acquires an upbeat implication stronger than its first appearance might suggest.

The first three harmonic areas (i, v and VII) are basically expository:

although they present some variations in temporal and pitch imitation, the
subject and the two-bar phrase unit are undisturbed. The area leading towards
the close in III (b. 107) is more developmental, exploring a wider range of
imitation, of dense texture, and of distant harmonies. The expansiveness of this
area is increased by adding an anacrusis to the subject, thus intensifying the
acquired upbeat implication of *l*, and overlapping the successive two-bar units.

This developmental function continues into a precipitous move to iv (bb.
107–12), and the subsequent section in that key neatly counters the preceding
tension by returning to more expository methods. Yet, through a remarkable
combination of contrapuntal and harmonic methods, it too becomes increasingly unstable.

Bars 112–18 combine melodic, rhythmic and harmonic repetitions to an
unprecedented degree (Ex. 50): three successive statements of the subject

Ex. 50   Sonata No. 11 (1683) in F minor (Z. 800): bb. 112–22

without the anacrusis emphasise the two-bar unit; the last two of these are at the
same pitch; the first two each express the same harmonic progression. This
degree of repetition demands some sort of response, which is provided in a
return to F minor involving a subtle overlap between melodic and harmonic
units.

Three successive subjects in B♭ minor would normally imply the following
harmonies, shown in Table 4:

Table 4. Largo from Sonata No. 11 (1683) in F minor (Z. 800): bb. 112–18

Subjects	1	2	3	
	i – V	i – V	i – V	expected i
Bars	112 – 113	114 – 115	116 – 117	118

However, in b. 116 the bass interrupts by going to G♮ instead of B♭. B♮ minor harmony is regained via a vi(iv)–V–i in bb. 116–18, but is instantly destabilised by violin II entering on F with the subject form of *a*, which, with the bass driven by inverted repetitions of *a*, turns the B♭ to function as a pre-dominant in F minor (Fig. 1).

Fig. 1. Largo from Sonata No. 11 (1683) in F minor (Z. 800): bb. 112–20

	Subj.	Subj.	Subj.		Subj.	Ans.
Bar	(112)	(114)	(116)		(118)	(120)
In iv	i –	V – i –	V– vi⁷(iv⁶)	– V – i		
In i					iv – V – i	
Therefore .... iv					V – i	

Clearly, the F minor still needs to be stabilised and to be balanced against the length of the previous sections, and this is achieved by a series of statements, firmly in that key, in bb. 120–34.

The care taken over the publication of the *Sonatas of Three Parts*, and the lofty claims of the preface, show that Purcell had high hopes for these pieces – by turns flawed and brilliant. This might explain the revisions of some of the other sonatas, for it is possible that he intended to produce a second set, consisting of pieces written both before and after preparations for the *Sonatas of Three Parts* were complete. The famous chaconne, *Sonata No. 6 (1697) in G minor* (Z. 807) fits this picture, for in the seventeenth century such sonatas were sometimes used to finish off published sets of pieces: Corelli's sonata on 'La Folia' is perhaps the most famous example, and Kühnel, who lived in London during the early 1680s, also wrote sets of variations under the title 'sonata'.[11]

After the *Sonatas of Three Parts*, Purcell published no more instrumental music until the mid 1680s. From this point, small pieces of keyboard music, often transcriptions of songs which had become famous in other contexts, become frequent in his output. From 1683 his main focus as an instrumental composer shifted towards the odes and, towards the end of the decade, the theatre. It is in those areas that he most consistently pursued the innovations so forcefully essayed by the sonatas.

CHAPTER SEVEN

'Bassani's genius to Corelli joyn'd'[1]: instrumental music in the odes, the anthems and on the stage

THE INSTRUMENTAL MUSIC PURCELL wrote for his odes and anthems offers the most generically consistent indicator of his compositional development. The earliest such pieces are the symphonies and ritornelli written for early anthems such as *My Beloved Spake* and *Behold, Now Praise the Lord* (Z. 28 and 3), all in a style conforming to the rather conservative methods of the verse anthem. Not so the odes, for even in his first court ode, in 1680, we see a more experimental side to Purcell, keen to use this fairly new genre as a platform for innovation. One of the most revealing of such works is the symphony to his second court ode, written in 1681, *Swifter Isis, Swifter Flow* (Z. 336), for which he reworked an earlier overture, which survives in a non-autograph, but generally reliable, source of early Purcell, BL MS RM 20.h.9 (Ex. 51 (i) and (ii)).

The many changes of detail in the part writing are at first minor and in the interests of clarity, but from b. 8 they become radical. The starting point is in violin II, where the revision (Ex. 51 (ii)) fills in a G–F descent to stress F♯. Purcell picks up this descending chromaticism to fill out the bass descent from D to A, imitated in canon by the second violin one bar later. The revised version of the first violin line is also much more effective, largely because of the way it projects the unresolved A on the downbeat of b. 9 and picks it up two bars later (*x*), resolving it and the tension between high and low registers through a linear descent to D. This line too is imitated canonically one bar later, the entry being highlighted by the preceding rest. The result has less of that seamless flow of which the young Purcell was inordinately fond, but it gains in motivic economy and in harmonic direction.

The year before this revision, Purcell had essayed a very different approach to combining his elaborately polyphonic ideals with periodic phrasing and motivic economy. The symphony to his first court ode *Welcome, Vicegerent* (Z. 340), begins (Ex. 52) with a strongly directed yet metrically ambiguous melodic

Ex. 51   Overture in G (Z. 336.1): bb. 7–12

(i) Early version

(ii) as in *Swifter Isis, Swifter Flow*

Ex. 52   Welcome, Vicegerent (Z. 340), opening symphony: bb. 1–4

Ex. 53   Welcome, Vicegerent: Ritornello (Z. 340.5) after 'But Your Blest Presence'

sequence in violin I, the tension of which is intensified by the ties at the beginning of each unit, and by its being set against a metrically clear bass and viola, and an even more irregular version of the sequence in the second violin. Within a four-beat bar, violin I begins with a three-beat unit (*a*), which is repeated (*b*) and then shortened to two beats (*c*); this shortened unit is in turn repeated and extended to four beats (*d*) by the addition of a new figure *e*.

This new figure sets up an emphatic release of these tensions on the downbeat of b. 4, as the stress patterns of all parts coincide for the first time, which turns the ascent just as the line reaches B♭, a pitch with an inherent descending pull, especially given the E in the bass. Bars 4–5 resolve the tensions of bb. 1–3 with a much more regular descending line, which reaches down as far as A in b. 7 for a close in the relative minor.

A forcefully polyphonic approach to metrically regular material can be seen in the other large instrumental piece in this ode. The ritornello after the chorus 'But Your Blest Presence' (Z. 340.5) is a fifty-six-bar rondeau based on eight-bar phrases – A1, A2, B, A2, C, A1, A2 – in which A1 ends with a half close, and A2 with a full close. The strongly periodic phrasing is based on multiples of two bars and on texturally saturating repetitions of two motifs x and y (Ex. 53). The graceless predictability which afflicted a number of comparably periodic instrumental pieces from the early 1680s, is here avoided by causing many of the compositional processes, particularly the harmonic, to cross the boundaries between phrases.

Purcell's flair in extracting so many possibilities from x is astonishing – note the differences in the harmonisations at the beginnings of A1 and A2 (Ex. 53 (i) and (ii)) – but it is ultimately more significant that such variation is directed towards continuity of overall design. So section B is a response to the vigour of A1 plus A2. It ends with a full close in ii and, through using the part writing to connect directly into A2 (Ex. 53 (iii)), articulates a progression ii–V–I in C across the phrase boundary.

Just as B was a consequence of the first A1 + A2 statement, so C is a consequence of this A2. It ends with a full close in IV, which overlaps into the next statement of A (Ex. 53 (iv)). But this statement turns out to be not A2 but A1, and it maintains the strong inflection to ii for some bars, as a preparation for the half close at its end. A2 then comes to close the piece. Given the inexorable rhythmic drive and the twofold use of A2 to preface further development, the end of the ritornello naturally runs straight into the next verse and chorus.

Outside the *Sonatas of Three Parts* there is no more striking indicator of Purcell's expanding stylistic practice than the symphony to the late 1682 ode *What Shall Be Done?* (Z. 341). The first section opens with a protracted descending scale in the first violins, from high B♭ to a close onto chord V in b. 12 (Ex. 54). This is immediately turned to the minor mode, in which transformation it acts as ii of E♭. The power of this intrusion is proportional to its structural significance: the A♭ is the highest note since the opening B♭; the sudden leap to it articulates a connection between the E♭/F minor move and that original register, with its concomitant B♮ harmony. This connection gives rise to some of the most characteristic local features of the second section and generates one of the most important elements of its large-scale harmonic structure.

The intensely active texture of the second section derives much of its

Ex. 54   *What Shall Be Done?*, (Z. 341) opening symphony: bb. 1–17

coherence from the large-scale pitch processes generated by varied repetitions of
material based on the subject and countersubject. The subject's definitive
function is underlined by its metrical regularity (Ex. 55). Its descending scale
reworks the descent which opened the first section and is a matrix for most of
the piece. Its strong drive towards the tonic derives partly from there being no
attack on a downbeat until the second bar, by which point the scalic descent *x*

Ex. 55   What Shall Be Done? (Z. 341) opening symphony: bb. 25–34

is underway; the tonic is emphasised through enclosure by the supertonic and leading note.

Each phrase in this section presents in the outer parts a derivation of this matrixal scale, using variations on either the subject (bb. 44–8, for example) or countersubject (bb. 48–50 and 60–8, for example), and tends to concentrate on a distinctive range of combinatorial possibilities. The inner parts, and some of the long-term pitch processes in the outer parts, continue across the boundaries articulated by intermediate cadences, all of which have the characteristic enclosing ending, and are graded so as to produce processes larger than the span of any one phrase. That in C minor (b. 48), for example, is subordinate to the much stronger one in F (b. 52) by the continuity of pitch process in the outer parts and by the strength of the longer-term progression which connects all the principal closures in the piece.

The relationship between subdominant-oriented harmony, the counter-subject, and long-term pitch process is particularly trenchant. The A♭ in the answer (b. 30) is not an inevitable consequence of the imitation – A♮ would at least be grammatical: but by its sheer distinctiveness, it sets up one of the most important harmonic gestures of the piece, and links it to the countersubject, which here is being presented for the first time. The minor dominant harmony moves directly to E♭ harmony and its near relation C minor.

The crucial issue is that any E♭ (or C minor) harmony resulting from the prominent A♭ does not in fact go to V. In the long term this prevents the setting up of V of I, and is especially important once excursions to other keys begin.

Significantly, on the only two occasions when F major harmony occurs soon
after the A♮ instigator (bb. 35–7 and 62–5), it is turned into a local tonic.

The economy of Purcell's concentration on this concept is extraordinary.
There are just two places where the matrixal scale is broken, and both coincide
with E♭ harmony. On the downbeat of b. 40 the scale reaches G and E♭, in violin
I and bass respectively (b in Ex. 56). The leap down to E♭ from G breaks the

Ex. 56   What Shall Be Done? (Z. 341), opening symphony: bb. 39–44

scale by omitting F and going down to D. The countersubject then dominates
the texture and picks up the missing F (*a*), then the D and resolves down to B♭,
but as part of G minor harmony. Similarly, the break in the scale in b. 62 creates
a strong disturbance which presses through to the close in F in b. 65.

Thereafter, for the first time, the texture is dominated by the countersubject.
Its metrical irregularity is now used to focus onto a close in B♭. The break at E♭
(C minor harmony) in b. 62 therefore functions as the first element in a
protracted ii–V–I progression, the first such in the symphony. The dominant is
prolonged by sequential patterns from the countersubject. The outer parts start
in canon (Ex. 57), and their non-coincidence of stress patterns, and progressive
lengthening of units, mean that the required coincidence is all the more telling
when it comes (b. 69).

Finally, the cadential function of the descent from high B♭ (bb. 68–9) is
articulated by the bass moving up by step. The concluding phrases continue the
descent to B♭ using a metrically and harmonically unambiguous scale in the
tonic, based on the subject.

Ex. 57   *What Shall Be Done?* (Z. 341), opening symphony: bb. 65–70

Purcell wrote no second section of a symphony, indeed no orchestral music of any sort, quite as Italianate as this piece, until, in 1687–8, he began a more general use of overtly Italianate textures. In the meantime he concentrated on applying to instrumental textures more closely related to his native style, those repetition techniques so successfully used in *What Shall Be Done?*. In doing so he had to learn to let go of the literal repetition techniques which, in his earlier days, seem to have been a point of pride.

The second section of the symphony to the late-1683 ode *Fly, Bold Rebellion* (Z. 324), for example, is of a distinctive type which he had essayed earlier that same year in *From Hardy Climes* (Z. 325), though with less convincing results, largely because the studied avoidance of intermediate closes, and the tendency to proliferate secondary material, obscure the function of many gestures.

In both odes the section begins with fugal imitation – in *From Hardy Climes* there are four complete entries of a two-bar subject – but soon abandons strict restatements of the subject in favour of sequential work based on elements of it. Purcell's methods, especially in *Fly, Bold Rebellion*, are closely related to those used earlier by Blow, in the New Year ode for that same year, *Dread Sir, Father Janus*. Indeed, the second sections of Blow's symphony and of Purcell's for *Fly, Bold Rebellion* are based on strikingly similar subjects;[2] but Purcell's grasp of harmonic structure and voice-leading is much stronger and, through carefully building on precedent, he gives the seemingly extravagant approach to dissonance a compelling purposefulness.

Until b. 17 (Ex. 58) most dissonances are resolved by step, but this orthodox

Ex. 58   Fly, Bold Rebellion (Z. 324), opening symphony: bb. 12–24

approach is gradually abandoned by building on the events of b. 18. The second violins' 9–8 at the beginning of that bar is developed from the first violins' much less dissonant *m* in b. 16, and the struck 7 on the downbeat of b. 19 is a further derivation. This 7 is resolved by subtle motivic working in the second violin and the bass: the former's motif *t* is an inversion of *x*, but also is an imitative continuation of the same part's *s*. The bass in the meantime sets off on a scalic descent *u* derived from the subject's *r*. In the process it resolves the A to G, while violin II readily ascends to B♭. The second beat of the bar takes a similar approach to the violas' F, which is resolved in the bass as the viola itself plays *v*, a further derivation from *s*.

No less subtle is the exploration of the I–ii–V harmonic structure of the subject. This progression is repeated at varying temporal intervals in the early stages of the section, but with differing functions each time: bb. 14–15 see it presented I–II–V, while bb. 15–17 rework this with a much stronger thrust towards the dominant. Thereafter related patterns recur, such as the VI–ii–V–i in the relative minor, bb. 20–2, and the strong lead to the final dominant pedal offered by the I♭⁷–IV–II–V of bb. 28–9. Many of the melodic and harmonic sequences are based on developments of the same progression, such as that beginning in b. 22 which, in the subdominant, sets off I⁶–IV–ii–V⁷.

The metrical ambiguity inherent in the subject, with its stress on the second and third beats, is exploited at the first departure from the immediate tonic-dominant areas, producing the duple units *d*, *e* and *f*. It becomes more explicit in the next phrase, which presents four duple-time units grouped into two quadruple units (*a* and *b*), coincident with a harmonically mobile progression moving from IV to I. Triple-time units return on the break in the melodic sequence at the downbeat of b. 25, which also is the point at which F major returns as the local tonic. The piece is replete with other such metrical dislocations, often with the outer parts in metrical counterpoint, as in bb. 22–3, where the bass is grouped in duple units one beat later than violin I (*k* and *l*).

From around this time, the free yet impeccably controlled part writing of such pieces helps to expand the expressive range of instrumental music. This can be seen in the anthems as well as the odes – in *Unto Thee Will I Cry* (Z. 63) bb. 126–53, for example. Perhaps the finest such movement from around 1683 is the symphony which introduces the G minor section of *I Was Glad* (Z. 19.4).

The expressive tone of the piece is derived from the text, but this cannot explain the coherence of an upper line which seems to break every rule in those books Purcell would have known, such as Simpson's *Compendium*. It constantly modifies a protoline which is sometimes implied, sometimes stated, and which forms a straightforward harmonisation of the bass, all of which can be seen in the opening phrase (Ex. 59).

The melody ornaments this line in three main ways: it might leap to other notes of the relevant harmony; it might ornament harmony notes with passing notes, which might be approached by leap; or it might superimpose elements of adjacent harmonies. This last can be seen in b. 151, where the G is held over from the preceding harmony, using the G–D motif which has featured prominently since the beginning of the anthem. The bass progression E♭–D is

Ex. 59 I Was Glad, G minor symphony (Z. 19.4) and protoline

given three interpretations (bb. 152–3, 156–7, 172–3), each presenting a different conflation of possibilities. The propensity to leap to and from dissonance is developed in the first few bars by introducing progressively more intense passing notes. Invariably, where a dissonance is approached or quitted by leap, a 'correct' preparation or resolution, or both, is implied in the continuo.

The sinuous melodic line is bound together by pitch and harmonic projections such as the D in bb. 155–7. Such projections become even more important in the second section, where an ascent to F♯ (b. 166) prepares for a return to G minor after an extended passage in B♭. A break in the line projects the F♯ across the strong subdominant inflexion (bb. 167–8) essential for the primacy of G minor; it is picked up in b. 169 and resolved in bb. 170–3.

A comparably free approach can also be seen in a type of ritornello common to most odes after 1683 – the running-quaver, duple-time ground bass, based on a preceding song. From the 1683 odes *From Hardy Climes* and *Fly, Bold Rebellion* onwards, in 'The Sparrow and the Gentle Dove' (Z. 325.8) and 'Be Welcome Then, Great Sir' (Z. 324.11) respectively, Purcell included such a song and ritornello in almost all his odes, and similar pieces emerged elsewhere, most famously in 'Oft She Visits' from *Dido and Aeneas* (Z. 626.25).

From the outset Purcell tended to view such ritornelli as a further set of variations, rather than as a filled-out restatement of the song; and this is especially shown in the way they include what seem to be his first attempts to transpose a ground. The over-experimental, lumpy result in pieces such as 'The

Sparrow and the Gentle Dove' in *From Hardy Climes* (Z. 325.8) and 'With Him He Brings' in *Ye Tuneful Muses* (Z. 344.11) of 1686, shows that this was something of a rocky road.[3] Yet its direction is clear, for Purcell moved from the somewhat over-worked complexity of the ritornello after 'Be Welcome Then, Great Sir' from *Fly, Bold Rebellion* (Z. 324.11) – where the opening bars rework the song's welcoming fanfare while the texture is characteristically peppered with references to its distinctive rhythm and the arpeggio figuration – to the superb duet and ritornello 'Let Caesar and Urania Live' from the 1687 ode *Sound the Trumpet* (Z. 335.5).

In the latter, the repeated notes and semiquaver turns of the duet's opening are the basis for the whole ritornello, which combines cellular repetitions on these figures at varying temporal and intervallic levels, while the texture is far more Italianate than any earlier such piece. It is nevertheless packed with characteristically independent details such as the second violins' F♮ *échappée* in b. 35 and the violas' B♭–A in b. 37.

Even by the standards of his age, Purcell was unusually style-conscious, and the path he took to a wider range of instrumental practice is inseparable from an increasingly free view of the relationship between genre and style. The second section of the opening symphony to *I Was Glad* (Z. 19) is a good case, one of the first in which Purcell begins to move away from the top-line-dominated, dance-like second section which had been the norm in his verse anthems with strings. While the dance character remains, the texture is overtly imitative, using the material which will form the basis for the opening verse section.

Comparable methods are seen much more compellingly in the second section of the symphony to the 1685 coronation anthem *My Heart Is Inditing* (Z. 30). After a less-than-exact series of imitative entries (Ex. 60), the upper line *a* reaches D (bb. 35–6) on a strong I–V. A consequent begins on V of I, and ends in a close in vi in bb. 41–2.

In the meantime a series of subtle motivic developments has been underway, the emergence of the end-motif *x* in bb. 38 and 42 being particularly important. In the close in b. 42 the descending third is ornamented in the second violin (*y*), partly as an imitative response to violin I's figure *z*. This bar presents the two main melodic elements for the following harmonic and melodic sequences: the arpeggio figure *m* – developed out of the earlier ♩.♪ figuration; and *y*, which becomes *n* in the next bar and for the rest of the sequence.

In the sequence the stressed pitches of the outer parts describe the ascending lines *b* and *c*, but these are broken in b. 45 by inverting the outer parts at the D minor stage of a harmonically mobile sequence. The inversion sets in train a series of circular harmonic and registral events which end in b. 50 with a close onto D minor, picking up the pitches left at the point of inversion; it is notable

Ex. 60   *My Heart Is Inditing* (Z. 30), opening symphony: bb. 27–45

in particular, how although the close stresses D on the downbeat of b. 50, the F of line *b* is picked up in the next bar by using *n* in the first violins. The continuations of *b* and *c* lead to a close in the subdominant (b. 55), a harmonic area whose prominence throughout the symphony is reflected in numerous gestures which have their ancestry in the B♭ of b. 1, and in a general tendency to close into the subdominant more readily than the dominant.

The methodological link with the symphony to *Fly, Bold Rebellion* is clear, but the scale of events is significantly larger. Indeed, none of Purcell's music before *My Heart Is Inditing*, instrumental or vocal, is so dependent on harmonic and melodic sequence as a primary means of expansion except, perhaps, some of the less-successful Italianate sonatas. Moreover, these methods find room for finely detailed inner parts which, when they are not pairing off with one of the outer parts, go their own sweet way with cogently derived details, some of which drive across the periodic boundaries – the viola's B♭ in b. 36, for example, is derived from the first violin two bars earlier and from the B♭s which have been prominent since b. 1.

A year after *My Heart Is Inditing* Purcell applied its techniques of free repetition to a more consistently fugal texture in the second section of the symphony to *Ye Tuneful Muses* (Z. 344.1b). Its up-to-date structural methods are especially founded in using harmony for long-range projection, and in the way thematic entries articulate function. The bass entry in b. 48, for example (Ex. 63), articulates F major as the main function in the approach to a close in B♭. As with most such entries, function is intensified by the preceding rest, in contrast to the seamless flow of earlier practice.

The complex yet clear functions of the opening phrase's motivic material are tenaciously reworked throughout the piece. The first violin line consists of an eight-bar phrase made up of two four-bar sub-phrases. The main pitches of the first are the descending line *a* (Ex. 61) and, because of the motif *z* at the end, this

Ex. 61   Ye Tuneful Muses (Z. 344), opening symphony: bb. 24–31

sub-phrase is open-ended. The beginning of the second is defined by the leap to high G and the phrase itself by the move away from and back to that G (*b*). In *a* the descent articulated by repetitions of *x* is more distinct than that articulated by *z*. Descents generated by repetitions of *x* can be extended at will to an intermediate close; *z* and derivations from it can be used to modify the patterns generated by such descents.

Repetitions of the second violins' motif *m* fulfil a similar descending function

Ex. 62   *Ye Tuneful Muses* (Z. 344), opening symphony: bb. 70–8

(c). This similarity means that motifs *x* and *m* are to some extent inter-
changeable, and that either can precede or follow *z*. Motif *z* can be replaced by
derivations such as the rhythmic reversal *o*. The whole phrase is a distinctly
articulated prolongation of G minor.

Subsequent phrases are either harmonically closed, like this one, or they are
mobile and expand into new harmonic areas. The closed phrases almost always
prolong harmonic functions, either by elaborating upon a single harmony, or by
embarking on an enclosed harmonic circuit. In most of them, motion is
intensified by some element pushing across boundaries – in b. 31, for example,
the bass enters with *a*.

A more complex, harmonically enclosed phrase is exemplified in Ex. 62. Here
D major is prolonged by an eight-bar circuit which establishes that harmony's
function as V. The beginning of the prolongation is articulated by breaking out
of the sequential pattern preceding it, which led away from a close onto C
minor, but which had not established G minor as the tonic. The possibility that
this C minor could function within a long-term iv–V–i progression is reinforced
by bb. 74–5, and in particular by the stressed iv⁶–V in bb. 77–8. The expanded
register in b. 78 gives the dominant a tension which can be resolved only by
closing back within that register. This happens during the next eleven bars,
which prolong D yet again, but now securely as V of i.

The harmonically mobile type of phrase is exemplified in bb. 42–53 (Ex. 63).
After the close onto D minor the return to G minor is highly unstable: the
harmony in b. 44 is in first inversion, while the appearance of *z* in violin I and

Ex. 63   *Ye Tuneful Muses* (Z. 344), opening symphony:.bb. 40–53

a contrary motion descent in the bass push on through this bar; in b. 45 motif
c needs to be completed and is therefore pushing across the weak closure
articulated in the lower parts. Crucially, it has reached high B♭, which here and
elsewhere (bb. 25 and 36) begins a descent generated by repetitions either of *x*
in prime or inversion, or of *m* or *z* (cf. Ex. 61). This descent ends with a strong
close in B♭.

The next year's birthday ode, *Sound the Trumpet* (Z. 335), includes Purcell's
largest purely instrumental piece outside the stage music. The significance of the
Chaconne in F (Z. 335.7) for the development of Purcell's instrumental practice
lies as much in the use to which it is put as in its purely musical merits. Back in
1681, in *Swifter Isis, Swifter Flow* Purcell had used an instrumental piece to
portray the approach of the royal barge (the prelude to 'Hark! Just Now My
List'ning Ears', Z. 336.5). Here he uses the chaconne as a homage 'to the
monarch of Britain and Lord of the Ocean', a superb release of the tension

accumulated during the preceding items. The appearance in 1687 of a piece evidently indebted to French models, in an ode which in most other respects is his most Italianate to date, symbolises the extent to which Purcell's new-found stylistic confidence was essential in order for instrumental music to play the dramatic role it was to assume within the next two years.

Stylistic confidence and, by implication, an increased distinction between style and genre, are also symbolised by the appearance, in that most conservative of genres, the verse anthem, of opening symphonies in an Italianate style. The earliest seems to be *Behold, I Bring You Glad Tidings* (Z. 2) which, according to the Gostling manuscript, was written for Christmas Day 1687.[4] Purcell was to go on to much better things than that symphony, but its control of Italianate texture for dramatic effect and its virtuosic treatment of the material make it notable for its period.

The long-range focus which makes possible its extreme levels of repetition is taken somewhat further, and with musically superior results, in *O Sing unto the Lord* (Z. 44), which dates from around 1688. Both the first and second sections put their material through its paces in a manner similar to that of the earlier anthem, but the second section is at first much more concerned with literal repetition of the subject. Its opening bars emphasise the subject's metrical stability by pairing the first and second entries a bar apart and both beginning on C, and by doing the same one and a half bars later with the third and fourth entries, beginning on F.

It is a neat irony that material which begins with such metrical stability ends up being fraught with metrical tension. Entries at the half bar in the run up to the close in ii had begun a process which culminates in stretto entries one crotchet apart. Release comes with the fragmentation of the subject into its component motifs, and the pairing of the texture once again, beginning in b. 32 and well established by the half close in bb. 34–5.

Dido and Aeneas (Z. 626) was Purcell's first opportunity to concentrate into one work the expressive possibilities of his new-found confidence in a range of instrumental styles. Most of the independent instrumental pieces are superb applications of techniques already well established in the odes, and however effective they are in context – the 'Sailors' Dance' (Z. 626.30), the 'Echo Dance' (Z. 626.22), the 'Witches' Dance' (Z. 626.34), the 'Triumphing Dance' (Z. 626.13) and the preludes for Acts II and III (Z. 626.14a and 29a) – it is their function in the drama which sees Purcell at his most innovative.

Purcell had taken a more obviously radical step in the early months of 1689 with the first of the six odes he was to write for the birthdays of Queen Mary. The opening symphony to *Now Does the Glorious Day Appear* (Z. 332) is the first in an ode to feature five-part strings and to have an opening section in Italian sonata style.

Its approach to 'trumpet' style is far removed from the block-harmony methods of most of the pieces which almost certainly inspired it, for the irregular imitation on strongly periodic material produces extraordinarily complex layers of metrical counterpoint. In this respect at least, its methods are anticipated by the second section of the symphony to O Sing unto the Lord. The hammer-blow chords in the openings bars (Ex. 64 (i)) define the principal metrical units; yet the imitation cuts across these, occurring in the first instance every one and a half bars and then more closely, driving the expanding texture, which at first is based solely on a tonic chord. As the top line reaches high A in b. 6 the bass begins to move, beginning a harmonic circuit which touches on the dominant before closing back in the tonic. An episodic passage based on the predominant rhythm leads to another series of statements, including one on a weak beat (viola, b. 15, Ex. 64 (ii)) and an augmentation in the bass.

It is possible, though unlikely, that Purcell's first piece actually written for trumpet is The Cibell (NPS, vol. XXXI, p. 95);[5] but it is not typical of his practice for the instrument. This really began in late 1689 or early 1690, in the opening symphony to 'The Yorkshire Feast Song' Of Old, When Heroes Thought It Base (Z. 333), where he wrote the first in a long line of distinctive pieces for what was then a comparatively new sonority in art music.

Purcell gives the two trumpets the same thematic material as the strings, making in effect a six-part texture. There is plenty of evidence that Purcell's instruments and players made a much smoother, lighter sound than is commonly associated with the modern trumpet – a sound that might also have been somewhat different from that of most continental players. This might explain why in this, his first piece for two trumpets and strings, he tended to treat the (typically) six instrumental lines more or less equally so that, rather than tension between the two sonorities, we have a vibrant timbral mélange amongst equals, and an approach very different from that of his possible models. It is significant that he was later to adopt a different course; but the new sound must have made a big splash with the audience at the first performance, on 27 March 1690. This ode is also important for featuring Purcell's first large-scale use of oboes, which in 'The Pale and the Purple Rose' (Z. 333.6) are used as a concerted group against the strings, as part of a depiction of battle.

Queen Mary's birthday ode of the same year, Arise, My Muse (Z. 320), shows a sharply contrasting approach. The opening symphony, also in the main trumpet key of D and scored for two trumpets and five-part strings, is a more convincing piece than the opening of Of Old, When Heroes Thought It Base, largely because Purcell has concentrated on those musical qualities which, in large ensembles, trumpets can deliver best.

The trumpets have the same material as the strings, but their distinctive sound is judiciously used to articulate important events. In the second section, violin

Ex. 64   *Now Does the Glorious Day Appear* (Z. 332), opening symphony:

(i) bb. 1–7

(ii) bb. 15–19

I leads off with a five-bar idea. In each successive bar the next lowest part enters, using mainly the first two bars of this idea, until all five string parts are in. While the uppermost part continues projecting a two-bar unit, the lower parts constantly work against this with independent phrasing which dominates the texture. The trumpets do not enter until the fourteenth and sixteenth bars of the section, using the earlier two-bar theme. Crucially, these entries articulate the two-bar phrasing, and although by the twenty-first bar they have submerged themselves under the strings, the brief stability they bring is an important element in preparing for the first close in the tonic, produced by the strings in bb. 22–3. A subsidiary idea is then launched by the trumpets, re-entering in thirds at a high pitch. Purcell must have been pleased with this piece, for he reused it the following year in *King Arthur*.

Significant as this symphony is, the main achievements in instrumental music from 1690 are in *Dioclesian* (Z. 627), which in both the Second Music (Z. 627.2) and the chaconne 'Triumph, Victorious Love' (Z. 627.38), features the earliest certain instance of Purcell using simultaneously the full Baroque orchestral forces of strings, trumpets, oboes (including the tenor oboe) and bassoon. Moreover, these forces are disposed as concerted groups. The result is a considerable improvement on his use of strings and flutes in 'And Now Every Tongue' from *What Shall Be Done?* (Z. 341.3c), and is impressively sturdy.

Such technical innovation is perhaps less important than *Dioclesian*'s self-conscious displays of stylistic virtuosity. The 'Chaconne – Two in One upon a Ground' (Z. 627.16), for example, is the nearest Purcell approaches at this time to the enthusiastically conservative virtuosity shown in some early works. Then there is the 'Dance of Furies' (Z. 627.14), which captures those creatures' harrying energy by having each section in a distinct style, each traceable to generic models outside dance music proper. The 'Soft music before the dance' (Ex. 65 (i)) is pure *stile antico*, an emphatic re-creation especially of the first section of Fantasia No. 5 (Z. 736), including its strong inflexions to the minor dominant. The rapid runs and dotted rhythms of the dance proper are almost certainly based on French string practice, and on the French overture in particular. The third section (Ex. 65 (ii)) features the more slow-moving, seemingly homophonic, textures commonly found in the third sections of some overtures. The repeated semiquavers and martial rhythms of the fourth (Ex. 65 (iii)) are a reworking of *stile concitato* such as Purcell might have encountered had he known pieces such as Monteverdi's *Il combattimento di Tancredi e Clorinda*, and also are based on trumpet-style pieces from Italian sonatas and in some French operas. The fifth reworks the first section of the dance to make it end in the tonic.

Each section ends with a full close and each, except for the first, is linked to its neighbours either by overlapped endings and beginnings, or by the endings being in the dominant. Also, there are underlying features common to all. In particular each describes an elaborated melodic progress from the tonic to the dominant and back again (usually accompanied by a move towards the dominant key), while the prominent melodic figuration of ascending or

Ex. 65 *Dioclesian*, 'Dance of Furies' (Z. 627.14):

(i) bb. 1–11

(ii) bb. 27–30

(iii) bb. 44–7

descending fourths (e.g. *a* in bb. 10–11, F♯–B in bb. 29–30, A–E and F–C in b. 48) is derived from the scalic movement *x* of the 'Soft music before the Dance' (C–F in bb. 2–3, Ex. 65 (i)).

The First Music (Z. 627.1) is an overture in the Anglo-French style which Purcell had practised since the mid 1670s. In the first section, modern features – the directness of the harmonic structure (i–VII–V of i), the consistent underlying presence of a basic one-bar periodic unit, the tendency for the bass to outline harmonic support rather than be involved in the nitty-gritty of motivic imitation – are combined with distinctively conservative elements such as the stepwise sweeps of the upper line, the constant motivic imitation throughout the texture, and imitation which drives across punctuations.

Then there are character pieces such as the hornpipe which functions as the First Act Tune (Z. 627.4) – a superb combination of sturdy rhythmic energy and piquant minor-mode harmonies – and the 'Country Dance' from Act V (Z. 627.25), which combines rustic roughness with technical artifice.[6] With such forceful characterisation, Purcell's instrumental style was expanding well beyond the expressive boundaries of *Dido and Aeneas*.

After the success of *Dioclesian*, Purcell was busy with music for a number of plays which required overtures, dances and act tunes, and it was probably to ease his load that for some of these he revised earlier music. For a minuet in *Distressed Innocence* (Z. 577.8) he reworked a piece which could be from as early as 1683,[7] by shortening the second half, turning its complex melodic patterns into a simpler yet more strongly directed line, and providing a vastly superior bass to the first half. It was probably also around this time that, for use in *The Gordian Knot* (Z. 597), he reworked three pieces: the first Air (Z. 597.2) is from the 1682 ode *What Shall Be Done?* (Z. 341.4b) and the second (Z. 597.4) from the apparently incomplete *Suite in G* (Z. 770.1c); in both, the changes result in a clearer structure, less burdened with detail. Fewer changes were made to the 'Rondeau Minuet' (Z. 597.3), one of his finest instrumental pieces from the mid 1680s, originally a ritornello from the 1685 ode *Why, Why Are All the Muses Mute?* (Z. 343.9).

The super-charged energy of much of this music is typified in the third Air from *The Gordian Knot* (Z. 597.7), with outer parts full of irregular periodic units which, after the double bar, move onto a leaping figure very different from the largely stepwise movement of the first strain (Ex. 66 (i) and (ii)). No less important is the relationship between the outer parts and the strikingly independent inner ones. In bb. 1–2, for example, the impeccably shaped lines of the second violins and viola prominently ornament tonic harmony, respectively with A–B–A and C♯.

In the overture to this play these features are seen with an effect more substantial than in perhaps any other music written between *Dioclesian* and

Ex. 66   The Gordian Knot, Air (Z. 597.7):

(i) bb. 1–4

(ii) bb. 10–13

The Fairy Queen. Its technical complexity and motivic concentration might seem far removed from the simple characterisation of most instrumental music for the stage. But it nevertheless is forcefully direct, largely because its contrapuntal manipulations are underpinned by clearly focussed harmonic prolongations.

In the second section, most of the prolongations are effected through repetitions of the main theme (*x* in Ex. 67). The four initial entries prolong the tonic across bb. 17–23, though this is characteristically peppered by references to the dominant, produced by entries of the answer (b. 20) and subject (b. 21). The strong up-beat harmonic rhythm (♩ ♩) of b. 22 imparts stress to the downbeat of b. 23, articulating the end of the tonic prolongation, and the start of a quasi-sequential pattern which, as the figuration leaves subject-based material, moves towards the relative major. This harmonic area is then set up as a longer-term goal by a prolongation of its own dominant, running from b. 27 to b. 32. The beginning of the prolongation is articulated in bb. 26–7 by changes of melodic patterning, by the bass-line's thrust towards the downbeat of b. 27, and by the repetition of dominant harmony in bb. 26 and 27.

The section consists largely of such prolongations, the Protean energy of which depends on the technical diversity underlying them and on the extraordinary subtlety of articulation. In bb. 36–46 (Ex. 68) and 51–7, for

Ex. 67   The Gordian Knot (Z. 597), Overture: bb. 17–33

example, most bars begin with pitches of the local tonic chord; but the
functioning harmony is that key's dominant. In the first case, for example, this
is because the downbeat of b. 36 is stressed through being preceded by the same
up-beat figure which three bars earlier had approached the close into III,
because it begins another series of imitative exchanges based on the subject and
because of the upper parts' tendency to stress A, especially in bb. 39–40.

But perhaps the most highly developed prolongations are in bb. 42–6 and
58–70. In the former (Ex. 68) various inflexions of iv and ii of D minor are used
as pre-dominants while the overall function of V is articulated throughout,
partly because of the specific-pitch connections between bb. 41 and 46 (Ex. 69
(i)). The latter instance is still more elaborate and is particularly interesting in
that it prolongs functions other than the dominant – the earliest such instance
I have so far traced in Purcell's work. Here too, specific-pitch connections are
central to the process (Ex. 69 (ii)).

Ex. 68   *The Gordian Knot* (Z. 597), Overture: bb. 35–47

In both cases the posited connections are grammatical, but in context the results would be faulty, for the strength of these prolongations depends very much on their length. Moreover, in a piece which has featured so many dominant prolongations, something such as the pre-dominants of bb. 58–66 is needed to set up a final close. We might note that the third section of the overture complements the scale on which these processes have unfolded, by prolonging the tonic.

Simple harmonic structures reach a new level in the opening symphony to the 1692 birthday ode *Welcome, Welcome, Glorious Morn* (Z. 338), which follows the example of *Dioclesian*'s 'Triumph, Victorious Love' (Z. 627.38) in having separate parts for strings, oboes and trumpets, and in being in C. The second section revels in extracting as much as possible from the harmonic limitations imposed by trumpets, for almost every progression is between tonic and dominant harmony; and the piece is driven by the rhythmic irregularities caused by varying periods of imitation, by the overlapping of motivic entries, and by the

Ex. 69 The Gordian Knot (Z. 597): prolongations in second section of Overture

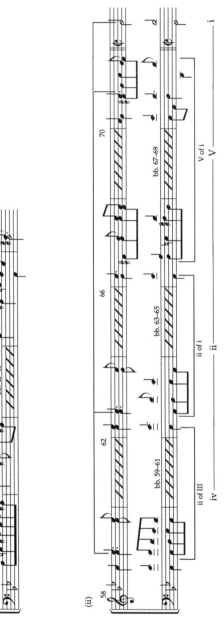

constantly varied concerted imitations between the three instrumental groupings.

To accompany the spectacular stage effects which were a central ingredient of
dramatic opera, Purcell was, by 1691, able draw on a vast array of stylistic
resources. In the large stage work of that year, *King Arthur* (Z. 628), the C major
symphony (Z. 628.33) after 'Ye Blust'ring Brethren' is an outstanding example.
The sources are unclear as to instrumentation, but the top line can be played on
the trumpet in C, while the other two parts have the same range, but include
notes which will not fit the trumpet. It seems inescapable that commentators are
correct in asserting that it was intended for one trumpet, two violins (perhaps)
and continuo – just the sort of technical challenge Purcell would have relished.[8]
Certainly this fits neatly with the piece's function as 'a soft tune' to accompany
the rise of Britannia's island. No bombastic fanfare this, but a superb use of that
'sweet sound' of the trumpeter, Shore, to suggest at once salutation and
tranquillity after the storm of 'Ye Blust'ring Brethren'.

Contrapuntal skill is neatly allied to instrumental resourcefulness. The
continuo opens with a plain, independent bass, though the trumpet characteristically enters with a varied augmentation of the continuo (Ex. 70), and even

Ex. 70   *King Arthur*, trumpet(?) symphony (Z. 628.33): bb. 1–6

the continuo's simple crotchets and minims concentrate on reworkings of the
opening bars. The trumpet is very much the first amongst equals: it has the first
entry, it leads off the stretto imitations on rapid figuration (b. 10) and it drives
the harmonic motion across the strongest move towards the dominant (bb.

12–16). The material seems unpromising for imitation, but various stretti on the subject and on the rapid fanfares are superbly calculated to screw up tension, driving towards closes into V and vi (bb. 17 and 20) and to an inflexion to the minor dominant (b. 25).

In the Second Music (Z. 628.2) Purcell confidently handles those Italianate styles of texture and melodic material which he had used in the symphonies to *O Sing unto the Lord* (Z. 44) and *Now Does the Glorious Day Appear* (Z. 332), but with a significantly less complex surface and with a rather more strongly projected harmonic structure. As with so many aspects of Purcell's development, this is question of degree rather than substance. The first section uses, as its main means of expansion, dialogues (possibly between groups of strings and wind[9]) based on the statement-plus-answer phrase structure of the opening two bars, producing a cogent sequence of tonic-dominant-tonic cycles, within and then around the tonic area: i – III (bb. 5–6) – iv(IV) (bb. 7–8) – v(V) (bb. 9–10) – i. The tension caused by the harmonic discursion and spasmodic phrasing finds apt relief on the return to the tonic, when elements of the opening are translated into a much more connected dialogue which reworks some of the earlier progressions.

One of the most important results of Purcell's ever-growing stylistic confidence is the emergence between 1690 and 1693 of pieces which rework aspects of his earlier style, invariably by grafting conservative textural features onto modern structural methods. Examples are the 'Soft music before the dance' (Z. 627.14a, Ex. 65 (i)) from *Dioclesian*, the instrumental section of 'Pursuing Beauty' from *Sir Anthony Love* (Z. 588.2), and the 1692 birthday ode *Love's Goddess Sure* (Z. 331).

In the main stage work from 1692, *The Fairy Queen*, this is most clearly seen in the 'Dance for the Followers of Night' (Z. 629.15). Every bit as cerebral as the 'Chaconne – Two in One upon a Ground' from *Dioclesian* (Z. 627.16), this piece nevertheless has a much more directed expressive purpose, for its strangeness is clearly intended to reflect the scene on the stage. It is perhaps more of a homage to the mentor of his youth, Locke, than to himself, for it is clearly modelled on the somewhat quirky four-in-two canon provided by Locke for the conclusion of *The Tempest* (1677). Purcell pairs the violins, while the violas and basses follow them a bar later. The opening establishes the unusual harmonic language of the piece by having a straightforward C minor arpeggio set against a descending line which suggests a decidedly Dorian version of the key. The harmonic twists produced by the shifting between flat and natural forms of A and B infuse the first strain. Yet the structure is essentially modern, being strongly periodic and single-minded in its harmonic focus on C minor.

Purcell's conflation of elaborate polyphony and modern structural methods reaches extraordinary levels in *The Fairy Queen*'s Second Act Tune, an Air in

C (Z. 629.16). Amongst the most significant processes are those involving the changes away from and back to the predominant rhythmic pattern of its first violin line. The repetitions of the rhythm *a* (Ex. 71) produce a uniform stress on

Ex. 71   *The Fairy Queen*, Second Act Tune (Z. 629.16): bb. 1–14

the first beat of each bar. This repetition is alleviated by occasional bars of quavers as at *b* which, throughout the piece, are in groups of at least two bars and always occur where impetus is especially needed. In bb. 5 and 6 the rhythm *a* would fit but, on the downbeat of b. 5, would lose that drive across the end of the first phrase and towards the downbeat of b. 7 which begins the next sequential pattern. In b. 10 *b* drives on through the end of the harmonic and melodic sequence of bb. 7–9, towards the close into V.

   In the bass there are two main types of motion, also with distinct functions. Minims, often with some octave leaping, usually appear at passages of maximum harmonic stability, such as the opening bars and the sequence in bb. 7–10. Crotchets, which feature much stepwise movement (the quavers in bb. 10 and 11 notwithstanding) tend to produce intensified motion, such as bb. 5–6. The core issue here is not so much the motivic concentration of the outer parts as their relation to each other. Half way through the first violins' first phrase the bass begins crotchet movement, which pushes the phrase on towards the stronger driving patterns of bb. 5–6. The downbeat of b. 10 is a point of arrival, articulated by the way in which the bass breaks the pattern of octave leaps in the preceding bar. To intensify movement towards the close, the bass then uses quaver figuration derived from the upper part to ornament what is still basically crotchet movement.

The downbeats of the outer parts make straightforward counterpoint, outlining unambiguously forceful harmonic progressions of a type which could readily have belonged to contemporary Italian music. This clarity is essential, for it projects the fundamental pitch and harmonic progressions against which the often elaborate part writing can unfold. The way in which the motivic working complements this fundamental movement is underlined by the recurrence of the same bass pattern in bb. 4 and 6, both of which use secondary dominants to approach the following crucial downbeats, although the first violin line is different in each bar.

Purcell's progress in instrumental style between *King Arthur* and *The Fairy Queen* is epitomised in the fourth act tunes of both works (Z. 628.11 and 629.38). Rhythmically economical as the tune from *King Arthur* is, it is by far the less sophisticated concept. In *The Fairy Queen* the first violins repeat the rhythmic motif ♩ | ♫♫♩ ♩ | every one and a half bars, thus stressing successively the first then second pulse of the bar. This ambiguity is deliciously complicated by the bass, which runs along in canon at the octave a bar later. Approaches to closes are marked by the outer parts breaking out of this ticklishly fraught rhythm into a conformity underlined by motivic changes in both parts, while a few bars before the end of the piece the canon changes to run at the fifth.

The nonpareil of motivic economy is the prelude to Juno's song 'Thrice Happy Lovers' which begins Act V (Z. 629.39). Just sixteen bars long, it is repeated in its entirety, even though the first twelve bars of the bass consist of a one-bar figure transposed and varied to suit the harmonic context, while throughout the same bars, the upper strings repeat a half-bar figure. Even by this composer's exacting standards the motivic concentration is extreme; but it is also expressively cogent, for it throws pitch and harmonic progressions, spiced with piquant detail, into high relief.

Whatever the merits of this and other pieces, the instrumental centrepiece of *The Fairy Queen* is the symphony which opens Act IV (Z. 629.27), a full-blown

Ex. 72   *The Fairy Queen,* Canzona from symphony to Act IV (Z. 629.27b): bb. 16–30

Ex. 72 Continues on facing page

Italianate orchestral sonata, and apparently Purcell's first to be specially composed for a stage work. The opening, quasi-homophonic, texture for strings and trumpets is given characteristically polyphonic treatment, and is followed by a fast fugal movement based on two subjects and headed by the composer's first use in some eight years of the title Canzona. It is followed by a B minor slow movement for strings alone, then an Allegro which perfects the use, as subjects

for fugal imitation, of those fanfare-style motifs at which trumpets excel. Two statements of this movement surround a brief, chromatic Adagio for strings alone, which plumbs the depths of chromatic elaboration.

Compared with earlier pieces for trumpet and strings, this canzona seems to have stepped onto another plane of operation. It thrives on the tensions offered by various motivic endings on A, F♯, E or D, and by changes of texture away from and back to the densely fugal opening style. Its thematic material and many other aspects of its operation are derived from the first section, the first theme (a of Ex. 72) being closely related to the figuration which approaches the two closes in I and V (bb. 5 and 9), and the arpeggaic second theme b coming from the end of the section.

The first theme of the canzona picks up the D which ended the first section, opens with the traditional canzona rhythm, and smartly reverses the mainly descending patterns which dominated the first section. The contrast between it and the second theme – the ascending line of a rises from D and stresses the final A, and the arpeggio figuration of b descends to stress D – is one of the main animating forces of the piece.

As the opening section reinforces high A through its incessant repetitions of a, some sort of balancing statement is required to return to a stable D. Despite its initial close on D, b is never presented in a form strong enough to acquire that function; indeed, the more it fails to do so, the less likely it becomes that it can. The progress of the piece is intimately bound up with developing a progression which will achieve that necessary closure.

The canzona is in three main sections defined by closes (Table 5). The close of A1 is set up in bb. 26–7, where for the first time the stress patterns of all parts come together, partly through concentrating on b, and articulate the beginning of a dominant prolongation from b. 27 to the resolution on the downbeat of b. 30 (Ex. 72).

The first bars of section B are dominated by sequential patterns on c (Ex. 72), a derivation of the repeated notes in a. But it also sees the emergence of y (Ex.

Table 5. The Fairy Queen, *Canzona from Act IV Symphony (Z. 629.27b)*

	A1	B	A2
bars	16–30	30–36–38	38–51
	I—I	I—V—I	I—I

Ex. 73   *The Fairy Queen*, Canzona from symphony to Act IV (Z. 629.27b): bb. 36–40

73), a scalic filling of the descending fourth which was so prominent in the first section (bb. 10–15). This has the strongest closural potential of any motif so far, a possibility pressed home by its being used in the approach to the close into V (bb. 35–6) and to the tonic close in bb. 37–8 (Ex. 73).

Section A2 incorporates a more expansive derivation *z*, and combines this with extraordinarily elaborate reworkings of *a* and *b*. The prominence of *z* in the lower parts is a throwback to a more distant originator of *y* – the two scalically descending fourths in the second violin in b. 20 (Ex. 72).

In bb. 36 and 37 the trumpets had entered in parallel thirds and had picked up the harmonic tension of the close onto A (bb. 35–6) to turn that harmony back to V of I. So now the close into I on the downbeat of b. 48 begins another statement of *y* and its derivations to close the piece, again via a dominant prolongation. But the closural properties of *y* are now made much stronger. Significantly, *x* (Ex. 73) does not appear; instead closure is achieved by a slowed-down version of *y*, in the rhythm ♪♩. ♪|♩ ‖ and by a concluding entry on high A in the second trumpet. Although F♯ is uppermost in the final chord, convincing closure is achieved by the first violins and trumpet wedging in towards D, by the slowing of motion in the penultimate bar, and by the timing of the second trumpet's entry, which makes its version of *y* work as an ornamentation of the fundamental movement down to D.

The final Allegro is the most compressed working of fanfare figures which Purcell ever executed on a large scale. The strings and trumpets are treated as two distinct groupings and the two-bar units of the material are adroitly overlapped both within and between these groupings. It is entirely in D, and the boundary between its two main sections is articulated by the strongest intermediate close and by the beginning of the customary inversion of the material, though this quickly reverts to its original form. A superb example of populist appeal – thunderous sonorities after the slow movement for strings – combined with artifice for the connoisseur, its wears its technique on its sleeve, and is full of quirks of detail which impart a much more abrasive quality than Italian equivalents.

Later that same year, at the annual Cecilian celebrations, Purcell had an unparalleled opportunity of demonstrating that, as far as modern instrumental style was concerned, no English composer could outdo him. The ode *Hail, Bright Cecilia* (Z. 328) begins with another symphony in the same style as that from *The Fairy Queen*, at least as virtuosic in technique, and even larger in size, mainly because of several repetitions of movements, which are, however, not casual inflations of scale. The open-ended close of the Adagio, for example, demands a balancing return to D major, provided at first by a return to the Canzona. The next statement of the Adagio exploits this relationship for a second time, and D major is now provided by the final Allegro, which in turn is repeated after a brief chromatic Grave.

The first section of the symphony is far more polyphonic than its apparently homophonic texture suggests. It is dominated by a single melodic and rhythmic motif, set up in b. 1 by the A–D–A move (trumpet I, Ex. 74) and answered in the strings with D–G–D in the bass. Repetition of the opening bar articulates this statement-plus-answer as a periodic unit, the harmonic functions of which are defined by the opening and closing harmonies. The section is driven largely by increasingly aberrant versions of the unit's stress patterns, which destabilise the metre, a process resolved only in the coincidence of stresses at the final cadence.

Other than the swapping of parts between the trumpets, the first two units are identical, and this repetition establishes their pitch and harmonic content as the focal area of the movement. The third unit begins with the upper trumpet at a higher pitch, and this sets in train the first break in harmonic constancy between trumpets and strings. The strings enter on dominant harmony instead of tonic (b. 3), which disturbs the stress patterns of the unit, partly by drawing attention to the string progression at the expense of the trumpets. Although this is to some extent diverted by the unanimous presentation of the dominant in the fourth unit, it is picked up in unit 5, where the basses invert the rising-fourth figure to underline V–II–V, so articulating a local tonicisation of V. Unit 6 presents dominant harmony as unanimously as 1 and 2 did the tonic. Unit 7 reverses this

Ex. 74   Hail, Bright Cecilia (Z. 328), opening symphony, first section

pattern with V–I, but also disrupts the pattern of instrumentation, for the kettle-drums now accompany the strings so that, although the tonic has returned, it is highly unstable. The entries of trumpet I and the strings (with kettledrums) are capped by trumpet II's entry a beat early, followed by trumpet I on the 'right' beat.

The harmonically open ending of this first section is not resolved until well into the canzona, for although the first theme (*a* in Ex. 75) is firmly in D major,

Ex. 75   *Hail, Bright Cecilia*, Canzona from opening symphony (Z. 328.1b): bb. 11–14

the massive A major close is still a live issue. Theme *b* acquires the strongest potential for resolution, by picking up the high A of b. 10 and bringing it down scalically to E in b. 14, thus setting up D as the main potential pitch, although on this occasion at least, the E goes to F♯.

The distinctive properties and pitch emphases of the two themes produce some of the core features of the canzona. Theme *a*'s purposeful move from D to A makes it particularly useful to articulate a move away from D or, using the answer form (A, F♯, D, E, A, D), back to D. The sequential patterns of *b* are used as a primary means of generating rhythmic energy, especially when stretti occur on the 'wrong' beats. The deflected ending of *b* becomes the starting point for another ascent to A (cf. bb. 14–15 and 21–3). As with most such ascents, this A is articulated by a V–I in that key and the approach is inflected to the minor mode. A further move towards D follows.

So we have cycles of ascents and descents, groupings of which are articulated by carefully graded full closes into the tonic. Each grouping concentrates on specific combinatorial possibilities, and tensions between strings and trumpets are used so that, on the whole, the grading of closes depends largely on the trumpets' role.

The intermediate tonic closes are in bb. 21, 28, 32, 40 and 44; of these the first is the weakest. It inaugurates a series of entries which feature stretti on *b*, in both prime and inversion, and which enter at the crotchet, the dotted minim and the semibreve.

The greater strength of the close in b. 28 is articulated by the rhythmic unanimity between outer parts during the approach and by its being the only one to end with the tonic pitch uppermost in the trumpets. After it there is a single arch away from D to A and back again, the episodic, essentially circular function of which is articulated by its being set for much lighter scoring, though it is rhythmically unstable because stretti on *b* tend to enter on the 'wrong' part of the bar.

After the tonic close in b. 32, which resolves some of this rhythmic tension, the gradual departure from the melodic forms of the opening bars reaches its peak on the reduction of *b* to its most sparse identifiable component, an upbeat quaver and crotchet downbeat (𝄾 ♪♩), a three-part imitative discourse on which ends in b. 40 with another close in D.

Given such a context, the entry, at the close in b. 40, of an answer form of *a* in trumpet I, produces a strong return to stability, not least because this form of *a* has the strongest potential yet for a close into D. So the several stretti on it make a convincing approach to the final close in b. 44. Even so, F♯ is uppermost; but now it does not weaken the close, the strength of which is derived from the approach, the unanimity of stress patterns, and the comparative absence of ornamental movement which has, especially in the case of *b*, been a forceful agent of rhythmic instability. The canzona ends with tonic and dominant repetitions on quaver-crotchet rhythm and, although the last chord has A uppermost, the ending is sufficiently conclusive for the section, largely because the bass reaches the first low D of the piece.

The Adagio, in A minor, follows the then-ascendant concerto practice of using two groups of instruments, in this case two trios – one of two violins and cello, the other of two oboes and viola. It is primarily concerned with reconciling these two groups by a process that is mechanical in concept yet astonishingly subtle in execution.

Themes are scarcely an issue; instead there are just two motifs, both seminally presented in the first phrase, which melodically circulates around E. Throughout the movement the opening motif is repeated sequentially on different harmonic and pitch levels to articulate harmonic mobility, and is increasingly associated with chromatic alteration. By contrast, the phrase's concluding motif articulates, through full closes, many of the more important harmonic areas, while repetitions of it can articulate large-scale harmonic sequences, e.g. the I (i.e. V of IV)–IV of bb. 65–9.

The first two phrases (bb. 47–56) set a pattern of the oboes answering the violins with a variation harmonically more mobile than the violins' statement. As the movement progresses, the string phrases tend to reinforce or modify the harmonic areas opened out by the oboes, but do not move to radically new areas. So, while the strings at first lead the instrumental dialogue, progress is increasingly dominated by the harmonic lead offered by the oboes' phrases, to the extent that the end of each oboe phrase could lead directly into the beginning of the next, conjoining phrases 2, 4, 6 and 8, for example. The dialogue is destabilised by the irregularity of the phrase lengths and by the increasing harmonic mobility. This reaches its peak in b. 83, where the violas join the violins, while in b. 85, just as the harmony is reaching for the tonic area for the last time, the oboes enter to make a tutti. The movement ends with an extraordinary chromatic peroration, with the final full close prefaced by a 'neapolitan sixth' – as Purcell himself said, 'a Favourite Note with the Italians'.[10] The D major Allegro is dominated by the frenetic, sonorous energy of the two main instrumental groupings, as they work in consort and contrast. Not as evidently sparse in its motivic material as the equivalent movement from *The Fairy Queen*, it nevertheless is an extraordinary example of motivic concentration, being based on just three motifs, derivations of which emerge only gradually, while the four-square phrasing which the material tends to suggest is avoided by adroit contrapuntal manipulations.

Until the last year of his life, in *The Indian Queen* (Z. 630), Purcell was to get no further opportunity for such a large instrumental piece, at least in the stage music. But the new methods of compositional economy represented both by these two Italianate symphonies, and by the shorter instrumental works of *The Fairy Queen*, are central to the methods of the several large sets of pieces composed between 1692 and 1695, for plays such as *The Married Beau* (Z. 603) and *Abdelazer* (Z. 570), and for the symphonies to odes such as *Come Ye Sons of Art* (Z. 323) and *Who Can from Joy Refrain?* (Z. 342).

Some sets of dances and act tunes are dominated by a specific range of compositional concepts. For example, in the pieces he provided for Congreve's comedy *The Double Dealer* (Z. 592), which was produced in November 1693, Purcell apparently revives details of his old style in a much more trenchant way than in the 1692 ode *Love's Goddess Sure* (Z. 331).

In the overture, while parts pair off for most of the time and the harmonic structure is decidedly modern, the relationship between the pairs and the behaviour of the occasional independent part can be extraordinarily tense. The opening (Ex. 76 (i)) sets the scene by pairing the inner parts in thirds and sixths against the first violin and bass. Resolving the $\frac{6}{4}$ in b. 1 produces stress on the downbeat of b. 2, and the first violin picks up the resolving figure but half a bar later, thus tending to stress the second beat of b. 2. The consequent metrical tension is intensified by the bass setting off in canon with the first violin, at the beginning of the second bar. It takes several bars to sort out this disparity, by which time we are embarked on a broad harmonic circuit around F major.

The nervously jumpy subject of the second section is in striking contrast to the forcefully driven stepwise lines of the first (Ex. 76 (ii)), but it is nevertheless

Ex. 76   The Double Dealer (Z. 592), Overture:

(i) bb. 1–4

(ii) bb. 16–26

(iii) bb. 35–7

one of the section's more stable elements, for the elaborately syncopated secondary material gradually stretches the metre to breaking point. This is brought to an end by a strongly prepared close in the dominant, and thereafter direct statements of the subject disappear (Ex. 76 (iii)).

The last piece to do this so obviously was the early Overture à 5 in G minor
(Z. 772); but in *The Double Dealer* the function is entirely different and the
result much more cogent, for the loss of the unstable texture is palpable relief,
the apparently new material being a more stable way of filling out the thirds
which dominated the subject. A broad harmonic circuit which includes a strong
close in the relative minor (b. 41) and a prolongation of the dominant (bb.
46–50), expunges the earlier metrical tensions, especially because the harmonic
rhythm is the same as in the bars before the close into the dominant, and the
coincidence of stress patterns in all parts produces a clear long-range drive.

Brazen blends of old detail and new structure reach a peak in the A minor
Hornpipe (Z. 592.5). In the second half (Ex. 77) the violins begin in thirds, and,

Ex. 77   *The Double Dealer*, Hornpipe (Z. 592.5): bb. 5–12

with the bass, provide all the essential elements of the texture. The viola sets off
with a line largely consonant, yet determinedly independent in rhythm and
shape. On the downbeat of b. 6 a viola G would produce parallel fifths with the
first violin; to avoid this Purcell has a 9–8 which, however, has a bite altogether
greater than such pragmatism would suggest. The other parts take this rugged
independence as a cue increasingly to go their own way: the struck dissonance
of b. 6 is picked up by the second violin in b. 7; the viola climbs up a scale, and
the second violin responds with a descending one; this causes the 4–3 in the V–I
of C major to be struck against its own resolution.

But this is an extreme approach, and a rather more balanced meld of conservative and modern elements, and a much greater level of integration across pieces, can be seen in the music for Crowne's 1694 comedy *The Married Beau* (Z. 603).

The first section of the overture is dominated by a motif almost identical to that which opens *The Gordian Knot* (Z. 597). But the results are much less suave, largely because *The Married Beau* allies *The Gordian Knot*'s structural strengths – a powerful, economical harmonic structure and the use of a few motifs in parallel motion – with a texture driven by its lines, packed with irregular phrase lengths and full of surprising twists of detail.

In the second section of the overture, the three main motifs are strongly differentiated and articulate just two types of fundamental movement: the agile scalic motion and distinctive rhythm of the main subject (*a* in Ex. 78), the

Ex. 78   *The Married Beau* (Z. 603), Overture: bb. 21–30

definitive character of which tends to dominate the texture, and the descending scale step, which is mainly articulated by the two subsidiary motifs *c* and *d*, of which the former includes rhythmic elements drawn from *a*. While the countersubject *b* is abandoned after the initial series of entries, it is the clear originator of the scalic motion in *c* and *d*.

The phrase structure is strongly periodic, while the single-minded harmonic practice is advanced by contemporary English standards. After the initial statements of *a*, all other statements are diatonic to F. Yet there is no close in F, and D minor returns via an inflexion in b. 33, a statement of *a* beginning on D in b. 34, and an enormous dominant prolongation from b. 38. This harmonic simplicity gives strong support to the resourceful jugglings of the motivic material and to the extended sequential patterns which are a primary means of achieving scale.

The music for *The Married Beau* has more links between pieces than any earlier set of instrumental music for a play. Perhaps the most obvious of these is the reworking of the overture's opening motif in the F major Air and the C major March (Z. 603.4 and 8). Several pieces also continue the overture's concentration on D minor and F major. The 'Slow Air' (Z. 603.2) juxtaposes a four-bar phrase (bb. 1–4) with a tonally propositional, varied repetition in F, and the D minor Hornpipe (Z. 603.3) takes this further by having its first strain entirely in D minor, while its second sets off anew in F major; to return to D minor, the first bar of the concluding four-bar phrase is in F and the second bar repeats it in D minor. The most memorable of these instrumental pieces is undoubtedly the 'Hornpipe on a Ground' (Z. 603.9), which in the ground and the opening of the first violin line picks up the notion of descending lines which was such a prominent feature of parts of the overture and the C major March (Z. 603.8). Like so many pieces in this set, the hornpipe is dominated by third-based figuration.

Such pieces show complete mastery in the instrumental character piece, and underline how dependent this development was on the free yet concentrated repetition techniques typified earlier in the Prelude to 'Thrice Happy Lovers' in *The Fairy Queen* (Z. 629.39a). The upper parts of the C minor Air written around this time for *The Virtuous Wife* (Z. 611.4), for example, consist of constantly varied repetitions, in quaver rhythm throughout, of the arpeggio figure from the first bar. Packed with quirky detail which gives the piece much of its forcefulness, they are supported by a bass which strides along in simple crotchets. Then there is the March from *The Old Bachelor* (Z. 607.8), which opens with imitations on a repeated-note figure. But these are less concerned with contrapuntal elaboration than with reinforcing a generally mock-pompous tone, epitomised by the march being in triple-time.

The character-piece concept underlies many, perhaps most, of the smaller pieces of instrumental music which Purcell wrote during the last year or so of his life. *Abdelazer* (Z. 570) was premiered in April 1695, and Purcell's music is perhaps most famous for the air 'Lucinda is Bewitching Fair' and for the famous Rondeau (Z. 570.10 and 2). Several of the dances take their cue from the overture's first section, which uses the opening motifs as the basis for a long series of harmonic and melodic sequences, economical in their exploration of related keys and strongly periodic in phrasing. The subject for the second section is itself sequential, and the section is preoccupied with explorations, not of the subject's combinatorial possibilities, but of differing contexts for varied

versions of it. So after the opening entries, the first violins use the subject to cross
the boundaries of a strong V–i in the tonic D minor (bb. 25–6), and to launch
a harmonic progress in which the subject is supported by material which also is
sequential, but which, by its distinctly accompanimental nature, highlights the
main material. The goal is a close into the relative major (bb. 32–3), articulated
by all parts assuming subject-based figuration. Similarly sequential patterns are
a dominant feature of other movements, including the Rondeau and the G
major Air (Z. 570.2 and 4).

Such sequences are, of course, part of late Baroque vocabulary; but Purcell's
use of them is distinctive. In the first strain of the $\frac{3}{4}$ Hornpipe from *Bonduca* (Z.
574.5), the three upper parts are entirely consistent in their motivic details, and
one of the main driving forces behind the sequential patterns of bb. 3–5 is the
strong up-beat thrust produced by violin II's and viola's rhythm (Ex. 79). The

Ex. 79   *Bonduca*, Hornpipe (Z. 574.5): bb. 1–6

same rhythm appears in bb. 1–2, but the bass avoids an entirely plausible and
motivically consistent crotchet motion until the sequence gets under way. The
strong i–V outlined in the first two bars by the sustained dotted minims of the
bass thus imparts extra energy to the sequence once the crotchets get under way
in b. 3. The release of energy in these bars is intensified by the harmonic tensions
of the first violin's G–D against tonic harmony, and G–E♭ against the dominant
in bb. 1–2. All this passes in a flash, of course, but the momentary, motivically
generated tension is real, and persists through the second strain in the form of
highly unpredictable twists in the motivic sequences.

Purcell had not yet finished with flamboyant displays of good old-fashioned
contrapuntal prowess. A year or so earlier, for the opening symphony to the last
of Queen Mary's birthday odes, *Come Ye Sons of Art* (Z. 323), he had turned
yet again to the canzona style. But he outdid himself in simultaneously using
three contrasted subjects, and while their character and the manner of treatment
produce a less extrovert effect than the canzona in *The Fairy Queen* (Z.
629.27b), the concentration on material is no less virtuosic or well-judged.

His swan song in these techniques was to come in the 'Trumpet Overture' from *The Indian Queen* (Z. 630.16). Like that in *Come Ye Sons of Art*, this canzona has a suavity of texture which seems somewhat removed from the gritty concentration of earlier examples. But the techniques remain as sophisticated as ever, and have a particular interest in that the piece uses a variant of a subject which had first appeared at least ten years before, in the canzona from the Sonata No. 7 (1697) in C (Z. 808.3b), a movement which had itself had been revised at least once (Ex. 80 (i)).

The changes in the subject are significant: they avoid the earlier work's clipped, two-bar phrasing, by adopting the characteristic up-beat rhythm at the opening and by having an ending which can readily be extended (Ex. 80 (ii)).

Ex. 80 (i) Sonata No. 7 (1697) in C, Canzona (Z. 808.3b): bb. 1–3

(ii) *The Indian Queen*, Trumpet Overture (Z. 630.16): bb. 15–27

The initial entries reflect this in the varieties of temporal imitation and in the ease with which parts pair off in thirds when using the semiquaver figure. Such pairings are generally set against more slow-moving figuration, which itself might be paired off.

The result is an unusual lucidity of texture, which highlights the entries of the subject to the extent that they tend to sound rather like a solo line, a characteristic strongly underlined by the way the trumpet's first entry is set up via a long dominant pedal. The prominence of these entries is also reinforced by the large-scale harmonic organisation, for while there are shifts between tonic and dominant, each section of the canzona focusses mainly on the local tonic concerned, with little interest in harmonic variety within the section. This sectional emphasis is pushed home by the strength of the articulating closes, by the extended harmonic prolongations and by harmonic mobility being confined to sections which do not concentrate on the subject as such.

The result is a structure which sounds rather like a series of expositions, each in a related key. At the first departure from straightforward statements of the subject, for example, sequential imitations drive towards the relative minor (bb. 29–33), and a close into that key is neatly set up by the trumpet's entry (Ex. 81).

Ex. 81   The Indian Queen, Trumpet Overture (Z. 630.16): bb. 32–40

Note in particular how the bass prolongs the dominant by leaving the low register in b. 36 to state the subject, and by picking up that low F♯ in b. 38.

Such methods represent the consolidation of a new phase in Purcell's instrumental practice. It was only the composer's premature death which prevented him from carrying further what seems to be a step into a defining technique of late Baroque style.

CHAPTER EIGHT

Early mastery: sacred music to *c.* 1685

ANTHEMS

CRITICAL OPINION HAS BEEN DIVIDED on the quality of Purcell's church music: Arkwright regarded it as at least equal with the theatre music and court odes, while Westrup's views were generally unfavourable.[1] Yet some of Purcell's anthems are amongst his best known and most frequently performed music; moreover, a few never entirely disappeared from the Anglican repertory, a durability to some extent explained by convenience and by the matchless conservatism of Anglican music, but it also is a testament to their quality. Some of the earlier anthems in particular stand in the same relationship to the composer's vocal music as the fantasias do to his instrumental music – a late and extraordinarily fine product of that English polyphonic tradition which Purcell esteemed so highly.

Most of the very early anthems, dating from 1676–9, are for voices and continuo alone, perhaps because a young composer was more likely to get a performance if he used smaller forces.[2] They include solidly competent and occasionally beautiful pieces such as *Lord, Who Can Tell?* (Z. 26) and *Who Hath Believed Our Report?* (Z. 64), which link the young Purcell directly into the mainstream of post-Restoration verse anthem practice. Nevertheless, the differences between these pieces, plus the wide range of practice shown in less successful early anthems such as *Let God Arise* (Z. 23) and *O Lord Our Governor* (Z. 39), reveal an eagerness to experiment and a natural curiosity in stretching the expressive boundaries of an inherently conservative medium.

Lord, Who Can Tell? pre-dates 1679 and is typical of most anthems in that the chorus is subsidiary to the soloists (two tenors and bass): in this instance it appears only in the final 'Gloria', after three contrasted verse sections. The first section sets the generally penitential tone with descending leaps (Ex. 82),

Ex. 82   Lord, Who Can Tell? (Z. 26): bb. 1–21

notably the descending diminished fifth in 'offendeth', and skilfully works two
contrasted points in a dialogue which increases the pace of entries to drive
towards a close.[3] After a complete entry in each voice, a series of modified
repetitions on 'who can tell?' accumulates tension across a two-bar prolongation of V of III (bb. 11 and 12), thus setting up a full close in that key. To
counter this assertive questioning the next line is set to a scalically descending
point, combined in stretti to produce double suspensions. After the drawn-out
descent from high E (b. 16) the inevitable resolution of V is given a final,
deliciously pathetic twist in the triple *échappée* of b. 18.

Purcell's skill at driving a line for calculated expressive effect can also be seen
at the end of the last verse section: the plea on 'O Lord' is intensified by a
repetition (Ex. 83, bb. 75–6) which ornaments the two lower voices'

Ex. 83   Lord, Who Can Tell? (Z. 26): bb. 71–8

fundamental progression F$\sharp$/A–E/G with a prominent *échappée*-like G/B
beneath D$\sharp$, while the textual emphasis on 'strength' is captured by a linearly
driven combination of B, D$\sharp$ and G. In both cases the D$\sharp$/G dissonance
intensifies the drive towards resolution. The second one, for example, neatly
mixes the sounds of a $^6_4$ and a $^5_3$ over B.

Another early anthem, *Who Hath Believed Our Report?* (Z. 64) is a very
different type of piece. Its unusual uniformity – each portion of the long text
(Isaiah 53: i–viii) is defined by a strong close, all sections except the last half
(bb.103–28) of the penultimate one are in $\math혰{C}$ time, and the vocal writing is

consistently declamatory – is neatly ameliorated by using changes in scoring to define structural boundaries. The seven sections (Fig. 2) are a succession of verses for ensemble (A, C1 and D) and successive soloists (B and E), with the choral reworking (C2) of the central thought 'All we like sheep have gone astray, and the Lord hath laid on him the iniquity of us all' appearing twice, to act as the defining pillars.[4]

Fig. 2. Who Hath Believed Our Report? (Z. 64)

	A	B	C1	C2	D	E		C2
Closes	i – iv	iv – i	V of i – i	i – i	i – v	i – i		i – i
Bars	1 – 22	23 – 54	55 – 67	68 – 78	79 – 85	86 – 96 – 103 – 128		129 – 39
Scoring	at¹t²b	t²+t¹+b+a	at¹t²b	SATB	at¹t²b	t²+t¹		SATB
Time Sig.	¢ 31						**C**	¢

Each section reworks the harmonic premises set out by the opening one, which sets three portions of text, each marked by a close and disposed so as to make the most of its possibilities for dramatic expression.

Fig. 3. Who Hath Believed Our Report? (Z. 64): first section

Who hath believed our Report?, and to whom is the arm of the Lord revealed	(X)
For he shall grow up before him	(Y)
as a tender plant, and as a root out of dry ground.	(Z)

Text	| X |	X	| X |	Y	| Z |	
Closes	i –	V of i –	III –	v(V) –	III –	iv
Bars	1	5	9	13	18	22
Scoring	| t¹ |	b	| at¹t²b |	at¹t²b with solos |		
Main closes	i .... v iv					

Dialogue technique is here used to highlight the contrast between verse solo and verse ensemble. So the first two appearances of 'X' are for single voice, but during the close into III, the ensemble entry interjects with 'Who'. While the technique is not particularly subtle, it is an effective way of accumulating tension to set up another section, and establishes the pattern for the setting up of Z, which neatly contrasts short solos with the predominant ensemble writing.

If *Lord, Who Can Tell?* is indebted to Locke and *Who Hath Believed Our Report?* to Humfrey, other early anthems explore possibilities from farther afield. *Let God Arise* (Z. 23) strings together illustrative devices derived from early-seventeenth-century Italian music, while similar sources might have suggested to Purcell that the text of *O Lord Our Governor* (Z. 39) needed a departure from the most common scoring of three soloists, typically *atb*, in favour of three trebles and two basses. The trebles aptly sing 'Out of the mouths of very babes and sucklings' while the basses express the more robust acclamations of praise. But in both anthems the emphasis has drifted too far away from musical concentration, towards local text illustration; Purcell's superb later setting of O Lord Our Governor as a sacred partsong (Z. 141), using a metrical version of the text, is a telling improvement.

In the verse anthem without strings this early interest in the dramatic possibilities of scoring finds its most compelling result in Blow up the Trumpet (Z. 10), scored for eight-part choir and seven soloists, to which is added the possibilities for spacial contrast offered by decani and cantoris groupings and by varied doublings between the ten staves of the score. The anthem is in C, one of the two trumpet keys, and its seven sections are in three groups, the ends of which are defined by choral reworkings of recently heard material. The first group dramatically contrasts the major-mode, fanfare figures for 'Blow up the Trumpet', and the elaborate working of minor-mode, declamatory lines for the prophet Joel's exhortations to 'Sanctify a fast, gather the people and sanctify the congregation'. The anthem brilliantly sustains these contrasts by using a distinctive harmonic gesture to pivot between the major and minor modes, both between and within sections.

The harmonically propositional I–V–I of section A1 (Fig. 4) is strong enough to project across substantial subsequent deflection. So B opens with a declamation to 'Sanctify a fast' which juxtaposes G major harmony to E♭. This opens up Janus-like possibilities for G major, which in bb. 20–2 is used to return to C, now in its minor mode, to set up the choral reworking of 'Blow up the Trumpet'. It returns at a number of central expressive points, such as the preparation (b. 61) for the cry 'Spare thy people', where it neatly deflects the tension accumulated by the chromatic twistings of 'let them weep between the porch and the altar'.

Fig. 4. Blow up the Trumpet (Z. 10): first three sections

	A1				B				A2		
Harmonies	i – V of I		V – I		V of I	V of III/v(V)	– i		I – V of I	– I	
Bars	1	7	8	14	15	20	22	29	30	34	37 – 40
Scoring		Verse				Verse				Chorus	

From 1681 onwards the verse anthem with strings was the dominant type in Purcell's sacred music, but we know at present of only three such pieces with fairly reliable datings from before 1679. Of these – My Beloved Spake (Z. 28), Praise the Lord, Ye Servants (Z. N68), and If the Lord Himself (Z. N66) – only Z. 28 is complete. One other anthem is likely to pre-date 1680 – Behold, Now Praise the Lord (Z. 3) – but one section of this too is incomplete.[5]

My Beloved Spake exists in two versions, both of which date from these early years; the main substance of the revision lies in changing the first section of the symphony, and seems designed to deal with the challenges of musical cohesion inherent in the genre. Although Purcell would have got the idea of sectional repetition from earlier anthem composers, his use of it and of motivic referencing between sections is unusually developed. The symphony repetition, for example, marks no significant textual point, unlike many such cases in Humfrey and Blow; but it does have intrinsic musical significance.

Like most anthems, *My Beloved Spake* is concentrated around a single tonic, in this case F major or minor. Purcell uses juxtapositions of the two modes for complementary musical and poetic purposes. The first two verse sections (Fig. 5), one in the major and the other in the minor, establish the principle of the contrast, while the next section, 'The flow'rs appear' (Z. 28.4), articulates a new beginning (*a*) by its similarities to 'My beloved spake' (Z. 28.2) in scoring, key and melodic pattern. The subsequent massive expansion of F major through 'And the time of the singing of birds is come' justifies the extremity of the harmonic shifts in 'And the voice of the turtle' (Z. 28.6), for in order to repeat the modal contrast first expressed in *a–b*, without recourse to a long F minor section, something extravagant is essential. The repetition of the symphony (*c*) marks both the closure of this first half and initiates a new beginning.

The return of 'rise my love' (*d*) is overlapped into the previous section in what is probably Purcell's earliest surviving example of a device he was to use extensively in his mature dramatic music. A return is called for by the text, but the musical result is a true recapitulation of the first section. The mode contrasts which have animated most of the piece are now expunged, a point underlined by the major mode of 'My beloved is mine' (Z. 28.9), the 'Alleluia' (Z. 28.11) and the choral reworking (*e*) (Z. 28.13). This is in keeping with the implication that everything from 'My beloved is mine' onwards is a response to the earlier part of the text.

It seems likely that the symphony was revised to tighten structure, for references to its opening bars recur at a number of important points: the prominent E♭ is a feature of the 'Alleluia' and of the ritornello (Z. 28.5d and e) preceding 'And the voice of the turtle', while the leaps of a third which are prominent in both versions of the symphony come back forcefully for the final group of items, from 'My beloved is mine' onwards (Z. 28.9–13).

Throughout the anthem there is a tendency for vocal sections to begin and, less consistently, to end themes on the mediant of the key or chord concerned. Endings or beginnings different from this pattern may articulate a significant change or a closure: the symphony ends on the tonic; the first phrase for Bass I ends on the root of C for the close onto that chord, and this generates the change into a new phrase and line of text – 'rise my love, my fair one and come away'. The same characteristics can be seen in the last sections: 'The fig tree putteth forth' begins and ends on A, but the succeeding triple time passage ends on F and inaugurates the return to a varied form of 'rise my love'; 'My beloved is mine' and the 'Alleluia' sections begin on A. Other melodic and rhythmic

Fig. 5. Structure of My Beloved Spake (Z. 28)

SYMPH.	VERSE & RIT.	VERSE & RIT.	VERSE	VERSE CHOR & RIT.	VERSE & RIT.	VERSE	SYMPH.	VERSE	VERSE & RIT.	VERSE & RIT.	VERSE & RIT.	CHOR. VERSE & CHOR.
										d		*e*
	'My beloved spake' and 'Rise my love'	'For lo, the winter'	'The flow'rs appear'	'And the time'	'Alle-luia'	'And the voice'		'The fig tree'	'Rise my love'	'My beloved is mine'	'Alle-luia'	'My beloved is mine' and 'Alleluia'
F	F	Fm	F	F	F	F/Fm	F		F	F	F	F
c	*a*	*b*	*a*			*b*	*c*		*d*	*e*		*e*

Ex. 84   My Beloved Spake (Z. 28): melodic and rhythmic connections

Fig. 6. My Beloved Spake (Z. 28): phrase structure and scoring in 'And the time of the singing of birds is come'

1 *Verse*	I – I		I – V		V – vi	II – V – I		
bars	95	99	100	103	104	107 108		111
2 *Chorus*	I – IV		IV – ii		V – I			
bars	111	115	116	119	120	123		
3 *Orch.*	I – IV		IV – V		V – I			
bars	123†	126	127	130	131	134		

|_____ Verse _____|

†The orchestral parts begin with the downbeat which ended the previous phrase, rather than with a long upbeat, as in the preceding vocal phrase. There are textual problems with this part of the score (*NPS*, vol. XIII, pp. 114 and 162) which do not, however, affect the substantive issue.

connections are plotted in Ex. 84. Note the rising line A–C–D prominent in the first and last extracts.[6]

This anthem's tendency towards strongly periodic structures is evident at the local level in 'For lo the winter is past' (Z. 28.3) and in 'And the time of the singing of birds is come' (Z. 28.5): indeed, Westrup cites the latter as an example of 'the new homophonic style, in which all the joyousness of secular song is brought into the service of the church's hymn of praise and thanksgiving'.[7]

The young Purcell skilfully avoids the predictability which can so easily come with such textures. Its three sub-sections are in principle for verse, chorus and orchestra respectively. Although all begin and end in the tonic, each is different in its harmonic emphases (Fig. 6) and in details of pitch and scoring. The masterstroke lies in setting the last phrase of the third sub-section for verse. The unexpected change in itself generates tension, which is increased by the altered harmonic and melodic patterns, in particular by the upper line's six repetitions of the supertonic (cf. end of sub-section 2). Release from this tension is provided by the move into the 'Alleluia's, which themselves generate a new series of tensions.

A much more concentrated approach to technique can be found in some verse anthems without strings, defined as a group by their complex contrapuntal textures, exceptional degree of concentration on a limited amount of thematic material, and by penitential texts. The earliest could date from around 1677; between then and 1682 some of them were revised at least once and, it seems likely, Purcell wrote some more in similar vein. The group comprises *Bow Down Thine Ear* (Z. 11), *Hear Me, O Lord* (Z. 13A and B), *Let Mine Eyes Run Down with Tears* (Z. 24), *Save Me, O God* (Z. 51) and the funeral sentences *Man That Is Born of a Woman* (Z. 27 and other versions); a case also can be made for including *Blessed Is He Whose Unrighteousness Is Forgiven* (Z. 8). All these pieces are in the autograph volume Fitzwilliam MS 88, except for *Let Mine Eyes Run Down with Tears*, which might be slightly later than the others.

Of the earlier version of *Hear Me, O Lord* (Z. 13A) only the first section survives. But the reasons for the revision (Z. 13B) nevertheless seem clear, and typify many of the changes made in other anthems in the group; though not all revisions so convincingly improve on the original, if at all. In Z. 13, Purcell changed the second part of the opening verse to deal with problems of harmonic progression and with a weakness which is perhaps inherent in one of the points of imitation.[8]

In Z. 13A, the introduction in b. 11 of the point for 'hide not thy face from me' emphasises the ii–V of bb. 11–12, and this inaugurates a series of far-ranging progressions featuring mode flexibility and secondary dominants. (Ex. 85 sketches the main harmonic functions of both versions.) Things begin well enough, but go awry in bb. 13–14. The G minor of b. 13 is turned to the major mode, and this dominant function is given an interrupted resolution to Ab. Then, via IV of C (b. 14), G major harmony returns and repeats the move to Ab, now treated as IV of Eb, which key is reached via a full close in bb. 16–17. From here D minor is regained smoothly enough.

These progressions are locally coherent, and their somewhat circular gropings might be an expression of the despair of 'them that go down into the pit'. However, the internal balance is unconvincing, largely because the repetition of the G–Ab progression, the most prominent gesture of the piece, is self-defeating: because the first achieves nothing, the second inevitably sounds tautologous.

In Z. 13B the point for 'lest I be like unto them that go down into the pit' is virtually unchanged, but 'hide not thy face from me' is set to a more strongly directed, chromatically ascending line which contrasts well with the scalic descent of the other point; its inherent leading-note properties help to articulate

Ex. 85   Hear Me, O Lord, (Z. 13 A & B): continuo of bb. 11–20/21

the richly ornamented harmonic progressions from b. 11 onward. In the process we lose the fine ending to Z. 13A, but this is amply compensated by the more controlled harmonic structure.

Some of these anthems show a particularly sophisticated use of the 'dialogue' method. The first section of *Let Mine Eyes Run Down with Tears* (Z. 24) (Ex. 86) sets three distinct units of text to three phrases, in each of which a gradually increasing pace of movement towards the cadence focusses attention on the harmonic function of that cadence:

$$i - V \text{ of } i - III - i \text{ (I)}$$

bb. 1   10   17   20

One of the most important gestures is the approach to dominant harmony via a strong subdominant: it is the first harmonic progression of the piece (x in Ex. 86) and varied forms of it appear at the approaches to the most important dominants, those in bb. 9–10 and 18–19.

Ex. 86 *Let Mine Eyes Run Down with Tears* (Z. 24): first section

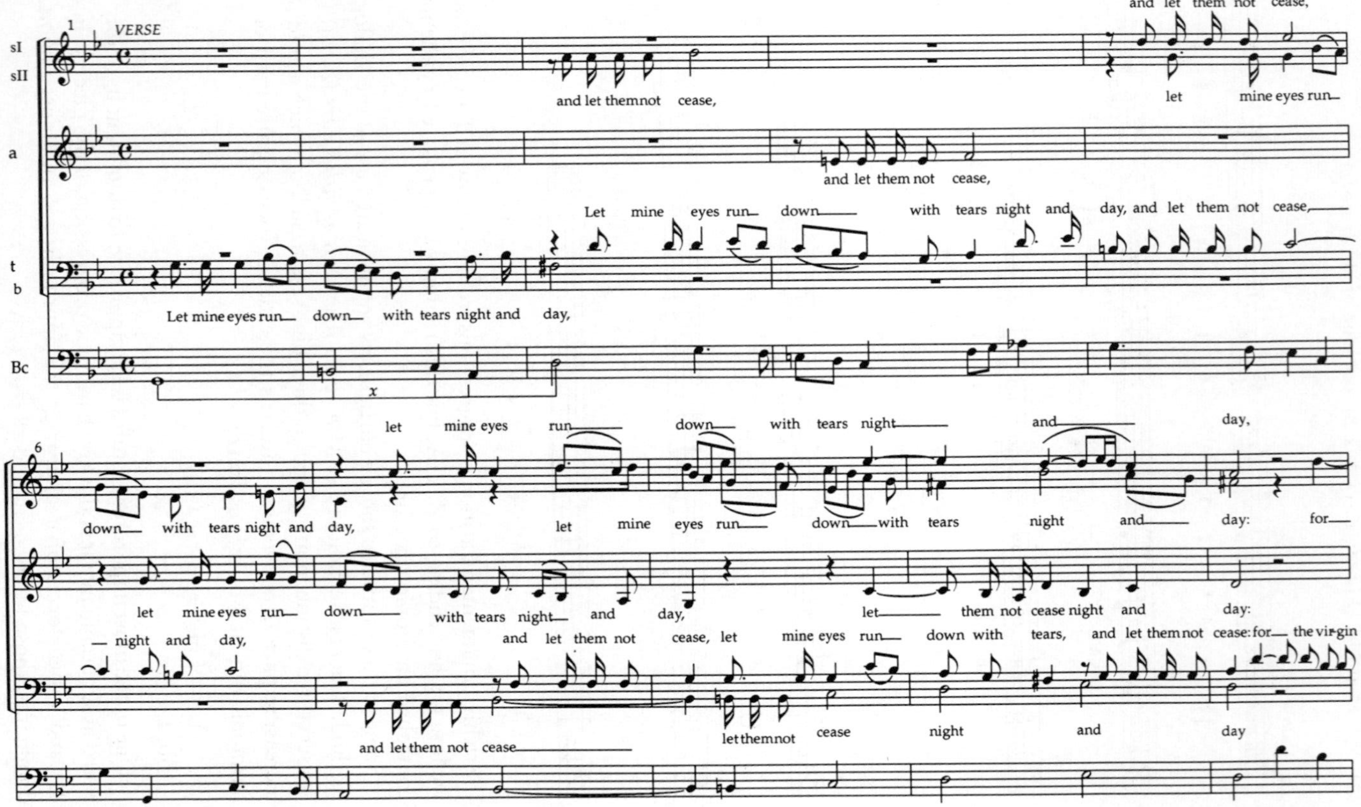

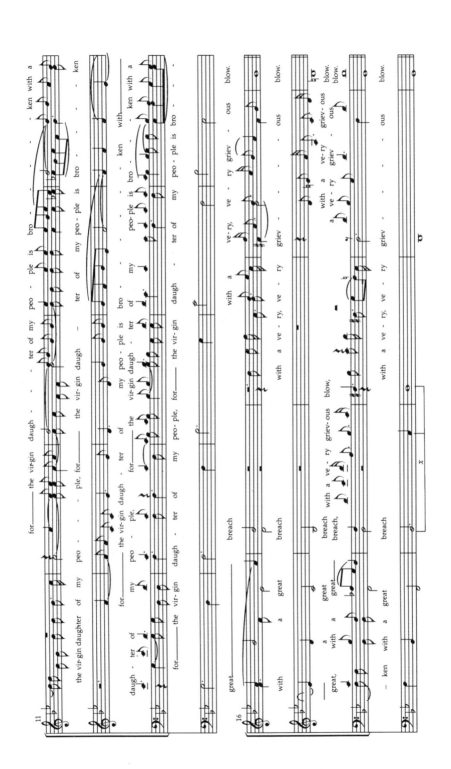

The two points in the first phrase have distinct functions. That for 'and let them not cease' aptly generates movement towards the stressed minim on 'cease', and therefore is often used to articulate significant pitches, especially in bb. 1–6; but the most important role in the generation of pitch process belongs to the broadly sweeping opening point.

The roles of high D and the adjacent E♮ in forming the most important pitch process of the section emerge gradually, as the density of the texture increases, as follows:

(1) In the opening theme the E♭ on the third crotchet of b. 2 tends to imply a resolution to D. The leap of an augmented fourth to A highlights the A, the D resolution appearing in the continuo as the A moves to F♯.

(2) One octave higher, soprano II picks up this A and resolves it to B♭ (b. 3), this being the first explicit statement of the semitonal movement which is to be so important.

(3) This first dialogue is answered by a similar one between tenor and soprano I (bb. 3–5), which includes the first explicit statement of the D–E♭ relationship, derived from the A–B♭ semitone of b. 3. (The alto entry in b. 4 ornaments this main dialogue.)

(4) The soprano II and alto statements of bb. 5–6 are at a lower register than the D and E♮ of b. 5, which sets up a 'vacuum' between the registers.

(5) This is filled as soprano I and soprano II, enter on C and D, pick up the high D and E♭, and fill in the gap with the descending scales of bb. 7–8.

(6) The E♭ is reinforced by the repetitions in sopranos II and I (b. 8) on 'run' and 'night'.

(7) The upbeat E♮ (b. 8) needs resolution, and this is projected through to the downbeat of b. 10. Yet here the expected D in soprano I is avoided in favour of A.

The entire phrase is thus open-ended, not only harmonically (ending on V of i), but also in terms of the large-scale pitch processes. During bb. 7–10 the main features of this process are articulated by the entries of the point for 'Let mine eyes run down with tears', which gradually takes over from the other.

As the phrase progresses the entries of this main point are compressed to produce an acceleration in the process itself, for although bb. 1–6 use the point for 'and let them not cease' to make most of the prominent pitch connections, their pacing is generated by the entries of the other point. The acceleration operates thus: bb. 1–2 a two-bar unit; bb. 3–4 a two-bar unit; bb. 5–6 two one-bar units; bb. 7–8 four half-bar units. (By now the entries are so closely associated with the word 'let' that the Alto entry in b. 8 functions as a complete entry.) Resolution of these reinforced E♮s, is drawn out over the whole bar to increase the release offered by the D major harmony in b. 10.

The setting of 'for the virgin daughter' continues the same pitch processes, but is otherwise very different. The D which should have ended the previous phrase is picked up by soprano II, foreshadowed by the tenor at the lower octave. The speed of entries here is evenly paced, so the main driving forces are derived from harmonic tension, both from the B♭ orientation of the entire phrase, which does not resolve the open-ended harmonic pattern of bb. 1–10, and from the tensions generated by the local progressions and their internal polyphonic conflicts. These conflicts are a reworking of the semitonal pitch movements of the first phrase and emerge immediately in the E♭/D clash between the tenor and soprano II (b. 11). Here the E♭ functions as an unprepared appoggiatura to the G minor harmony, and during the phrase this relationship is amplified into repeated soundings of prepared appoggiaturas against their resolutions. The pitch oscillations from E♭ to D continue (bb. 13–15), but B♭ is increasingly important (cf. b. 3 soprano II) especially after the scalic connection from D to a close onto that pitch (bb. 15–17).

After the close into B♭ the scalic approach to D (*x*) resumes its significance. The bass reinforces dominant harmony by imitating the tenor on V of G minor (b. 18); but soprano II, in tenths with the bass, repeats the point in its original form (cf. bb. 17 and 18), and is followed by soprano I, pressing home the thrust towards the close through the F/F♯ clashes. The high Fs are the first time that the sopranos have gone higher than E♭, and are unresolved within the overall voice-leading. The consequent tension produced is released in the harmonic stability of the cadence, though even the final bars are given a twist by the alto entry in b. 19.

The extravagant chromaticism characteristic of many parts of these anthems plumbs unique expressive depths. Westrup notes that in the early version of *In the Midst of Life* (Z. 17A) Purcell experiments with the traditional device of chromaticism to indicate 'the bitter pains of eternal death', and also shows a 'characteristic disregard for euphony when the movement of the parts seems to him more important' (Ex. 87 (i)).[9]

Yet merely placing parts together, however strongly directional they might be, does not necessarily create strong progression. This passage works partly because all parts are following a point which justifies its independent existence through the simple strength of the proposition – the chromatic filling out of a rising fourth – and partly because contrapuntal independence presses harmonic function (Ex. 87 (ii)) to the limits of comprehensibility – bitter pain indeed. In his revision of this anthem (Z. 27.2 and 3) Purcell altered this passage, but the bass remained the same, and the treble was altered only to improve the articulation of the rising line, while the changes in the inner parts improve rhythmic momentum, and some rather odd word underlay. So the harmonic and contrapuntal principles of the first version remain.

Fitzwilliam MS 88 includes another unique group of anthems, probably

Ex. 87   In the Midst of Life (Z. 17A):

(i) bb. 22–8

(ii) harmonic reduction

slightly later than these. With their *basso seguente* continuo and severe counterpoint, they are true *stile antico*, and an explicit reworking of those compositional features which Purcell seems to have found interesting in those works of Byrd and Gibbons to be found in the same autograph. They also are very closely related to anthems by Blow in the same style.

On the evidence of that manuscript, *Hear My Prayer, O Lord* (Z. 15), *Lord, How Long Wilt Thou Be Angry?* (Z. 25), *O God, Thou Art My God* (Z. 35), *O God, Thou Hast Cast Us Out* (Z. 36) and *O Lord God of Hosts* (Z. 37) were composed in 1680–2.[10] They begin and end with extended choral sections, surrounding one or more verse sections between which there may be further substantial choruses and, partly because of this unique arrangement, have been described as 'full anthems with verse'.[11] Much of their expressive power comes from skilful contrasts between the rich polyphony of the choral sections and the less obviously contrapuntal but nonetheless line-driven verse sections. Thus, in *O God, Thou Art My God* (Z. 35), the affirmatory opening is for four-part chorus, the imploratory statement 'My soul thirsteth for thee', is for *atb* soloists, and the return to confidence is expressed by the chorus singing 'Thus have I look'd for thee in holiness, that I might behold thy pow'r and glory'.

These anthems seem to have been Purcell's last concentrated involvement with the verse anthem without strings. From about 1681 onwards he was mainly involved with the verse anthem with strings. Some two dozen or so examples of such anthems survive additional to the four documented early ones – a change of emphasis which might be a reflection of his increased status, and in particular his appointment in July 1682 as one of the organists at the Chapel Royal.[12]

The preoccupations of Purcell's earliest anthems with strings are continued in these works. The opening symphony often anticipates the expressive emphasis of the text. So *In Thee, O Lord* (Z. 16) begins with a densely worked symphony on a ground bass: solid repetitions of the ground, persistent crotchet movement and steady forward drive – surely these represent the unchanging character of God, the very reason why the psalmist could put his trust in Him. *Rejoice in the Lord Alway* (Z. 49) features a superb imitation of pealing bells, while in *My Heart Is Fixed* (Z. 29) Purcell adopts a procedure he would use with much greater effect, in the 1685 ode *Why, Why Are All the Muses Mute?* (Z. 343). The anthem opens with soloists, and the instruments come in later as a response to 'Awake up my glory, awake, lute and harp'.

After the opening symphony, Purcell's anthems typically consist of a mix of verse, chorus and instrumental movements, which usually follow the organisational and large-scale harmonic methods of Purcell's earlier anthems. Large-scale processes depend largely upon melodic propositions which cross the boundaries of sections, and upon careful balancing of sectional repetition and contrast.

I Was Glad (Z. 19), for example, consists of three large units, each textually distinct and consisting of a balanced series of sections. The first deals with the psalmist's response at being asked to go 'up to the house of the Lord' at Jerusalem; the second (bb. 80–149) praises Jerusalem's attributes; the third requests prayer for Jerusalem. Their internal organisation is typified in the first, in which almost all material is derived directly from bb. 1–7 of the symphony; most of the melodic material of the later units is derived from the first.

The opening proposition is developed from the matrixal scale outlined by bb. 1–3 of the first violin (*a* in Ex. 88 (i)). The *échappée* motifs (*x*) are a recurrent feature. Like many basic propositions, the line *a* is fundamentally regular, but contains local irregularities which define its character: Ex. 88 (ii) shows how a regular continuation of the sequence set up by *x* would end on the same pitch and temporal position.

The important difference between the hypothetical and real versions is that sustaining the B holds up the next step in the trochaic movement D–C, C–B; A is therefore more strongly accented, the B is weakened and the F♯ also is strong. The open function of the matrixal line is therefore partly derived from its clear outlining of dominant harmony. The second phrase transfers this F♯ to the higher octave, and repeats the matrixal line (*b* in Ex. 88 (iii)) in a varied, closed form.

The triple-time section picks up the D–G progression, which in the first section was a long-term one, and makes it a prominent local feature (*A* in Ex. 88 (iv)). A precursor of this occurred in b. 4 (*n* in Ex. 88 (iii)), and this precursor is more explicitly stated later in this first theme (*f* in Ex. 88 (iv)).

From b. 13 the theme gradually emphasises D at the expense of G, in both pitch and key. This change is articulated especially by *B* (Ex. 88 (v)), the first scalic ascent of the piece, in which *e* is an inversion of *g* and *d*, themselves a compression of the descent in *a*. These motivic changes and the harmonic inflexions towards D in bb. 13–14 culminate in a full close in D in bb. 22–3, which uses a number of developments from earlier themes (*C* in Ex. 88 (vi)).

An immediate return to G is articulated by a restatement in bb. 23–8 of a variation on bb. 7–10 (cf. Ex. 88 (iv)). The moves towards D in bb. 12 and 20 coincided with the first prominent Es in the section, so E reappears in b. 29 as the pivotal pitch in tonicising G via a reworking of C. The section closes on high G, which gives local harmonic and rhythmic closure, but as the posited point of rest is the lower G, there is a consequence, which comes in the form of the alto's reworking of bb. 7–35.

The solo extends the material of bb. 7–35 by introducing a new theme (*D* in Ex. 88 (vii)). The cadential implications of *D* are considerably stronger than those of *C*, so it is later used to rework the matrixal scale in a form which, for

Ex. 88 I Was Glad (Z. 19): melodic connections in first unit

the first time since bb. 1–7, closes that scale firmly on the low G, special emphasis being given to the cadential B–A–G move (bb. 63–5, 67–9). The short concluding ritornello closes the unit through two complementary means: the instrumental texture is a return to the resources with which the section opened, and the closing theme is presented twice, this repetition of cadential function emphasising that function over any previous closure.

A number of anthems contain considerably more sectional repetition than *I Was Glad*. Some, such as *It Is a Good Thing to Give Thanks* (Z. 18), include repetitions of vocal sections which, although not in the original text, reinforce its central message. In the best instances there is a complementary relationship between poetic implication and musical function. So *Rejoice in the Lord Alway* (Z. 49) contains perhaps more repetition than any other anthem, but the various restatements of the opening material are distributed between the soloists, strings and chorus in such a way that the final statement for full resources is brilliantly climactic.

The scoring of *I Was Glad* is typical of most verse anthems with strings – *SATB* chorus, four-part strings, *atb* soloists, and continuo. A few are for larger forces: *Praise the Lord, O My Soul, and All That Is within Me* (Z. 47) uses four-part choir and six soloists, arranged in two contrasted groupings, *sst* and *tbb*. But this is unusual, and it is notable that even here pragmatism rules, in that the boys' voices are reserved for easier passages. Nevertheless, the piece is something of a landmark in Purcell's use of resources, for it is remarkably successful at using rapid changes between contrasted groups of singers and instruments to accumulate tension.

In this and most other respects, the 1685 coronation anthem *My Heart Is Inditing* (Z. 30) surpasses Purcell's earlier achievements. It is scored for larger forces than any other of his sacred compositions – four-part strings and continuo, eight-part choir and eight soloists[13] – and uses these forces in an overtly dramatic way. It is the only anthem with strings to use the chorus for the first vocal entry – and with impressive effect. Indeed, apart from the use of a string orchestra, the arrangement of the sections and their styles owes as much to Purcell's earlier full anthems with verse as to the verse anthem with strings; for solo sections in recitative style, common in earlier and later anthems, are here entirely absent. This unique combination of styles and resources marks *My Heart Is Inditing* out as a summation of much of Purcell's earlier sacred music; but the piece also gives hints of the burgeoning dramatic composer.

The repetition techniques which are so prominent in the second section of the symphony set the style for most of the anthem, which features a highly-developed version of the cumulative dialogue technique that Purcell developed from Humfrey.

In the verse after the symphony repetition, the text 'Hearken, o daughter, consider, incline thine ear, forget also thine own people' (Z. 30.6), is set for all eight soloists who, in various combinations and in $\frac{2}{2}$ time, pass around the exhortations to 'hearken, o daughter'. As they come together on the approach to the cadence, the part writing produces a simultaneous F♯/F♮ clash between tenor II and treble I, exquisitely timed to occur on 'own', which may not be the most stressed word in natural speech (it is set on the second minim of the bar), but which implies the bitter-sweet aspects of the bride leaving behind all that she knows and accepting a new family. The verse moves to triple time for the positive consequences – 'Instead of thy fathers thou shalt have children'. Purcell's masterstroke is to interject the earlier exhortations, now in the new metre and different in other ways too from their earlier appearances; so that as well as positive encouragement, there is a memory of earlier implications.

This is the first anthem to make any significant departure from the simple, long-range harmonic organisation seen thus far in the verse anthem with strings. It works out on a large scale the subdominant-related harmonic emphases posited in the opening bars of the symphony. These persist in the avoidance of moves to the major mode of the dominant; by contrast, the dominant minor occurs frequently, often in a context oriented towards ii or IV, and where the major-mode dominant does occur, it is invariably transitory. Although a number of later anthems also show an interest in harmonic concentration, none matches this one for consistency and for profundity of concept, in this area or in any other. It is an impressive landmark in Purcell's compositional development.

SERVICES

We know of three service settings by Purcell, the *Te Deum and Jubilate in D* (Z. 232) from 1694, the Evening Service in G minor (Z. 231) of unknown date, and the Service in B♭ (Z. 230), composed before October 1682, almost certainly for Westminster Abbey.[14]

Service setting presented unique compositional challenges, for the length of the texts involved, especially for the morning service, and the time limits imposed by the liturgy meant that there was little opportunity for musical expansion. In the Service in B♭, Purcell's resourceful response is typified in the opening sections of the *Te Deum* (Z. 230.1a). The general pace of events is considerably faster than in most of Purcell's sacred music: in particular the alternations between verse and chorus sections are more rapid than in most of the full anthems with verse, to which this service is related in many ways. The pattern of alternation is, in principle, governed by the poetic structure, usually occurring across a pair of verses. But Purcell is nevertheless responsive to textual nuance, so the universality of 'the holy church throughout all the world' is represented by full chorus, rather than *decani* alone, which would result from following this pattern.

The main structural punctuations are made by chorus sections, but to maintain an expansive progress these are kept open-ended, in most cases by harmonic means, so that the harmonic structure is in units considerably larger than those defined by the scoring differences. Occasional large-scale repetitions consolidate overall design, as in bb. 44–52, where 'Heaven and earth' appropriately uses the same material as 'All the earth' in bb. 9–18.

Purcell's flexible approach to the text and his capacity for dramatic response find a particularly fruitful outcome in the Benedicite (Z. 230.3), the text of which, with its thirty-two repetitions of 'bless ye the Lord: praise him and magnify him for ever', presents considerable musical challenges. The opening words 'O all ye works of the Lord' are set for a three-bar declaimed solo; the chorus entry with the words which are to be so often repeated is therefore highlighted. The rest of the piece consists of groups of verses which alternate the full text with amenable conflations. So two or more verses might be combined by omitting all or part of the refrain, as in 'O all ye Fowls of the Air, o all ye Beasts and Cattle, bless ye the Lord: o ye Children of Men, bless ye the Lord: praise Him and magnify Him for ever'.

For all the note-against-note setting, the Service in B♭ is a masterpiece of contrapuntal ingenuity. The main sources often proclaim this proudly: the gloria of the Benedictus is marked 'Canon 2 in 1 by inversion', and 'O go your way into his gates' from the Jubilate is 'Canon 4 in 2 per arsin et thesin'. As Westrup says, they are 'pure music, not crabbed puzzles – to delight the craftsman's heart'.[15]

This service must have delighted Purcell's heart, for the care he bestowed on it shows a labour of love. Nowhere is this more evident than in the relationship between it and the anthem O God, Thou Art My God (Z. 35), explicitly indicated in two important sources of the anthem (Fitzwilliam MS 117 and the Chapel Royal part-books).

Like the Service in B♭, the Evening Service in G minor (Z. 231) is related to the full anthems with verse, especially in its disposition of chorus and verse sections. While its methods are not markedly different from the Service in B♭, it is contrapuntally less complex than the equivalent sections of the morning service, tending to emphasise purely melodic features. The sources offer us no help with dating the piece, while it presents a problem of authenticity in that the 'Gloria' commonly attached to the 'Nunc dimittis' is almost certainly not by Purcell.[16]

MOTETS

Purcell never used the term motet, but it is convenient thus to distinguish his few sacred compositions in Latin from the verse anthems. Their distinctive style is almost certainly due to a complex blend of Italian and English influence and, while we do not know if they were written for a specific time or place, it has been suggested that they were for private performance. In this respect it may be significant that he wrote his neat copies not in his book of liturgical music, Fitzwilliam MS 88, but in his collection of vocal and instrumental domestic music, BL Add. MS 30930.[17]

We know of three such pieces: the justly famous *Jehova, quam multi sunt hostes* (Z. 135), the much less accomplished *Beati omnes qui timent dominum* (Z. 131) and the incomplete *Domine non est exaltum* (Z. 102). The two complete motets follow structural principles similar to the full anthems with verse, in that an opening chorus is followed by a series of sections for soloists and chorus in which the latter is dominant. But the similarities end there, for unlike the full anthems they are *stile moderno*, the instrumental bass is *continuo* rather than *seguente*, and the solo sections involve just one singer at a time.

Given this background, it is interesting that the choruses in *Beati omnes* show many of the problems Purcell experienced in some of his more Italianate sonatas. The work suffers from over-regular phrasing and the contrapuntal operation is mechanical, so that the repeated distinctive sonorities, especially the sound of the augmented triad, are done to death.

Not so *Jehova, quam multi sunt hostes* (Z. 135), which sets verses from Psalm 3 to music of extraordinary intensity and drama, and which shows a remarkable sensitivity to textual nuance. As always in such cases, these qualities depend on context as much as on the local colour of progression. It is in A minor, and the fifth verse – 'I laid me down and slept, and rose up again: for the Lord sustained me'[18] – includes superb responses to the concepts of sleeping and rising, epitomised first in 'Ego cubui et dormivi', moving from instability to relative stability and then, in 'ego experge feci me', opening out to a new harmonic area, and thus requiring a response. The effect of these passages is highlighted by the drop in register after the vigorous choral writing of the previous verse. Fine as this first part of the verse is, it is the second – 'quia Jehova sustentat me' – which sees Purcell's sensitivity to the inner meaning of a text at its height, as the trebles sing in high parallel thirds over a slow-moving continuo, and are replied to by the lower voices, in sliding $\frac{6}{3}$s. In Baroque opera parallel thirds were a standard device to express the unanimity of lovers; here they stand for the relationship between the psalmist and Jehova.

SACRED PARTSONGS

Twelve sacred partsongs have survived, all except one in the autograph volume BL Add. MS 30930, where they keep company with the fantasias and other domestic instrumental music.[19] Some of them present a complex source history and some are incomplete; all except three are settings of John Patrick's metrical psalms, published in 1679. The dominance of Patrick has led Nigel Fortune to make the plausible suggestion that Purcell's settings, like Patrick's texts, were intended for performance at the Charterhouse School, where Patrick was chaplain. They are designed for solo voices, and even the one piece, *O All Ye People* (Z. 138), which has no parts evidently for soloists, is more likely to be for groups of soloists than for a larger body. They feature a variety of vocal arrangements, only three of them using the *atb* scoring typical of the verse anthem.[20]

The majority of solo sections are recitatives, and reveal a remarkable ability to reflect detailed textual nuance. In *Hear Me, O Lord, the Great Support* (Z. 133) the tenor solo (Ex. 89) emphasises meaning, rather than following the word

Ex. 89   Hear Me, O Lord, the Great Support (Z. 133): bb. 24–7

accentuation of everyday speech. 'Lord' is stressed by the ascending leap and its long note value, 'righteous' is emphasised by the upward appoggiatura, 'special' by the rhythm and the melodic contour, and 'favour' by the unexpectedly long note value. From the beginning of the section, the second and fourth pulses of the bar have been stressed at the expense of the first and third. A 'natural' musical consequence of this would be to set the second line to the following rhythm:

with spe-cial fav-our own

By lengthening the first syllable of 'favour' Purcell restores emphasis to that word without losing the stress on 'own', thus bringing out the crucial message – that righteousness has its reward.

Several partsongs show highly developed applications of the dialogue technique commonly associated with the verse anthems. Fortune points out the most remarkable of these: in *When on My Sick Bed I Languish* (Z. 144) the text is rearranged between the voices so that the poet responds directly to the encouraging words of the 'gentle spirit'.[21] This sense for dramatic potential, no less than their extraordinary technical skills, makes the partsongs stand out as one of the young Purcell's highest compositional achievements.

CHAPTER NINE

Brilliance and decline: sacred music
after *c.* 1685

Of the seventy or so anthems known to have been composed by Purcell, only around twenty date from after 1685, and most of those pre-date 1689.[1] The Chapel Royal's loss of prestige once James II came to the throne must have had a hand in this; and even with the greater political stability under William and Mary it did not regain its former status, for the focus of musical activity in London was shifting decisively towards the stage, concerts, and other forms of public music making.[2] Purcell's increasing reputation in these areas probably left him with insufficient incentive to expend much energy where there was little to be gained. Certainly this would go some way towards explaining the marked decline in quality observable in so many of his anthems written after 1689.[3]

It might have become harder to get a four-part string orchestra together on a regular basis after 1685, but it was still possible when the occasion demanded it. So, the verse anthem with strings *Blessed Are They That Fear the Lord* (Z. 5), scored for *ssab* soloists, four-part strings and *SATB* choir, was composed in early 1688 for the 'Thanksgiving appoint'd to be observed ... for the Queen's being with child', and it was probably for the coronation of the new king and queen, just a year later in 1689, that Purcell was able to draw on an *SSATB* choir and five soloists, in addition to full string forces, for *Praise the Lord, O Jerusalem* (Z. 46).[4]

Changed circumstances are a possible explanation for Purcell's return to the continuo verse anthem around 1685, having largely neglected it during the preceding five years. Many of these pieces are amongst the finest of Purcell's smaller sacred works, but it might be significant that some authorities have dated most of them, including *O Consider My Adversity* (Z. 32) and *Thy Word Is a Lantern* (Z. 61), before 1687.[5]

Nevertheless, it is in these continuo anthems that those compositional problems emerged which almost certainly are closely linked to Purcell's declining interest in church music. In the opening phrase of *Blessed Is He That Considereth the Poor* (Z. 7), which probably dates from around 1688 (Ex. 90),

Ex. 90   *Blessed Is He That Considereth the Poor* (Z. 7)*: bb. 1–5

the chromatic bass is a standard, competent response to the word 'poor'; but there is no sign of the boldly formed lines characteristic of the sacred partsongs, which include several examples of this formula. Similar weaknesses, but combined with the problems of triple-invertible counterpoint which dogged some of the sonatas, are evident later on, in the setting of 'The Lord comfort him' and 'make thou all his bed' (Z. 7.3 and 7.4). In this anthem and in most others from this period, the melodic writing is more melismatic than in most pre-1686 anthems, but the necessary repetition techniques are sadly predictable.

More successful, but nevertheless problematic, are the two anthems *The Lord Is King, the Earth May Be Glad* and *Sing unto God* (Z. 54 and 52) written for a solo bass, most likely the Revd John Gostling. Comparison of the better of them, *The Lord Is King*, with some of the more-or-less contemporary sacred songs published in 1688 in *Harmonia sacra* – the nearest Purcell got elsewhere to these solo anthems – is revealing, for it shows that it was difficult to develop the anthem in a comparable direction without compromising its function. Few anthems lasted much more than ten minutes. For reasonably large, multi-sectional pieces such as those under consideration here, scale was usually achieved by setting a single verse of Biblical text (usually from a psalm) to one musical section, by exploiting opportunities for musical illustration and by extending the section through one or two varied repetitions of phrases, often on different harmonic and pitch levels. Each section usually began and ended in the tonic key.

But the vocal writing in *The Lord Is King* rests uneasily with these conservative structural methods. It uses melismas and elaborate ornamentation (Ex. 91) more flamboyant than most earlier anthems – gestures which have their

Ex. 91   *The Lord Is King, the Earth May Be Glad* (Z. 54): bb. 72–8

origin outside the English anthem, in genres where purposefulness derives from operating against a different, larger-scale kind of structure. In the anthem they therefore tend to have only a superficial function, and while their genteel restraint might be appropriate to their ecclesiastical context, it carries little expressive conviction in comparison with many sacred songs.

Most of the better anthems from after 1685 are verse anthems with strings. The resources offer more opportunity for dramatic contrast, and in at least two instances, *O Sing unto the Lord* (Z. 44) and *Praise the Lord, O Jerusalem* (Z. 46), Purcell seems to have responded to the demands of a special occasion. By far the most accomplished is *O Sing unto the Lord*, which was probably written in 1688.

This anthem follows on from *Behold, I Bring You Glad Tidings* (Z. 2) of late 1687 in showing the 'whole-hearted adoption of what may be called the Italian oratorio manner'.[6] Rather than the Anglo-French symphony which was characteristic of most anthems before 1685, here we have a piece more like an Italian orchestral sonata and which, even more than the symphony to *My Heart Is Inditing* (Z. 30), provides the main material for the first vocal section. (Some derivations are indicated in Ex. 92.) Also, the first two verse sections are reworkings of the opening phrase of the symphony, and the solo 'Declare his honour' (Z. 44.3) reworks the harmonic structure and many melodic statements of the symphony's first section.

Ex. 92   O Sing unto the Lord (Z. 44): motivic connections

Just how effective the periodic phrasing and expansive harmonic methods of these years could be in sacred music is shown by the F minor verse and chorus section 'O worship the Lord'. Its expressive impact is deeply dependent on the vivid colouring imparted to harmonic function by exact motivic imitation, mostly in parallel thirds or sixths, which convey the text with matchless clarity.

Immediately afterwards, the dramatic potential of the forces bursts out powerfully, as the bass soloist turns to F major for 'Tell it out among the heathen that the Lord is King', and the chorus and strings do the telling with vigorous homophonic discourse on 'The Lord is King'.

A number of later verse anthems were to use the techniques of *O Sing unto the Lord*; but none matched it. *O Give Thanks* (Z. 33)[7] is typical in showing a discourse between soloists and chorus which manifests a similar flexibility in its use of resources. But the result is routine, and only confirms that on the whole Purcell's talents had by then found much more fruitful outlets. Viewed in this way, the perfunctory quality of works such as *The Way of God Is an Undefiled Way* (Z. 56), which seems to have puzzled Westrup,[8] becomes easier to understand.

Purcell's swan-song in sacred music lies entirely outside these critical strictures. For the funeral of Queen Mary in Westminster Abbey on 5 March 1695 he composed *Thou Knowest, Lord* (Z. 58C), his second setting of these words, even though some fifteen years before he had revised his earlier setting. We have no firm evidence as to why Purcell was not content to reuse his earlier revision. However, it is of less consistent quality than the other funeral sentences, and Purcell might have felt that the occasion demanded a piece which would have a more straightforward appeal, in keeping with the public mourning decreed and, it would seem, genuinely felt, at the death of a much-loved monarch.[9] Moreover, processional performance in Westminster Abbey might have been intended, for which the rhythmic simplicity and note-against-note texture of this later setting are far more suitable. Recalling the first performance, Tudway states that the piece was 'accompanied with flat Mournfull Trumpets', these being the same instruments which had played the Funeral March and Canzona (Z. 860).[10]

Tudway described the work as being 'compos'd ... after the old way'. It seems that, just as Purcell looked to his early instrumental music for inspiration when composing *The Indian Queen* (Z. 630) and other late dramatic music, so now he turned to the *stile antico* to express penitence in the face of human mortality.

Amongst Purcell's anthems *Thou Knowest, Lord* is unique in seeming to begin and end in different keys – the first chords are E♭, but the work ends with a plagal close in G minor (the last chord is, of course, major), an outline workable with almost any combination of the various versions of the funeral sentences, but not evidently tied to any one in particular. However, as in the fantasias, tonal views of harmonic structure do not fit reality.

The piece is constructed of a series of registral arches which constantly shift their harmonic ground, often suggesting an approach to stability on the pitch G, the first uppermost pitch of the piece, but always being deflected from it. The

crucial pitch is A, which always rises to B♭, B♮ or D, from there opening up
further explorations. This persists until the A falls to G, on its way to F♯ (b. 41)
for 'at our last hour'. With impeccable poetic sensitivity, the musical argument
is resolved at this point, save for the balancing cadential phrases on 'for any
pains of death to fall from thee'.

This piece possesses that same rarefied beauty as the choruses in Schütz's
passions, also 'after the old way'. For each composer, the re-creation in his
maturity of *stile antico* is a testament of personal and musical priorities. The
very persistence of *stile antico*, as a remnant of a past age, made it peculiarly apt
for the expression of eternal values.

For the final comments on this anthem we can again turn to Tudway, for his
memory of the occasion remained vivid over twenty years after the event.

I appeal to all that were present, as well such as understood music, as those that did not,
whither, they ever heard anything, so rapturously fine, so solemn, and so heavenly, in the
operation, which drew tears from all; and yet a plain natural composition, which shows
the power of Music, when 'tis rightly fitted and adapted to devotional purposes.[11]

Purcell was perhaps at his most inconsistent in his anthems. But the best of
them can take equal rank with much of his dramatic music, and reveal that same
power which so moved Tudway.

SERVICES

Purcell's last large composition for the church was the *Te Deum and Jubilate in
D* (Z. 232), written for the Cecilian celebrations of 1694. It is full of the elaborate
affective vocal gestures at which Purcell had by then become a master, and
features massive orchestral and choral effects from the *SATB* choir, strings and
trumpets. Today it seems strange that this was for many years one of Purcell's
most popular pieces of any genre for, while it contains wonderful moments,
Westrup's comments are substantially correct:

It cannot be denied, however, that its plush and gilt have faded with the passage of time.
The reiteration of the chord of D major, however glorious the choir and however
magnificent the trumpet-playing, no longer excites us as it did Purcell's contemporaries
and the audiences of the eighteenth century, to whom such magnificence was still novel
and striking. The weakness of the *Te Deum and Jubilate* is not merely its reliance on
largely superficial effects but also the disconnected structure of the whole. The continual
succession of short movements – some very short indeed – destroys any impression of
unity.[12]

Late-seventeenth- and early-eighteenth-century musicians seem to have been
enthralled mainly by the *Te Deum*'s figurative virtuosity, especially in the
opening sections. After a twelve-bar prelude for the orchestra the *atb* soloists

discourse on 'We praise Thee, O God, we acknowledge Thee to be the Lord', gradually expanding the registral range over some seven bars before ending on a full close in D three bars later. Instantly the chorus enters with a compressed version of the registral ascent, climbing one voice at a time up the tonic arpeggio from low D to high F♯ with repetitions of 'all'. By presenting seven more or less equally stressed crotchets, the sense of metre is weakened. As the F♯ is reached the full consort of voices and instruments comes in with 'All the earth doth worship Thee', restoring the metrical stability, to stunning effect. A generous contrapuntal working on 'the Father everlasting' balances this.

For the cherubim and seraphim's acclamations 'Holy, Holy, Holy: Lord God of Sabaoth', Purcell used an extraordinary, overlapping discourse between solo trebles and full choir. Surpassing even his typical enthusiasm, in a breathless description of this passage, Tudway declared of 'this most beautiful, and sublime representation', 'I dare challenge, all the orators, poets, painters etc. of any age whatsoever, to form so lively an idea of choirs of angels singing and paying their adorations.'[13]

Thereafter, most movements suffer from the problems described by Westrup, but even if the quality of the overall result is inconsistent, there are plenty of instances of Purcell taking delight in deliberate contrapuntal display. 'O go your way' is pure *stile antico*, featuring an elaborate canon at the fifth. In the concluding 'world without end' we see the bass entering with the subject in augmentation, a device Purcell had already used in the odes *Welcome, Welcome, Glorious Morn* (Z. 338) and *Of Old, When Heroes Thought It Base* (Z. 333), and to brilliant effect in the ode *Hail, Bright Cecilia* (Z. 328). Not content with these single and double augmentations, the *Jubilate* has the subject in triple augmentation (crotchets become breves).

Most of the church music Purcell wrote during his last years does not represent the composer at his best. Nevertheless, while Westrup's comments above remain substantially true, the *Te Deum and Jubilate*'s forceful deployment of figuration and display of peerless technical skill deserve our acclaim. Surely it is significant that the composer achieved this comparative success when writing, not for a musically indifferent monarch, but for a wider public, including his fellow musicians.

CHAPTER TEN

'The energy of English words'[1]: independent songs for one or more voices

INDEPENDENT SONGS TO C. 1688

Strophic and related settings

While the vast majority of Purcell's songs are in the odes and stage music, his independent songs include distinctive practices, especially in ground bass, recitative and in songs for two or more voices. Consequently they reveal much about the paths he took to attain that mastery for which he was to become, and remains, famous.

Most of Purcell's independent songs can be dated with some reliability, for after 1678 he regularly contributed to anthologies. Since we know when most of these were published, dates of compilation or completion can be assessed, which at least gives a terminal date for a song's composition.[2] The only significant exceptions appear to be some of the songs for two or more voices and some published in the two books (1688 and 1693) of *Harmonia sacra*. The earliest songs of certain authorship are the five published in the 1679 edition of *Choice Ayres ... The Second Book* which was completed in 1678.[3] They comprise the two song types which were to dominate Purcell's vocal music until around 1688, namely the single-section, largely strophic song, and the recitative song.

Of the former, *Since the Pox* (Z. 471) typifies Purcell's early practice. While neither it nor the other three short songs are profound pieces, it is a polished achievement for such a young composer and, like many of the early songs, ends with a chorus for two voices.[4] The effectiveness of Purcell's text setting is especially dependent on his control of context, and this can be seen in the way the expanding register of the opening phrase (Ex. 93) goes hand-in-hand with an unobtrusive motivic concentration on repetitions of *a* and *b*, the latter in both prime and inversion (bb. 4 and 7) and the former in a range of melodic variants.[5]

Ex. 93   *Since the Pox* (Z. 471): bb. 1–14

The effectiveness of gestures such as the descent on 'lie down' depends on a keen awareness of the relationship between motivic and harmonic development, and the progress of the text. In b. 4 the continuo fills in the main D–E progression with an aptly disturbing E♭ on 'inconstancy'. This is taken much further in the second line, where the inflexion to the minor mode of the dominant coincides with 'trouble', and imparts an appropriately dark colouration to the rest of the line.

The musical structures of larger strophic settings from these years feature some adroit harmonic balance. The 1680 setting *I Take No Pleasure* (Z. 388), for example, disposes its five couplets across a single section in A minor which moves i–v–III–iv–VII–i. The first line of each couplet ends in a half close, mostly in the same key as the full close which ends the second line. But Purcell 'bends' the harmonic progress for expressive purposes, as after the close in iv, where the harmony seems to be aiming for the tonic or relative major; but with a leap in the bass from F to C♯ there is an apt, disturbing return to iv for the setting of 'For though condemned and fetter'd here'.

For all its structural neatness, this song shows some problems characteristic of many of Purcell's early quadruple- or duple-time strophic settings. Typical are the lumpy vocal line and expressively unfocussed cross-relations of the *c.* 1680 song *Amintor, Heedless of His Flock* (Z. 357), which are even less satisfactory on repetition for the second and third stanzas.

Purcell was not alone in this, perhaps because he and others, including Blow, were attempting to produce a style more expressive and tuneful than the measured declamatory methods of their predecessors.[6] Perforce, they retain the small scale of the older styles, for the means to expand the size of periodic components had not yet been developed in English strophic setting. It is perhaps significant that it was in the more contextual world of stage music and the ode that Purcell first applied this style effectively, in 'The Gate to Bliss' from *Theodosius* (Z. 606.3a) and 'Rivers from Their Channels Turned' from *Fly, Bold Rebellion* (Z. 324.5), for example.

That he was aware of some of these difficulties is suggested by the unusual, recitative-like approach to a strophic text adopted later in 1680 for 'Retir'd from Any Mortal's Sight' (Z. 581), composed for Tate's play *King Richard II*. But he was not to do anything quite like this again until around 1692, in 'Ah Me! To Many Deaths Decreed' from *Regulus* (Z. 586); and by the mid 1680s he was exploring new methods of expanding the expressive scope of strophic setting, largely by developing voice-leading techniques to bind together expressive leaps and twists, and by applying methods of motivic repetition which had first been mastered in instrumental music. A central component of all this was the use of large-scale harmonic tension to help produce an increase in scale.

This can be seen in *Spite of the Godhead* (Z. 417) from early 1687, which sets three four-line stanzas to a single twenty-two-bar section. As usual in such songs, projection of specific pitches and modifications of their resolutions underlie many of the expressive gestures. For example, the V–i onto A minor in bb. 18–19 is unexpected because of the strong preparation for E minor and the strong approach to E (*a* in Ex. 94). In b. 19 the B quaver anticipates the harmony

Ex. 94   Spite of the Godhead (Z. 417): bb. 15–22

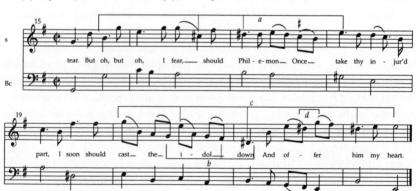

over D♯, but does not properly resolve the unstable C. The full resolution of iv onto V is at the beginning of b. 21, immediately after the register below the C has been filled out scalically.

As a setting of 'cast the idol down', the octave transposition of a basically scalic line is apt. The quavers leap to consonant pitches and set up a line *b* at the lower octave which ends on D♯, an octave transfer of the D♯ which might be expected after the stressed G–E (*c*). This low D♯ is, however, resolved in the higher octave: the G–D♯ progression of *b* is reversed (*d*), and the D♯ is approached by G–F♯ quavers, as in b. 20, before resolving onto the tonic.

At around the same time as this song or soon thereafter, Purcell gained, apparently quite suddenly, proficiency in an entirely different type of strophic setting. The distinguishing features of *Sylvia, Now Your Scorn Give Over* (Z. 420), *Ah! How Pleasant* (Z. 353), *Phillis, I Can Ne'er Forgive* (Z. 408) and *Love's Pow'r in My Heart* (Z. 395) – all published in 1688 in the second book of *The Banquet of Musick* – are brevity, simplicity (though Purcell still manages quasi-canonic imitation in Z. 408), a regular periodic structure and, except for *Love's Pow'r in My Heart*, duple or quadruple time. The word setting is mostly one beat per syllable, and the overall impression is of a piece of dance music to which the words happily fit, or of a popular song perhaps.

The easy surface of these songs hides the subtlety of high art. The melody of the delightful *Sylvia, Now Your Scorn Give Over* (Z. 420) for example, just eight bars long, is based on developments of one motif, with the independent bass occasionally taking part in motivic debate. Its methods of motivic repetition are, in essence, those which Purcell's songs were to use for the rest of his life.

Motif *a* (Ex. 95) is a filling-out of the rising third *x*. Its stressed pitches are always harmonic, although not necessarily consonant – note the C of b. 4. Motif *b* is *a* inverted and rhythmically retrograded; its first quaver is always, with one significant exception, non-harmonic. Repetitions of *a* and *b* generate the line *m*, which changes direction in b. 2 through *a* being replaced by *b*. At the end of b. 3 the harmonic pitches in *b* are D and C, but the drive of the motivic repetition on *b* presses on through the C, to A, which is highlighted by the change to motif *a* in b. 4. The C and A thus enclose the stressed cadential pitch B. The continuation down to G, using *b*, is expedient for the two-syllable word and provides continuity into the next phrase.

In bb. 5–8 the melody's different course balances the ascent and larger descent of bb. 1–4. The G–C of b. 5 is a response to the close onto G and breaks the continuity of line established in bb. 1–4. It also initiates the closural process by setting up a pitch wedge which connects the song's high and low registers, for in the context established by the first line it is unstable. The ascent after C uses motif *c*, an unstable development of *b* which ornaments a dissonant D. The A of b. 6 connects partly to the G of b. 5, and is partly a filling in of the G–C leap;

Ex. 95   *Sylvia, Now Your Scorn Give Over* (Z. 420): bb. 1–8

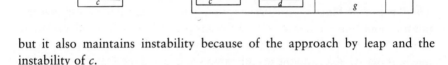

but it also maintains instability because of the approach by leap and the instability of *c*.

The last two bars wedge in to resolve these unstable pitches. F picks up from the preceding E (*f*); as in b. 2, it is the turning point for the direction of the pitch process. The A in b. 7 picks up the previous bar's A, wedges up towards the C (*e*) and joins with the less strongly articulated line (*f*) for the close. This repeats the *c* pitches of b. 6, but in a harmonically and melodically closed form, with D now consonant with the bass.

The relationship between continuo and voice is characteristically meticulous. In the last four bars the continuo leads off with *c*, which also follows the voice's reply. In b. 7 motif *d* presents yet another way of filling out a third, this time derived from *a*, and perfectly designed so as to articulate the beginning of the dominant prolongation in bb. 7–8. The continuo's phrasing in bb. 5–8 cuts across that of the voice, and takes two and a half bars to articulate the F–G–C move (*g*).[7]

Recitative songs

Purcell was to become the unequalled master of English recitative in his or any other age, and while this reputation was born of much effort, even in his teens he had an exceptional sensitivity to the style's special requirements. His earliest known song of this type, like the earliest strophic songs, comes from Playford's 1679 publication *Choice Ayres and Songs*. *What Hope for Us Remains?* (Z. 472) is subtitled 'On the death of his worthy Friend Mr Matthew Locke … who Dyed in August 1677'. The vocal line is remarkable for its impeccable pointing of not only the text's stress patterns, but also its meaning. This depends on a range of musical techniques, particularly the projection of specific pitches in both melody and bass (Ex. 96). The relationship between leaps and stepwise movement is

Ex. 96   *What Hope for Us Remains?* (Z. 472): bb. 1–9

particularly important in this, the bass moving mostly by step and by leaps of fourths or fifths to generate the solid progression *m*. In both parts, leaps other than these intervals usually reinforce significant pitch functions: the descending sixth in b. 5 highlights the leading-note function of B; the D and B♮ of b. 8 'enclose' the dominant C; the vocal leap from C to E in b. 7 stresses the latter, and picks up both the projection of E articulated by the ascending sixth of b. 2 and the strongly approached dominant function left on the downbeat of b. 6.

Purcell sustains intensity in delivering the text, maintaining strong forward thrust. In bb. 4–5, Ex. 97 would have been a commonplace progression of the

Ex. 97   What Hope for Us Remains? (Z. 472): conjectural harmonisation of bb. 4–5

time; but Purcell's stepwise descent to F♯ drives across the textual, rhythmic and melodic downbeat and pushes into the next phrase, appropriate to the links in meaning between the lines, brought out in 'Ev'n he…'

This large-scale view of the text is reflected in a broad harmonic structure.

i – III – iv – i – v – VII – ½ in v – ½ in III – i
bars   9   13   15   18   22   25   27

Potential hiatus at the tonic close in b. 15 is neatly evaded by the voice being on the upper D, an octave higher than the closural D posited by bb. 1–2 and at a register which has been associated with generation. Moreover, for 'His lays to anger and to war could move', bb. 15–16 arpeggiate the martial harmony D major, neatly followed by a ⁶₃ over D to 'Then calm the tempest'. As Ian Spink says, such highlighting of the text's antitheses is the mark of a master.[8]

It must have been soon after this song that Purcell began working on the sacred partsongs, an integral link in his development of recitative style. At the same time, or soon after, around 1682, he began publishing a fairly regular output of songs which use recitative as the centrepiece of a multi-sectional structure. The single-mindedness with which he concentrated on specific notions in any single song, suggests a restless, innovative, yet purposeful mind.

Urge Me No More (Z. 426) is in two sections – a long recitative and a shorter, triple-time jaunt. It dates from around 1682 and is a compelling, but isolated, attempt at using harmonic gesture to achieve emotional intensity, the extravagant leaps of the vocal line in the first stanza and the restless harmonic motion being designed to capture the poet's 'untun'd fortunes'. The second stanza's intensification of expression is highlighted by its varied repetition of the opening, using the same distinctive rhythm, and 'a similar arpeggio figure, though this time rising instead of falling'.[9] The subsequent wide-ranging harmonic motion reflects the dismal, grief-laden text and has no parallel in Purcell's solo vocal music, though there are equivalent passages in some of the sacred partsongs such as *O Lord Our Governor* (Z. 141) and *Ah! Few and Full of Sorrows* (Z. 130); and, as in the latter, the return to the home key is rather abrupt and less expertly handled than the preceding bars. For all the song's

Ex. 98   *Amidst the Shades* (Z. 355): bb. 40–51

boldness, it suffers from a superfluity of extravagant expression, and thus from rapidly diminishing returns.

A much more successful approach to extreme expression is seen in *From Silent Shades* (Z. 370), subtitled 'Bess of Bedlam'. This is Purcell's earliest known example of a recognised genre in seventeenth-century literature and music, the 'mad song', a defining feature of which, at least in the later seventeenth century, is the use of extreme contrasts to represent the character's state of mind.[10]

Purcell avoids the problems of *Urge Me No More* by using much less chromaticism and a more repetitive harmonic structure to generate a background continuity based on large-scale harmonic units and on similarities between sections in common tempo, metre and style. Within such unifying recurrences he uses extreme juxtapositions to portray 'the manic obsessiveness which underlies Bess's superficial, abrupt changes of mood'.[11] The most marked similarities are between the sections in triple time, while some sharply contrasted sections are linked by being a single harmonic unit. So the second, in 𝄴 time, moves from I to V and the third, in C3 time, complements this by returning to I.

Purcell's eagerly experimental approach to recitative is nowhere more evident than in four songs written around early 1683, *No, to What Purpose?* (Z. 468), *Beneath a Dark and Melancholy Grove* (Z. 461), *Amidst the Shades* (Z. 355) and *Draw Near, You Lovers* (Z. 462). Here, success in intensifying expression lies primarily in supporting detailed gesture with a clear background which spanned two or more sections, as in *Amidst the Shades* (Z. 355), which encloses a section in A major and 𝄵 time within two extended A minor recitatives, the second of which reworks many ideas from the first.[12] As in other angular, expressive lines, elaborate detail derives its strength from modifying a basically diatonic proto-line (Ex. 98 – cf. Ex. 59). The modifications can stress important words and may provide local illustrative points, as in 'In grief oppress'd' (b. 45). The modifications can be radical: bb. 42–3 see a descending leap to D♯ for 'sad' and, instead of an immediate return, a protracted ascent back to the register of the proto-line. This inflexion towards E minor is delicately balanced so as not to destroy the underlying move from the tonic to the major mode of the dominant (b. 44), for as bb. 42–3 do not assert E minor as a new area, the G of b. 43 is a chromatic filling out of the route back to the main pitch G♯, which is not reached until the next bar and the beginning of the next phrase.

In *No, to What Purpose?* (Z. 468) Purcell extends this experimentation to the tuneful middle section, in that he breaks free from the regular phrasing inherent in the triple-time air by adopting from Blow a device used in the pre-1681 ode *Awake, Awake My Lyre*. Both at the ends and in the middle of phrases he incorporates hemiolas, with results which, as in the Blow, are too self-conscious, though perhaps 'a necessary stage in the emancipation of triple time from the rather rigid mould he had inherited'.[13]

At around the same time as Purcell was writing these songs, he produced a number of sacred recitatives which were to be at least as important as the secular pieces in developing his recitative style. They are more consistently successful than the secular, possibly because the young Purcell tended to be better at expressing unremitting melancholy than at dealing with more wide-ranging expression. In *With Sick and Famish'd Eyes* (Z. 200), from around 1683, an elaborate vocal line is built around a strong harmonic progression set up by the first ten bars (Ex. 99). These bars form a single paragraph which, in bb. 1–3, sets up G above middle C as the 'home' pitch – note how the line circulates around it without any stable stress. The strong move towards the relative major in b. 5 is never stabilised: instead a rising line *a*, replete with rhythmic irregularities and chromaticism, reaches inexorably for high G. The instability of the G is countered in the answering turn back towards the opening pitch and harmonic premise, an expressive masterstroke, in that it picks up the B♭ which was implied by the A of b. 5 (*r*) and ends on the F♯ below the home G.

These events are superbly knitted into the text. The stressed pitches in the ascent (bb. 6–9) set the semantically connected words 'cries', 'groans', 'sighs' and 'ascend'. But the music finds no more release than the poet's heavenward pleas, and ends in the original gloom-laden register. The turn to B♭ in b. 11 offers no real respite, for it picks up the harmonic emphases and the high D which began the line *a*, and this time reaches B♭ in a full close in b. 14.

Purcell's next secular recitatives, *They Say You're Angry* (Z. 422) and *Cupid,*

Ex. 99   *With Sick and Famish'd Eyes* (Z. 200): bb. 1–10

the *Slyest Rogue Alive* (Z. 367), use large-scale harmonic circuits and prolongations to support an expanded range of vocal roulades and other elaborations. But these practices are taken much further in three recitatives written between 1685 and 1687, which encompass revealing differences of style and quality. The long, multi-sectional 'Sighs for our late sovereign King Charles the Second' *If Pray'rs and Tears* (Z. 380), consists of a series of large recitative sections and shorter triple-time ones. It deploys a remarkable range of rhetorical devices over a much larger span than earlier recitatives. But the effect is strangely antique, largely because Purcell avoids overtly modern figuration and gesture, and because the stylistic contrasts between sections are not strong.

More radical and successful is *I Came, I Saw* (Z. 375). But Purcell's finest effort from this period – indeed, one of his finest solo songs from before the late dramatic music – is inspired by gratitude to and grief for a colleague and mentor, much as *What Hope for Us Remains?* (Z. 472) had been by Locke's death some eight years earlier. *Gentle Shepherds* (Z. 464), 'A Pastoral elegy on the death of Mr John Playford',[14] dates from the winter of 1686–7 and controls contrast by reinterpreting across the six sections a number of distinctive melodic and harmonic propositions. The voice begins on low E (Ex. 100), and many of the vocal phrases are broad arches which begin or end on this note – bb. 9–11 and the opening of the second recitative section, for example. The elaborate vocal and harmonic details are underpinned by simple, clearly projected pitch and harmonic projections in the bass (*a* and *b*).

Table 6. Sections in Gentle Shepherds (Z. 464)

Style	Recit.	Ground	Air	Ground[15]	Recit.	Chorus
Time sig.	C	₵	3	2	C	3
Harmonies	i–V–i	i	i–v–iv–i	III–(v)–III	i–VII–i	I–ii–v–I
Bars	1–8	9–32	33–50	51–63	64–74	75–106

Ex. 100   Gentle Shepherds (Z. 464): bb. 1–12

In terms of 'real' time the two recitatives are slightly shorter than the other sections. However, their pivotal role is reflected in the musical similarities between them (Table 6) and in their texts. The first section commands the shepherds to lament; this they do in the next three sections, which concentrate on minor-mode keys until bb. 46–7, where a reference to C major precedes the close in A minor. This major-mode colouring is picked up by the second ground as we turn away from grief towards a more eternal prospect – 'And when those short liv'd glories wither, crown it with a lasting verse'. The association continues into the second recitative which, although it too starts in A minor, turns to the relative major and its dominant as the poet reminds us that 'Theron's name ... an endless fame shall meet.' Therefore the turn to the tonic major for the chorus is both musically and textually apt as we are told to 'waste no more in sighs your breath'.

The beautifully languid energy of this piece is to some extent a product of Purcell's increasing command of stylistic contrast. A year or so earlier he had

Table 7. Sections in Awake and with Attention Hear (Z. 181)

Style	Recit.	Air	Recit.	Recit.	Air	Recit.	Air
Time sig.	C	₵ 31	C	C	2	C	₵ 31
Harmonies	I–I	I–I	V of ii–I	i–i	I–I	I–~	I–I
	1–41	42–82	83–121	122–38	139–60	161–89	190–228

produced a landmark in this progress, *Awake and with Attention Hear* (Z. 181), which shows sacred settings moving away from lyrical penitence towards a more extrovert, dramatic style.

Cowley's text is a paraphrase, in the style of a Pindaric ode, of the thirty-fourth chapter of Isaiah, and in length far exceeds that of any other solo song by Purcell except the cantata for solo voices and three-part chorus *In a Deep Vision's Intellectual Scene* (Z. 545). It occupies 228 bars comprising seven sections, and there is no text repetition (Table 7; see also Exx. 20 and 22 (ii)).

To dispatch the long text, Purcell uses that highly dramatic form of *secco* recitative which first appeared in *From Silent Shades* (Z. 370); but now it takes on a much larger scale, and seems to base many details of figuration on Italian practice. Harmonic movement tends to be slow, supporting short note values in the voice, including roulades of a length unusual for Purcell at that time. The airs are less interesting, but the opening of the first one, with its one-note incantation on 'God does a solemn sacrifice prepare', gives a hint of the style Purcell was to use so successfully in ritual scenes from the stage works. In the last recitative Purcell stretches the harmony as far from the tonic F as B minor, and ends with an extraordinarily chromatic link into the last section.

But *Awake and with Attention Hear* escapes by the skin of its teeth, its length and flamboyance resting uneasily with its rather short-breathed phrasing. While it contains striking passages, and while the sectional organisation and the breadth of the harmonic circuits are evidence of Purcell's architectonicism, the piece achieves scale by layering modernistic figuration over repetitions of harmonic techniques essentially suited to earlier songs such as *With Sick and Famish'd Eyes*.

Much more convincing are the slightly later songs, also published in *Harmonia sacra*, such as *Begin the Song* (Z. 183) and the beautifully lyrical *Great God and Just* (Z. 186). The first of these, yet another setting of Cowley, uses a range of affective contrasts at least as wide as *Awake and with Attention Hear*, but with a much stronger relationship between musical design and expression. A single harmonic prolongation can be used to support motivic elaboration on one expressive idea, such as the V of vi for 'My music's voice shall bear it company', though sometimes prolongations cross the boundaries of ideas, to a radically greater extent than anything found in music of two or three years earlier. The twist to F minor for 'Unhappy most, like tortur'd men', after a close in the tonic C, is a good example, for it turns out to be part of a massive prolongation of the tonic which holds together the extravagant gestures and elaborate ornamentation of this part of the song.

Multi-sectional, non-recitative songs

As Purcell's stylistic practice expanded, he became increasingly involved with various types of multi-sectional structure which could grapple with a wider expressive range. This had been anticipated in a number of recitative songs from the early 1680s, but setting up contrasts of non-recitative styles was a different proposition, and he seems not to have tried it often before the last half of the 1680s.

It had been foreshadowed in songs for solo and chorus such as 'Blow, Boreas, Blow' from *Sir Barnaby Whigg* (Z. 589) and *Farewell, Ye Rocks* (Z. 463), but did not become the norm until around 1687, with *This Poet Sings* (Anacreon's defeat) (Z. 423). The three stanzas are set to one section each, and Purcell's use of repetition is especially interesting, for it is his first consistent application of large-scale repetition to solo song.

The song expands through an aggressive, developmental dialogue between voice and continuo, with constantly irregular imitation (Ex. 101), all of which extends phrases and drives across phrase endings, producing a series of juxtaposed harmonic statements based on the tonic C major and its dominant, and on the relative minor and its dominant. The patterns coincide for 'verse that dares' (b. 9), and set up a two-bar prolongation of V of vi. The consequent emphasis on the resolution of this harmony is the strongest close thus far, and an appropriate point to begin the repeat of the entire text (bb. 10–11). Now it is the turn of the continuo to articulate closure while the voice cuts across the downbeat with a variation of the opening phrase. These ideas are developed further, and a strong move to V (b. 15) precedes the first undisturbed full close in the tonic. This closes the section, which is then repeated.

The second section, in a slowish triple time, turns to C minor and touches strongly on the relative major, and on iv and VII. Each of the two couplets is repeated to a variation of the first setting, and the last line is repeated at the end to close the section.

The last section is much more four-square, almost jaunty. Although it remains in C minor, its arpeggio figuration and its repetition of text and music are reminiscent of the opening section. A pathetic slow section of just four bars, for 'Each dart his mistress shoots, he dies', concludes the piece.

The repetition or varied repetition of entire phrases was not new: it was especially common at the end of a song. But *This Poet Sings* is Purcell's first song

Ex. 101   *This Poet Sings* (Z. 423): bb. 1–11

See commentary in *NPS*,
vol. XXV, p. 293.

to use varied repetition of whole themes, and perforce whole lines of text, as the main agent of expansion. It is a landmark complementary to *Sylvia, Now Your Scorn Give Over* (Z. 420) but, on the whole, is less successful, partly because its eccentric key scheme and the self-conscious complexity of the first section do not achieve that expressive directness for which it seems to be aiming.

Ground-bass songs

Perhaps Purcell's earliest solo song on a ground is *She Loves and She Confesses Too* (Z. 413) from 1680, which seems to have been a response to Reggio's setting of the same text to the same ground.[16] Within stanzas, Purcell's ingenious combinations of techniques ensure continuous flow, while the more large-scale musical design neatly reflects textual structure. Although the end of the first couplet has a strong close coincident with the end of the ground, thereafter

melodic closure into the tonic coincides with the end of the ground only at the
end of a stanza. Each stanza is separated by a statement of the ground, complete
at the end of the first, but interrupted by the vocal entry thereafter.

This piece and the sweeping, elegant, though not profound *Let Each Gallant
Heart* (Z. 390) from late 1682, wear their technical prowess easily, but are
insignificant in comparison with *O! Solitude* (Z. 406) from 1684–5, which has
aptly been described as Purcell's 'first truly great vocal ground'.[17] The bass and
a number of melodic gestures are derived from the opening symphony to the
verse anthem *In Thee, O Lord* (Z. 16), which is also in C minor. But the song
produces greater continuity by overlapping the endings and beginnings of
successive bass statements.

The poet Katherine Philips (1631–64) might have felt that in solitude she
could 'learn Apollo's lore / Without the pains to study it';[18] but Purcell's
treatment of the text must have been the result of considerable labour. In
particular, the choice of repeated words and phrases shows exceptional skill at
highlighting the central features of the long and rather rambling poem, which he
distils by selecting just two verses and four lines from a third.[19] Within the first
line of text, extensive repetition of a few distinctive melodic patterns generates
a thirteen-bar phrase over three statements of the ground, with the end of the
phrase articulated by a full close on the tonic. These patterns become
punctuating gestures for a series of four massively constructed paragraphs, each
of which is articulated as a single musical thought mainly through their
revolving around and closing onto the high C, which in b. 13 was set up as the
main point of stability. Restatements of the opening material are subtle, some
of them only hinting at repetition, as in 'O how agreeable'; but that is enough
to emphasise the central point – that solitude is the poet's 'sweetest choice'. The
conclusion, a full-scale reworking of the opening, aptly brings the musical and
poetic statement full circle.

Another technique for expanding scale was to transpose the ground, which
Purcell seems to have tried first in the odes, though with mixed results. *Cease,
Anxious World* (Z. 362), written probably just before *O! Solitude*, was another
early attempt which does not entirely come off. There are six statements in the
tonic of the four-bar ground, juxtaposed directly to a statement in the relative
major, and giving the harmonic change a strong propositional quality. Single
statements follow in III, iv and v, the last leading directly to three statements in
the tonic. Although the piece is in two sections (3 and 𝄵 time) and is technically
resourceful, the ground's four-square phrasing tends to be paralleled by the
vocal part, with rather short-breathed results. It is not surprising that Purcell did
nothing quite like it again.

The two ground bass sections of *Gentle Shepherds* (Z. 464) show an
experimental approach to maintaining continuity in the vocal ground. Neither

transposes the ground, and movement is generated partly by metrical instabilities. In the first, the vocal phrases rarely coincide with exact multiples of the one-and-a-half-bar ground. The first line is repeated so that the section attains a reasonable length, and then leads directly into the second line. The second ground uses the same bass as the symphony to *Rejoice in the Lord Alway* (Z. 49), but the minim which concluded the anthem ground is replaced by a crotchet, so that statements end alternately on weak and strong beats. The repetition patterns are almost identical to those of the other section. Although the ground is entirely in C major, Purcell's ingenuity results in half closes in iii and V.

A very different approach is shown in the sacred song *Now That the Sun Hath Veil'd His Light* (Z. 193), which was published in the 1688 volume of *Harmonia sacra*. The ground's repeated motifs (Ex. 102) generate a descending scale and

Ex. 102   *Now That the Sun* (Z. 193): bb. 1–11

have only to span a third to retain their identity. The first move away from the tonic G is brilliantly timed. As the believer asks 'and can there be?', the vocal phrase suggests a new key, rising through C♯ to D, and the second bar of the ground begins on B instead of F♯. Further modifications set the voice so out of phase with the ground's phrasing and so harmonically restless, that the believer's hoped-for 'sweet security' will be rest indeed. This is reached with a full close in the dominant (b. 43), while 'Then to the rest, O my soul' is illustrated by two stable statements in V.

The return to I is equally well timed. The concluding downbeat of the second statement in V is also the first note of an inversion of the all-pervasive descending third. As this rises D–E–F♯, the upper parts descend in preparation for a statement in G major. The extended 'Alleluia's are Purcell's own addition to the text, and balance the size of the first G major section and the quite substantial move towards V.

Songs for two voices and continuo

Approximately forty of Purcell's songs for two voices and continuo have
survived. Most of them can be dated, either through publication or through
their position in the autograph manuscript BL RM MS 20.h.8. He concentrated
on only a few of the many seventeenth-century song types for two voices – there
are, for example, very few strophic settings. He followed the practice of most
post-Restoration composers in tending to avoid two high voices and continuo
in favour of one high and one low voice, or tenor and bass.[20] There is also very
little evidence of the melodic awkwardness so common in duple- or quadruple-
time solo songs of the early 1680s, perhaps because Purcell could exercise
himself in that area in which he was a proven master – the polyphonic interplay
of parts. Nor was he slow to exploit the dramatic possibilities of the genre, most
evidently in following the well-established tradition of England and the rest of
Europe by producing a number of dialogues for the usual mythological figures.

Only three dialogues are known with any certainty to date from 1685 or
before, *Sit Down, My Dear Silvia* (Z. 509), *While You for Me* (Z. 524) and
Haste, Gentle Charon (Z. 490). In the last, Orpheus makes his first approach to
Charon in lyrical recitative; but when he sees Charon asleep he breaks into a
more arpeggaic style, which, with its shorter note values and imitation between
voice and continuo, produces a suitably rousing motion. The following twist to
the tonic minor neatly illustrates the pains of parted lovers.

From around 1685, harmonic contrasts become integral to such inherently
dramatic treatment. The opening section of the dialogue between Love and
Despair, *Hence, Fond Deceiver* (Z. 492), consists of four broad paragraphs, two
for each character: Despair begins, but Love has the last word, of course. Each
paragraph has a strong, non-repetitious harmonic structure, the final close of
which articulates one of the main harmonic areas, i–v–III–i. Each character's
entry begins in the preceding key but is immediately inflected to new areas as he
or she contributes something new to the argument.

The balance between local harmonic colour and overall design is particularly
subtle. After Despair's close onto III, Love declares 'If then thou would'st
victorious prove, And with success thy wishes crown, With bold assurance
speak thy love, And make thy gen'rous passion known'. Appropriately, this
begins with fanfares on D, the major mode of the tonic, presented sufficiently
strongly to be implied as a local tonic. But in the longer term it functions as IV
of A minor: on 'crown' the harmony changes to a $^{4\sharp}_{2}$ over D, which provides
appropriately intense colour, and which functions as V of A minor, this being
affirmed at the close on 'known'.

Two-part songs with instruments

Purcell wrote a number of songs for various combinations of instruments and voices, spread across the early and middle 1680s. *How Pleasant Is This Flow'ry Plain* (Z. 543) is a fine example, in which the two flutes play the part of 'the wood's choristers on ev'ry tree', and a garishly coloured series of secondary dominants is used to set 'gaudy pomps and vanities'.

But by far the most remarkable of these songs is *See Where She Sits* (Z. 508), which Purcell may have written to demonstrate the superiority of his skills over Reggio's setting of Cowley's text. It has no exact equivalent elsewhere in Purcell's output: the vocal style is that of some two-part songs without instruments, but for much of the time the texture is in five parts, with the instruments having the same material as the voices and in most respects being treated equally with them. The complex texture is given a broad purposefulness by economical harmonic design (Fig. 7).

Fig. 7. Sections in *See Where She Sits* (Z. 508)

Scoring	s, b, Vlns	Vlns	Repetition for s, Bc	b, Vlns	s, b, Vlns
Time sig.	C	¢		C	
Harmonies	i – v – vii(VII) – i	i – III – i	i – III – i	i – III – v – i	i – III – iv(IV) – i
Bars	13 22 28	29 39 49	50 59 69	70 74 81 83	83 87 96 104

The conservative approach to texture is epitomised in the part writing and in the way polyphony generates tension across phrases. As in the In nomines and other conservative early music, each phrase accumulates tension through increasingly dense textures, and this is released in a cadence. Bars 83–7 are typical: the surface activity increases, and the register widens to its maximum at the end of b. 86 (Ex. 103). The cadence is articulated by the subsequent wedging-in of the outer parts and the comparative stasis of the voices. Characteristically, the second violin brings in the point for the next line of text during the close.

Purcell seems to be primarily concerned with a continuous unfolding and growth of ideas, of which thematic statement is just one aspect. At its first appearance (b. 89), the point for 'ah, what does it avail' includes a diatonic, ascending semitone on 'avail' which sets off a chromatically ascending sequence on successive crotchets: in the vocal bass, E♭ moves to E; in the soprano we have A♭ instead of A, which moves to A♮ in violin II. Because the point for 'That she weeps tears so wond'rous cold' goes with the rising line, that text becomes the focus for chromatic alterations which gradually permeate the texture and affect other melodic ideas and texts. The chromatic alteration now needs less introduction and, picking up the cue from the faster pace of imitation, begins to saturate the texture, touching on areas as harmonically distant as B♭ minor (b.

Ex. 103   *See Where She Sits* (Z. 508): bb. 83–96

Ex. 103 continues on facing page

93). However, this is an entirely contextual harmonic excursion, which colours vividly, as an illustration of her weeping 'tears so wond'rous cold', the main progression from G minor to C minor.

The last phrase also unfolds ideas gradually. It culminates in a neat piece of textual and musical linkage: as the voices finish with 'that I admire they fall not

hail', they use a closed reworking of the prominent C–A–F♯ leaps which in the first section set 'drops tears'.

Cantatas

The cantatas, all settings of pastoral texts, are distinguished from the two-part songs with instruments by their invariable use of a three-voice chorus, and by the rarity of duets. Four have survived complete, plus the opening symphony and chorus of another. One, the extremely long *In a Deep Vision's Intellectual Scene* (Z. 545), has no independent instrumental parts; the others include symphonies and ritornellos and, in addition to the continuo, are scored for two violins, or flutes, or both. Further defining features are the freedom with which their sections move across the contemporary styles: most types of solo song can be found, while the opening symphonies can be of the anthem or the ode type. All these pieces are in BL MS RM 20.h.8, where their position enables fairly accurate dating.[21]

In *Hark How the Wild Musicians Sing* (Z. 542) it seems likely that, unconfined by the expressive demands of the court ode, Purcell felt he could let his hair down, appropriately enough considering the text. Voices and instruments open together in a dramatic setting of the first line. The agitated rhythms are 'wild' enough, but the dramatic quality is particularly evident in the contrasts between and within sections. The last section provides one of the most striking examples of the latter, rather more complex than would have been acceptable in the odes, but certainly appreciable by committed musicians, who would have relished a musical complexity and expressive intensity achieved partly by brilliant exploitation of textual and musical antitheses. Thus, 'To yonder cool shade my Dorinda we'll fly' includes a chromatically descending line, the softness of which is superbly countered by the assertive, sequentially rising line for 'the greatest of blessings', to bring the piece to a confident conclusion.

But by far the most interesting of these pieces is the Latin setting *Laudate Ceciliam* (Z. 329), which was written for St Cecilia's day 1683. The piece and its somewhat polyglot stylistic background are discussed in detail elsewhere,[22] but here we might note that its unusual structure, with two repetitions of the opening chorus enclosing a range of highly Italianate verse sections, and its unusual notation, unique in Purcell's autographs, suggest a deliberate essay in the Italian style. It is particularly successful at tying together contrasts between recitative, air, solo and ensemble, and at making sectional repetition a product of large-scale process, as well as an articulation of it. Even more than *Hark How the Wild Musicians Sing*, it would have appealed to those with inside knowledge, and has some significance for being perhaps the first indubitably successful vocal piece by Purcell to absorb Italian elements wholesale.

THE LATE INDEPENDENT SONGS

During 1688 and 1689 the free repetition techniques seen in *Sylvia, Now Your Scorn Give Over* (Z. 420) are applied to larger songs. From the same time there is a marked decline in the quantity of independent songs, especially those for two or more voices. Given the dramatic potential of the few he did write, such as *Dulcibella* (Z. 485) and *When Myra Sings* (Z. 521), it is not surprising that Purcell's later development in this genre tends to be concentrated in the stage music.[23]

Another striking feature of these years is the apparent gap in composition of independent solo songs, between *High on a Throne* (Z. 465) of 1689 and *Fly Swift, Ye Hours* (Z. 369), published in 1692. There is no comparable gap elsewhere in Purcell's career as a song composer. The hiatus may indeed be due to 'an accident in transmission'; but it seems at least as likely that the odes and stage works of those years gave him every opportunity he needed in this area.[24]

Strophic settings

Purcell wrote only a few short strophic settings during his last years; as before, these tend to be much less effective when the second strophe has the same music – *She That Would Gain* (Z. 414) is one example. This seems to have concerned Purcell, for of his two settings of Colonel Henry Heveningham's text *If Music Be the Food of Love*, the first exists in two versions, and the second of these addresses this very issue.

Both versions date from around 1691–2, but the A minor version (Z. 379B), although published later, is almost certainly the earlier.[25] In places, the second strophe fits rather awkwardly (b. 24, for example), while in the G minor version (Z. 379.A) the music for the two strophes is slightly different and fits better; moreover, in Z. 379A, the music for the second strophe is printed in full, leaving no doubt about the slight alterations required.[26]

More sustained evidence of Purcell's concern for a faithful relationship between text and music is offered by his increasing use of multi-sectional structures for strophic verse, and by his propensity to set two-verse strophic poems as a single section in binary form. The latter is seen in *When My Amelia Smiles* (Z. 434), written at an unknown date between 1690 and 1695, and which uses extensive repetition to achieve greater length than the brief poem would have produced in the largely syllabic settings of earlier years.

In its first line (Ex. 104) the roulade is made of repetitions of two motifs distinguished by their natures and functions: x is consonant to the harmony and ornaments stepwise descent; y fills out a third from the end of x and the first note is dissonant. The roulade is in two melodic units, a descent from and then back to E (a); and a repetition of b. 3 carried down to an unstable ending (b). This instability – produced partly by not ending on the tonic and more particularly

Ex. 104   *When My Amelia Smiles* (Z. 434): bb. 1–11

by the distinctive ascending resolution of B and the leap down to F♯ – is
balanced by a more stable close onto V at the end of the next line.

The two four-line verses are disposed across a harmonic structure defined by
closes at the end of each couplet:

$$i - \tfrac{1}{2} \text{ in } i - III \quad : \| : \quad III - iv - i \quad : \|$$

b. 11   25   36

Those at the ends of odd-numbered lines are mostly half-closes in the key
tonicised one line later, while most of the even-numbered lines prolong the
immediately preceding dominant. The similarity to the methods of the 1680
song *I Take No Pleasure* (Z. 388) is self-evident; but the harmonic design is
much more economical and cogent.

After about 1692, the year of *The Fairy Queen*, motivic repetition expands
onto a much larger scale.[27] In *Lovely Albina* (Z. 394), one of Purcell's last songs,
a prolongation of the dominant is articulated after the close in bb. 7–8 (Ex. 105).

Ex. 105   Lovely Albina (Z. 394): bb. 5–12

It begins as a local tonic (b. 8), changes to V of I, and finishes by reaffirming its
former function much more strongly than before (bb. 11–12). The figuration is
almost entirely derived from the arpeggio *a* and from fillings out of this by
semiquaver ornamentations (*b, c* and *d*). Continuo and voice take equal part in
motivic debate.

One further type of repetition remains to be considered – the restatement of
a phrase on, or its alteration to lead to, another harmonic and pitch level. This
extension of those harmonically propositional methods which first appeared in
the sonatas, begins to emerge in songs around 1687–8 and becomes much more
common around 1692.

A particularly large-scale application can be seen in the 'Bell Barr' *I Love and I Must* (Z. 382) of 1693, though depending on methods as unusual as the song's unexplained subtitle.[28] The song is in a single section of 106 bars. The distinctive two-bar figure with which the continuo begins is treated as a 'motto' opening, and the first half or so of the song consists of a number of large phrases which begin with this motif set to successive lines. Together with the intermediate cadences, the harmonic and pitch levels of these repetitions articulate the large-scale harmonic functions which define the song's structure.

Ground bass songs

The stage works provided many opportunities for strict and free ground bass. Within the independent song Purcell increasingly used the technique in one section of a multi-sectional structure. The first section of *Fly Swift, Ye Hours* (Z. 369) is an outstanding example, where extraordinary energy is derived from the speed of surface movement (an important source, Bod. MS Mus.Sch.c.61, indicates 'brisk time'), but more substantially from the non-coincidence of phrases in voice and continuo, as the two lines' rushing scales chase one another canonically in a classic figurative depiction of flight. This reaches a peak during the period of maximum harmonic tension, the approach to A minor in bb. 6–9.

Only one independent song written entirely on a ground bass is certainly from this period, and this, significantly, is a revision of a work which could be much earlier. The two versions of *What a Sad Fate* (Z. 428A and B) differ markedly, and what is almost certainly the later version (Z. 428A) is closely connected with the so-called 'Guildhall' autograph.

For a few songs this manuscript is the unique source; for rather more it is the only authoritative one. Most of the songs are taken from the stage works and the odes, and so can be dated fairly precisely.[29] Many are transposed, and in many the ornamentation is more elaborate than in the better-known version; but whatever the substance of the revision, the purpose would seem to be the intensification of expression. None of the revisions, however, is as far-reaching as that of *What a Sad Fate* which, together with the other revisions, forms a unique demonstration of Purcell's compositional priorities in solo vocal music during the years 1692–5.

In the C minor version (Z. 428B) almost all the lines have motivic and pitch emphases in common, but the latter in particular are over-insistent on high G and on various patterns of descent from there. This is emphasised by the numerous rests and repetitions for, while these are a neo-madrigalian representation of anguish, they break up the line of the song to such an extent that the piece falls well below the architectonic virtuosity of *O! Solitude* (Z. 406), written perhaps just a few years earlier (though, given these weaknesses, it would not be surprising to discover that Z. 428B itself was written in the mid-1680s).

The A minor setting (Z. 428A) has a similar pitch emphasis on high E, but the shape of the lines is on a larger scale, generated not least by concentrated motivic repetition which drives in large sweeps across the boundaries of the ground; also, there are fewer and much more judiciously timed 'gasps'.

In this context the returns to high E have a strong generative quality: indeed, given the uniform rhythm and unchanging repetition of the bass, the phrase endings and beginnings of the vocal part have the most important structural pitches. Bars 1–22 articulate a prolonged tonic by having successive phrases which end on i (b. 10), V (b. 17) and i (b. 22). Thereafter until b. 51, V of i is prolonged by three phrases which end (bb. 32, 38 and 44) on various pitches of dominant harmony, and is resolved by a fourth phrase which resolves onto the tonic at the close in b. 52. Thus, even though the ground is not transposed, Purcell articulates large-scale harmonic statements, all within the tonic area.

Multi-sectional and recitative songs

In the last six years of Purcell's life the stylistic trends suggested by songs such as *This Poet Sings* (Z. 423), are taken much further. The differing approaches to large-scale structure seen in *High on a Throne* (Z. 465) from 1689 – Purcell's last song with a chorus – and *Fly Swift, Ye Hours* (Z. 369) from 1692, show just how fundamental were the changes which took place during the intervening years.

The intensified contrasts between sections, which are such a defining feature of the later song, remain characteristic of all Purcell's later songs of this type, and reach their peak in the second setting of *If Music Be the Food of Love* (Z. 379C), which probably dates from around May 1695. This is one of the greatest songs in English, by Purcell or anyone else, a quality which seems to have been born partly of his extended interest in the text. Apart from that for the anthem *Thou Knowest, Lord*, it is the only text for which he revised a setting and produced a completely new setting some time later.

Instead of the elegant strophic setting of some three years earlier, we have a tri-partite, multi-sectional structure, with the second strophe divided between the second and third sections. Stylistic contrast is a feature not only between sections, but within the first, which fluently breaks out of recitative – very florid on key words like 'joy', 'move', and 'pleasure' – into free arioso, as the continuo breaks into running semiquavers, a development of ideas from the G minor setting of the first version (Z. 379A).

The large-scale pitch and motivic connections required by such diversity are maintained in the second verse, which reworks a number of ideas closely related to the third section of *Fly Swift, Ye Hours*. The opening themes are especially similar,[30] but in the later song pitch and harmonic functions operate on a much larger scale.

The second strophe sets up two-plus-two bars as the normative periodic unit (Ex. 106), but even within this, the seeds of the section's expansive phrasing are

Ex. 106   *If Music Be the Food of Love* (Z. 379C): bb. 30–9

sown by the imitation one bar apart between voice and continuo (bb. 35–6). Thereafter the periodic units of bass and voice coincide only to articulate the beginnings and ends of the large harmonic prolongations which dominate the piece. The close on the dominant in b. 60, for example, (Ex. 107) is preceded by a ten-bar prolongation of its own dominant. The next prolongation of comparable length is that of F in bb. 72–83, which in turn leads to the Bb harmony which opens the last section. The connecting processes between these involve several multi-layered harmonic functions and some of the most protracted pitch progressions Purcell ever essayed.

In the bass, two voices *a* and *b* operate simultaneously, distinguished by register. The principal harmonies are articulated by *a*, which is defined by the stressed pitches. The connections between the pitches of *a* define function: the melodic minor patterns *c* and *d* make the D function as a dominant; the more oblique patterns of bb. 63–6 mean that the G ultimately functions as vi in Bb.

The voice articulates a complementary line *e*, but its phrasing and that of the bass overlap. The way in which *e* is altered on its transposed repetition *f* (bb. 65–8), so as to arrive at a close on F, is particularly subtle. Instead of a G in b. 68 we have F, and, at least as far as b. 70, F major harmony is implied as a dominant rather than a tonic. But bb. 67–72 build upon a change in the voice-leading of the bass so as to increase the possibility of its functioning as a tonic.

After each stage in the main process *a* (bb. 60 and 63), the bass has gone down an octave to articulate the secondary line *b* (bb. 60, 63 and 66). But in b. 67 it leaps up, and remains at the higher octave, articulating a stepwise descent

Ex. 107　　*If Music Be the Food of Love* (Z. 379C): bb. 60–90

Ex. 107 continues on facing page

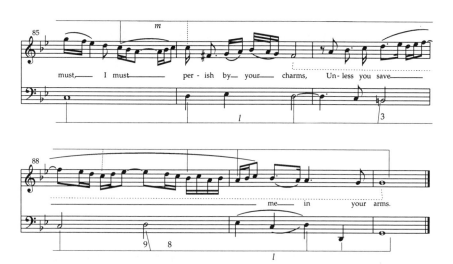

towards F (*g*), and breaking the process *b* just as the implied harmonic function is ii. The precipitate descent to F in b. 70, driven by the close imitation on *x*, adds the vocal C to the bass C as the imperfectly resolved elements (*b* and *j*), so that, although the voice-leading and the drive of the overlapping imitation produce a strong stress on F, that pitch remains unstable. The repetition of this phrase (bb. 72–6) reinforces F major, but neither it nor the prolongation of F (bb. 76–83) expunge the implied dominant function (N.B. the E♭ in b. 72), largely because bb. 76–83 are so harmonically static and so rhythmically repetitious.

Therefore the move to B♭ for the final recitative is a long-term resolution (*f* and *k*) of the ii of b. 67 and the subsequent F major. Thereafter G minor re-emerges. The B♭ harmony is weakened by having the bass on D (b. 84), which with B♮ encloses C. This in turn functions as the subdominant element of a repeated I–iv–V in the home key (*l*). The voice reinforces this with a cadential descent *m* to G.

As always, figurative detail is concerned with the single word; but what ultimately moves us and commands our attention is the song's sustained, rapt intensity; and this is inseparable from the way in which harmonic and pitch functions are projected, in a truly polyphonic way, over spans that, for the late seventeenth century, are large indeed. True that 'the treat is only sound', for here Purcell has attained a consummate relationship between textual meaning and musical concept.

CHAPTER ELEVEN

A new genre: odes to 1689

THE ODE[1] WAS THE ONLY large-scale genre which produced a consistently committed response from Purcell for almost the whole of his compositional career. Except for 1688, he produced at least one in each year from 1680 to 1695, mostly for the court, though a few were written for other prestigious venues. The ode thus offers an unmatched opportunity for observing the development of his vocal and instrumental styles.

In the earlier part of the seventeenth century, pieces which could be described as odes were closely related to verse anthems. The verse anthem was ostensibly for the praise of God and the ode explicitly for the praise of the monarch; so their purposes were sufficiently similar to make the verse anthem structure the natural choice for a composer intending to set the secular text.[2] An early example of the genre is *Do Not Repine, Fair Sun*, believed to be by Orlando Gibbons, and composed for the arrival of James I in Edinburgh in 1617.

This link continued after the Restoration, as in Henry Cooke's 1666 ode *Good Morrow to the Year*, the earliest post-Restoration ode for which both text and music have survived.[3] Its structure is as follows:

(1)   'Synfony' – two violins and continuo
(2)   Verse – bass and soprano
(3)   Chorus à 4
(4)   'Synfony' – two violins and continuo (not the same as 1)
(5)   Verse – soprano, tenor and bass, the end of which is reworked by Chorus à 4
(6)   Verse bass – the end of which is reworked and extended by Chorus à 5

Like most Restoration odes, this one consists of a series of units (just two in this case) which, typically, increase in density by beginning with verse and move towards a summatory chorus; the latter often amplifies the ending of the verse which has just been completed, and might be followed by a symphony. There is however no fixed sequence of events: in cases where the text called for an impressive opening, a chorus might appear immediately after the symphony, as in Blow's 1679 ode *Great Janus, Though the Festival Be Thine*, discussed below.[4]

The secular context gave the court ode a potential for musical expression more extravagant than that of the verse anthem; but it could achieve this only if it could develop into a sustained, quasi-dramatic musical structure, and grapple successfully with the challenges posed by the typically long texts. It was Purcell above all who succeeded in doing this. Indeed, the impact he made on this genre when he entered the lists in 1680 was comparable to that which his later dramatic music was to make on the English stage.

The time was ripe for such an intervention. Many odes by Humfrey, Locke and Blow are overtly experimental, especially Blow's, for it was he, above all, who set the trend for the future by expanding the range of movement types, by setting movements in contrasting keys, and by disposing movements in an inherently dramatic way. The results are often uneven, but show a resourcefulness and imagination which clearly inspired Purcell's practice.[5]

Blow's New Year ode of 1679, *Great Janus, Though the Festival Be Thine*, draws on a number of practices not normally associated with the verse anthem.[6] The opening symphony eschews the dance-like, binary-form second section which had hitherto been the norm in the anthem, in favour of a fully worked fugal texture; the chorus and verse sections have independent string parts; and differing harmonic areas help articulate structural units (see Table 8).

Purcell's first ode, *Welcome, Vicegerent* (Z. 340), is evidently indebted to Blow's practice. It was written in 1680, possibly around the same time as the four-part fantasias, and its instrumental music often shows a comparable assurance. Yet taken as a whole the ode is uneven, being a fascinating mixture of brilliantly judged dramatic gestures, at least one superlative instrumental movement, some lumpy choral writing, two duets – one beautifully elegant, the other occasionally perverse – and an unbalanced harmonic structure.

In an attempt to tighten the relationship between the symphony and the opening chorus Purcell adopts a blatantly contrived device. The second section of the symphony, featuring tightly worked fugal textures interspersed with passages of chordal writing, is repeated as a concertato accompaniment to the chorus. It seems likely that Purcell wrote the chorus movement first and extracted the instrumental parts later; and while the result is energetic, it suffers from otherwise inexplicable peculiarities. In the symphony, for example, the series of off-beat chords is deprived of the metrically strong choral passage which gives it its function.

The high levels of contrast inherent in the new approach to the genre sometimes work well, especially the use of minor-mode duets: stylistically 'Ah!

Table 8. Sections in Great Janus, Though the Festival Be Thine

UNITS	SCORING	TIME SIG.	HARMONIC AREA
(1)	Symphony (four-part strings)	₵ – 31	Dm–Dm
	Chorus *SSATB* with strings†	31	Dm–Dm
	Verse *ssatb* with strings		Dm–Am
	Chorus *SSATB*		V of Dm–Dm
(2)	Verse *atb* + ritornello (from verse)	$\frac{6}{4}$	Dm–Gm
	Verse + chorus: *ssb* + *SSATB*		
	+ *atb* + *SSATB*		Gm–Gm
	Symphony (two vlns + cont.)*	₵	Gm–V of Dm
		31	Dm–Dm
(3)	Verse *a* + ritornello (from verse)		Dm–Dm
	Chorus *SSATB*		Dm–Dm
(4)	Verse *t* + chorus of whole verse +		
	ritornello from same	31	Dm–Dm
	Chorus *SSATB* with strings		Dm–Dm

† It is likely that in most choruses without independent parts, strings doubled. This description indicates one or more independent parts, in this case the first violin.
* Not directly derived from the preceding material.

Table 9. Sections in Welcome, Vicegerent *(Z. 340)*

UNITS	SCORING	TIME SIG.	MATERIAL	HARMONIC AREA
(1)	Symphony	$\frac{8}{4}$	A	C maj.
		31	B1	
	Chorus		B2	
(2)	Verse *ab* + rit. (from	₵	C	C min.
	end of verse)			
	Chorus	31	D	C maj.
	Ritornello		E	
	Verse *t* with chorus		F	
——	Continuo link	2		C–G
(3)	Verse *ss*		G	G min.
	Chorus	₵	H	G maj.
	Verse *t* with chorus	31	J	
——	Continuo link			G–C
(4)	Ritornello		J	C maj.
	Chorus + verse *ab* +		K	
	chorus with strings			

mighty Sir' is similar to the roughly contemporary two-part song with instruments *See Where She Sits* (Z. 508), but is much less successful in controlling false relations and dissonance. More convincing is the charming duet for two sopranos 'When the Summer in His Glory' (Z. 340.8), a short binary piece, the mellifluous thirds and sixths of which emphasise the heavyweight impact of the following chorus.

Like Blow's *Great Janus, Though the Festival Be Thine*, the organisation of *Welcome, Vicegerent* raises many moot points. In its representation in Table 9 the differing key areas are viewed as articulating the most important divisions. This view has the consistency that each unit ends with a chorus, and the two central units begin with the only minor-mode movements – both duets. However, it also highlights an unconvincing repetition of material between units 3 and 4.

Purcell's structurally self-conscious approach is amply demonstrated in the last two units of the ode. The tenor verse 'Music the Food of Love' (Z. 340.10a) follows directly after, and in the same key as, the G major chorus, and is a pleasant example of the graceful triple-time air at which the young composer was adept. It uses the same method of alternating between verse and chorus as Blow had done in his 1678 ode *Dread Sir, the Prince of Light*, disposing the two four-line strophes across a single musical structure:

Strophe 1 – Tenor verse I – V. Repeated by chorus.
Strophe 2 – Tenor verse V of I – I. Repeated by chorus.

It is with the following ritornello that problems begin, for its function is confused. The continuo link separates and looks forward, expecting a complementary response; the ritornello responds harmonically by being in C; but melodically it is identical to the preceding section, tending thus to sound like an out-of-key member of the previous unit.

The final item perpetuates the harmonic confusion, which is unfortunate, for in other respects it is a fine early example of Purcell's dramatic skill, especially in the way in which it deploys rapid changes between solo and chorus during a jaunty, triple-time setting of the text:

> His absence was Autumn, his presence is Spring
> That ever new life and new pleasure does bring,
> Then all that have voices, let 'em cheerfully sing,
> And those that have none may say: 'God save the King'.

The first two lines end in V and are given to the chorus. The alto soloist has the third line, which ends on ii, and in the fourth line the bass soloist gets as far as V of iii on 'may say:'. Then the chorus bursts in with the final acclamation, and rounds off the ode with a conflation of the last two lines: 'let 'em cheerfully sing "God save the King".' The impressive sound is given a suitably clamorous quality by the addition of elaborate, independent string parts.

This last chorus uses a chain of secondary dominants to return to C major. But the pace of events remains unchanged until the end, and as the final C major harmony is not differentiated other than by resting on it for three bars, it tends to sound as if the piece is ending in the subdominant. It might be argued that, as other music by Purcell from this period shows a comparably local view of harmonic structure, this is not an inherent weakness but a product of style. It is, however, significant that, although the next year's ode *Swifter Isis, Swifter Flow* (Z. 336) shows a similar imbalance (the final chorus is so infused with a minor-mode excursion that the G major ending is harmonically inconclusive), Purcell was thereafter careful to avoid such features. Certainly, the strongly periodic structures inherent in the ode concept tend to emphasise them.

Swifter Isis, Swifter Flow is nevertheless replete with structural experiments which show a keen awareness of the genre's dramatic possibilities. For the opening symphony Purcell reworked a piece written a year or two earlier (see Ex. 51) and produced the most convincing instance yet, in any ode, of using scoring for diversification and to generate a large structure.

The symphony's second section has a full working of a scalic subject, which is proved apt for the text by a thirty-bar alto solo, and then shown amenable to a fully accompanied choral working, plus instrumental postludes. After some further high-falutin salutations, we turn to the tonic minor for 'Land Him Safely on Our Shore' (Z. 336.4), which follows the example of 'Hark, Behold the Heavenly Quire' from the previous year's stage play *Theodosius* (Z. 606.4), in being scored for bass and two recorders, an effective contrast with the massive forces of the opening items. As the bass finishes singing of the 'loss they mourned' during the King's absence, the string basses enter in C, 'loud', with a steadily moving arpeggaic line which sets the scene for the poet's response as he hears the royal barge – 'Hark, hark ! just now my listening ears / Are struck with the repeated sound / Of labouring oars', and which is the ground bass for a large instrumental piece, alto solo and string postlude.[7]

It is interesting to see, after this item, an arrangement of highly contrasted movements in an orderly sequence of keys, similar to that of the *Sonatas of Three Parts*. The C major unit is followed by a bass recitative in A minor, a verse, chorus and ritornello in F, an elegant soprano duet in D minor, and a concluding chorus in G.

In 1682 Purcell wrote two odes, *What Shall Be Done?* (Z. 341) and *The Summer's Absence* (Z. 337). The former is especially notable for its opening symphony, by far the best such piece Purcell had written thus far, and a superlative conflation of English and Italian stylistic features. It also sees Purcell's first use of flutes and strings in contrasting groups and, perhaps more

significantly, closes with an elaborate rondeau-like structure which uses
contrasts of scoring to enliven the inherent repetition, a clear anticipation of the
methods used in 1686, in 'From the Rattling of Drums' from *Ye Tuneful Muses*
(Z. 344.9), and in the late dramatic works.

Purcell's composition of odes reached a qualitative turning point in 1683,
when he composed at least three: the Cecilian ode *Welcome to All the Pleasures*
(Z. 339), *From Hardy Climes* (Z. 325) and *Fly, Bold Rebellion* (Z. 324). Some
of the new techniques still present problems, especially in *From Hardy Climes*.
The one really important number from this ode is the solo 'The Sparrow and the
Gentle Dove' (Z. 325.8) which, like 'These Had by Their Ill Usage Drove' (Z.
337.10) from *The Summer's Absence*, uses a quaver bass in common time, but
now treats it as a ground.

This elegant setting is far superior to any independent ground bass song
before *O! Solitude* (Z. 406). The melody effortlessly avoids coincidence with the
stress patterns of the bass, and although the ground remains in D minor
throughout, Purcell manages to suggest shifts to related keys, while the
elaborate ritornello shows Purcell making what is probably his first attempt to
transpose a ground bass.

This might well have been inspired by the technical ingenuity of Blow's 1681
ode *Great Sir, the Joy of All Our Hearts*, in which the massive concluding
chorus with instruments is preceded by a ground for alto and strings. Blow's
deployment of string and solo forces is ingenious, while of the eleven statements
of the ground, the sixth and seventh are substantially altered to achieve a change
of key.

In 'The Sparrow and the Gentle Dove' Purcell does not produce the loose
structure and harmonic lassitude of the Blow; but in an apparent desire to stick
as closely as possible to the ground he produces bumpy transitions which sit
oddly with the broadly conceived phrasing of the song.[8] Over the next few
years, Purcell was to make several further attempts at transposing the ground,
but complete success eluded him until he had the maturity to abandon the
dogma of exact repetition, and to adapt the bass for a more fluid change of key.

By contrast, *Fly, Bold Rebellion* is much the finest court ode to date, by
Purcell or anyone else. Westrup comments on the 'firmer grasp and ... bolder
imagination'[9] shown in individual movements; but the balance between these
movements, Purcell's keen response to the text's many opportunities for musical
imagery – all these also are part of the picture. Unit 1 in Table 10 declares
against rebellion, and for the King; the shorter second unit spells out the
subjects' need for their king's presence; the third unit – by far the most
elaborate, musically and textually – is principally concerned with the proper
relationship between king and subjects; the fourth and last unit declares a
welcome to the King.

Table 10. Sections in Fly, Bold Rebellion *(Z. 324)*

UNITS	SCORING	TIME SIG.	HARMONIC AREA
	Symphony	₵ −$\frac{9}{6}$ (sic)	F–F
(1)	Verse *aatbb* + rit. 'Fly, Bold Rebellion'	3	F–F
	Verse *b* 'The Plot Is Displayed'		F–F
	Chorus 'Then with Heart and with Voice'	$\frac{6}{4}$	F–F
	Continuo link	₵	F–Dm
(2)	Verse *a* + rit. 'Rivers from Their Channels Turned'		Dm–Dm
	Chorus 'For Majesty Moves'	3	Dm–Dm
(3)	Verse (recit.) *b* 'If Then We've Found'	C	B♭–C(m)†
	Verse *t* + rit. 'But Kings Like the Sun'	3	Am–Am
	Verse *ssa* + rit. 'But Heaven Has Now Dispelled Those Fears'		F–F
	Verse *atb* 'Come Then Change Your Notes'	2	Fm–Fm
	Chorus 'But with Heart and with Voice'	3	F–F
(4)	Verse *a* + rit. (ground) 'Be Welcome Then, Great Sir'	₵	F–F
	Verse *ssaatbb* + chorus *SSAATBB* 'Welcome to All Those Wishes Fulfilled'		F–F

† This minor mode ending is an elaborate inflexion of the functioning major mode.

The opening verse is evidently based on Blow's New Year ode from the previous year, *Arise, Great Monarch*.[10] Purcell gives the contrasting elements of the main idea to different voices, making, in effect, two themes (Ex. 108), while the broadly conceived harmonic progression gives elaborate local detail a long-range purposefulness new to the verse sections of the odes.

Contrast between movements is especially strong in the third unit, the beginning of which is articulated by a bass recitative (cf. *Swifter Isis, Swifter Flow* and *What Shall Be Done?*), prefacing an A minor tenor verse and ritornello. The disquiet created by the King's necessary absences is then eloquently dispelled as the *ssa* verse enters, in mellifluous counterpoint and F major, with the continuo operating in the same register as the alto, and mostly *seguente*. The next verse brilliantly exploits the change in poetic tone. It admonishes the rebellious crowds to 'change your notes', which duly occurs as the music turns to F minor with D♭, D♮, E♭ and E♮ in close proximity, for a sombre, chordal *atb* setting.

The concluding verse and chorus (unit 4) is one of the most elaborate Purcell ever wrote, and brings events full circle by returning to a texture related to that of the opening verse, though the pace of events is generally faster. To highlight the main closes Purcell prepares for them with passages of extraordinary complexity, thus emphasising the release of tension on the concluding

Ex. 108   Fly, Bold Rebellion, opening verse (Z. 324.2): bb. 1–9

downbeat. Such textures were to recur in a number of later, massively scored pieces, most notably *My Heart Is Inditing* (Z. 30); but as far as the odes are concerned these were a 'one-off'.

Purcell's Cecilian ode *Welcome to All the Pleasures* (Z. 339) was almost certainly the first of its kind by any composer, and was one of at least two pieces he wrote for the celebrations that year.[11] Not surprisingly, the presence of many distinguished contemporaries at the celebration encouraged him to produce one of his most finely crafted early pieces, shorter than most royal odes, with a consequently less complex overall structure, and well enough thought of to be published the following year. The symphony is a masterpiece, combining in both sections the most sophisticated invertible counterpoint with strongly conceived overall design.

Two other movements are particularly notable. The alto air 'Here the Deities Approve' (Z. 339.3) is much the most elegant of the three melodies so far conceived over an andante ground bass, and the most successful yet at avoiding the regular patterns outlined by the ground. The ritornello repeats the melody almost exactly but nevertheless includes imitation between the melody and the inner parts. The song was acknowledged by inclusion in the first book of

Orpheus britannicus (1698) and in subsequent editions; also, Purcell's own keyboard transcription appeared in *Musick's Handmaid* (1689).

The last movement of this ode is an imaginative *SATB* chorus which culminates in massive tonic and dominant fanfares on 'Io Cecilia', and ends with arpeggiations of the tonic chord on which each part drops out in turn until the basses alone are left to sing 'Cecilia'. The choral texture is augmented by two string parts which take part in the contrapuntal discourse on an equal basis with the voices. From now on such concertato textures were to be a regular feature of the court ode.

The odes were the first genre to benefit directly from Purcell's experience with the trio sonata and from the consequent increased range of stylistic contrast. One movement evidently grounded in that experience is the opening verse section of the 1684 ode *From Those Serene and Rapturous Joys* (Z. 326.2), which begins as a recitative but, after a few bars, becomes an air, the bass line of which is constructed largely from varied repetitions of a few motifs derived from the vocal part (Ex. 109). While Purcell might well have picked up the idea

Ex. *109*   *From Those Serene and Rapturous Joys*, opening verse (Z. 326.2): bb. 1–11

from Blow, this air is significant in being his earliest surviving attempt to apply to solo vocal music in English the sonatas' repetition of small motifs – a technique which was to be important for the development of his vocal style (cf. *Laudate Ceciliam*).[12]

Also related to Italianate methods are the chorus 'Welcome Home' (Z. 326.4) and the concluding D major piece 'With Trumpets and Shouts' (Z. 326.11). The latter has a certain rugged strength, and is imaginative in its use of resources and figuration. But 'Welcome Home' is rather less happy, for the occasional enlivening details such as the irregular phrase lengths and the sometimes dissonant inner parts in chorus and strings cannot ameliorate the plainness of the setting. The timing of this chorus is neat, however. The text is taken from the last line of the preceding song – 'And men and angels bid him welcome home'. The chorus thus achieves a twofold purpose, articulating the end of a musical unit, and representing the communal acclamations. More significant still is the repetition of the chorus to end the next unit. It is not called for by the text, but neatly rounds off a series of verse solos and ensembles dealing with images of welcome.

The text for these solos and ensembles plumbs the depths of sycophancy, especially when claiming that Charles' return is more welcome than was life to Lazarus! Yet here Purcell produces his best ground bass song to date, if it precedes *O! Solitude* (Z. 406). The E minor bass touches on A minor and G via their own dominants, and Purcell's vocal line articulates these areas, as well as half closes in the tonic which do not coincide with the bass closures. The restless harmonic movement of the bass plus the sinuosity and complicated phrasing of the vocal part give the setting a peculiar quality which manages to suggest at once Lazarus' sepulchral resting place and the extraordinary energy of his preternatural resurrection.[13]

For his first ode for King James II, *Why, Why Are All the Muses Mute?* (Z. 343) from 1685, Purcell used a much-improved example of a technique essayed in the anthem *My Heart Is Fixed* (Z. 29). The ode begins with alto solo, singing the first three lines of text in expressive recitative; a more lively triple time enters for the fourth and fifth lines, and the 'vocal choir' (*SSATB*) bursts in with an extended reworking of these.

> Why, why are all the Muses mute?
> Why sleeps the viol and the lute?
> Why hangs untuned the idle lyre?
> Awake, 'tis Caesar does inspire
> And animates the vocal choir.

Ex. 110   Why, Why Are All the Muses Mute?, 'Accursed Rebellion' (Z. 343.7): bb. 1–5

With the muses now roused the ode proper can begin; so the symphony follows. This overtly dramatic approach continues both in the expression of detail and in the large-scale structure. The text is disposed across six units, defined by key:

1	2	3	4	5	6
Dm	D	Gm	E♭	C–Am	Dm

The first urges that all should be preparing to welcome the King. The second turns to one of the 'trumpet' keys to declare Britain's greatness and the King's role in it, and is joined directly into the G minor of the third, dealing with Monmouth's rebellion. (The effect of this juxtaposition is underlined by the song's being Purcell's most dramatic 'Gostling' solo yet.) The fourth, dealing with the King's milder, gentler virtues (just when he had seen off the rebels in most bloody fashion), is prepared for by a gentle rondeau for strings, still in G minor, after which a beautiful move to the more genial colour of E♭ inaugurates the depiction of these virtues. A rapid move to C (exploiting the relationship between E♭ and C minor), begins the triumphant fifth unit, which incorporates two songs, the second in A minor. This readily leads back to D minor for the concluding unit.

Purcell's unerring grip on large-scale structure depends partly on balancing conglomerations of short pieces against single items which punctuate by massivity of effect, if not always length. The G minor solo 'Accursed Rebellion Reared His Head' (Z. 343.7) is a good instance, followed as it is by a series of subtle contrasts depicting the King's 'milder virtues'. It is by far Purcell's most flamboyant ode solo to date, and considerably more aggressive in impact than *They That Go Down to the Sea in Ships* (Z. 57), written just a few months earlier. And well it might be, for the text is packed with violent imagery to which Purcell had a ready response (Exx. 110 and 111), with the first four lines in recitative and the next four in bravura style, taking full advantage of Gostling's range. Like some contemporary independent songs, size results from extensive repetition of lines on different harmonic and pitch levels and from some extended harmonic prolongations. Moreover, economy underlies elaboration: the descending thirds on 'down' are derived from the scales of 'avenging thunder' (Ex. 111).

Ex. *111*   *Why, Why Are All the Muses Mute?*, 'Accursed Rebellion' (Z. 343.7): bb. 34–48

Such confident compositional virtuosity becomes a feature of most later odes. *Ye Tuneful Muses* (Z. 344) from 1686 has one of the finest opening symphonies of these years, but is more famous for the technically ingenious use of the popular song 'Hey Then, Up Go We', as an obbligato to the air 'Be Lively Then' (Z. 344.5). Purcell's use of this tune has been much commented upon,[14] but bears repetition and some amplification.

Like most dance tunes, 'Hey Then, Up Go We' has entirely regular phrasing which fits nicely neither with Purcell's general compositional aspirations, nor with the text's irregular metre; but he exploits this potential tension to produce a dramatised setting. With the tune in the bass, the soloist summons the muses, who might also be seen as representing the King's loyal subjects. His first line coincides with the dance's phrasing and is repeated, but thereafter an ingenious combination of text repetition and thematic variation causes vocal and continuo phrases to overlap. Similar features recur in the chorus' communal clamourings, during which the tune appears in an independent violin line. The soprano part begins with a variation on the opening phrase of the bass solo, but continues with a more regular line which is largely coincident with the tune's phrase structure; here it is the alto and tenor parts which maintain movement across the phrase divisions. The concluding ritornello returns the tune to the bass, and maintains the sumptuous textures of the chorus; but it negates the chorus' studied complexity by revealing the popular tune in its true colours, regular phrasing and all.

This ode shows some striking developments in the use of resources. As the chorus sings 'Tune all your instruments', the violins scrub on the four open strings to form a series of secondary dominants, leading to a chorus in E minor which summons loyal subjects to a celebration of the King's return.

The celebration proper takes place in the massive chorus with soloists and instruments 'From the Rattling of Drums' (Z. 344.9), which uses *SATB* chorus and *ssatb* soloists plus orchestra to create by far Purcell's largest ode movement to date. It is an enormous rondeau in C, one of the two trumpet keys and, during the refrain, the bass thuds away on tonic and dominant to imitate martial kettle-drums.[15]

The structural concept common to most rondeaux – typically AABACAA – is subtly modified to meld into one group no less than three statements of this basic structure (eight bars each to A, B and C). Each is varied in its scoring, with the last A of the first and second groups functioning also as the first of the second and third respectively (see Fig. 8). The first statement is given by the orchestra, with A on four-part strings (see Ex. 25 (ii)), and B and C on violins and viola. The second statement begins when the alto solo stands in for the repetition of A for orchestra, while B and C are for *sst* and *atb* verse respectively. In the third, A is for chorus and orchestra throughout, with B and C for violins and viola.

Table 11. Sections in Sound the Trumpet *(Z. 335)*

	TIME SIG.	KEY
Symphony	₵ –3	Am–Am
Verse *ab*+chorus with strings 'Sound the Trumpet'	₵	D–D
Verse *t* 'Crown the Year' (ground)	3	Bm–Bm
Chorus with strings 'To Caesar All Hail'	₵	G–D
Verse *aa*+rit. 'Let Caesar and Urania Live' (ground)		Dm–Dm
Verse *tb* 'What Greater Bliss'+Chorus with strings		
'With Plenty Surrounding'	3	F–F
Chaconne (strings)		F–F
Verse *b* with strings 'While Caesar' and 'His Fame'	C–3	Am–Am
Verse *aattbb*+Chorus with strings 'To Urania and Caesar'		Am–Am

Fig. 8. Structure of 'From the Rattling of Drums' (Z. 344.9)

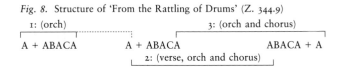

The birthday ode for 1687, *Sound the Trumpet* (Z. 335), is a logical result of the tendency, from 1684 onwards, to increase the size of individual items. While it might be open to interpretations other than that essayed in Table 11, it shows a clear propensity to move away from building a unit from accretions of small pieces, towards a smaller number of larger pieces, which might nevertheless be arranged in a series of climactic cycles.

Purcell's methods of culmination are ingenious. By fine control of phrasing, vocal and instrumental forces, and harmonic circuits, he makes the two choruses 'Sound the Trumpet' and 'To Caesar All Hail' lead towards subsequent events rather than act as a point of culmination. The musical emphasis is thus on the two ground bass numbers, 'Crown the Year' and 'Let Caesar and Urania Live'. The latter is the larger and more elaborate, and is followed by a verse duet 'What Greater Bliss' which leads directly into the chorus 'With Plenty Surrounding' (Ex. 112).

The expansive repetitions in this chorus mark it out as the culminating point of the implorations and exhortations in earlier numbers. It sets the text

> With plenty surrounding and loyalty sounding
> Io Pæns of joy,
> We'll pay our devotion
> To the monarch of Britain and lord of the Ocean.

and is followed by an enormous chaconne, during which dancing would presumably have reflected the subjects' devotions.

Ex. 112   *Sound the Trumpet*, 'With Plenty Surrounding' (Z. 335.6b): bb. 12–22

How can one follow such a musically compelling climax? Purcell's judgement is unerring. The bass solo, 'While Caesar Like the Morning Star' begins as an A minor accompanied recitative, whose character and key foil the preceding chaconne without negating it. The rapid changes of mood and texture in the recitative require some resolution, which duly happens in the triple-time section 'His Fame Like Incense Mounts the Skies'. This song, one of Purcell's finest bass solos (almost certainly for Gostling), depends for its effect upon flamboyant, extrovert performance, the strenuous yet brilliant effect of which represents an individual and more specific continuation of the acclamations expressed in the dance. It is topped off with the massive ensemble number 'To Urania and Caesar Delights Without Measure'.

This ode's increase in scale is closely linked to the unprecedentedly extensive use of harmonic prolongation. Ex. 112, from the chorus 'With Plenty Surrounding', includes an eleven-bar prolongation, neatly foiling the harmonic mobility of the preceding phrase. The IV–I–V in bb. 12–14 articulates the beginning of the prolongation by being much the most stable progression thus far, and by ending on the most heavily stressed dominant of the chorus. (But note how the alto characteristically suspends F over the phrase boundary.) The $\frac{5}{3}-\frac{6}{4}-\frac{5}{3}$ of bb. 14–18 are not resolved onto the tonic harmony of bb. 19–21, for the vocal parts continue to stress C, making that pitch function in those bars as an inverted pedal. Finally C major is cadentially affirmed by its own dominant before returning to the tonic (bb. 23–4).

Another method of expansion can be seen in the ode's final item, 'To Urania and Caesar' (Z. 335.9) (Fig. 9). The statements of A fulfil a function similar to rondeau-style repetitions, but they and B are varied on each repetition to span a different harmonic circuit. These changes are neatly allied to the text: on its first appearance, B functions as a balancing, harmonically closed consequent of A which expands by repetition in the last line, via by the aptly long melisma on 'o'erflow'.

The first statement of B includes harmonic excursions which reach their extremity on a six-bar prolongation of the subdominant. This builds upon the instability injected by the phrase repetition to destabilise the B section as a whole. It is significant that the entire passage marked X in Ex. 113 could be omitted, leaving us with an eight-bar, balanced, but rather inconsequential phrase. Purcell's approach is infinitely more subtle, as the prolongation is quitted via a precipitous, three-bar close which, being both metrically and harmonically unstable, produces a return to A, but of just eight bars.

Because much of the material consists of repetitions of small motifs, it can be transferred to a variety of harmonic and pitch contexts and a variety of textural types, while maintaining its fundamental identity. So, the already established function of B as the area of expansion is exploited at its second appearance to touch on new keys. In conjunction with a new scoring for six soloists, the material of 'o'erflow' is counterpointed against the rhythm of ''Tis but just'. The parts are invertible, and this, together with dramatic alternations between various groupings of soloists, expand this section to no less than thirty-three bars, and the choral reworking expands to an even larger scale.

The ode's two ground bass songs also show a confidence in applying harmonic tension as a structural generator. The tenor solo 'Crown the Year'

Fig. 9. 'To Urania and Caesar' from *Sound the Trumpet* (Z. 335.9)

To Urania and Caesar delights without measure,
With empire no trouble, and safety with pleasure; } A
Since the joy we possess to their goodness we owe,
'Tis but just our best wishes like that should o'erflow. } B

Verse

atb	*a*	*atb*	*t*	*aattbb*
A	B	A	B	⟶
2 × 8				
bars: 16	18	8	11	22
i – III	III – i	i – VIII	VII – V of i	V of i – i

*Chorus SATB with strings** (also verse)

Chorus	*a*	Chorus	Rit.	Chorus
A	B			
2 × 8				
16	4	21	7	14
i – III	III – V of v	~	VII – III	III – i
	V of v – v – v(V) – i – VII			

*The strings mostly double the chorus parts.

Ex. 113   Sound the Trumpet, 'To Urania and Caesar' (Z. 335.9): first statement of B

(Z. 335.3) is different from any previous ground in that the five-bar chromatic ground is not only transposed, but also altered and extended, moving away from the B minor tonic, to a close in the relative major. Fine as this is, the duet 'Let Caesar and Urania Live' (Z. 335.5) is a masterpiece. It exploits the arpeggaic, quaver style of bass found in many earlier songs and features an entirely convincing transposition of the ground, achieved by twisting its end to cadence first in the dominant and then to touch on other keys.

CHAPTER TWELVE

Consolidation and maturity: odes from 1689 to 1695

AFTER *Sound the Trumpet* Purcell wrote no more court odes for nearly two years, almost certainly because of the increasingly unstable political situation. The new monarchs William and Mary acceded to the throne on 13 February 1689 and Purcell set a fine precedent for the future by celebrating the Queen's birthday on 30 April with *Now Does the Glorious Day Appear* (Z. 332), the first in a line of six distinguished birthday odes. It is replete with evidence of the stylistic changes in Purcell's practice over the previous two years, notably his pervasive and convincing absorption of Italianate features. As Westrup has said of the finale, 'Here is the work of a composer who knew exactly what he wanted to do and did it without fumbling.'[1]

The symphony is the first in an ode by Purcell to feature five-part strings and an opening section in Italianate sonata style. In this it follows examples set by Blow in the 1688 New Year ode *Ye Sons of Phoebus*, by Draghi, and by Purcell himself in several post-1687 anthems. He also set himself new standards in making structural capital out of his fanfare-based, D major material. In all the early movements in that key, the opening motifs feature the rising third D–F♯ and a continuation either to the dominant or to C♯, the third of dominant harmony, while there are several common rhythmic figures. He balances unity of motif, key and metre (𝄵) against a triple-time tenor solo in A minor, 'This Does Our Fertile Isle' (Z. 332.4), which features a two-note free ostinato in the bass – a rising fourth E–A from the third beat of one bar to the first beat of the next, and readily transposable onto other pitches to express different harmonic progressions and areas. The last line of this song, 'Far above all, let this [day] the calendar adorn', sets the cue for the return of the chorus 'Now does the glorious day appear', not called for by the text, but neatly rounding off the opening celebrations.

Of the remaining movements the triple-time finale is the most compelling. As in earlier odes, opening imitation gives way to more homophonic writing; but it is of a sort far more sophisticated than any earlier example, largely because the strings and chorus are treated as overlapping groups which drive one another in an inherently polyphonic way.

After a series of phrases in the tonic D, a phrase concludes with a close in ii as the chorus sings 'And make heav'n's mighty concave ring'. 'Ring' is stated on four successive crotchets, on the last of which the strings set off with repeated chords of their own. Both the choral repetitions and the string chords are descriptively apt and, being called for neither by the text nor by any imbalance in phrasing, introduce a degree of disturbance sufficient to greatly expand the scale of an otherwise ordinary choral phrase. This process is repeated to end on V and finally on I.

Such integration of instrumental and vocal writing is seen also in *Dido and Aeneas*, on which Purcell could have been working at around the same time, and in *Celestial Music* (Z. 322), described in the principal source (BL MS RM 20.h.8) as 'A song that was perform'd at Mr Maidwell's, a schoolmaster, on the 5th of August, 1689, the words by one of his scholars'.[2] As a whole this work is pleasant but inconsequential, the best movement being the ground bass alto air in C minor and triple time 'Her Charming Strains' (Z. 322.3).

It would have been not long after this that Purcell completed a much more important private commission, this time for the Yorkshire Feast held annually in London, and which, in 1690, was used also to celebrate William's and Mary's accession.[3] *Of Old, When Heroes Thought It Base* (Z. 333) is Purcell's most innovative ode before *Hail, Bright Cecilia* (Z. 328), and has many interesting points of comparison with the first of his dramatic operas *Dioclesian* (Z. 627), which was premiered soon after the Yorkshiremen's celebrations on 27 March 1690. It is Purcell's first piece with extensive parts for solo oboe, and might be the first time he had written for solo trumpet (the only other contender is *The Cibell*), almost certainly in response both to foreign music he had encountered and to the rapidly rising skills of native trumpeters such as John Shore. Instead of conglomerations of small items, it consists of some twelve highly contrasted, full-size pieces for varying resources, with a repetition of the opening symphony separating those verses dealing with the honourable past of the city and county of York, from those praising its part in the recent Glorious Revolution. Past and the present are musically linked: after the symphony repetition has set the appropriate D major scene, the present hero William is honoured in the duet for two altos and two trumpets 'And Now When the Renown'd Nassau' (Z. 333.9), and this picks up musical material related to 'Brigantium, Honour'd with a Race Divine', which dealt with Constantine, a hero of the past.

This ode is also the first in which solos have extensive instrumental preludes, precedents for which had been set by *Dido and Aeneas* (in the opening of Act III, for example) and were continued in *Dioclesian* and other stage music from this time onwards. Some preludes, such as 'Brigantium, Honour'd with a Race Divine' and 'The Bashful Thames' (Z. 333.3 and 4), work material based on the first line and are around eight bars long; in 'So When the Glitt'ring Queen of Night' (Z. 333.11), the upper parts form a single twelve-bar phrase consisting of transposed and varied repetitions of the two-bar ground, while the bass has six statements of the ground in its original form. By contrast 'The Pale and the Purple Rose' (Z. 333.6) presents the entire song.

From around 1690, various types of binary movement become increasingly common in solos and duets from the odes and stage music; but in this ode, every verse movement except the opening one (Z. 333.2), is some sort of binary structure. In many, Purcell is happy to use the regular phrase structures of dance music; in others he aims for a much more complex scheme.

When all these innovations are added to the expressive strengths of the music, we have a piece more concerned with musical display than any ode to date, and a virtuoso progression of expressively calculated stylistic contrasts. In the second part, for example, the bass duet 'They Did No Storms' (Z. 333.10) is in the predominant D major; but it modifies the triumphalist atmosphere with its extensive minor-mode passages (A minor and B minor) and with imaginative text illustration, such as the deliciously grumpy yet menacing low-pitched parallel thirds during 'in the grumbling air'. The next movement, 'So When the Glitt'ring Queen of Night' (Z. 333.11), is in the relative minor and in triple time, like the slow movements of many of Purcell's later D major symphonies. In this suave, elegant ground bass setting which breathes a nocturnal atmosphere similar to that in 'See, Even Night' from *The Fairy Queen* (Z. 629.11), almost every note of the instrumental parts is derived from the two-bar bass. After the twelve-bar introduction, violins and viola repeat motifs derived from the ground to circulate around the same pitches so that D–F♯–E are uppermost in each bar. Yet these one-bar units are set against the two-bar units of the ground and the more mobile viola part, a combination of circular repetition and different phrase lengths which produces an hypnotic continuity against which the voice unfolds with purposeful freedom, as in the A♮/A♯ clash of b. 19, which intensifies the approach to the cadence and the release on it.

The range of genre, style and technique is unprecedented in any earlier work by Purcell. 'The Pale and the Purple Rose' (Z. 333.6) refers to the houses of York and Lancaster respectively, and to the Wars of the Roses. A rhythmic ostinato in the bass (| ♩ ♪ ♪ ♩ |), each statement on one pitch, represents the drums of battle, and in an unusual application of concerto principles, the prelude splits the melody between violins and oboes in such a way that one can never be sure who is the principal, though they come together for the concluding and mid-point cadences.

For all the modernity of much of the ode's material, details of execution are replete with polyphonic methods founded in Purcell's earliest music. The opening phrase of 'And in Each Tract of Glory'[4] is generated from the two-bar motif *a* and the four-bar consequent *b*, both of which are open ended (Ex. 114).

Ex. 114 *Of Old, When Heroes Thought It Base,* 'And in Each Tract' (Z. 333.7): bb. 1–12

The former defines the basic periodic unit of two bars; the latter, as it begins with an upbeat and is twice the length of *a*, crosses over the boundaries articulated by the three presentations of *a* (bb. 1–8). The effectiveness of this method of generating a large phrase out of comparatively small units depends on the continuo articulating clearly the harmonic meaning of the whole without doing violence to the independence of the vocal parts. So, the bass pattern *e* complements the open ending of *a* + *b* in bb. 1–6 of the tenor; yet *c* complements the presentation of *a* in the bass. The consequent, increasingly strong articulations of dominant harmony (bb. 4, 6 and 8), through an elaborated Bb–A in the bass (*d*), produce a dominant prolongation lasting from b. 4 to b. 8. The close onto V in b. 8 is articulated as the strongest phrase ending thus far because all parts have a punctuation of some sort at the beginning of that bar.

Yet it is open both harmonically and melodically, the latter because the presentation of *a* in bb. 7–8 produces an expectation of its consequent *b*. The stress patterns in all parts now agree (*f*) as a new harmonic and pitch emphasis is sought, ending in a close on F.

Such music has a technically studied air which can easily become over elaborate, though here Purcell avoids this rather more successfully than he did in *Dioclesian*. 'And Now When the Renown'd Nassau' (Z. 333.9), for example, audaciously balances harmonic stasis against various types of motion, to generate an irregular binary structure, each 'half' of which sets one couplet (Fig. 10); and while it lacks the polish of later pieces which do something similar, it is nevertheless accomplished and forceful.

Fig. 10. 'And Now When the Renown'd Nassau' (Z. 333.9)

	A1	A2		B	C
Bars	1 – 11	11 – 23 │ │	23 – 33	33 – 36 – 41
Harmonies	I – I	I – V – I │ │	I – IV – ii	(V) – I – I

The first phrase (bb. 1–6, Ex. 115) is derived entirely from an arpeggiation of D major harmony, and from various ways of filling it in, notably the opening continuo motif. Its rhythmic activity at first generates considerable momentum, but with repetition the motion become circular: the only changes are in density and register as each part (the continuo excepted) ends its phrase with an F♯ downbeat. To halt this, Purcell just stops the rhythmic activity on the downbeat of b. 6, a crudity of gesture which perfectly matches the preceding phrases. Something different has to happen; so the same motifs (b. 6) and developments of them (bb. 7–8) are now set over a harmonically mobile bass. Bars 8–9 see the first true close of the piece, which is reinforced through repetition by the trumpets.

The repetition of A (A2 in Fig. 10) is written out in full and is altered so substantially that its identity is not immediately evident. The first few bars feature different and more complex imitations between voices and trumpets, and the roulades at b. 14, the equivalent of b. 5, are extended to lead to a half close, and bb. 6–9 are transposed to the dominant. Bars 6–11 are then repeated in their earlier version to restore the tonic.

Most of the ode texts Purcell had to deal with were poor stuff, and D'Urfey's are only a little better than average. But one of his strengths, in the odes and elsewhere, was in offering possibilities for a wide range of dramatic expression, as can clearly be seen in Queen Mary's 1690 birthday ode *Arise, My Muse* (Z. 320). The first vocal entry is an accompanied recitative for alto and strings (Z. 320.2) which, like most earlier recitatives of this kind, such as 'While Caesar, Like the Morning Star' from *Sound the Trumpet* (Z. 335.8), has a strong preludial quality which is derived partly from the piece itself and partly from its

Ex. 115 Of Old, *When Heroes Thought It Base*, 'And Now When the Renown'd Nassau' (Z. 333.9): bb. 1–9

context. Both recitatives follow a substantial orchestral movement, and for all their elaborate surface motion and detailed rhetorical gesture, their pace of fundamental movement is extremely slow. In such a context, and as the alto soloist has been urging the muse to rise, something else has to happen. This is accomplished in the fine, elaborately worked chorus 'Ye Sons of Music' (Z. 320.3). This reaches a strong half close which resolves back to tonic harmony as the choir declaims 'Then sound your instruments'. The full consort of trumpets and strings blazes away with four bars of fanfares in D major, ending with a full close.

Despite its sheer massivity, this closure is open-ended, largely because the choral and orchestral closes burst in upon the ample unfolding of the earlier part of the chorus and do not match its scale. A D-major duet for tenor and bass therefore follows, beginning with 'Then sound your instruments', but now completing the rest of the text. As a climactic conclusion the chorus repeats the song, doubled by the trumpets and strings. The move into a second 'movement' (so described in the published text) is articulated by the strongest stylistic change yet, into the relative minor for the ground bass air 'See How the Glitt'ring Ruler of the Day' (Z. 320.5).

Westrup is undoubtedly correct in identifying the D minor alto solo with two obbligato flutes 'But Ah, I See Eusebia Drown'd in Tears' (Z. 320.9), as the musical and dramatic highlight of the ode.[5] D'Urfey's text personifies the Anglican church[6] as Eusebia, mourning the pending departure of her champion. (William was about to leave on a military campaign.) The alto soloist becomes Eusebia herself, pleading with William not to go. The bass soloist enters in D major, urging William to 'go on ... / Illustrious man; Leave not the work undone'. After a brief yet assertive setting the alto solo returns in D minor, picking up the beginning of Eusebia's pleas and paraphrasing them by omitting some flute phrases and some vocal repetitions. The bass soloist has another go, but manages just five bars before Eusebia's pleas, 'no, no, Fate must some meaner force employ', intrude again. The sound of strings, flutes and chorus wins out as the material of the bass solo is worked into an elaborate conclusion for the work – if it indeed is the end, for, after all that has passed, William's departure makes a somewhat odd ending, and Purcell seems not to have set D'Urfey's final lines, with their chorus in praise of the Queen and hopeful for the King's return. Presumably, as in other odes, Purcell would have used the full consort of instruments.[7]

Purcell was slow to move the court ode towards the methods of *Of Old, When Heroes Thought It Base*, with its large single items. But it nevertheless remained fruitful ground for structural innovation, and in this respect few odes match his 1691 effort for the Queen's birthday, *Welcome, Welcome, Glorious Morn* (Z. 338).

This ode was written when Purcell was struggling with the concepts of scale and communication posed by the rise of dramatic opera, a rise in which he had played a primary role. In *King Arthur* he essayed solutions through the imaginative and economical uses of concertato techniques between voices and instruments and through new repetition techniques; and all these influenced his choices profoundly when it came to composing *Welcome, Welcome, Glorious Morn.*

Connections with *King Arthur* are at their most explicit in the opening vocal item. The arpeggaic motifs (Ex. 116) are similar to those in 'Hither This Way' from Act II of *King Arthur* (Z. 628.12), and the dotted-note roulades on 'glorious' are comparable to Philidel's 'Down you fall a furlong sinking' in the same piece. Both works begin with a solo featuring a pair of obbligato instruments, these being oboes in the ode and possibly in the stage work also.[8] Both pieces also use the material of the song as the basis for an elaborate chorus, follow the chorus with a contrasting piece for two and one solo voices respectively, and conclude with a varied repetition of the chorus.

This overspill from Purcell's concern with musical cohesion in stage music results in one of his most tightly organised odes. The opening symphony's astonishing motivic compression is continued by the ground bass figure of 'Welcome, welcome', just one and a half bars long, with internal motivic repetitions and a strong V–I at the end (Ex. 116).

The knotty conciseness of the opening becomes a springboard for progressively larger phrases, in the voice alone at first, but then in a complex, constantly overlapping discourse between the three sonorities – oboes, continuo and voice. One of the most potent tensions is the rhythmic counterpoint between these phrases, between the repeated brevity and closure of the ground every three minim pulses, and the tendency for the melodic material to suggest periodic units in multiples of two minims.

The descending vocal arpeggio has no balancing phrase. Instead, the oboes respond with a rhythmically and harmonically closed version. Already, Purcell is juggling the combinatorial possibilities, as the oboes enter at the beginning of the second ground statement rather than the end and conclude with the G–E quavers with which they opened. But the voice enters where it did before, and ornaments the descending arpeggio with the semiquaver rhythm from b. 2. These push the phrase onto the roulade which acts as a consequent to the earlier vocal phrases, and which presents the first phrase to be longer than one ground statement. As before, it and the instrumental reply end on G, so maintaining the openness of the phrase.

The next line of text and a new motif enter before the oboes close. Open-ended phrasing is now taken further: the D on 'smiles' is resolved neither here nor in the instrumental repetition, but is picked up in the next phrase and

Ex. 116   *Welcome, Welcome, Glorious Morn*, opening verse (Z. 338.2): bb. 1–9

resolved in an ornamented descent to A. This, plus a modification of the ground, produces a move into A minor, in which key there are two ground statements, followed by an overlapping return to the opening phrases as they were in b. 3.

The expansive methods of the solo are taken further as the chorus enters, again overlapping the end of the preceding phrase (cf. 'Hither This Way'), reworking the solo, and exploring most combinatorial possibilities. Rhythmic drive is intensified as the imitation drives across what formerly were gaps in the vocal or instrumental texture, and as the repetitions of 'welcome' enter on successive beats. The close imitation is perpetuated into the subsequent points, culminating in b. 22, where, in A minor, the alto imitates the soprano one beat later and a sixth lower, producing simultaneous tonic and subdominant leading notes, C♯ and G♯.

Just how different these late odes can be from one another – far more so than earlier court odes – is underlined by the very different expressive and compositional concepts Purcell adopted for the 1692 ode *Love's Goddess Sure* (Z. 331), which is particularly notable for its more intimate manner, prompted no doubt by Sedley's text,[9] and for its calculated use of sonorities and textural types derived from Purcell's early music. As with the opening symphony, these borrowings are surface features, and their expressive effect depends very much on their modern context. This is particularly clear in the final group of choral and verse items, which epitomise Purcell's capacity to convey simultaneously the immediate and the longer-term meanings of a text.

> May she to heaven late return,
> And choirs of angels there rejoice.
> As much as we below shall mourn
> Our short, but their eternal choice.

For the first couplet the ode's preference for the minor mode is set aside in favour of G, the tonic major, thereby seeming to set the scene for a triumphant conclusion. But at the third line the tonic minor returns for a remarkable lamenting verse which ends on V of i, extended by chromatic appoggiaturas. The festive tone of the earlier chorus returns as the V resolves back to G minor at the beginning of the last line, with a similar texture and tempo to the G major chorus; but now, in the minor mode, it is shot through with the sorrow of those left on earth after the Queen's death.

For the verse section Purcell harnesses the penitential spirit and some techniques of the sacred partsongs and the funeral sentences. The two imitative points (Ex. 117) have distinct functions. In any one voice the opening of 'As much as we below' defines the stable pitch area of the next few bars and the unstable descending leap on 'below' sets up the need for a balancing ascent. This is provided by the ascending chromaticism for 'shall mourn' which, in the first two presentations, terminates on the pitch which preceded the leap (cf. bb. 2–5 in tenor; bb. 2–6 in alto).

Much of the piece's intensity is produced by an impeccably judged conflict between consistent melodic patterns and a clear harmonic background. When the soprano enters, for example, it avoids the D–E♭ version of *a* (cf. tenor, b. 1) and instead picks up the rising chromaticism of 'shall mourn' and the mediant-uppermost sonority (cf. b. 3), to go to F, even though the main harmonic function is V. Such line-driven tensions set the scene for the C♯–D of b. 8 and the inversion of the 'shall mourn' theme at b. 13.

Ex. 117   Love's Goddess Sure, 'As Much As We Below' (Z. 331.9a)

Ex. 117 continues on facing page

The main source of harmonic tension is an increasingly complex presentation of i–iv, which seeks to resolve to V. The i–iv–i alternation in bb. 1–3 is intensified by the i(I)–iv of bb. 4–5. This iv is itself intensified to the major mode and then moves to V, which is prolonged over a dominant pedal. The resolution to i in b. 9 is unstable because of the soprano and alto appoggiaturas and the bass entry. The subdominant is now elaborated to alternate with ii, producing

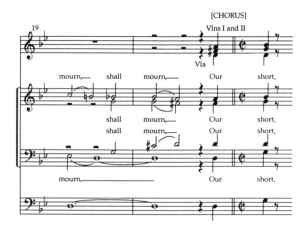

a stronger predominant function and a consequently stronger move onto V (b. 13). Again the dominant is prolonged, this time by the descending chromatic bass. It is not resolved until the next chorus and, significantly, the chorus' final V–i is preceded by the subdominant/supertonic sonority which featured so strongly in the verse, in this case a $^9_7$ over C.

Finally, the wealth of surface detail acquires its strength from articulating economical voice-leading, which projects across the span of the movement. In the preceding G major chorus, D a ninth above middle C was prominent and the chorus ended through a series of descending arpeggios which brought the D down to a close on G. The verse opens on D an octave lower and the first melodic statement leaves this unresolved (*a* in Ex. 117). The texture expands to the higher D (bb. 6–7), which is picked up again in b. 10, remains unresolved, and is finally dealt with by the chromatic descent in bb. 14–20, which brings it down to A. Descent from high D to G occurs only at the end of the ode, passing through that A.

Later that same year, and after the success of the premiere of *The Fairy Queen* (Z. 629), Purcell had a matchless opportunity to display his talents to his fellow musicians, unfettered by the requirements of the court ode. For that year's Cecilian celebrations he composed *Hail, Bright Cecilia* (Z. 328), which in complexity and quality far outstrips any earlier efforts by Purcell or anyone else. He missed no opportunity offered by the rich, though rather obvious, musical imagery of Nicholas Brady's text; indeed, Peter Dennison has justly claimed that Purcell 'wrote no work of comparable length that is so richly scored for voices and instruments, so diverse in technique and texture, or so unfailingly imaginative in the wealth of its musical invention'.[10] In these respects it exceeds even the finest scenes from *The Fairy Queen* which had been composed earlier the same year. It attracted much attention: the first performance was reported on by Motteux in *The Gentleman's Journal* of November 1692; many songs from it were published over the next thirty or so years; and Purcell's autograph score, with the names of singers written on it, was the basis for many subsequently made copies of the whole ode or extracts from it.[11]

If the overall design of the ode is based on any earlier methods, then it is those of that other notable non-court ode *Of Old, When Heroes Thought It Base* (Z. 333). So, progress through *Hail, Bright Cecilia* depends largely upon contrasts between different types of movement, all conceptually unified by a common literary and musical purpose. The progress is rendered explicit by various linking descents, in most cases through a descending scale in the continuo; between 'Soul of the World' and 'Thou Tun'st This World' (Z. 328.5 and 6) the move from B♭ to its relative minor needs no such defining; between 'With That Sublime Celestial Lay' and 'Wond'rous Machine' (Z. 328.7 and 8) what would seem to be an ascent (C major to E minor) is turned into the opposite by a marked drop in register for the E minor beginning and by the comparatively open conclusion of 'With That Sublime Celestial Lay'.

The one case which eschews descent is the move from A minor to D major between 'In Vain the Am'rous Flute' and 'The Fife and All the Harmony of War' (Z. 328.10 and 11). But this is consistent with the gradual return of the opening symphony's festive spirit, articulated partly in the I–i–I keys of respectively 'The Fife and All the Harmony of War', 'Let These Among Themselves Contest' and the 'Hail, Bright Cecilia' chorus (Z. 328.11, 12 and 13), and partly in the fast–slow–fast tempi of the same three movements. Finally this return is made exhilaratingly explicit in one of Purcell's most enthusiastic, text-driven displays of technical skill, where he reworks one of the opening symphony's main themes into the choral texture.

Hail, Bright Cecilia opens with an Italianate orchestral sonata featuring a canzona movement and impressive use of trumpets and drums. It is in D, and its ending is neatly devised so as to leave certain pitches unresolved and suggesting a move from A (a sixth above middle C) to D.

These same pitches are picked up at the beginning of the D minor recitative, which consists, with one exception, of a series of open-ended sections which continue to posit this D as a point of closure. The preludial quality of the recitative and its reworking for chorus, is largely a product of rhythm. The off-beat, repeated statements of 'Hail' emphasise the salutation without stressing the word at the expense of 'Cecilia', and accumulate enormous rhythmic tension, which needs a strong, sustained downbeat on D minor.

Non-resolution to D is maintained through the choral and orchestral working of 'Fill every heart', largely by changes in scoring which drive across D minor closes (bb. 23 and 34). The emphatic harmonic movement articulated by the augmented subject in bb. 38–40 of the bass makes the D minor close in b. 42

much the strongest of the movement, and a true resolution of the dominant projected at the end of the recitative; yet it is also destabilised in a most subtle way.

A minim's-worth of tonic harmony plus a minim rest, or a full semibreve on the tonic, would close the piece. Instead, tonic harmony lasts for just a minim and cuts to dominant harmony on the second half of the bar, and for continuo alone. The destabilising effect and the suspension of harmonic motion during the long pedal points of 'That thine and music's sacred love' stand in marked contrast to the earlier part of the piece, and the longer this disparity persists, the greater the tension becomes. The sudden increase in the pace of harmonic motion for 'May make the British forest prove' releases this tension into a more harmonically discursive passage which reaches an unalloyed tonic close in bb. 60–1, though by then even more D minor is needed for stability, which is provided by an orchestral reworking of the material.

'Hark Each Tree' (Z. 328.3) is one of two ground bass pieces in the ode, and as far as elaboration within strict ground bass techniques is concerned, it is *ultima Thule*. Like most of Purcell's grounds ameliorable to the alteration necessary for key changes, this bass consists largely of sequential repetitions; so extra bars can be added, or it can be curtailed, repetitions being defined largely by recurrences of the distinctive opening figure. Form is articulated primarily through the disposition of voices (alto and bass) and instruments (violins and flutes) and through the changes of material at successive lines of text, producing three large sections, each in a distinct harmonic area:

Section 1: (Line 1)   66 bars (1–66) A minor
Section 2: (Lines 2–4)   49 bars (67–115) C–Em–G–Em
Section 3: (Lines 5–6)   45 bars (116–60) ~–A minor

The alto solo ''Tis Nature's Voice' (Z. 328.4) is perhaps the most famous movement from the ode, partly because a contemporary account of the first performance suggests that Purcell himself sang the part.[12] Intended as a virtuoso display of both performance and compositional prowess, it pillages the bottom drawer of rhetorical devices, and in this respect stands in the same relation to English recitative as 'Possente spirito' from *L'Orfeo* does to the Italian *stile nuovo*.

The extreme surface differences between and within phrases cohere largely because of an impeccable relationship between textual structure, ornamentation, and musical structure, this last being especially dependent on the comparative weighting of full and half closes. The most elaborately ornamented passages, for example, tend to be underpinned by harmonic prolongations. So, the second part of the song (bb. 30–56) is in F minor and its repetition of 'and straight we grieve or hate' ends on a Phrygian close in C minor (b. 36), this

Ex. 118   Hail, Bright Cecilia, 'Soul of the World' (Z. 328.5): bb. 1–8

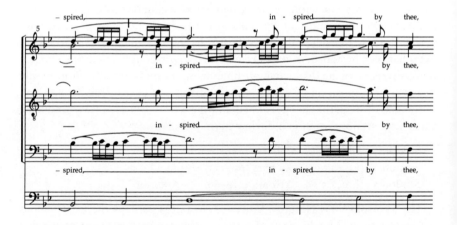

dominant then being resolved after a four-bar roulade around C minor to set 'rejoice or love'.

A whole chapter could be written on Purcell's use of rhetorical figuration in this song. Westrup points out the internal pedal representing the captivating power of music;[13] the 'gasping' rests of the upper part, which revolves around just three notes as the bass descends by step across a tenth are derived from Italian madrigalian and operatic practice, but the application is entirely original. As always, usage depends on context – in this case on the increased pace of harmonic movement, for it is the only time that there has been a harmonic change every crotchet. We might also point out the stark simplicity of the opening, which uses that natural acoustic phenomenon, the major triad, to present nature's voice.

Brady's third verse – 'Soul of the world! inspir'd by thee, / The jarring seeds of matter did agree' – opens, with stunning effect, through a move from F minor to the massively scored major mode and the key of B♭ for one of Purcell's truly great choruses (Ex. 118). It has three sections, defined by concluding full closes in I (b. 11), iii (b. 26) and I respectively, and by a distinct break before the second and third sections. Each section is binary, the first parts tending to be elaborately contrapuntal and the second more chordal. The first parts of the first and third sections end with a half close (bb. 8 and 37) and that of the second with a full close in vi (b. 22), inherently unstable due to the sudden move to that key.

Such structural clarity and conformity is an essential component in creating unity out of great surface diversity, while the opening's cosmic impression is appropriate to its function of presenting a motivic core – various ways of filling out a third – which runs through the whole chorus. The stasis of the opening fundamental pitches is followed at 'inspired' by more elaborate third-based patterns, whose fundamental pitches articulate a slow ascent over a tonic pedal. The ascending lines, moving mostly by step, increasingly conflict with the pedal, and when the bass moves to C and D, after building up enormous tension through its stasis, the consequent harmonic movement has prodigious strength.

The second and third sections follow this pattern of using both fundamental and ornamental ways of filling out thirds, and the virtuoso displays of contrapuntal skill reach a peak in the last section. From the outset, 'Made up of various parts' is, appropriately enough, presented in prime and inversion and in increasingly elaborate stretti, and its closing bars feature a dominant prolongation which ends (bb. 36–7) with the definitive G–C leap and IV–V harmony which ended the first section (bb. 10–11). The setting of 'one perfect harmony' which follows is a consummation of the propensity for contrapuntal passages to be foiled with chordal writing. The dissonances on the repetitions of 'one perfect' (bb. 38–9) stress the second word and embody its meaning in rhythmic uniformity throughout the texture and an exact canon three in one, over a dominant pedal and using a point (bb. 39–41) which augments the earlier quaver pattern for 'various'.

The next movement, 'Thou Tun'st This World' (Z. 328.6), is in some respects the most straightforward in the ode. It follows the pattern of a few pieces from the stage works in having an instrumental prelude (two oboes and continuo), a song, and a chorus, all on the same air. The extensive repetitions of motifs and phrases in the air articulate some extended pitch connections. That between the F♮ which ends 'the spheres above' (b. 40) and the F♯ which ends a varied repetition of that phrase (b. 43) is a striking example, which justifies the otherwise rather odd melodic pattern immediately preceding the F♯. But perhaps the main interest of the piece lies in the three differing harmonisations of the melody, each of which features a different range of contrapuntal manipulations, such as the prelude's canon at the crotchet in bb. 15–18, which appears in the bass and voice during the song.

The trio 'With That Sublime Celestial Lay' (Z. 328.7) sees one of the few applications in secular music of the verse anthem's dialogue technique, a technique well suited to dispatching a text fairly quickly. The ten lines of text are set in two sections. The first has four large phrases, the first three of which each set one couplet, begin with a single voice, and finish with all three. The fourth phrase has one couplet and one line and is set for one voice alone. This aptly contrasts with the second section, for three voices throughout, in triple time and at a faster tempo – 'Brisk without lightness, without dulness grave' – and compensates for its textural uniformity with harmonic discursiveness.

The precipitous ending leads readily into the bass solo, with obbligato oboes, 'Wond'rous Machine' (Z. 328.8), the second ground bass of the ode, but entirely different in technique and design from 'Hark Each Tree'. Perhaps its most prominent feature is its rhythmic energy, derived from projection against the ground of sharply differentiated rhythmic variations upon a single melodic idea.

The first two statements of the ground and the oboes' two-bar idea present material which will dominate the piece. The bass outlines the two-bar periodic unit against which all phrases are projected, and its shamelessly mechanical character, reinforced by no-less mechanistic repetition, is singularly apt. The relationship between the vocal parts and the oboes is a judicious mixture of mechanistic similarity and marked contrast, and tends to run in four-bar cycles which end as the ground begins a statement. Set against the incessant repetitions of the ground, this continuous generation of material assumes an ecstatic quality well suited to the text.

Perhaps the most accessible song in the ode is 'The Airy Violin' (Z. 328.9); yet beneath its easy melodic grace lies a motivic economy scarcely less tight than that of Purcell's more highbrow contrapuntal works. It is concerned mainly with concerted imitations between voice and violins and with departure from, and return to, core motivic patterns. The latter coincide fairly exactly with departure from, and return to, the tonic C, and consist mainly in various ways of filling out thirds via differing rhythmic patterns, and dotted rhythms in particular.

The opening three-bar phrase epitomises these methods, beginning with arpeggiations of the tonic C, each bar being concerned with a different interval, C–E–C, E–G and E–C respectively. As in other such songs we see an expressively apt use of the standard 'motto' opening: the 'airy violin' is announced and then enters. The longer repetition of this phrase maintains the third-based patterns to reach the dominant, and then sets 'quit the field' by abandoning them and the barely gained key in a precipitous one-bar descent from G to C.

'In Vain the Am'rous Flute' (Z. 328.10) is one of the most expressively subtle pieces Purcell ever wrote, and is certainly one of his finest duets. By far the most complex vocal duet in the odes or the stage music, it combines imagery which in other contexts might be used for the lament of broken-hearted lovers, with that which can express the intensity of their passion.

The form is basically binary, plus a flute prelude and postlude which paraphrase the material of the first and second parts respectively. The prelude also sets up the pitch propositions which dominate the movement, and the metrical disturbances which are a primary means of expansion. The opening A–E, and the E–A answer in the second flute, set up the main referential pitches for the upper parts (Ex. 119). The descending semitone, prominent in b. 4, becomes the progenitor of an extended discourse based on stepwise movement. But as the semitone was used to begin a hemiola close (bb. 4–6), the discourse picks up the distinctive duple-time patterns to create a finely calculated metrical disturbance. At the end of b. 7 this too becomes blurred and not until the bass moves through an upbeat F to a downbeat on E (bb. 8–9) is the metre re-established. The phrase ends with a close on the relative major, but A minor is clawed back via an ascending line in the bass which aptly reverses the descending patterns predominant thus far to reach V of that key (b. 14).

At the concluding cadence (bb. 17–18), and that at the end of the first phrase (bb. 5–6), the bass approaches E through D, a move which is to be a feature of all important closes. In the upper parts, full closes onto A are approached by a descending scale from C. This too is carried into the duet proper.

Cecilia was commonly pictured playing the organ, and the text declares that the efforts by the flute and guitar to 'inspire wanton heat and loose desire' cannot match the power of that instrument's 'chaste airs'. In an extraordinary piece of rhetorical subtlety, Purcell has the musical process of the song reflect the futility of their labour by using devices such as chromatic progression and close-harmony suspensions to convey amorous intensity, within a large-scale design which persistently negates all attempts to move away from the tightly circumscribed pitch area outlined at the beginning.

The duet's opening picks up the earlier E–A (b. 19 in Ex. 119); varied repetition produces an unstable F–B in the next bar. This F posits resolution on E, and although the register is regained by subsequent ascent, the E in b. 22 remains unstable because of the following leap. All this is reinforced by the alto's repetition of exactly the same pitches, though the phrase is extended in b. 29 to produce a comparatively stable scalic descent which resolves the E down to the lower register. This then is the nature of the process – to set up laboriously gained, ascending pitch progressions away from the tonic A, and then to cancel them by reasserting the original register comparatively quickly.

So 'Jointly labour' expands the register to include high G and an occasional

Ex. 119   Hail, Bright Cecilia, 'In Vain the Am'rous Flute' (Z. 328.10): bb. 1–30

Ex. 119 continues on facing page

A. It modifies the setting of 'am'rous' to suit 'labour', with suspensions and metrical irregularity in the upper parts. Such irregularity is used more intensely to set 'wanton', using material from the end of the flutes' prelude. The second half of the text contrasts the 'chaste airs' with those of the flute and guitar. So the song stabilises E as the alto goes to E minor, though A minor wins out (bb. 52–7) albeit with less emphatic effect, on the tenor's reply. The setting of 'Seraphic flames and heav'nly love', as much as any moment in the entire ode, shows that quiet mastery of text and music which gives Purcell his unparalleled reputation.

The ascent to A on 'flames' in bb. 57–8 is the first time that this pitch has been reached by scalic ascent, and is the first high A in a predominantly A minor context. It is thus the ultimate intensification of the former E/F pitch barrier. To some extent the rapturous quality is due to this and to the colour caused by using the descending form of the minor scale to ascend. Yet this also means that the A is unstable, a situation which is sealed by the tenor's entry a fifth lower, and the 4–3 in b. 81. So the A, like the F and E before it, is drawn down to the lower register.

The flutes' postlude reworks at the higher octave the material of the last line. But the cadential pitches of the prelude return, the high C in particular (b. 96), and this is intensified by going up even higher to E before closing down onto A. In the approach to the close, the D–E bass progression is also intensified, by a preceding C♯.

These languorous beauties are blasted away by the trumpets and drums of 'The Fife and All the Harmony of War' (Z. 328.11), yet another original exploitation of the harmonic limitations imposed by trumpets. Each of the three lines of text receives two or three statements, beginning with repetitions of single motifs and expanding to a complete phrase; most repetitions are varied in some way from the original. The second and most evident means of expansion is the trumpet passages. Peter Dennison has rightly described these as interjections, since for most of the piece they are insertions into a phrase structure generated by the voice alone – a purely musical depiction of war between instruments and vocal forces, brilliantly set up by the opening contest between trumpets and drums.[14]

The duet for two basses, 'Let These Among Themselves Contest' (Z. 328.12), is one of the finest of this type, which became something of a speciality in the odes. As in many of the earlier ones, a predominant driving force is the rhythmic energy of the two vocal parts against a slowly moving harmonic background. The two voices persistently 'contest' with one another, and to offset the restless motion, the main closes of this binary structure are particularly prominent:

i – V of i   : ‖ :   i – VII – III – i   : ‖

The text's mention of 'diff'ring graces' is an offering Purcell was hardly likely to refuse. Each voice goes its own way with ornamentations on middle C and the D above. These constantly rub against one another as the bass moves, in an imaginative elaboration of the 'third and fourth together, to introduce a Close', which Purcell enjoyed as a 'Discord used by the Italians'.[15]

In the printed source of the text the last verse is headed 'Grand Chorus', and grand Purcell's setting certainly is. The ABCA arrangement of the four sections covers, respectively, a declamatory chorus which ends with powerfully simple polyphony, an elaborate fugal section, a sensuous slow section for *aatb* soloists, and a repeat of the first chorus. Purcell wrote no other large ensemble piece which shows so concentrated a skill at using concerted instrumental forces, vocal scoring and timing of main events; and few pieces by him, maybe none at all, can match its combination of great surface diversity and pitch progressions which cross the span of the movement.

The massive breadth of the opening (Ex. 120) depends on manipulating text-derived rhythm across a large-scale pitch and harmonic progression. In each of the opening phrases, groups of instruments accumulate tension with imitative fanfare figures culminating on a 'Hail!' from the chorus. In the process they engage in motivic dislocations, as in bb. 6–7, where the bass imitates the trumpets' figuration just one crotchet later, and these drive towards and sometimes through the choral exclamations. The timing of the choral entries is crucial. The first three, on I, V and I respectively, articulate two-bar units. The next statement is at one bar, and the remaining three at one and a half bars.

These seven chords outline a circuit from I to V of I and a long-term D–C♯ pitch progression in the soprano. The enormous energy of bb. 12–14 is due partly to their metrical stability after the increasing instability of the approach, and partly to the clear presentation in the soprano of pitch progressions almost identical to those of the exclamations, but at a much faster and more regular speed. The bass too has a role, for its descending line is an augmented and varied version of the previously unstable instrumental motif.

The energy of this progression is appropriate to its function. It greatly

Ex. 120 Hail, *Bright Cecilia*, 'Grand Chorus' (Z. 328.13): bb. 1–25

Ex. 120 continues on next page

strengthens the A major harmony without tonicising it, and projects it with sufficient force to sustain an elaborate prolongation across the rest of the section.

In a small-scale reworking of the principles operating in the repetitions of 'Hail!', the repetitions on 'great' (bb. 15–16) give enormous impetus to the descending scale for 'Great Patroness'. The high As, which in the instruments have become increasingly prominent, now pass to the voices (b. 18) for an intensified and lengthened version of the descending scale, with E and C♯ especially prominent, so as to intensify the approach to D which has been projected ever since bb. 12–14 (cf. 'one perfect harmony' from 'Soul of the World').

The fugal section sets just two lines, presented as a double fugue with two expositions, separated by an orchestral passage (cf. 'Let Music Join in a Chorus Divine' from *Of Old, When Heroes Thought It Base* (Z. 333.12)). Both themes have close relationships with earlier material. 'Who whilst among the choir above' features the D–E–F♯–D shape prominent in the first section of the finale, while 'Thou dost thy former skill improve' – arguably the most extraordinary piece of self-conscious technical display in Purcell's output – reworks the second theme from the opening canzona, a relationship which becomes even more explicit in the instrumental ornamentations later in the section.

The section gradually accumulates density of texture and breadth of register through piling up entries on the two themes and bringing in the instruments gradually – trumpets do not enter until the instrumental interlude, for example. In the second vocal exposition the basses have the theme in double augmentation (quavers become minims), but with a result far superior to that produced by the same technique in *Of Old, When Heroes Thought It Base*, nearly two years earlier: not only is it textually apt in going further than the virtuosity of the first exposition, but the bass also outlines a more tonic-oriented reworking of the end of the first exposition, with the I⁶–IV–IV♮⁷–II–v(V) of bb. 32–5 becoming I⁶–IV–ii⁶–V (bb. 41–3), to create an impeccably focussed approach to the final close. Moreover, the registral span of this passage is wider – the voices go as high as G – and the trumpets gradually assume greater prominence to bring the whole to a massively dense conclusion.

In the third section, the tempo, the close harmony in B minor, and the parallel thirds, are a superb evocation of 'rapture' and 'infinite felicity'. Characteristically, it includes false relations and dissonances arising from independent part writing, often motivated by exact imitation, and in purposeful conflict with the harmonic circuit from vi to iii of D. After such chromatic intensity, the comparative harmonic stability of the first section brings the piece to an impressively solid conclusion.

Purcell's only ode after 1692 which can approach the consistently high quality of *Hail, Bright Cecilia* is his last for Queen Mary, *Come Ye Sons of Art* (Z. 323), though it does not equal the expressive scope of the greatest of all Cecilian odes. Perhaps this was inevitable, for the functions of the birthday ode meant that neither *Come Ye Sons of Art* nor the 1693 ode *Celebrate This Festival* (Z. 321) could engage in such high-flown musical display.

Then there are the fragments, possibly by Purcell, of *The Noise of Foreign Wars*,[16] and the lost New Year ode for 1693, *Light of the World* (Z. 330), of which the text alone has survived, though it has plausibly been suggested that the so-called *Sonata for Trumpet and Strings* (Z. 850) is the opening symphony.[17] If so, the rest of the ode remains a desideratum to tantalise musicological sleuths, for the sonata is a fine piece, and in his late years Purcell usually produced work of fairly consistent quality within a single ode.

This consistency extends even to the weakest of his late odes. *Great Parent, Hail* (Z. 327) was written for the centenary celebrations of Trinity College, Dublin, held on 9 January 1694. The symphony has a slow and a fast section, both with highly Italianate textures. Like the rest of the ode it is technically solid, but musical interest is unevenly sustained across the considerable length of Nahum Tate's text; and that length seems to be one of the piece's central problems, for it left Purcell little chance to engage in the large-scale numbers featuring extensive repetition, which were a hallmark of most of his big compositions at this time. Perhaps the most interesting items are the portentous bass solo with strings 'Awful Matron Take Thy Seat' and the soprano solo with flutes 'The Royal Patrons Sung' (Z. 327.5 and 9), the latter especially so for some elaborate vocal ornamentation.

For the opening symphony to *Celebrate This Festival* (Z. 321), Purcell reused the first two sections of the symphony to the 1692 St Cecilia ode, but transposed to C, doubtless to suit the range of the sopranos in the first vocal movement. This ode's expressive directness and simplicity of texture are deeply dependent on a range of repetition techniques unmatched in any other, but plainly linked to those seen in the music written for that year's production of *The Fairy Queen*.

The work sees the court ode's cumulative structural methods at their most subtle and elaborate. The first unit stretches just four lines of text across more than a hundred bars, with each line set to music consistently distinct in character and function (Fig. 11). Purcell neatly reverses the order of Nahum Tate's first two lines (as printed in the *Gentleman's Journal* for April 1692), in order to concentrate on celebration. The first four bars of A (Ex. 121) consist of a two-bar phrase of fanfare figures plus a varied repetition, all on tonic harmony; and the pitch apex of these bars – the dominant in b. 4 – is pivotal in many subsequent processes. In bb. 5–8, for example, the semiquaver repetitions on 'celebrate' descend from the dominant and this is spun out so that the opening four bars are answered by 4 + 4 bars.

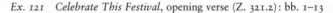

Ex. 121   Celebrate This Festival, opening verse (Z. 321.2): bb. 1–13

So, in A, pitch movement is all, for harmony simply switches between tonic and dominant. By contrast, B is more harmonically mobile, and is used to move from I to V as a local tonic. The scoring associations set up in these bars, with A on *ss* and B on *atb*, will become a primary generator of later developments.

Medium- and long-term repetitions tend to have differing functions, and these are evident in the various recurrences of A. After a close into the dominant at the end of B, the first four bars of A are repeated in that key, thus throwing its definitive properties into sharp relief, albeit in a developmental way. But Purcell now sets up a discourse between the two groups of soloists so that plain statements of A are driven by interjections of 'Hark' from B. After just nine bars the sopranos' strong close into G is destabilised by the continuo's descent through F♮, to set up a discourse between B and A in the tonic – a return to the home harmonic area, but without the stability which only a plain statement of A can give.

The forceful progress of this discourse leads to the first presentation of Tate's lines in their original order BA. This includes the first appearance of 'to', which is set as an upbeat to a two-bar, varied form of A (A^2 in Fig. 11). But any suggestion of closure at the end of this variant is weakened, partly by ending

Fig. 11. *Celebrate This Festival* (Z. 321): first unit

Hark, hark, the muses and the graces call   B
To celebrate this festival.   A
Britain now, thy cares beguile,   C
Bless the day that blest our isle.   D

Scoring:	VERSE				CHORUS WITH INSTRUMENTS†	VERSE			OBOES CONTINUO	CHORUS WITH INSTRUMENTS†
	ss	*atb*	*ssatb*	*atb*	*SATB*	*ss*			*SATB*	*SATB*
Text and music:	A	B	A+B	B+A	B	A²	A	C	D	C	A	A
Number of bars:	12	10	9	5	2	12	2*+12	10	12	12	12
Harmonies:	I–I	I–V	V–V	I		I–I	vi			vi	I–I	I–I

$$\text{i–v–i}\quad \text{i–III–V of i}\quad \text{i–v–i}$$

†strings, oboes and trumpets   *continuo introduction

with the mediant uppermost, and, rather more subtly, by the setting for *atb*, instead of either the fuller scoring, or *ss*, which precedent might suggest.

The presentation by chorus with instruments, including oboes and trumpets, achieves closure by returning to A in its original form, and by reinforcing its properties through sheer weight of numbers. The restatement of A after the duet (C and D) does essentially the same thing, though this time the return of the chorus is set up by a presentation on oboes.

This inherently dramatic use of resources can be seen in a number of other movements. The short soprano solo with trumpet sets just one line, ''Tis sacred, bid the trumpet cease': the soprano keeps singing 'bid the trumpet cease', but the trumpet insists on continuing to enter. Eventually the chorus casts off the trumpet's flight and adapts the text to order it – 'Cease, trumpet, cease'. In the alto solo 'Return, Fond Muse' (Z. 321.13) the viola acts as a high bass line for two flutes. The vocal phrases are unaccompanied except for the continuo, and the entire song consists of alternations between these two groupings, which come together only at the final close.

There are many other notable movements, such as the soprano solo 'Crown the Altar' (Z. 321.7), a ground bass which ends with a repetition of the opening section. The bass solo 'Expected Spring' (Z. 321.8) has a dance-like vocal line, and ends with a chorus which overlaps its regular periodicity with elaborate imitative roulades in voices and instruments. The extraordinary eight-part chorus 'Repeat Maria's Name' (Z. 321.13c), does just that, with many repetitions of 'repeat', over a seven-bar dominant pedal.

Celebrate This Festival is an undeservedly neglected piece. In complete contrast, Queen Mary's last birthday ode, *Come Ye Sons of Art* (Z. 323), is one of Purcell's best known works, a fame which rests partly on its consistently high quality and also on the more modest forces required; in particular it has no elaborate trumpet obbligato, and requires just four soloists and four-part choir. The symphony is one of the most remarkable of Purcell's late instrumental pieces, the second section being in canzona style, and outdoing even that from *Hail, Bright Cecilia* in being based on three simultaneously presented subjects. The text also apes the style of *Hail, Bright Cecilia*, its references to musical instruments producing imaginative responses from the composer which, while they might not have the extraordinary subtlety of the earlier piece, have a straightforward brilliance and communication entirely appropriate to the court ode's function.

The repetition of the opening verse, sandwiching the alto duet 'Sound the Trumpet' (Z. 323.3), is a simpler application of the structural techniques seen in *Celebrate This Festival*. The robust energy of the melody readily withstands these repetitions, especially because of imaginative contrasts between instrumental and vocal groupings. In most other respects though, this ode marks

Ex. 122   Come Ye Sons of Art, 'Sound the Trumpet' (Z. 323.3): bb. 20–8

a move towards the 'separate number' methods which were already pre-dominant in the non-court odes of the previous four years or so.

Most of the movements use techniques developed primarily in stage music. In 'These Are the Sacred Charms' (Z. 323.8), for example, the text says how Mary's 'darling hero' William is protected on the field of battle. Rather than concentrating on the love of the royal couple, Purcell chooses the imagery of battle, realised in energetic contention between the metrically irregular ground bass and the bass soloist. Packed with imagery of a much more subtle kind is the soprano solo with oboe obbligato, 'Bid the Virtues' (Z. 323.7), which picks up the text's mention of 'graces' to produce elaborate ornamentation, with voice and oboe sharing as equals.

'Sound the Trumpet' (Z. 323.3) is Purcell's last shot in this genre at the running-quaver style of ground bass which had been a feature of almost every ode since the early 1680s. It is by far his most concentrated piece of this kind, a virtuoso combination of strong periodicity, motivic concentration and repetition – qualities underlined by each half of the binary structure being repeated. The opening vocal figuration uses a characteristic trumpet-style gesture almost as common as the arpeggaic fanfare – the long note on the dominant followed by descent – and turns it into one of the piece's primary generative elements. This opening phrase, setting 'Sound the trumpet', ends with a stress on the mediant F♯ rather than the tonic, and the second, setting the complete line 'Sound the trumpet 'til around', closes on the E below that. The second line, 'You make the list'ning shores rebound', re-emphasises the high register until this first half closes by passing through the E to a full close on D. No less important for generation is the vocal imitation in close harmony, as first one voice and then the other takes the lead, but with the temporal intervals constantly changing.

The bass, with its repeated high Ds, rhythmic constancy and forceful two-bar phrasing, is transposed but otherwise unchanged beyond the addition of a half bar or so to move from one harmonic area to the other, and the first half of the song is in D throughout. Moreover, while the vocal phrasing frequently crosses that of the ground, there are enough coincident closes for the succession of ground statements to be much more strongly marked than in most of Purcell's strict ground bass pieces; consequently the added bars also stand out.

This all seems calculated to underline the large-scale harmonic progressions produced by the transposed statements. So instead of a steady progress around the harmonic area, as in 'Music for a While' (Z. 583.2) for example, we have a series of quasi-propositional statements in I, V and vi, plus a return to I. These boundaries are further marked by each statement's coinciding with a move to a new line of text.

The dividing line between phrase elision and articulation is especially fine at the moves to vi and back to I. The former follows the close into V after the two ground statements in that key which open the second half. The bass figure a (Ex. 122) could readily lead back to D and the opening figure for 'All the instruments of joy' would work over that form of the ground; but another half bar link is added to produce a palpable drop into vi. The close into that key then uses b, a variant of a, while the B in the upper voice carries over into the D major statement, thus eliding the pitch progression across two harmonic areas for the first time and stressing 'celebrate', the quintessence of the song and the ode.

After all this, the last of Purcell's surviving odes comes as something of a disappointment. *Who Can from Joy Refrain?* (Z. 342) was composed for the sixth birthday of the heir to the throne, the Duke of Gloucester, on 24 July 1695.[18] Stylistically it is in line with other music from this last year of Purcell's life – the huge opening solo, for example, with its widely separated restatements of material in tonic and dominant, is comparable to 'Wake, Quevira' from *The Indian Queen* (Z. 630.4b). But this and all other movements lack that flair in the application of ideas which distinguishes Purcell's better music, though the choral outbursts on 'Wondrous day' in the first movement are dramatic enough. The opening symphony is the same one as for *Timon of Athens* (Z. 632), though transposed to C.

As Westrup has pointed out, the massive concluding chaconne 'If Now He Burns' (Z. 342.7 and 8) is the most interesting movement.[19] Approaching the scale of *King Arthur*'s 'How Happy the Lover' (Z. 628.30), it features solos for trumpet, oboes and different vocal combinations. Its phrase structure is just a little too four-square, but it skilfully deploys its forces to accumulate energy and, in its use of interludes contrasting with plain statements of the ground, is rather more typical of many French chaconnes than most of Purcell's efforts. Other notable items include the duet 'For Though the Sun' (Z. 342.2e) and the bass solo 'The Father Brave' (Z. 342.4), both of which, along with a couple of other pieces, were published in *Orpheus britannicus*.

CHAPTER THIRTEEN

Background and beginnings: dramatic music to 1689

PURCELL'S STAGE MUSIC has attracted more interest and controversy than any other area of his output. Most writers have concentrated on the large works, on *Dido and Aeneas* (Z. 626), *Dioclesian* (Z. 627), *King Arthur* (Z. 628), *The Fairy Queen* (Z. 629), *The Indian Queen* (Z. 630) and the spurious music for *The Tempest* (Z. 631). Although many have therefore ignored much of the dramatic music, it is indeed these large works which tend to raise the more fundamental issues surrounding our understanding of Purcell's compositional development and of English music for the seventeenth-century stage.

Until the mid 1960s many, perhaps most, Purcell scholars tended to view his dramatic music in the light of continental opera, and to see it as the most important contribution to a generic progress from single songs and masque-influenced scenes, through the imperfect conventions of 'dramatic opera' (as *King Arthur* was called), towards an English version of Italian opera in which, at the very least, the principal characters would sing and the larger part of the drama would be carried by music; this progress was cut short by the death of Purcell and by the subsequent influx of Italian opera.[1]

Within the last thirty years, several studies of Purcell's dramatic music have led to important reassessments of the chronology and authenticity of some works, while others have concentrated on developing a sound critical basis for reassessing the relationship between music and drama.[2] These studies have shown that the older view is fundamentally flawed. Firstly, it assesses the relationship between music and drama by holding, as cynosure, concepts incompatible with those which motivated English seventeenth-century playwrights and composers. Secondly, it tends to underestimate the influence of French opera on seventeenth-century English stage music. Thirdly, in order to do justice to the self-evident dramatic brilliance of Purcell's music, one is forced to minimise those musico-dramatic points which, by one's own definition, are the stage works' most serious flaws. Finally, this view no longer matches the musicological evidence: in particular, the culminating point of its gradualism, namely the music for *The Tempest*, is now known to be almost certainly not by Purcell.[3]

Moreover, in terms of both dramatic practice and musical models, the older view ignores the effects on stage music of the seventeenth- and eighteenth-century controversies surrounding the roles of music in Classical Greek tragedy. These controversies, so arcane to modern readers, were central to theorising dramatists of that time, whose varying views helped produce a wide range of interpretations across Europe. The early Italian pioneers for example believed the whole drama was sung, whereas in England, as well as France, many held it was the choruses only. As Richard Luckett has said, clear statement of the real issues has not been helped, then or now, by the partisan standpoints adopted by the protagonists.[4]

So keen are modern scholars to make up for this long-standing imbalance, that there is now some danger of bending over backwards in the opposite direction; of failing to engage in critical appraisal of the concepts underlying some of the plays and dramatic operas for which Purcell provided music.[5] The following chapters engage these controversies, though their primary concern is with Purcell's compositional responses to the texts he had before him and with how his musico-dramatic concepts developed. They contend that, whatever the conventions of the late-seventeenth-century English stage, Purcell had a natural interest in a close relationship between drama and music; that where possible he sought to parallel dramatic development and musical development; and that he tended to do this with various adaptations of that musically organic thinking which had informed his earliest music.

* * * *

The earliest firm evidence of Purcell writing music for the stage is associated with Nathaniel Lee's *Theodosius* (Z. 606), which dates from early 1680. Purcell provided music in this play for several strophic songs and for a ritual scene in which some of the secondary characters have singing parts. By far the most popular song was 'Hail to the Myrtle Shade' (Z. 606.8), which went through a number of editions and, as late as 1774, was reused as a vehicle for political skits.[6]

Other strophic songs make an interesting comparison with Purcell's contemporary, independent ones. The soprano solo 'Sad as Death' (Z. 606.6a) avoids altogether the lumpy, inelegant line which affected so many independent songs in quadruple or duple time. Its expressive melodiousness in many ways

anticipates the methods of much later songs and shows a strong grip on voice-
leading. In the last line, for example (Ex. 123), the scales of the penultimate bar

Ex. 123   Theodosius, 'Sad as Death' (Z. 606.6a): bb. 13–17

iron out the tensions of the preceding bars, these being generated out of the
A–F♯ of b. 13 and the implied resolution to G.

The way in which Purcell dealt with the text of the ritual scene, in which the
royal maidens, Marina and Favilla, are inducted into a convent, shows that,
even in his early twenties, he had a sense for an intimate relationship between
musical and dramatic progress. Lee gave each woman three four-line strophes,
in which they express their differing responses to their prospective fate. Purcell
eschews the obvious approach, of repeating a short strophic setting, in favour of
rolling the verses together so that each character's lines come out as a single
thought, and he aptly sets Favilla's lines as a variation of Marina's. Marina's
three verses, beginning with 'The Gate to Bliss' (Z. 606.3a), feature prominent
false relations between F and the F♯ leading note, all superbly harnessed to
textual accentuation and apt for her inner struggles; Favilla's first two verses
subtly shorten Marina's vocal line, with most of the false relations ironed out in
keeping with her less tortured response, while her last verse, 'Haste then, O
haste! and take us in' is set as a triple-time duet, representing resolution of the
women's inner struggles.[7]

Most famous of the music for *Theodosius* is the bass solo and chorus 'Hark,
Behold the Heavenly Quire' (Z. 606.4). The flutes which accompany Atticus
throughout have already been heard, in the solo (also for Atticus) and trio
'Prepare, Prepare' (Z. 606.1) at the beginning of the scene, and now return, after
the women's minds are resolved; so that they not only represent the angelic
choir, but also bring the rites full circle. The flutes and continuo play a twenty-
two-bar, binary piece; Atticus responds with a repeated 'Hark!' before moving
into a syllabic setting of 'Hark, Behold the Heavenly Quire' (Z. 606.4), singing
the bass line of the prelude. Compared with the best of Purcell's contemporary
sacred and instrumental music, this is all rather stiff, albeit appropriate for its
purpose.

Eight years were to pass before Purcell made another contribution to stage
music as large as that to *Theodosius*. In the meantime, later in 1680, he wrote

'Retir'd from Any Mortal's Sight' (Z. 581) for Nahum Tate's adaptation of Shakespeare, *King Richard II*, a song remarkable for applying recitative style to a strophic setting. Then in 1681, for Thomas D'Urfey's *Sir Barnaby Whigg*, he wrote 'Blow, Boreas, Blow' (Z. 589), which anticipates many methods of the mad songs and the recitative songs written around 1683, while some of its details were to be reworked some thirteen years later in 'Let the Dreadful Engines' from *Don Quixote* (Z. 578.3). Apart from a few more single songs for plays, there is no more stage music after 'Blow, Boreas, Blow' until the several songs written for Thomas D'Urfey's *A Fool's Preferment* (Z. 571) of 1688, a paucity which almost certainly had far more to do with theatre politics than with Purcell's compositional skills.[8]

None of the eight songs which Purcell contributed to D'Urfey's play (April 1688) approaches the expressive profundity of many later pieces. But the group is nevertheless a landmark in his development as a dramatic composer, not least because of its range of stylistic types. Such variety was partly a product of convenience, for the tension between singing actors and acting singers was at least as strong then as it is today. Present vagueness over exactly how many songs were performed in the first production has arisen perhaps because of changes Purcell had to make when he misjudged the skills of the people he was working with.[9]

The delightful dialogue 'Jenny, 'gin You Can Love' (Z. 571.7) is in the style of popular song or dance, and could have been sung by anyone who could make a pleasing sound. Yet the treatment is full of art: the quasi-canonic imitation in the bass overlaps the phrasing of the voice, in bb. 3–4 for example (Ex. 124); the

Ex. 124 *A Fool's Preferment*, A Dialogue by Jockey and Jenny (Z. 571.7): bb. 1–4

D against E of b. 3 shows a thoroughly polyphonic approach even to the regular phrasing and motivic repetitions of this melody. Such songs were to become increasingly common in Purcell's output, most often as some sort of pastoral dialogue.

This play includes 'I'll Sail upon the Dog Star' (Z. 571.6) which, perhaps because of its Italianate idiom, became one of the most popular of all Purcell's songs, being published as late as 1745 and 1805.[10] As in his most successful Italianate instrumental music, local repetition techniques are often disguised. So imitation of the continuo's 'motto' opening (Ex. 125 (i)) is exact at first, but

Ex. 125   A Fool's Preferment, 'I'll Sail upon the Dog Star' (Z. 571.6):

(i) bb. 1–8

(ii) continuo, bb. 8–12

thereafter is always altered in some way. The varied repetitions preserve enough for motifs *a* and *b* to remain readily identifiable, but generate an increasing tension as motifs overlap between voice and continuo and within the continuo itself (bb. 4–5), and as the voice progressively lengthens phrases while the continuo tends to shorten them.

The text's 'wild galactic imagery',[11] is superbly evoked by this knotty contrapuntal dialogue, epitomised in 'I'll climb the lofty mountain', where the voice's scalic ascent is imitated by inversion in the bass, with results far more subtle than an ascent in both parts. The end of each phrase in this treatment is marked by varied statements of the affirmative bass figure *c* (bb. 7, 12, 16, 22, 26 and 32), and the song's motivic concentration is epitomised in the second phrase, where the turn figure for 'chase' is imitated in the bass and repeated to articulate a move towards G major (Ex. 125 (ii)).

The compression and racy flair seen in this song were put to even better use the following year in *Dido and Aeneas* (Z. 626), Purcell's only true opera, and a remarkable conflation of precedents not necessarily associated with the stage. More has been written on it than on the rest of the dramatic music put together,[12] and for a number of reasons: it is readily performable with limited resources; it conforms to most popular images of opera and is therefore more easily understood by a twentieth-century audience than Purcell's other large stage works; it presents plenty of intriguing puzzles for the producer; and it is, above all, an outstanding piece of musical drama.

The opera has also proved an invigorating stamping ground for academic controversy. The sources of the work and their completeness or incompleteness, its allegorical nature, the quality of Nahum Tate's libretto, what types of singer took part in the first performance, why it was never performed in a public theatre during Purcell's lifetime, the dates of the first performance and of composition – all these and other subjects have produced lively and sometimes barbed comment.

While it is possible that some work on the music and text could date back to c. 1687, the evidence tends to favour 1689 as a date for both the composition and the first performance, with the latter probably occurring around April.[13] From this performance, which took place at the school for 'Gentlewomen' in Chelsea run by the dancing master Josias Priest, just one document, a printed copy of the libretto, survives. There is no evidence that during Purcell's lifetime Dido and Aeneas was ever performed in a public theatre, and when it did reappear, in 1700, it was in a much altered and dismembered form, as a series of masques inserted into Shakespeare's Measure for Measure, which was itself much changed. It was altered yet again to appear as a musical addition to the plays The Anatomist and The Man of Mode in 1704, and it was probably for one or more of these three productions that most of those changes from the original were made which survive to bedevil modern attempts to reconstruct the 1689 score.[14]

The full score nearest to Purcell's original seems to be the so-called 'Tenbury' manuscript, which was copied not earlier than 1748, but is almost certainly based on a manuscript from the first decade of the century, perhaps one of those used for the adaptations just referred to. The differences between 'Tenbury' and the original libretto are considerable, for it seems likely that Purcell set the libretto's long Prologue, for which no music survives, while within the three surviving acts, the music for the end of Act II and, possibly, several dances is missing; moreover, within the three acts there are discrepancies of detail.

It is more than likely that Purcell himself was responsible for some of the changes in Tate's directions, for many of them seem designed to tighten musico-dramatic relationships and to clarify the recurrent structural patterns so prominent throughout the opera; composers of opera have always engaged in such tinkering. While each scene of Dido and Aeneas has a distinctive emphasis, the principle behind the patterns is simple enough – a series of recitatives, airs and ensembles culminates in a large chorus, which is followed by a dance reflecting the predominant tone of the scene.[15]

Some of the dances may have been lost in the later adaptations, but it is equally likely that Purcell sacrificed some in the interests of structural and dramatic clarity. There are, for example, three possible explanations for the apparent absence of 'A Dance Gittars Chacony', indicated by the 1689 libretto after Belinda's air 'Pursue Thy Conquest, Love' (Z. 626.11): either it is lost, or Purcell never wrote it, or the direction is wrongly printed in the libretto. The first is possible, as is the second (Harris suggests that the dance might have been improvised);[16] but the air connects so neatly into the following chorus 'To the Hills and the Vales' (Z. 626.12), and the chorus is such an effective group-response to Belinda's urgings, that the music seems complete as it stands. In this rather carelessly printed libretto[17] the third explanation is by no means a remote possibility. But although the chorus is not a chaconne, 'The Triumphing Dance' (Z. 626.13) which ends the scene is a triple-time, medium-paced dance on a ground; so one can reasonably conjecture that instead of providing two dances, Purcell conflated them, and for 'The Triumphing Dance' used a chaconne-like dance such as was common in such celebratory contexts, and as he had already done in the 1687 ode *Sound the Trumpet* (Z. 335).

More specific evidence of Purcell's approach to the libretto lies in some changes he made in the opera's early stages, where the text is printed as follows:

BELINDA: Fear no danger to ensue,
2 WOMEN: The hero loves as well as you.
CHORUS: Ever gentle, ever smiling,
                   And the cares of life beguiling.
                   Cupids strew your path with flowers,
                   Gathered from Elizian bowers.

This comes at the end of a scene which, by the sheer speed of events, places exceptional demands on the audience's capacity to absorb both the facts of the plot and the expressive tone being set by the music. With impeccable timing, Purcell turns to C major from the C minor which had dominated the scene, freezes the action, and firstly sets all six lines as a duet for Belinda and the Second Woman ('2 Women' is almost certainly a misprint), using the first two lines as the refrain in a rondeau structure; secondly the whole is repeated by the chorus which, as the libretto specifies, can be danced. The result is long enough to allow us to absorb the import of what has gone before, and in its encouraging tone looks forward to the seeming confidence of the later parts of the scene.[18]

One of the most remarkable features of *Dido and Aeneas* is the extent to which a tightly wrought musical organicism reflects the detailed tensions and resolutions of the drama. To some extent this is helped along by associations between specific expressive concepts and types of musical progression, the most obvious example being the so-called 'grief' motif.[19] Then there is the use of key, especially changes of mode, within and between scenes. In the first scene, for example, Aeneas' appearance coincides with a strong move into G major after the C major jollity of 'Fear No Danger'. As he and Dido converse E minor becomes prominent, its darker colouring appropriate to the irony of a situation in which, while Aeneas resolves to defy 'The feeble stoke of destiny', we know that it is his and Dido's situation which is the weaker. The E minor chorus 'Cupid Only Throws the Dart' (Z. 626.9) is not as dainty as one might expect, featuring as it does a commonplace motif thrown around the texture in exact imitation, with results as barbed and disturbing as the seemingly innocent Cupid's arrows. Another short recitative moves back to G, but without dispelling the darkly ironic atmosphere, which is only veneered over by the turn to C major for Belinda's air, the chorus and the dance.[20]

Such neat associations are considerably surpassed in subtlety by the next scene. Like Dido and her court, the Sorceress and her Witches begin in the minor mode and end in the major, in this case F. But the moves away from F, and even the major-minor juxtapositions, have an aspect much more capricious than those of the first scene, entirely appropriate to the manic appearance of the Witches' behaviour but, like the Witches themselves, with a purposeful background.[21]

The brooding momentum of the string prelude in F minor sets the scene superbly, its expansiveness due to a combination of broad harmonic control and a single elaborated descent from high F, which covers no less than sixteen bars (Ex. 126); after this, the Sorceress' music seems an extension of the prelude, being an inverted paraphrase of this registral move. As the Witches appear in response to her summons, the harmony changes to B♮ – perfect in this context for the macabre jollity of the 'Harm's Our Delight' chorus. They are, of course, at one with the Sorceress' aims, so the chorus returns to F, via a D–E♮–F ascent articulated by repetition of the 'Harm's our delight' phrase.

The Sorceress can now readily enter in the original F minor, to the strains of some of the most remarkable accompanimental work in Baroque opera. As she sings 'hate' over yet another F pedal, violin II and viola ornament the fundamental $^{5}_{♮3}$–$^{♭6}_{♭4}$–$^{5}_{♮3}$ over F by moving out of phase and driving a stressed A♮ against violin II's D♭. Then there is the first violins' delicious semitonal drop from D to D♭ on 'sunset', reinforced by the violas' step up F–G, the potency of which is set up by the preceding close ending on B♭ major instead of minor, to express 'prosperous state'.

This time, the move from minor to major goes to C, as the Sorceress declares that Dido will be 'Deprived of fame, of life and love'. The exultant tone of her fanfare figures, in one of the 'trumpet' keys, continues through the first 'Ho, ho' chorus, which underlines its continuity of purpose by prolonging C major: although it touches on F and even B♭, its ending on C is very much as V of F.

The major mode has now become associated with the Witches themselves and, more particularly, with their impending triumph. It therefore continues

Ex. 126 *Dido and Aeneas* (Z. 626): Act II, Scene I

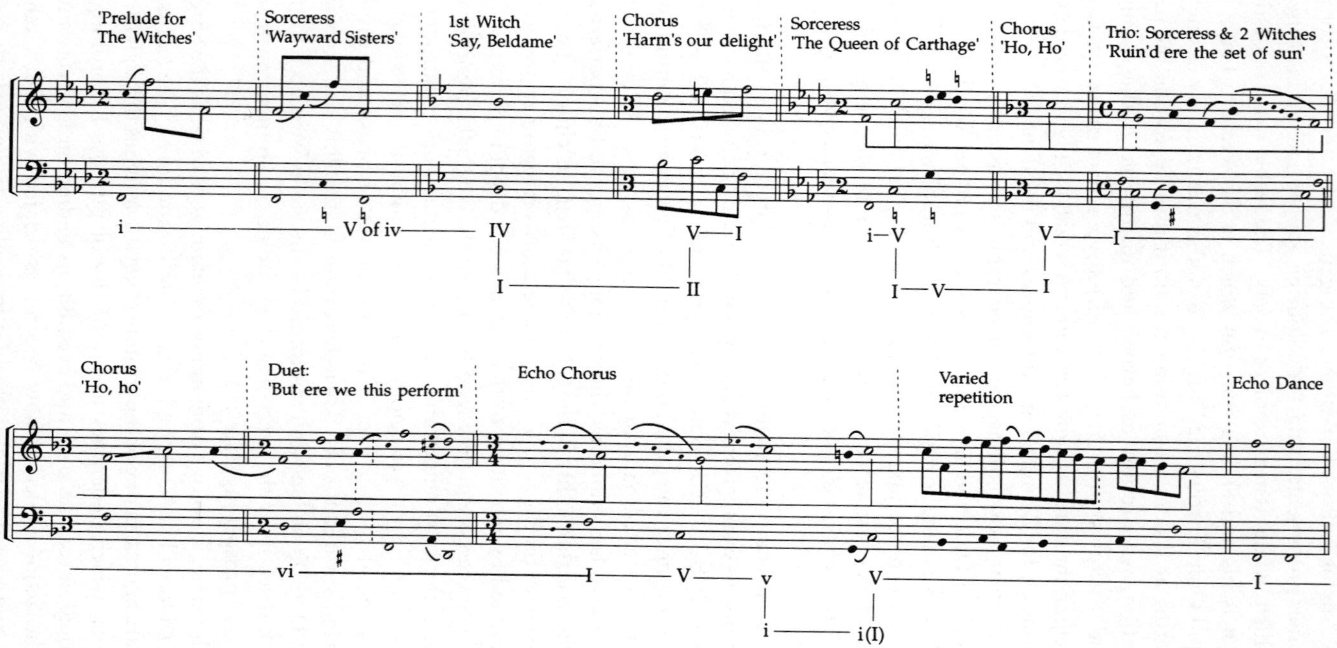

into 'Ruin'd ere the set of sun' until, in a suavely menacing move to G minor, we hear what will happen to Aeneas, a passage which includes the brilliantly timed musical hiatus on 'Hark' which has attracted much comment.[22]

Thus far all sections of this scene have been open-ended. But now the Sorceress concludes her account of Dido's and Aeneas' fates with 'And charge him sail tonight with all his fleet away', set to an ornamented yet remorseless cadential descent from high E♭ to F. The second 'Ho, ho' chorus prolongs this closing tonic, but its rhythmic energy and its conclusion with A uppermost demand something further to draw to a close the range of contrasts put forward thus far. This A resolves as V of D minor for the rollicking duet 'But Ere We This Perform' (Z. 626.20), a surprise move to be sure, but also a brilliantly judged side-step which plays a central role in producing a satisfactory finish to the scene.

In the duet, either low or high D can function as the main closural pitch, with the high remaining marginally less stable. The second half of the duet is strongly oriented towards F, and reaches D minor only in the last four bars, and then it is on the high D. All this, plus the energetic motion right up to the final downbeat renders the duet open-ended, with its local harmonic and pitch tensions resolved onto A at the end of the first phrase in the following 'Echo Chorus'.

This A is the same one which ended the previous 'Ho, ho' chorus, and the approach to it is a reworking of the prototype descending scale from D which ended both the Sorceress' last recitative and the 'Ho, ho' chorus (cf. also 'to the musical groves' from 'To the Hills and the Vales'). The chorus completes resolution to F via two main types of variation on this progression – scalic fillings-out of a fourth or fifth (e.g. 'the charm we'll prepare') and arpeggaic variations on this (e.g. the second statement of 'In our deep vaulted cell').

The echoes are additions to the basic two-bar units précised in Ex. 127, and become increasingly prominent and irregular in length: at '3' for example, they greatly prolong the inflexion to the minor mode. It is the echoes themselves which give the piece its extraordinary character as they distort this fundamental structure and importunately turn an inflexion into the central feature of the piece, while their repetitions underline the grotesque subtlety of the Witches' turns to the minor mode of the dominant.

As a means of balancing the obviously sinister aspect of the chorus' first half, the second half's diatonic lucidity and straightforward F major orientation, impart a darkly ironic atmosphere much more effective than any intensification of the preceding perturbations could have been. To articulate the local and long-term functions of the chorus' ending, it finishes with an impeccably diatonic scale descending from the high D of the duet, through the A which resolved it, to the first stable low F since the beginning of the scene.

Ex. 127   *Dido and Aeneas*, Echo Chorus (Z. 626.21): main material for first half

Completion of the musical process seals the dramatic argument – the Witches' triumph is now inevitable, and this prospect needs now only to be celebrated in dance. The 'Echo Dance of Furies', as it is called in 'Tenbury', consolidates this harmonic and pitch stability by being firmly in and around F. Its distorted echoes, inspired by the chorus' own methods, have been much commented on, and work as well as they do in this context largely because of the contextual stability.[23]

For musico-dramatic consistency the Witches' scene is matched only by the opera's conclusion, from Dido's entry on 'Your counsel all is urg'd in vain' (Z. 626.35a). Here the libretto's rapid pacing of drama and emotional contrast would be a serious challenge to the talents of any composer. Purcell's setting is unmatched in English music for its consistent equivalence of musical gesture and dramatic implication, which provides a thread running through the wide range of surface variety. Thus Purcell conveys in rapid sequence Dido's fatalism, Belinda's loving hope, Aeneas' weak protests, and the chorus' commentary, at once detached yet intimately observant.

This scene in particular embodies the essence of tragedy: the outcome is known from the beginning; it is the responses of individuals before powers greater than they which command our interest and, ultimately, our compassion. The dominant fatalism is embodied in the recurrence of G minor at crucial points, articulated within the scene by strong closes with G uppermost, but subtly anticipated by the last section of the frenetic 'Witches' Dance', immediately before Dido's entry.

This dance is in three short, contrasted sections, the first two of which are in B♭. The second, in triple time, ends with a half-close in that key, and leads directly into a sudden outburst on V of G minor, in ¢ time and with a strong metrical dislocation which is not resolved for fully six bars, by which time G minor is clearly on top. Indeed, B♮ is regained only in the last four bars of the dance, so that harmonic primacy at the close is, to say the least, ambiguous; and when Dido enters it is in G minor, a colouring which goes right back to her fatalistic minor-mode singing in the first scene, and which articulates yet another link between her and the Witches, as inverse images of one another.[24]

The two most prominent pitches in Dido's part are low G and the D above it (Ex. 128). The apparent naturalness of the D–G repetitions on 'earth and

Ex. 128   *Dido and Aeneas*: Dido's final entry (Z. 626.35a)

heaven' hides the audacity of Purcell's methods, for the harmonic context of each is different and they establish the connection of D, both as a pitch and harmonic centre, with those aspects of Dido's character which are at once imperious and defiant, yet noble. It reappears in her and Aeneas' three statements of 'by all that's good' and, more intensely, in her lines 'Thus on the fatal banks of Nile, / Weeps the deceitful crocodile', in 'I'm now resolved as well as you', and in 'That you had once a thought of leaving me'. Finally it comes, with exquisite pathos, in the repeated 'remember me' of the lament. And while these aspects are noble, they also contribute to her downfall; so the tensions emanating from the D keep being pulled back to their fatal conclusion, musically embodied in the constant gravitation to G minor, and to the G above middle C in particular.

Purcell certainly does not miss a trick. At every principal statement concerning Aeneas' departure and Dido's downfall there is a G minor close with G uppermost; usually D is closely involved in the approach. The relative strengths of these closes are impeccably judged. Dido's first close on G minor separates the first four lines from those that follow, emphasising what is more or less the opera's central issue – 'Earth and Heav'n conspire my fall'. The harmonic change from G minor for 'To fate I sue' reflects Dido's turning in desperation, while the descent of her vocal line to low D matches the depths of her determined despair. The bright turn to B♭ for Belinda's lovingly hopeful interjection 'See, madam, see where the prince appears' ends no less inevitably, implying G minor. The immediate move to D minor for Aeneas' entry on 'What shall lost Aeneas do?' ends in G minor on 'we must part'. The chorus 'Great minds' begins in B♭ with D uppermost, and elaborates a descent to the same G minor harmony with the tonic uppermost, fatalistically underlining that 'Great minds ... shun the cure they most desire.'

This veering from major to minor mode – a reversal of the pattern which dominated the earlier acts – underlies many of the strongest musical tensions in the section: thus Dido's 'I'm now resolved as well as you' is in the dominant, inflected to the major mode and neatly embodying the peak of her headstrong stubbornness. Minor mode colouration returns on 'slighted flame', and the strongest G minor close since 'conspire my fall' brings this part of the dialogue to a close.

Aeneas' exit is one of the opera's main dramatic boundaries, and Purcell's music articulates it as such. For the first time an extended dialogue begins and ends in G minor – the course of events is already determined. Its ferocious pace as it touches on other keys and Dido and Aeneas rail at each other, does not change the inexorable progress of the story, and the end of argument is marked by both characters singing together after the long period of separate lines.

After Aeneas' departure G minor is pervasive; but even so there is a constant, inexorable descent to Dido's death. She sets it up herself in a setting of 'But Death, alas! I cannot shun' which recalls the descent to D minor heard earlier in 'To fate I sue', but now pressed on to low B♭ in the continuo as a preparation for the chorus 'Great minds' and by the chorus' continuation to and conclusion in G minor. The descent now passes into the continuo's scale from G down to C and then into Dido's own line, an exquisitely elaborated, chromatic descent from C to low D for 'Thy hand, Belinda'.

With the beginning of the lament, the personal conflicts of the tragedy are complete, and this is represented musically by passing the descending line to the instruments – to the chromatic ground – and by having the voice rework the D–G connection in a form almost entirely scalic, and purged of former tensions. The pitch emphases which encompassed the agitations of the earlier recitative are transmuted into an eloquent personal statement of sorrow and regret. The vocal part of the lament has phrasing much larger than that set out by the ground. Basically it consists of a double arch, the concluding octave descent of which is reworked in the orchestral ritornello. Its expansiveness gives time for contemplation on the dramatic events, and provides their musical consummation by combining the G–G descent with the chromaticism of the ground. The final chorus reworks the concept of descent, both local and long-term, but now purged of chromaticism. It is an elaborate binary structure, the first part suggesting moves to other keys, but always gravitating back to G minor, and ending with the half close at 'on her tomb'. Here the sopranos' descent has reached A. The second half reworks the first's harmonic structure, but now emphasising with full and half closes what were passing keys, and thereby articulating the long-term cadential descent to G much more strongly (Fig. 12).

Fig. 12. Dido and Aeneas: second half of final chorus

$$v - (\tfrac{1}{2} \text{ in III}) - \text{III} - (\tfrac{1}{2} \text{ in i}) - i$$

Upper pitch: D   C   B♮   A   G

The instrumental music in *Dido and Aeneas* is amongst the composer's finest to date and is his first large-scale use of that increasing skill at instrumental characterisation which was developing with his expanding stylistic range. But perhaps more remarkable still is the range of types used in the vocal music. The pace of the action and the consequent need for brevity fitted perfectly with Purcell's practice in the late 1680s, particularly with his comparatively recent development of non-doctrinaire, concentrated repetition techniques, as in 'I'll Sail upon the Dog Star' from *A Fool's Preferment* (Z. 571.6) and in *Sylvia, Now Your Scorn Give Over* (Z. 420).

So, 'Pursue Thy Conquest, Love' (Z. 626.11) is a miniature da capo aria, superbly realised out of just two lines of Tate's libretto, which respectively urge pursuit and declare that Dido's eyes 'confess'd the flame her tongue denies'. The continuo and vocal lines imitate closely throughout, in a neat representation of pursuit, and the move to the dominant for the second line is a musical assertion to support that of the text.

The three great ground bass arias, one in each act, have provoked more comment than any other pieces in the opera. As Westrup has said, Dido's lament is 'one of the great things in music',[25] but the technical resourcefulness of 'Ah! Belinda' and 'Oft She Visits' (Z. 626.3 and 25) is scarcely less astonishing. In the former, the switch from C minor to G minor at 'I languish' shows just how far

Purcell had come in using transposed versions of the ground for expressive effect, while the return to C minor, with its sudden introduction of A♮ – also on 'I languish' – into a vocal line which had been firmly in G minor, is arguably his most expressively cogent use of the technique of overlapping the phrasing of the ground and the vocal line.

In many respects *Dido and Aeneas* is the most complex yet most consistent manifestation of large-scale organicism in Purcell's output. The organicism holds together the pace of action and provides the long-range musical background partly responsible for what Westrup has termed a triumph over weakness.[26] The most obvious weakness, mentioned by almost every commentator, is the underdeveloped character of Aeneas: at his limp response 'Tonight?' to the Spirit's deceitful message, even Purcell cannot dispel the bathos. Nevertheless, *Dido and Aeneas* does much more than just carry the main drama along on music. The music itself is part of the drama, as it penetrates aspects of action, interaction and character not immediately evident in the text.

Whatever the splendours of his later music for the stage, it is regrettable that Purcell never again composed a true opera. Nevertheless, he did not turn his back on the musico-dramatic principles epitomised in *Dido and Aeneas*. Organicism as a means of expressing dramatic structure and implication remained a potent force in almost all his subsequent large dramatic works, to varying degrees and in differing ways in each. These works tend to lack the deeply personalised characterisation of Dido and Aeneas, epitomised above all in Dido herself; but this is amply compensated for in other areas.

CHAPTER FOURTEEN

'An English-man, equal with the best abroad'[1]: dramatic music from 1690 to 1691

A P A R T F R O M *Dido and Aeneas*, the only theatre music of which we have certain evidence in 1689 is 'Thy Genius, Lo!' (Z. 604.A), a song written for Lee's play *The Massacre of Paris*. It was the first of two settings of this text, the second dating from 1695; but it was small beer compared to the work Purcell would have been doing in response to an invitation from the managers of the Theatre Royal to set their magnum opus for the 1690 season. For this he again worked with the choreographer Josias Priest, while the text came from Thomas Betterton, who had adapted a play by Massinger and Fletcher, *The Prophetess, or the History of Dioclesian*, 'after the manner of an opera'.[2]

Betterton had a long and distinguished history in English musical theatre. Back in 1675 he had commissioned Shadwell to provide the text, and Locke and Draghi to provide the music, for *Psyche*, and in 1685 he had produced *Albion and Albanius*, the first full-length opera in English to be the work of a single composer: the text was by John Dryden and the music by Louis Grabu, the French-trained, Catalan composer whom Charles II, showing a nice ignorance of native talent, had appointed in 1666 as master of the King's English chamber music.[3]

Albion and Albanius had a run of just six performances, for reasons which, although the music is less than inspiring, appear to have been mainly political.[4] *Dioclesian*, as the 1690 work is commonly called, seems to have been an attempt to make up for this failure and, besides being well received by most contemporary commentators, was a financial success. Like *Albion and Albanius*, the music was published in a sumptuous full score, the only one of Purcell's large theatre works to be accorded such a rare honour.

Nevertheless, within modern times, no music attributed to Purcell other than that for *The Tempest* has produced such widely differing opinions. Though only one writer has unequivocally said so, most seem to regard *Dioclesian* as the least satisfactory of the large stage works.[5] Robert Etheridge Moore might be right to claim that its 'finer qualities...are purely musical',[6] but surely there is something fundamentally wrong with a concept which seeks to make music central to the total experience, when all the solos are sung by singers who have no real acting roles and not one musical scene furthers or even cogently symbolises any central aspect of the plot.

Such disparities seem not to have greatly worried the audiences of the day however, for all contemporary accounts, including that of Downes, enthusiastically stress the spectacular stage effects and the impressive music. This underlines the fact that, however indebted *Dioclesian* might be to *Albion and Albanius*, it is essentially a play with music, whereas Betterton and Grabu had aimed at an English equivalent of *tragédie lyrique*.

In the last twenty-five years it has forcefully been argued that the conventions of English dramatic opera do not require the same types of musico-dramatic integrity as 'true' opera.[7] It is undoubtedly true that we should not expect to find in *Dioclesian* the same types of musico-dramatic structure or expressive emphases as in *Dido and Aeneas*. But Purcell's responses to dramatic opera reveal an eagerness to make the most of any possibility of tightening the relationship between music and drama, and, while the weaknesses of *Dioclesian* might well have something to do with his inexperience in the newly developing genre of dramatic opera, the problems presented by the text would probably have proved insurmountable even if he had composed his music some years later. It is not just the superiority of individual items in *King Arthur* and *The Fairy Queen* which makes these later (1691 and 1692) works more convincing: music and drama are more integrated, and for the most part the composer produced musical structures which had a clear relationship to dramatic function, a relationship which gave these items a context against which their expressive qualities could focus.

But there are more problems in *Dioclesian* than its lack of such integration: Dent found that 'Considered in detail, [it] suffers to some extent from over-elaboration.'[8] Movements for large ensemble are the most obvious casualties. In the first vocal piece of *Dioclesian*, 'Great Diocles the Boar Has Kill'd' (Z. 627.5), the complex string textures and affectively vivid bass solo have a quasi-religious, pompous detachment more suited to the court ode or the anthem than to the stage,[9] a connection reinforced by the chorus which, like several from the odes, has 'Iô' fanfares and a densely worked, polyphonic texture.

During the solo, the motivically saturated orchestral texture, complete with theme inversions and much overlapping of lines, even at main closes, is an extreme case of technical overkill. The complexity undermines the clear pacing of periodic units and, by blurring the expressive focus of the words, hinders the direct communication necessary for stage music to make a proper impact.

Sometimes this over-complexity can be seen in the instrumental music. The
preludes to 'What Shall I Do?' from *Dioclesian* (Z. 627.18) and 'When I Have
Often Heard' from *The Fairy Queen* (Z. 629.23)[10] make a revealing comparison.
Both are trio textures, and in this later piece the second violin part complements
the melody by a judicious balance of parallel and independent movement far
preferable to the consistent and rather obvious independence of parts in
Dioclesian (Ex. 129 (i) and (ii)).[11]

Ex. 129   (i) *Dioclesian*, Prelude to 'What Shall I Do?' (Z. 627.18): bb. 1–8

(ii) *The Fairy Queen*, Prelude to 'When I Have Often Heard' (Z. 629.23): bb. 1–8

Purcell probably appreciated some of these difficulties well enough. Most of
the solo vocal movements are fairly short strophic settings, sometimes involving
instruments. Only the accompanied songs of Act II, 'Great Diocles the Boar Has
Kill'd', 'Charon the Peaceful Shade' and 'Since the Toils'(Z. 627.5, 6 and 13)
attempt detailed affective illustration, and much of this depends on elaborate,
evocative part writing between voices and instruments. Only 'Since the Toils'
makes any serious attempt at expansion by repetition, and that, significantly,
has a ground bass to keep a tight rein on musical development.

Of these songs in Act II much the best is 'Charon the Peaceful Shade' for,
while its dramatic purpose is somewhat vague, it is extraordinarily suggestive of
the text, partly because of the consistent exploitation of an ambiguity seminal
in the flutes' opening phrase, and explicitly posited by the vocal entry. The first
phrase (Ex. 130) moves towards B♭, driven in particular by the flute parts, which
emphasise the B♭–F pitch range. A downbeat on B♮ in b. 4 would seem to be the
goal of the phrase, but the bass breaks this, firstly by not going to F in b. 3, and
secondly by going to G in b. 4, just as the voice enters to articulate a new
beginning. The harmonic ambiguity and tension thus set up between G minor
and B♭ is not dispelled until b. 12 and is all the more potent in effect because of
the overlapping four-bar phrases in the flutes and the voice.

Ex. 130   *Dioclesian,* 'Charon the Peaceful Shade' (Z. 627.6): 1–15

The relationship of these tensions to the text is amongst the most subtle in Purcell's music of this period. The vocal entry does not use the first flute part, which embodied the F–B♭ harmonic ambiguity. Instead it picks up the second part, firmly in G minor, and thus sounding, appropriately enough, like a calm shadow of the flutes' phrase. The G minor character is now complete, as the bass C goes to D (cf. bb. 3 and 6).

The consequently clear ii–V–i in G minor (bb. 6–7), with the voice significantly ending on B♭ rather than G, is the starting point for two compressed reworkings of these relationships. The flutes imitatively rework bb. 1–4: the second repeats the D–F of b. 1, and the first enters on G producing a four-bar phrase which includes the F♮/F♯ tension posited from the beginning, but now more firmly within G minor. Its ending on V of i is the cue for the voice entering, now with the flute I line of bb. 1–4, but followed by the flutes imitating a bar later and purging all B♭ elements. For the first time the voice sets up low G as a point of closure, through the half close ending with low F♯ in the voice. The next phrase concentrates on the F–B♭ pitch relationship which was posited in bb. 1–4. But it is now unalloyed B♭ major, setting 'He hastes to waft him o'er' and managing thus to sound like a response to the 'invitation' offered in the first few bars.

One chorus which works especially well is that at the end of this first musical scene. The slowly rising, imitative lines of 'Let the Priests with Processions' (Z. 627.13e) produce a very slow expansion of register, driven by dissonant, independent part writing, and the effect is well suited to the ritual context. As in many ode choruses, elaborate polyphony gives way to more homophonic acclamations, here aptly applied as the full consort of woodwind and strings join together and reach their registral peak for 'All sing great Diocles' story'.

But a number of choruses show that over-elaboration which Dent identified. 'Let All Rehearse in Lofty Verse' (Z. 627.23a) from Act IV, for example, combines some engaging ideas and rather obvious, short-breathed alternations between choral and orchestral groups. Each phrase is concerned with one specific type of motif or figuration and, while the technical prowess is impressive, the emphatic closes and the coinciding shift to a new idea are too mechanical.

Much of the best music in *Dioclesian* is in the concluding masque. This is, of course, an insertion into the play, and as such does not 'rely on the play for survival'. Although it is possible that the elaborate scenery worked against the best interests of Purcell's music, this was the only place where, unencumbered by speech, he was free to pace events as expansively or as briefly as he wished, and where he could extract his own imagery from the text.[12]

The prelude and chorus 'Behold, O Mighty'st of Gods' (Z. 627.28) epitomises Purcell's sureness of touch. Perhaps its most important feature is its masterly use of distinct groups of strings and oboes, in all three possible combinations, and featuring irregular phrase lengths across a broad harmonic circuit.

The tutti is the normative sonority, established by the opening phrase (bb. 1–8, Ex. 131 (i)). It posits a close into C minor by ending on V of i, this being particularly stressed through being preceded by its own dominant, and by violin I's protracted descent from G to D. But now the oboes take off on their own, and the resulting tension helps to kick off a broad harmonic circuit of irregular phrases, alternating strings and oboes. Return to the tutti comes, unexpectedly (b. 32, Ex. 131 (ii)), after a phrase on the oboes. It begins in E♭, but quickly returns to C minor (bb. 34–5) featuring the high G which began the prelude. A long, densely imitative final phrase extends to b. 44 and, at its very end, picks up

Ex. 131 *Dioclesian*, Prelude to 'Behold, O Mighty'st of Gods' (Z. 627.28):

(i) bb. 1–12

(ii) bb. 28–40

and resolves the G major harmony with D uppermost, which was left in b. 8. During this return to C minor, the scalic descent from G is outlined again, but now with a prominent prepared appoggiatura on D–C (b. 38).

In the chorus, which is somewhat simpler in scoring and harmonic structure, but contrapuntally more elaborate, this appoggiatura is a primary motif, and is especially associated with 'mighty'st' and 'gods'. The chorus also follows the prelude in ending its first phrase on V of i (b. 55) and using this as a starting point for a series of harmonically discursive phrases before picking up (bb. 74–88) that unresolved dominant. C minor is tonicised by a reworking of the opening material.

Perhaps the finest vocal piece of the Masque is the duet for two sopranos 'Oh the Sweet Delights of Love' (Z. 627.30). Like 'Fear No Danger' from *Dido and Aeneas* (Z. 626.7), also for two sopranos, it is a rondeau, but on a larger scale, and it uses a flexible musical design not immediately suggested by the original text, but perfectly suited to the expressive purpose (Fig. 13). The song is extraordinarily suggestive, not just because of the gasping imitations on 'oh' during the refrain A (Purcell's adaptation of the original text's 'Ah'), but also because of the ways in which A returns. Such returns are, of course, one of the typical features of rondeau structure; but in this case their effect is intensified by the atypical irregularity of the phrasing. Moreover, both B and C have 'clean break' starts, which emphasise the harmonic and pitch differences between them and A. So a return to the main tonic is projected even through their superbly focussed harmonic events; and when the return comes, in a musical equivalent of a wriggle of delight, it is elided into the closes of B and C, largely through a connecting line in the continuo.

Fig. 13. 'Oh the Sweet Delights of Love' from *Dioclesian* (Z. 627.30)

Section

Oh the sweet delights of love!†	
Who would live and not enjoy 'em? }	A
I'd refuse the throne of Jove,	
Should power or majesty destroy 'em, }	B
Give me doubts or give me fears.	
Give me jealousies and cares;* }	C₁
But let love, let love remove 'em.	
I approve 'em,	C₂
I approve 'em, }	
(But let love, let love remove 'em.) [omitted]	

Bars:	1 – 10	11 – 18	19 – 28	29 – 33	34 – 40	41 – 50
Section:	A	B	A	C₁	C₂	A
Harmonic				V of iv – VII	VII – v(V)	
structure:	i – i	III – III	i – i	V of iv	–	v(V)	i – i

†'Ah the sweet delights of love!' in printed edition of the play.
*'Give me sighs, and give me tears' in printed edition of the play.

Nevertheless, Price is correct in asserting that the best music in *Dioclesian* is in the dances,[13] though the overtures and act tunes are also notable. Even some of these seem too highbrow for their function, though. It is hard, for example, to imagine a theatre audience, already well into the large-scale and grand gestures of *Dioclesian* – literary and musical – settling down to listen to the beautiful but intimate and rarefied canonic chaconne 'Two in one on a ground' (Z. 627.16).

For all *Dioclesian*'s complexity and high purpose, its large-scale organisation shows little of the organicism which helps make *Dido and Aeneas* work. The opening sequence of numbers in Act II, for example, is in G major, and begins with a prelude for strings, before the accompanied bass solo 'Great Diocles the Boar Has Kill'd'. This song culminates in the elaborate accompanied chorus 'Sing Io's! Praise the Thund'ring Jove'. The soprano solo with flutes 'Charon the Peaceful Shade' is in G minor and leads directly into the imaginative C major sequence (Fig. 14) setting the quatrain:

> Sound all your instruments of war,
> Fifes, trumpets, timbrels play!
> Let all mankind the pleasure share,
> And bless this happy day.

Fig. 14. Setting of quatraine 'Sound all your instruments' from *Dioclesian*

Recit:	7 bars	Soprano	Lines 1 + 2
Symphony:	5 bars 'Very slow'	Trumpets + strings	
	29 bars 'Quick'		
Duet:	30 bars 31	Sop. + bass	Lines 3 + 4
Flourish:	C chord 'for voices only', singing		Line 1
	'Sound all your instruments',		
	omitting 'of war'		
	Direction to 'Flourish with all instruments in		
	C – fa – ut key'		
Chorus:	44 bars, reworking duet	*SATB*, strings,	Lines 3 + 4
		trumpets + oboes	

The insertion of the flourish is one of those seemingly simple touches by which genius can extract from a text the last ounce of dramatic possibility. But something of this sort is needed by this scene which, as a musico-dramatic concept, can at best be described as rambling.

It can be argued that this scene is an A1BA2 structure, in which B is 'Charon the Peaceful Shade', while the A sections are sequences of numbers defined by key (G and C respectively) and by their culmination in a chorus. But it takes more than an orderly sequence of keys and a reasonably symmetrical grouping of numbers to articulate a convincing musico-dramatic structure; and the ambiguous relationship between the music and everything which takes place before and after it in the play is an insurmountable handicap, as is the fact that, throughout the score, 'the music makes us feel nothing for any of the speaking characters'.[14] Too expressively unfocussed for a self-evident purpose to emerge, yet full of impressive pieces, *Dioclesian* is rather dissatisfying.

It was to be during the next two dramatic seasons, in the composition of *King Arthur* and *The Fairy Queen*, that Purcell learned to develop convincing musico-dramatic structures on a large scale. In both cases he was helped by working with a librettist who seems to have had a deeper understanding of the potential strengths of dramatic opera.

Bibliographic evidence suggests that, between the premieres of *Dioclesian* (June 1690) and *King Arthur* (May 1691), Purcell provided music for at least four plays: *Sir Anthony Love* (Z. 588), *Amphitryon* (Z. 572), *Distressed Innocence* (Z. 577) and, almost certainly, *The Gordian Knot* (Z. 597); while *Circe* (Z. 575) also comes from around this period. For most of these plays Purcell was concerned mainly with dances and other pieces of instrumental music, but there are a number of songs and, in the case of *Circe*, some impressive choral music.

By far the finest of these songs is 'Pursuing Beauty' from *Sir Anthony Love* (Z. 588.2). More compellingly than any song in *Dioclesian*, it uses the arioso and recitative techniques seen both in *Dido and Aeneas* and in some independent recitatives and dialogues, to paint a profoundly expressive, dramatically penetrating scene.[15] Like many of the independent songs, it contrasts an expressive opening arioso with a more regular, tuneful air, all beautifully tailored to fit the contrasts of the text; and in the prelude for two violins and continuo, style is perfectly matched to expressive purpose.

The instruments are evoking 'the distant shore', a metaphor for the mystique of feminine beauty. Its texture has that bold phrasing and simple, direct harmonic structure characteristic of Purcell's most up-to-date music; and the prelude, like that to 'We Must Assemble' from *Circe* (Z. 575.1), concentrates on repeated notes anticipating the forthcoming vocal line. The result is no airy Italianate portrayal, but a rarefied evocation of the old English style, especially the 'drag' section from Fantasia No. 11 (Z. 742.2), and the second and third strains of the Pavan in A minor (Z. 749). More obviously antique are the last few bars which, with their overlapping scalic imitations forming chains of $\frac{6}{3}$s, and their piquant flattened sevenths, look back to the last section of Fantasia No. 6 (Z. 737.4), the last strain of the Pavan in B♭ (Z. 750), and the last section of Sonata No. 4 (1683) in F (Z. 793.4).

King Arthur is unique amongst Purcell's large stage works in not being an adaptation of a play. By the time of its first performance, in May or June 1691, it already had a long history, for Dryden had worked on the text around eight years before. Except for one act, this text seems to have been substantially complete by late 1684. It was not performed in that version however; instead, the prologue was detached, inflated, and mounted in 1686 as the all-singing opera *Albion and Albanius*. The reasons for these changes and for the revival of the main part of the drama are complex, and deeply rooted in the politics of the time, as well as in Dryden's aspiration to produce a native equivalent of opera.[16] In the long run, it failed to become the forerunner of a distinctive genre, even though, if the number of performances over the next eighty years is anything to go on, it was the most commercially successful of all Purcell's stage works. Ironically the frequency of the revivals led to progressive corruption of the musical text and, since there is no autograph, not all the music has survived. Yet there are sources authoritative enough to give a clear idea of how Purcell's views of large-scale musico-dramatic structure were developing.[17]

Dryden and Purcell were at pains to avoid that flimsy relationship between music and the play's main action which marred *Dioclesian*. Even though Arthur does not sing, he is intimately involved with several of the musical scenes. Of his evil opponents Oswald, Osmond and Grimbald, the last sings, while all three are involved in the events surrounding the music in Acts I and II and, less directly, those of Acts III and IV. Moreover, the scenes in Acts II and IV are intimately involved in the main action and, while the famous Frost Scene of Act III has a somewhat tenuous connection with the main plot, it vividly draws out the tension as the evil Osmund attempts to seduce Emmeline.

Much has been made of allegory in the text and plot of *King Arthur*,[18] and there is no doubt that for contemporary listeners these were live issues. But the modern student or listener should exercise caution, for while an appreciation of such matters can lead us towards a deeper understanding of the dramatist's and composer's motivations, and can enhance our response to the work as a whole, it can have comparatively little to do with our immediate response to the music, for such knottily cerebral matters cannot thus be communicated, particularly when the allegory must be interpreted out of the text. However emblematic Dryden's and Purcell's characters might be, Purcell's music is not concerned with profound, communicable symbolism in the way that, for example, Wagner's is. Moreover, given the occasional function of music in *King Arthur* there is no reasonably continuous musical context against which our appreciation of such matters can unfold.

It is significant that in *King Arthur* personal matters are hardly ever given musical dress. Indeed, the one scene of true intimacy, the chamber duet 'You Say 'tis Love' (Z. 628.35), is sung by anonymous characters. Dent had a point when he claimed that in *King Arthur* 'Purcell was more concerned with setting the words themselves than in depicting the characters of those who sang them'.[19]

Nevertheless, even in this respect *King Arthur* does better than *Dioclesian*. Most of the characters involved in the music have at least some semblance of personality, and while the heroic nature of the drama means that their behaviour involves much posturing, they are sufficiently plausible to encourage some musical characterisation, particularly in Act II. This is even true of symbolic characters, for while the Cold Genius is a strangely affected and ponderous creature, and the Cupid can appear rather silly to late-twentieth-century minds, both characters nevertheless come across as imaginative metaphors of universal concepts; and while the dramatic rationale for the frost scene is flimsy, the characters are real enough within the fantastic, allegorical world of *King Arthur* as a whole.[20]

What the music may lack in intimacy it more than makes up for in boldness of imagination and aptness for its dramatic context. More than in any piece since *Dido and Aeneas*, the dramatic progress of musical scenes is propelled by an appropriate musical development unfolding against a distinctive background unity.

In the frost scene, for example, the musical context for later developments is set out by the instrumental prelude (Z. 628.19a) and the Cupid's first song. Predominant features of the prelude are various melodic and harmonic sequential patterns, highlighted by the texture's rhythmic uniformity, for they are thus the most prominent changing elements. The Cupid's song, 'What Ho! Thou Genius of This Isle' (Z. 628.19b) begins, like the preceding prelude, with a G–C leap and continues with an upbeat C, but which now goes to E instead of F. Thereafter the vocal line's expressive gyrations are linked to a harmonic circuit cast in four main phrases, ending on bb. 19, 23, 25 and 28, and articulating respectively IV, I, V of vi and I. The two circuits away from and back to C are eleven and six bars long respectively, proportions which approximate to those of the prelude's I–V (eight bars) and V–I (five bars). The song's last C major circuit touches on V of vi, and the three-bar phrase used to go there is reworked in C major to close. Throughout the scene such proportions – closing a section with a short reworking in the home key, and weighting the lengths of main harmonic divisions roughly two to one – are commonly used to generate movement from one item of the scene to the next.

Items are grouped by several means, including the relative strengths of closes and differences of scoring and key. The lop-sided ending already referred to links the prelude, 'What Ho! Thou Genius of This Isle', and the Genius' famous prelude and solo 'What Pow'r Art Thou?' (Z. 628.20). This last is comparatively even in phrase structure, but is in C minor, and far too massive to be closed off by the Cupid's acerbically witty response 'Thou Doting Fool' – an exquisitely proportioned, but short-breathed rondeau. By contrast the Genius' accompanied song 'Great Love' (Z. 628.22) has an emphatic conclusion which, added to the subsequent return of C major recitative for the Cupid ('No Part of My Dominion'), brings to a close the first part of the scene and the opens the second.

Musical characterisation mirrors dramatic progress. The Cupid sings to phrases which mostly begin with boldly confident leaps, and which include lively rhythmic variety. In 'What Pow'r Art Thou?' the Genius' part is almost entirely scalic, and is as rhythmically uniform as its accompaniment, suggesting immobility within a texture which manages also to convey portentous grandeur through the inexorable drive of the harmonic and melodic processes. When the Genius is won over by the Cupid's jaunty, engaging rondeau, his response 'Great Love' adopts the confident arpeggios of the Cupid's music; yet it remains a ponderous piece, managing to suggest at once the winning power of love and the Genius' character.[21]

The Cupid has achieved its first purpose; now it has to raise a people 'Of kind embracing lovers and embrac'd'. This is, of course, a reworking of the dramatic tensions which animated the first part of the scene; but the fact that the hard work has already been done is reflected in the stylistic parallels between the two parts of the scene and in the musical characterisation of this part of the scene.

Parallels between the two parts of the scene go much further than similarities of texture, such as that between the Genius' music and the 'Chorus of Cold People' (Z. 628.24b). The first recitative's moves towards the subdominant and relative minor are recast in the second ('No Part of My Dominion', Z. 628.23); after a phrase fully in C we turn to V of vi to begin 'E'en here I will a people raise / Of kind embracing lovers and embrac'd'; but now it acts as II of the subdominant's relative minor, for a deliciously languorous setting of these lines. In a direct parallel with earlier concluding phrases, these lines are repeated in C major, but with subtle modifications which make them turn away from this concern with amorous detail and look forward with confidence to the arrival of the summoned people.

The prelude for the 'Chorus of Cold People' (Z. 628.24) immediately picks up the recitative's confident arpeggios, while its uniform use of emphatic downbeat, and pressing upbeat patterns, and its reliance on melodic and harmonic sequence are further palpable links with the opening prelude – in particular the final phrases of both pieces ascend by sequence to a high A and precipitously fall to the tonic (cf. bb. 11–12, 155–9 and 176–7). The chorus features that strongly propelled part writing and harmonic movement, and the persistent repeated quavers, which distinguished the Genius' aria; but by a number of means Purcell suggests shivering stiffness without the Genius' reluctance. The determinedly long-range harmonic structure and melodic line of the Genius are replaced by a much less forceful design which only occasionally departs from C minor, and which tends to hover around a more limited pitch range – with the notable exception of 'Tho' quiv'ring with cold', the entire upper part lies within the minor sixth between B and G. Certainly the people are uncomfortable, most strikingly so in their augmented triads; but even here they are altogether less resolved than the Genius. Perhaps even that archetypal symbol of the cold characters, the repeated quavers marked tremolo (for that is the probable meaning of the wavy lines above the instrumental and vocal parts in 'What Pow'r Art Thou?' and in the 'Chorus of Cold People'), should be abandoned for their dance.[22]

The remainder of the scene is dominated by the Cupid's solo and chorus with instruments, ''Tis I That Have Warm'd Ye' (Z. 628.25–7). A catalogue of the numerous links between this ensemble and earlier parts of the scene would be dreary, but it is worth pointing out that the rhythm of the ritornello (Z. 628.25b) is clearly related to that of the opening prelude, and that it is dominated by sequential patterns of rhythm, harmony and melody, many of which are also related to the opening prelude and the Genius' aria. More obviously, the Cupid's solo picks up the opening of the prelude before the 'Chorus of Cold People' (Z. 628.24) (Fig. 15), and maintains the musical characterisation of the earlier part of the scene in that the now warmed-up Cold People and the bass singer, who almost certainly is the Genius, abandon their angular chromaticism and adopt the Cupid's arpeggaic figuration.

Purcell's response to Dryden's text is characteristically flexible. To underline connexions between the two parts of the scene he sets 'See, see we assemble' as a chorus rather than a solo for a 'Man'. In ''Tis I That Have Warm'd Ye' he ignores the subtlety of Dryden's final line ''Tis I, that have arm'd ye', which surely would have been missed in performance, in favour of a simple repeat of the first line, thus concentrating on love's warming power. He then intensifies the dramatic point of the entire scene by uniting the Cupid and (probably) the Genius to sing 'Sound a Parley' as a duet (Dryden gives it to the Cupid alone).

Much more remarkable is the musical structure he applies to Dryden's verse – a structure without precedent in his own music and, as far as I can ascertain, in any earlier music for the English stage. It uses an unusual amount of sectional repetition on different levels so that the chorus ''Tis love' (Z. 628.25c), which Dryden seems to have intended as a response to the Cupid's solo, becomes the summary point of the entire scene. By repeating that chorus after the duet 'Sound a Parley', the latter becomes the middle section of an elaborate ternary structure, the expansive techniques of which derive largely from rondeau methods (Fig. 15).

''Tis love' is a complex amplification of the Cupid's opening solo, and main harmonic functions are articulated by closes at the ends of phrases which, in principle, are four bars long or multiples thereof. Structural pillars are presented by recurrences of the opening line with its concomitant A1 material. By omitting statements of the closing version A2, which ended the Cupid's solo, and by using two variations on the first version of the ritornello, closure is avoided, and at A2's only intermediate appearance the same effect is obtained by having the ritornello set off again in the final bar.

Two statements of this complex combination of rondeau and ritornello

Fig. 15. *King Arthur*: structure of '"Tis I That Have Warm'd Ye' (Z. 628.24–7)

Prelude, Chorus, Dance and '"Tis I That Have Warm'd Ye'

	PRELUDE	CHORUS AND DANCE OF COLD PEOPLE	SOLO* '"TIS I'	STRINGS	CHORUS WITH STRINGS '"TIS LOVE'			FINE
Material	A	Z	A1 B A2	Ritornello	A1 Rit. A1 B A2	Rit.	B A2	
Number of bars	34	24 and 17	20	8	20	20	23	
Harmonic structure	8 + 8 + 10 + 8 / I–V I–I vi–vi–i	i~i / i~i i–Vofi~i	8 + 4 + 8 / I–V Vof11	I	8 + 12 / I–V I–ii–V	8 + 4 + 8 / I–V Vof1	8 + 4 + 8 / I–vi(VI)–Vof1 Vof1	5 + 6 + 4 + 8 / I–vi(VI) –Vof1 Vof1 I

'Sound a Parley'   Dal Segno ✿ al fine

	VLNS DUET†	DUET VLNS	DUET	VLNS	DUET	VLNS	DUET	DUET VLNS	DUET
Material	C C	D1	C	D2	C	E1	E2	C	C×2
Number of bars	40	17	15			20			19
	6 15 +1 15 +3	8 + 3	12 + 3	8 + 3 6	12 + 3	8 + 3 6 +1		12 7	
Harmonic structure	I 1–V(VofI) I – V	V of I–vi—	I	vi–VofI	I	V of IV–ii II–V(VofI)		I 1	I 1

* The Cupid's first solo is a reworking of the prelude before the 'Chorus of Cold People' (Z. 628.24a). The prelude concentrates on developments of the opening lines (A) of the Cupid's solo and thus neatly sets up the prominence of that material necessary for it to act as the refrain of a complex rondeau.

† All duets are accompanied by the violins.

techniques surround a more regular yet no less subtle rondeau structure, the duet 'Sound a Parley' (Z. 628.26) (Fig. 15). But here too, the lengths of the various sections are constantly changed. Like the earlier part of the movement, it touches strongly on V, ii and vi, while the opening material C is reused to set the final lines of Dryden's text as the last statement of the rondeau refrain. The ritornello comes in on the singers' final downbeat, and leads readily back to the chorus ''Tis Love', which is now a summatory response to Dryden's final thoughts – 'Love was made for a Blessing, / And not for a Pain'. (This repeat is designated Z. 628.27 in Zimmerman's *Analytical Catalogue*.)

It seems likely that the dance specified by Dryden took place during the performance of this elaborate piece. Certainly the ritornelli in particular could work as a dance suitably jerky for the recently warmed-up Cold People, and this seems more likely than that either of the pieces commonly regarded as the Third Act Tune[23] formed the culminating action of the scene, although the act tune might have been danced to anyway.

Only one other scene in *King Arthur* can match the frost scene's musico-dramatic integrity and consistent musical characterisation. In Act II Grimbald (a mortal opposed to Arthur), and Philidel (a repentant spirit), assisted by their attendant spirit creatures, compete to guide Arthur along paths that will lead respectively to destruction or safety. Immediately before the music starts Grimbald appears and passes himself off as a shepherd who can guide Arthur and his followers through the unfamiliar territory. Arthur sets off to follow him, but as he does so the instruments enter, and Philidel urges Arthur to follow him instead, with an apt use of the Italian 'motto' opening.[24]

Dryden's text neatly sets up the central dramatic point by having Philidel change the first line of Grimbald's preceding speech: 'Hither, this way, Briton's' to 'Hither this way, this way bend'. Crucially, it is Philidel who starts the music off; everything then hinges on the attempts of Grimbald's spirits to pass themselves off as well intentioned, by imitating the musical gestures of Philidel and his spirits.

There were Purcellian precedents for the musico-dramatic concept, notably in the Witches' music from *Dido and Aeneas*. But the approach here is far more subtle, based on various ways of setting:

> Hither this way, this way bend,   (x)
> Trust not that Malicious Fiend: (z)

In Dryden, Philidel immediately moves into the four lines beginning 'Those are false deluding lights'. But Purcell's approach is to set up these two lines as a refrain structured $x1$–z–$x1$–$x2$, with $x1$ finishing on V of i (b. 5), while $x2$ is closed, ending on i (b. 11). Both versions of x are just one bar long, and readily extensible by repetition and instrumental interjection.

Purcell's masterstroke lies especially in his translation of these two versions of phrase x into choral refrains for the two groups of spirits. The first choral entry comes after Philidel warns, through some chromatic excursions ending with a full close in the dominant, that Grimbald's 'false deluding lights' will 'in bogs and marshes leave ye'. Philidel's spirits enter as a chorus, with a version of $x1 + x2$, lengthened by a brief dialogue on 'This way'. A snatch of the dialogue plus the closing phrase $x2$ are then repeated by Grimbald's spirits.

Philidel gives further warnings in a second solo 'If you step no longer thinking', which ends on V of i, and urges them again to come 'Hither this way'. This entry acts as the first line of another chorus based on $x1$, z and $x2$, and with the first $x2$ deceitfully given to Grimbald's spirits. But their efforts are foiled by Philidel's spirits, who counter with z ('Trust not that Malicious Fiend') and a complete, closing dialogue on $x1$, $x2 + x2$. So Philidel has won musically, and he seems to have won dramatically too, as Arthur's supporters decide they should heed him. But Grimbald has another go, in his song 'Let Not a Moon-born Elf' (Z. 628.13). This almost persuades Arthur's companions,[25] but a repetition of the most recent version of the chorus, in which Grimbald's spirits have just a brief intervention, is sufficient to swing things in Philidel's, and thus Arthur's, favour.

The subtlety of Purcell's approach lies in the fact that Grimbald's spirits masquerade behind Philidel's music. The three phrases $x1$, z and $x2$ presented by Philidel are all securely based in D minor. It is not the urgings of Grimbald's spirits which depart from these securities, but Philidel's own accounts of what will happen to Arthur and his followers if they heed the deceiver, for the false spirits stay inexorably associated with Philidel's own text and music. To underline this Purcell altered part of the text: Dryden had the line given to Philidel's spirits – 'Trust not that Malicious Fiend' – followed by Grimbald's spirits saying 'Trust me, I am no Malicious Fiend.' As spoken discourse this makes perfect sense, but Purcell omits it and sustains the intention in music.

The main dramatic business of the scene is thus over, and the rest of it is brilliantly depictive, though less concerned with dramatic progress. Individuals and small groups from Philidel's spirits, led by Philidel himself as first soprano, sing the elaborate 'Come, Follow Me' (Z. 628.14), in which Purcell picks up the ancient notion of depicting pursuit with canonic writing. Again, a refrain-like structure is used, with solos and small ensembles coming between the refrains which, eventually, are set for full chorus.[26]

The other scenes in *King Arthur* include music which can be counted amongst Purcell's finest, though they all suffer from the incompleteness of the musical sources. This is particularly unfortunate in Act IV Scene II, which sees music playing a role rather more sinister than it did in Act II. While Arthur is ultimately able to heed Merlin's warning about the dangers lurking behind the illusions of beauty he will encounter, he first has to resist seductions in which music plays a central role.

As soon as Arthur declares 'But where's the Horrour! Sure the Prophet err'd', he hears 'Soft Musick' (lost). He realises that 'Hell entertains me, like some welcome Guest', and ignores the music's seductive powers. He is now confronted with something much more enticing as 'two Syrens arise from the Water; They shew themselves to the Waste, and Sing'. The first part of this piece ('O pass not on'), if it was ever set, is missing; but the duet 'Two Daughters of This Aged Stream' (Z. 628.29) has survived, and manages brilliantly to suggest the sinister motives behind this none-too-subtle attempt at luring Arthur.[27]

He responds to the extent that 'A Lazie Pleasure trickles through my Veins', but brings himself to his senses. Yet his trials are not over, for

As he is going forward, Nymphs and Sylvans come out from behind the Trees, Bass and two Trebles sing the following song to a Minuet.
Dance with Song, all with Branches in their Hands.

Here is one of Purcell's masterstrokes, for Dryden provides two verses which are divided by 'the same Measure play'd alone'. Purcell adapts Dryden's verse by missing out one line in the first and by altering the fifth and seventh lines in the second. Moreover, instead of providing a minuet, he sets the whole to a huge passacaglia on a four-bar ground, by far the largest single piece in *King Arthur*, and the most elaborate ensemble ground bass composition he ever wrote. It is an apt modification of Dryden's intentions, for a minuet could hardly have provided more seduction than the half-naked, singing syrens and their exquisite duet.

Despite its technical brilliance and resourcefulness, 'How Happy the Lover' (Z. 628.30) has limitations: as Price says, its effect is merely hypnotic and, while it probably made an impressive spectacle, the music eventually dulls the senses.[28] Perhaps it is meant to. Arthur's spoken response to this 'heavy rubber mallet' technique is inevitably anti-climactic:

And what are these Fantastick Fairy Joys
To Love like mine? False Joys, false Welcomes all,
Begone ye Sylvan Trippers of the Green;
Fly after Night, and overtake the Moon.

That the subsequent action, in which Arthur triumphs over Grimbald, takes place without the aid of music, reinforces the futility of these latest musical efforts.

The musical pageant in Act V was an opportunity for extravagant stage effects, and Purcell matched these with appropriately impressive music. Merlin waves his wand, and the scene changes to reveal 'the British Ocean in a Storm;

Aeolus in a Cloud above: Four Winds hanging, etc.'. What follows is in effect
a masque on the rising fortunes of Britain, with movements dedicated to various
aspects of native life. The incomplete state of the end of the scene is a problem,
but even what remains makes it clear that any attempt to see large-scale musical
order in it is fraught with inconsistencies. Whatever qualities the individual
movements might have, Dent was right in asserting that as a whole, the pageant
contains nothing truly dramatic.[29]

It nevertheless gets off to an arresting start with the baritone solo with strings
'Ye Blust'ring Brethren' (Z. 628.32), when Aeolus commands the winds to
'retire and let Britannia rise / In triumph o'er the main'. A number of
commentators have drawn attention to the astonishing vigour of the string
writing in the run up to Aeolus' entry; yet this music's power to command our
imagination rests on far more than frantic activity followed by change.[30] In
principle Purcell's methods revolve around creating a normative background
based on multiples of one bar, and setting against this events which, almost
from the start, are irregular. The one-bar metrical grouping is set up in bb. 1–2
by the violins' successive entries on middle C (Ex. 132). Irregularity comes with

Ex. 132   King Arthur, 'Ye Blust'ring Brethren' (Z. 628.32): bb. 1–7

the entries of viola and bass, on the dominant and tonic respectively, after intervals of one and a half bars. Throughout, the texture is dominated by motifs *a*, *b*, *c* and *d*, though not necessarily as part of a subject entry.

Purcell keeps the outer parts distinctly phrased yet almost perpetually out of phase with one another, while the inner parts tend to reinforce the general hubbub by scrubbing away on repeated notes, by running in parallel thirds or sixths with one or more outer parts, and occasionally by rubbing against the harmony implied by the outer parts. To articulate the approach to a close, the outer parts come into conformity. In b. 10, for example, the bass picks up the sequential repetitions started one bar earlier in the first violins. They run with these in parallel tenths, giving, for just one bar, two fundamental progressions per bar; but at this pace of events that is enough to set up distinctively cadential part writing in b. 11, as violin I circles around C and B, and the bass prolongs the dominant. The C major downbeat in the next bar is clear, but given the one-bar norm and the hectic speed, it spills on, with a full bar of C major scales, during which Aeolus enters.

The progress through quavers, then crotchets, to minims and finally semibreves as the winds retire, is part of a process continuous with that which started the scene. The quaver figuration uses augmented versions of shapes which were already prominent, notably the turn figure *b*. But there is far more to it than this, for Aeolus entered with an augmented variant of *d*, and from then on the priorities of the texture have been subtly changing.

This music's main driving force has been its non-conformity. Once Aeolus enters, the stress patterns of the outer parts and the voice become increasingly coincident. So the nature of the non-conformity changes, as Aeolus sings at his suitably imperious, slower pace, firstly with a phrase moving I–I (bb. 12–15), and secondly with one going from I–V (bb. 16–18), during the larger part of which his line follows the shape of the instrumental bass. As he commands the winds to 'retire', the few remaining disparities are removed, as the harmony returns to C major and the strings slow to quavers, then crotchets, and finally become even slower than Aeolus himself. The very musical process has been under Aeolus' command since his first appearance.

Command of a very different type of musical process can be seen in the duet 'For Folded Flocks' (Z. 628.36), one of the most frequently published pieces from *King Arthur*, and clearly dependent on Purcell's long experience with

Fig. 16. King Arthur: design of 'For Folded Flocks' (Z. 628.36)

Bars	1 – 12	13 – 19	20 – 5	:‖	26 – 31	32 – 6	37 – 40
Closes	half	full	full	:‖	full	full	full
	in i	in III	in v(V)	:‖	in iv(IV)	in VII	in i
Lines	1 – 3	1 – 3	4 – 5		1 – 2	3	4 – 5
	└──────── Stanza 1 ────────┘				└──────── Stanza 2 ────────┘		

Ex. 133   *King Arthur,* 'For Folded Flocks' (Z. 628.36): bb. 1–25

three-part and other ensemble songs. He changed a few details of the written
text which, in its published form is described as a 'Song of Three Parts':

1

For folded flocks, on fruitful plains,
The shepherds and the farmers gains,
Fair Britain all the world outvies:
And Pan as in Arcadia reigns,
Where pleasure mixt with profit lies

2

Though Jason's fleece was fam'd of old,
The British wool is growing gold;
No mines can more of wealth supply:
It keeps the peasant from the cold,
And takes for king the Tyrian dye.

The two stanzas are disposed across a binary structure, whose phrases are
defined by the closes indicated in Fig. 16.

There are three distinctive types of texture (Ex. 133), based respectively on the
expansive line, on repetition of one short motif, and on comparative homophony
with little or no repetition. Each of the above phrases uses one or two of these
types, and Purcell's mastery lies firstly in the way he deploys them and links their
use into the piece's long-range musical purposes, and secondly in his use of
musical ideas which are at once highly suggestive yet amenable to complex
elaboration without obscuring expressive clarity.

The first two textural types are set out in the opening phrase, beginning with
quasi-canonic entries in the bass and tenor, on an idea curiously suggestive of
lazy pastoral rapture, largely due to the slow pace of fundamental pitch
movement and to the bass pedal. While this phrase stays in the tonic D minor,
it will prove significant that the first harmonic progression (bb. 2–3) is a strong
inflexion towards III. The second part of the phrase (b. 8) picks up the dominant
harmony which ends the bass and tenor dialogue and marches off with the
second type of texture for 'Fair Britain all the world outvies'.

The texture is now more animated than in the first seven bars, partly because
of the apt repetitions of 'all', but more significantly because these generate a
change in the pace of fundamental movement. The stress on each repetition
articulates the beginning of a new metrical unit, which now has two pulses;
moreover, the beginnings of these units do not coincide in the bass and in the
two upper parts. This is resolved in bb. 11–12, where the parts come into
rhythmic ensemble – the third textural type – to return to triple time, and to
articulate the first strong close of the piece, a half-close in the tonic.

With consummate artistry, Purcell takes this as the cue for a return to the opening line; but now it is the alto's turn to lead, while the lower voices have a dialogue on 'Fair Britain all'. Such a radical reinterpretation of the first line's harmonic and rhythmic structures is more than just a feat of outstanding technical ingenuity: the text setting still has the clarity and tranquillity it needs, yet now it has an underlying instability caused by the lower voices' dialogues and by the inflection to the relative major, which occurs at around the same point (cf. bb. 3 and 14), but is now allied with a much more mobile harmonic design. The thrust onto the relative major for the close in bb. 18–19 thus aptly reflects the assertiveness of the text, yet finds its justification in musical precedent. The move to a comparatively homophonic texture for lines four and five is a neat contrast, highlights the structural importance of the close into the dominant, and sets the tone for the triumphant fanfares which open the second part of the song.

This second part reworks the same textural types as the first. The line 'No mines can more of wealth supply' gets particularly interesting treatment. It starts off with a motif which inverts that of 'Fair Britain all', but then has complex sequential imitations on 'No' which, like those on 'all', set up complex duple-time metrical patterns. In stretching this idea out for three full bars, Purcell aptly mines the depths of musical plausibility, with textures which owe much to the early seventeenth-century madrigal and to consort music. Such readily identifiable motivic links are only the surface aspect of the song's cohesion: beneath them lies a purposeful design, without which these reworkings would sound only like so much worthy doodling.

'The pride and darling of the stage'[1]:
dramatic music from 1692 to 1695

FOR THE 1692 SEASON, hoping to build on the success of *Dioclesian* and *King Arthur*, the United Company had Shakespeare's *A Midsummer-Night's Dream* 'made into an Opera', with results even more visually spectacular than *Dioclesian* and *King Arthur* had been. It is not known who adapted Shakespeare's text, but it was Purcell who provided the music, and who wrote some more for a revival the following year. Although there are some quite important variant readings between sources, and although some differences between the 1692 and 1693 productions are not clear, *The Fairy Queen* presents no textual problems as fundamental as those in *King Arthur*.[2]

The Fairy Queen has nevertheless been a source of lively controversy, mainly because its adaptation of Shakespeare has been anathematical to the twentieth century's puritan artistic ethics. Until very recently published opinion was almost entirely negative towards literary, theatrical and musico-dramatic aspects, and fulsome in its praise of the purely musical achievements. In recent years, radical reassessments of the concepts underlying the work, notably by Roger Savage and Curtis Price, have tended to see both the adaptation and the relationship between music and drama as having a distinctive integrity.[3] The musical scenes are thus no longer irrelevant or destructive interpolations: each is a masque, a gesture of celebration or illustration, featuring symbolic figures such as 'Night', 'Winter', 'A Chinese Man', etc. Moreover, at least in the 1692 production, the symbolic subject of each masque is central to the plot, the transition into it set up by the text, either by taking an expanded view of one of Shakespeare's calls for music, or by inserting a new one.

Whatever view one takes of the relationship between music and drama, few would contest that Purcell's music shows that impeccable equivalence between intention and result which underlies all great art. His stylistic range is here at its most ambitious; but underpinning its diversity are grandly simple structures which throw into relief the strengths of single items and the relationships between them.

The most impressive of these large-scale structures is the masque in Act IV (Fig. 17). The adapted act is an amalgam of Shakespeare's Acts III and IV and its musical strengths lie partly in the way it uses a subtle mix of genres, keys and scoring to reflect the progress of events on stage. After the ass's head is taken off Bottom, Titania calls

> Let us have all Variety of Musick,
> All that should welcome up the rising sun.

Variety is what we get. According to the playbook 'The Scene changes to a Garden of Fountains. A Sonata plays while the Sun rises'.[4] Purcell accompanied this feast of the stage designer's and machinist's arts with one of his finest instrumental creations, an Italianate symphony for strings and trumpets, full of terse motivic ideas which permeate many of the later pieces in the scene.

The Four Seasons and their attendants enter for the solo and chorus 'Now the Night Is Chas'd Away' (Z. 629.28). This ground bass piece balances solo, chorus and orchestra so that the whole culminates in a summatory, astonishingly vigorous series of variations for orchestra to which, perhaps, the company could have danced.

The duet for two altos 'Let the Fifes and the Clarions' (Z. 629.29) reflects a very different view of ground bass technique. While the first song regarded its nimbly leaping quaver bass as the starting point for variations of great diversity, this one has a bass of just five notes up and down the D major arpeggio, and vocal parts which manage to concentrate on similar fanfare motifs. Its extraordinary sparseness assumes an insistence which commands the move on to the 'Entry of Phoebus' (Z. 629.30):

> Let the Fifes, and the Clarions, and shrill Trumpets sound,
> And the Arch of high Heav'n the Clangor resound.

This dramatic link is brilliantly reinforced by the way in which many motifs from the duet are reworked during the thunderous symphony for strings, trumpets and drums played as Phoebus enters.

After all this D-major trumpeting, the move into Phoebus' solo is startling. Purcell picks up the notion of the 'cruel long winter' having 'frozen the earth' with an A minor setting for tenor, two violins and continuo, whose tortuously slow progress superbly captures 'imprison'd' nature seeking 'in vain to be free'. As Phoebus declares 'I dart forth my beams to give all things a birth', a rollicking triple-time solo leaves the violins, those symbols of winter's grip, silent.

How can the assembled company respond to these portentous claims?

Fig. 17. The Fairy Queen: Act IV

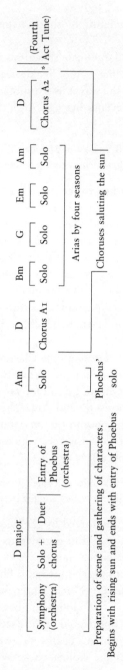

*The libretto specifies a 'Dance of the Four Seasons' at this point, for which no music survives, although it seems likely that Purcell did write it. See Zimmerman, *Analytical Catalogue*, p. 326 and Laurie, 'Purcells Stage Works', p. 103.

Purcell creates a suitable response by combining sectional repetition and variation with a slow progress through just four lines of text:

> Hail! Great parent of us all,
> Light and comfort of the Earth;
> Before thy shrine the Seasons fall,
> Thou who givest all beings birth.

The continuo's descending scale from D to A, which linked the opening D major area with Phoebus' A minor aria, is now answered by a descent from A to D, on which the full consort of instruments enters for a massively scored, declamatory chorus 'Hail! Great parent of us all', just five bars long and ending with a full close in the tonic. It is followed directly by a triple-time, fugal chorus on 'Light and comfort of the Earth' which, together with its instrumental postlude, ends in a full close in A. This sets things up neatly for the return of the descending continuo scale to return to the chorus 'Hail! Great parent'. As if in response to the declaration of the Sun's attributes, this is extended to nine bars to include the line 'Before thy shrine the Seasons fall' and now ends with a full close on A. Again it is followed by a triple-time chorus, this time a declamatory one, setting the last line of the verse and ending with a full close in D.

The four seasons make their obeisance as each sings an aria setting out its distinctive attributes. Winter (a bass, of course) has the last of the four contrasted pieces, at the end of which he 'Prays the Sun to restore him, and sings as before'. The full close in A minor is followed by the same descending scale which ended Phoebus' aria. Thus both music and text set up the return of the chorus 'Hail! Great parent' to close the scene. Purcell uses the version of the chorus which sets all four lines, thus bringing the homage full circle.

In the playbook a dance for the four seasons is specified next. No music survives for it, although Purcell might well have written it. Nevertheless, the cumulative effect of the scene – a series of varied cycles away from and back to the two massive D major paeans to the sun – remains.

Although no other 1692 masque is quite as elaborate as this one, they are all deeply concerned with musical cohesion. That in Act II has two scenes (described as 'songs' in the playbook), separated by Titania's command to sing her to sleep, in C major and minor respectively. The C major items are united by holding to precepts set out in the first prelude (Z. 629.7a), in which an extraordinarily subtle tension between figuration and metre underlies seeming rhythmic regularity. The two distinctive figurations (x and y of Ex. 134) open in dialogue between two instrumental groupings, respectively two violins and viola, and continuo. In both groups, the sequential repetitions produce a large-scale movement, predominantly across thirds (a and b) with E given special prominence in violin I (bb. 2 and 3–4), and producing a metrical grouping of three crotchets, which opens out into four only at the closes.

Ex. 134 *The Fairy Queen*, Prelude to 'Come All Ye Songsters' (Z. 629.7a): bb. 1–4

Similar dislocations drive the second phrase, in which the former lower figuration appears in the violins and the upper in the violas and continuo; it is longer and reaches a close on G mid-way through b. 9. Thereafter the three upper parts take up continuous semiquaver figuration while the continuo has the violins' opening figure, but now compressed to stress the first and third beats of each bar, and thus iron out the metrical dislocation. In just three bars this finishes with a close in C.

'Come All Ye Songsters' (Z. 629.7b) begins (Ex. 135) by paraphrasing the prelude's melodic movement G–C–E (*a* of Ex. 134) and, perhaps more significantly, aspects of its tensional methods. It was on high G that the prelude began part-inversion of the opening figuration (b. 4); in the recitative, stepwise movement emerges (bb. 14–15) as the voice reaches high G; and from then on the figuration of the recitative is dominated by third-based motifs (cf. *a* and *b*). G is also the pitch on which the recitative moves into the ground bass song proper (b. 19). As the ground enters, metrical and harmonic stability returns, as if the ground itself represents the songsters assembling.

Most of the other C major items maintain relationship with the prelude and opening song by using third-based motifs and by stressing E and G in their melodic lines. Both links are evident in the ground bass prelude (Z. 629.8a) and in the trio 'May the God of Wit' (Z. 629.8b) and, perforce, in the following instrumental 'Echo'. (From this prelude onwards the violas have no part to play until the 'Fairy Dance'; surely the trio textures are meant to represent the songsters?) The chorus 'Now Join Your Warbling Voices' (Z. 629.9) has similar pitch and motivic emphases, and the song and chorus 'Sing While We Trip It' (Z. 629.10) returns to the strong stress on G and also picks up the Scotch snap figure from the second prelude.

The opening piece of the second scene, 'See, Even Night' (Z. 629.11), reflects

Ex. 135   *The Fairy Queen*, 'Come All Ye Songsters' (Z. 629.7b): bb. 13–23

the dramatic context by reworking vigorous scalic figuration, taken largely from 'Now Join Your Warbling Voices', into somnolently descending lines. These appear in the second bar of 'See, Even Night', beginning on high G, and recur throughout the piece in a range of contexts (Ex. 138). Nevertheless, the first sound is an ascending third, while the Scotch snap descending third reappears in a deliciously languorous form for 'nothing', and the setting of 'noise and care' features the same high G which was formerly associated with maximum tension. Similar links can be found in all the other items, including the extraordinary 'Dance for the Followers of Night' (Z. 629.15) which ends the masque.

The 1692 version of the Act V masque makes an interesting comparison with the last act of *King Arthur*, for it shows Purcell aiming for a scene of palpable musico-dramatic unity in an essentially non-dramatic format. The music is a virtuoso exhibition of various kinds of ostinato technique, superbly set up in the opening G minor symphony for strings and in Juno's air 'Thrice Happy Lovers'. In the 1693 production the famous but dramatically irrelevant song 'The Plaint' (Z. 629.40) appeared next.[5] In both productions Oberon then calls

> Now let a new transparent world be seen,
> All nature joyn to entertain our Queen.
> Now we are reconcil'd, all things agree
> To make an universal harmony.

Two fine instrumental pieces, an Entry Dance and a Symphony (Z. 629.41 and 42) are played 'While the Scene is darken'd'. Then we see 'a transparent Prospect of a Chinese Garden, the Architecture, the Trees, the Plants, the Fruits, the Birds, the Beasts quite different to what we have in this part of the World'.[6]

The subsequent, basically cumulative progress is particularly dependent upon contrasts between solos and ensembles and between dramatic stasis and motion. The Chinese man and woman are exotic individuals which on the one hand represent the 'new Transparent World', and on the other personify 'Universal Harmony' in that they possess the same passions as the Europeans and fairy folk who have dominated the play.

The man sings the massive 'Thus the Gloomy World' (Z. 629.43), a da capo ground bass song, with trumpet obbligato, with the 'B' section in a different time and with a different ground. The woman sings the song 'Thus Happy and Free' (Z. 629.44), but instead of the long setting suggested by the text, printed as four three-line stanzas each repeated by the chorus, we get three presentations of a rollicking nine-bar, binary-form theme: the first is for four-part strings; the second gives the first two stanzas to the soloist; for the third and fourth stanzas the fully harmonised version returns, set for strings and chorus. The terseness of this treatment throws the emphasis forward onto the large solo 'Yes, Daphne' (Z. 629.45): it is not as long as 'Thus the Gloomy World', but its amazing technical wizardry – it is a freely treated ground bass – is scarcely less impressive.

An entrance and dance of monkeys (Z. 629.46) brings this display of exoticism to an end. The First and Second Women's long solos 'Hark, How All Things' and 'Hark! the Echoing Air' (Z. 629.47 and 48) are an apt, celebratory response to events in which the world does indeed seem 'to have one voice'.

The next piece of printed text is 'Sure the dull god of marriage does not hear', a response which would be fine if only it had been clear that he was ever intended to. Purcell inserts a solution of his own to counter the dramatic flimsiness. At the end of 'Hark! the Echoing Air' the chorus and strings enter for five homophonic cries of 'Hark!' These set up an expectation which imparts some tension to the transition into 'Sure the Dull God', and it is typical of Purcell, that a such bold gesture is based on an earlier, seemingly insignificant one, in this case the end of the trumpet's opening phrases, which overlap with the vocal entry at the beginning of the song.

This is the first moment of genuine dramatic tension. During 'Sure the Dull God Of Marriage Does Not Hear' (Z. 629.49a) the Women declare that they will 'rouse him' and the rest of the company join in for a superbly structured, cumulative ensemble number 'Hymen Appear!' (Z. 629.49b–e). He arrives to the strains of a sixteen-bar Prelude and, in a sombre E minor, declares (Ex. 32) how he has become disappointed by 'loose dissembled vows' and 'false flames'.

So, in 'Turn, Then Thine Eyes' (Z. 629.50c) the women urge him to be encouraged by 'those glories here'. It is almost certain that the traditional ordering of numbers at this point is wrong, and that the chaconne, traditionally regarded as coming after the trio 'They Shall Be As Happy' (Z. 629.50e) and being for the Chinese man and woman, is in fact the 'Grand Dance... of Twenty-four Persons' indicated in the playbook at this point. Certainly, that ordering makes more sense both of the purely musical structure, with 'They Shall Be As Happy' presented successively as a trio and chorus to end the masque; and of the dramatic scene, with Hymen – a somewhat mawkish progeny of Orpheus' reluctant Charon – won over by musical display.[7]

Taken as a whole, this masque can be seen as one section of dramatic action – the appearance and persuasion of Hymen – between the last two of three static tableaux, of the Chinese man and woman, the First and Second Women, and the final dance and chorus. Yet the musical arrangement is loose, for the key scheme does not coincide with these boundaries and despite the prevalence of ostinato techniques and third-based motifs, it is the quality of the individual item which ultimately impresses.

Many of the solo songs in *The Fairy Queen* are of unprecedented size, especially 'Hark! the Echoing Air' (Z. 629.48) and 'Hark, How All Things' (Z. 629.47). The long instrumental prelude of the latter (Ex. 136) foreshadows the

Ex. 136   *The Fairy Queen*, Prelude to 'Hark, How All Things' (Z. 629.47a): bb. 1–5

scale of things to come, and in its simple yet expansive harmonic structure, which uses permutations solely of I, V and IV, it establishes that forceful clarity of function which makes possible the setting of such a brief text to so much music (Fig. 18).

Fig. 18. The Fairy Queen: structure of 'Hark, How All Things' (Z. 629.47)

Hark how all things with one sound rejoice,
And the world seems to have voice.[8]

Prelude	A1	:‖	B		A2
bb. 1 – 19	18 – 36	:‖	39	– 55	56 – 84
I	I – V	:‖	V – (I – IV ~) – vi		I

Repetition occurs on just three words, 'sound', 'rejoice' and 'voice', each
with a characteristic motif. Like the opening bars of the prelude, the first vocal
phrase (Ex. 137) arpeggiates G to D. Motif *a*, used to set 'sound', can readily be

Ex. 137   *The Fairy Queen*, 'Hark, How All Things' (Z. 629.47b): bb. 17–41

Ex. 138   The Fairy Queen, 'See, Even Night' (Z. 629.11): bb. 23–32

altered, provided it retains its main identifying elements – the rhythm of b. 21 and the four scalic quavers. An inverted variant immediately follows (b. 22) and, in b. 32, a version closer to the original, though the new context enables it to fulfil a different function: instead of the regular scalic descent *m* of bb. 21–4 it becomes part of a large, irregular, descending pattern which, outlining dominant harmony, drives to a close in that key (bb. 35–6), and which neatly contrasts with the ascending patterns formed by the repetitions of *b* for 'rejoice'.

Repetition techniques are their most elaborate in the B section, where b. 40 sees a more radical modification of *a*, retaining just the four scalic quavers at the end of the bar (*s* – b. 40). In one of those happy matches between textual and musical structure which are characteristic of so much great text setting, the next extended melisma is on 'voice', rhyming neatly with that on 'rejoice' and including motivic derivations from *b* but contrasting with it in function.

As with *m*, the melisma describes a descending scale generated by motivic repetition. The bass is no less concentrated, consisting largely of developments of *t* (b. 21). The harmonic and motivic directions of each part are clear, and together tread an impeccable path between stretching and breaking the boundaries of harmonic possibility as they proceed remorselessly to a resolution on E minor, which is followed by the song's first section, reworked to end in the tonic.

A more obviously elaborate song is 'A Thousand Ways' (Z. 629.25) from Act

III. The inordinate repetitions of 'thousand' are only the most obvious response to the text ('A thousand ways we'll find to entertain the hours'). It is likely that it was originally a duet with the lower part almost identical to the instrumental bass;[9] certainly this would intensify the erotic suggestiveness, which depends partly on the somewhat breathless, quasi-canonic imitation between voice and bass, and partly on the suggesting of melodic progressions – especially those involving the sharpened or flattened sixth and seventh degrees of the minor scale – then turning them aside. The following chorus extends these notions by pairing off the vocal and instrumental parts to produce elaborate cross relations and a judicious sprinkling of augmented triads.

A related style of chromaticism is used, to comparably erotic effect, in the song 'If Love's a Sweet Passion' (Z. 629.17), which has attracted as much attention for the variety of the three harmonisations for strings, soloist and chorus, as for its melodic expressivity. Price justly remarks that the prelude and chorus are 'so casually dissonant that one supposes the composer could have hit upon half a dozen equally stunning harmonizations', and finds the indulgently saturated texture a comment on the dramatic context.[10] Casual it may be, but the over-the-top harmonisation of the chorus' lines 'When in striving to hide, she reveals all her flame', with its outrageous succession of secondary dominants, works because the successive harmonisations have increasingly pressed the boundaries of harmonic possibility for any given moment, while having a longer-term goal in view.

Night's solo 'See, Even Night' (Z. 629.11) bears comparison with that other outstanding piece of nocturnal evocation, the ground bass air 'So When the Glitt'ring Queen of Night' from the 1690 ode *Of Old, When Heroes Thought It Base* (Z. 333.11). In 'See, Even Night', Purcell creates a suavely floating, somnolent effect through rhythmic uniformity (Ex. 138), giving the voice practically the same material as the strings, and omitting bass instruments. The main idea *a* and immediate derivations saturate the texture, even when the voice has moved on anew. So the setting of 'And all her peaceful train is near' is in G minor and, while the voice repeats a single high D, the strings have the main material inverted. The result is a texture in which line is an extraordinarily potent force, as in b. 28 (Ex. 138), where the voice stresses elements of dominant harmony over the functioning tonic to create a subtle instability, emphasising the resolution onto dominant harmony in the next bar. This emphasis neatly sets up that harmony as the beginning of a long prolongation which ends with a close into the dominant (b. 42).

For the spring and summer of 1693 Purcell produced no new large stage work; instead *The Fairy Queen* and *Dioclesian* were revived, and one of his main tasks was the provision of extra music for the former. He also composed music for a number of plays, including Southerne's comedy *The Maid's Last*

Table 12. The Maid's Last Prayer '*No, Resistance Is But Vain*' (Z. 601.2)

No, no, no, no, resistance is but vain,	1
And only adds new weight to Cupid's chain:	2
A thousand ways, a thousand arts,	3
The tyrant knows, to captivate our hearts:	4
Sometimes he sighs imploys, and sometimes tries	5
The universal language of the eyes:	6
The fierce, with fierceness he destroys:	7
The weak, with tenderness decoys.	8
He kills the strong with joy, the weak with pain:	9
No, no, no, no, resistance is but vain.	10

Section	Line	Bars	Key	Time
A	1	1–20	i–v	Triple
	2	20–33	~–III	
	1	33–53	~–i	
B	3 and 4	54–62	i–III	Duple
C	5 and 6	63–72	III–iv(IV)	Triple
D	7	72–5	VII–VII	Duple
E	8	76–81	vii–V of iv	Triple
F	9 (1st half)	81–8	IV–III	Duple
G	9 (2nd half)	88–94	~–V of i	Triple
+A	10 = 1	94–112	V of i–v	
	2	112–25	~–III	
	1	125–45	~–i	

Prayer (Z. 601), which includes the superb duet 'No, Resistance Is But Vain' (Z. 601.2). The song's dramatic context is weak, but the text's imagery and general suggestiveness (the text is apparently by an MP, Anthony Henly)[11] elicited the composer's highest powers.

No multi-sectional song before this one so securely and cogently uses harmonic process as a primary means of providing continuity across wide stylistic variety (Table 12). Its methods in this and other respects were to become central to Purcell's later multi-sectional songs for the stage, such as those in *Don Quixote* (Z. 578) and 'Ye Twice Ten Hundred Deities' from *The Indian Queen* (Z. 630.13).

The repetitions in section A of the first line create an opening unit sufficiently defined to form the background against which subsequent events are focussed, with the two large statements of A sandwiching a number of contrasted smaller sections which dispatch the text comparatively quickly. These smaller sections have common motivic patterns; the triple-time sections are closely related to A, and all sections are dominated by scalic motion and by motifs which cover a

Ex. 139 The Maid's Last Prayer, 'No, Resistance Is But Vain' (Z. 601.2):
(i) bb. 1–10

(ii) bb. 28–39

third. The first line is distinguished from all except 9 (treated anyway as part of a sequence of rapid change) by beginning with a leap.

Purcell's control of context is impeccable. The opening motif *a* (Ex. 139 (i)) is set up as a defining agent firstly by the large, tonally propositional statement which begins on the dominant in b. 9 and secondly by its return after the C major close at the end of the second line (b. 33 in Ex. 139 (ii)). This return is superbly timed: the second line features, after b. 20, a series of overlapping, ascending melodic sequences in the voices, with audacious harmonic effect as each of the ascending fourths in the bass (every two bars) ends with a major third above, producing a gross over-burden of secondary dominants which ends on V of C and a prolongation of that function (bb. 29–32, Ex. 139 (ii)). It certainly adds new weight, but also cries out for relief.

After this calculated superfluity, the return in C major of the opening motif *a* is at once a relief and a submission. It keeps to its original form during the chromatic ascent of the bass, but as the latter reaches E (b. 37) the vocal pitches change to fill out a third, and this helps articulate the beginning of a prolongation which lasts through to b. 46, and which involves progression away from and back to the supertonic in the upper voice (bb. 37–46). The importance of the subsequent close is underlined by the Neapolitan harmony, produced by chromatically filling out B–A.

Aspects of this section justify the subsequent considerable contrasts. Duple-time sections follow the example of the first departure from the opening material (bb. 20–33) in concentrating on major mode harmonies. The chromatic approach to V of i after a close in C (bb. 32–6) receives a new and delicious twist in the first bars of the last section, G + A (Ex. 140): the bass falls a diminished fourth, and the voices use the same motif for 'weak' as was formerly used for 'add' in the over-strong progressions of the second line. The enervating chromaticism of bb. 88–94 suggests a move back to the tonic and in b. 94 picks up the high E which was such a prominent feature of the last few bars (bb. 89 and 91); this and the drawn-out B of bb. 93–4 come together on the C. This is, of course, b. 2 of the opening, so while the chromatic descent posits a resolution on A, this does not happen until the end of the piece, after a complete repetition of A. Purcell was neither the first nor the last composer to reap a great harvest from the obvious imagery of poor verse.

This song has little to do with the surrounding play, and here we have one of the central paradoxes of Purcell's music for the stage, for while he was at pains to make the most of musico-dramatic relationships, such as there may be, he was not in the slightest handicapped by their absence. This is highlighted by the quality of the music written for the 1693 revival of *The Fairy Queen*, much of which seems to disturb the plan of the 1692 production.[12] Yet the Act I scene for the drunken poet has become famous, particularly for Purcell's skill at making good entertainment out of material which could have been fatuous.

Like Night's scene in Act II it reworks a few closely related motifs throughout, and only occasionally goes outside the tonic. It is a masterpiece of timing, in which subtle differentiation of the music for the fairies and the poet plays a crucial role. The poet's music is dominated by steady arpeggaic figures, while

Ex. 140   *The Maid's Last Prayer*, 'No, Resistance Is But Vain' (Z. 601.2): bb. 86–96

the fairies have more nimbly moving lines derived from those of the poet: his bumbling repetitions on 'Fill up the bowl', for example, are followed by the agile repetitions of the fairies' 'Trip it in a ring', which fill out the poet's arpeggio patterns.

There are few better examples of how Purcell had learned to adapt his naturally elaborate polyphonic thinking to modern methods of construction than the concluding chorus 'Drive 'em Hence' (Z. 629.5l). The tension produced by constantly varied combinations of the two well-characterised subjects – a descending crotchet scale for 'Drive 'em hence' and trenchant arpeggiations for 'away' – drives two harmonic prolongations and a mobile sequence which in F major articulate V of I (bb. 1–5), V of IV (bb. 6–9), IV–II–V (bb. 9–13) and V of I (bb. 14–17). The subjects consist of repetition of small motifs, and are thus amenable to fragmentation without loss of identity.

The end of the chorus prolongs V of I (bb. 14–17), and is famous for its setting of 'Let 'em sleep till break of day'. The prominent E♮s, which are central to its expressive effect, are a continuation of the strong subdominant inflexions between bb. 6 and 9, which were quickly abandoned in the assertive move onto the dominant in bb. 9–13. So these closing E♭s pick up some of these unfulfilled implications, not as approaches to or aspects of subdominant function, but as a colouristic borrowing which neatly balances the assertive ending of 'Drive 'em hence away'. They are, of course, justified by imitation.

Such clear borrowings from Purcell's early practice also can be seen in two of his smaller dramatic contributions from 1693, the music for Dryden and Lee's *Oedipus* (Z. 583) and for Shadwell's *The Libertine* (Z. 600).[13] In the opening scene of the former, the first two refrains feature dissonance which lends a graphically sonorous twist to 'sullen powers'. The dissonance arises through the parts simultaneously presenting differing harmonic possibilities, in a manner strikingly reminiscent of that which was responsible for so many of the most dissonant passages in the pavans and fantasias.

This piece leads immediately into the celebrated 'Music for a While' (Z. 583.2) which, if its popularity can be taken as a guide, might indeed be the most satisfying in expression and technique of all Purcell's ground bass songs, except perhaps Dido's lament.[14] The ground's prominent use of both forms of the sixth and seventh degrees of the scale are derived from the remorselessly descending lines which at the end of the trio illustrate 'poor ghosts' being sent 'ten thousand fathoms low'.[15] Its more leisurely chromatic ascent neatly counters this as music seeks to sooth the 'sullen powers'.

The concept is beguilingly simple, but the execution reveals brilliant imagination and resourceful technique. Much of the ground's energy comes from tensions between the two voices generated by the single line and particularly from the chromatic ascent from dominant to tonic. Out of this grows a central tension of the piece: the voice begins with the same three notes as the ground – C, G, A♭ – but stretched out over a longer span; in the ground, G and A♭ began the chromatic shift, whereas in the voice they are treated as the registral peak, and always begin some sort of descent (Ex. 141). The first vocal phrase posits a link between these descents and a closural gesture: the setting of 'for a while' descends precipitately to D; 'shall all your cares beguile' balances this with a more leisurely line which picks up the D for a V–i coincidental with the end of the ground. Yet the stress falls on E♭ both here and at the reworking of this progression three bars later.

The notion that vocal closure is postponed by avoiding a stressed middle C at the end of the ground is a sublimely simple foil to the elaborate vocal figuration and to the harmonic thrust of the ground. While the C minor feel of the first statements is unalloyed, the first move outside the tonic (on 'and distaining to be pleased') sees the ground concentrating on the constant harmonic mobility which the chromaticism facilitates, rather than on statements

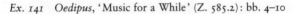

Ex. 141   Oedipus, 'Music for a While' (Z. 585.2): bb. 4–10

which are securely in another key. So the statement which begins in G minor
ends in B♭, and the statement in that key is immediately turned towards E♭ and
needs an extra bar to reach a close.

Throughout, Purcell's control of context is impeccable. After a brief linking
passage back to C minor, there is a statement in that key for 'Till the snakes
drop from her head', the end of which is given appropriate emphasis through
the voice's descending by step to a stressed middle C at the end of the ground.
But three factors prevent closure: the single statement is insufficient to counter
the sweep of the preceding harmonic mobility; the vocal descent has been from
G, not the A♭ which by now is strongly linked to closure; and the repeated
syncopations on 'drop' need balancing by the rhythmic connectedness which is
such a feature of the rest of the song. All this is reinforced by the impressive
swing to G minor in just one and a half bars for 'And the whip from out her
hand'.

Lee's poem is in one continuous verse and follows this line with a call to the
'sullen powers' to 'Come away, do not stay.' Purcell concentrates on the main
purpose of the song – to 'beguile' the powers' cares – and so repeats the
opening line to conclude the song, and sets 'Come away' as a separate ensemble
item. After such an expansive circuit away from C minor and the confirming
properties of middle C, a return to the material which set up those implications
is a perfect marriage of poetic meaning and musical function, and it brings the
song to an end on its only stable middle C. The song so dominates the scene that
the subsequent setting of 'Come away' and the summoning of Laius come as
something of an anticlimax.[16]

After the large productions of 1693, Purcell was mainly involved with several
large sets of instrumental music, including those for *The Double Dealer* (Z. 592)

and *The Married Beau* (Z. 603). For the 1694 season he concentrated on his contributions to the first and second parts of *The Comical History of Don Quixote* (Z. 578.1–8), which was premiered in May of that year. Into his several large vocal contributions he put his highest powers, while D'Urfey's strongly featured dramatisation also encouraged the other contributor of music, John Eccles, to his best efforts.

Apart from the strophic settings used for 'When the World First Knew Creation' and 'Lads and Lasses' (Z. 578.2 and 8), Purcell's songs in *Don Quixote* are amongst his largest vocal compositions. D'Urfey's play has been the source of considerable controversy, but there is no doubt about the importance of music's role in it, or about the intention that music should intensify central elements of the drama.[17]

To meet the musical challenges posed by the unusually long texts, Purcell devised simple yet ingenious solutions. 'Sing All Ye Muses' (Z. 578.1) is a response – gushing with energetic and violently contrasted imagery revolving around soldiers' storming of a wealthy town – to a call for 'the song in praise of arms and soldiery'. Price rightly observes that one of the strengths of Purcell's music for this play lies in its taking itself absolutely seriously, despite the irrational tendencies of the drama.[18] 'Pure in heart' this multi-sectional duet for alto and bass might be, but its expressive power, like that of most songs in *Don Quixote*, lies partly in the verve with which it stretches its musical material to the limits of coherence, neatly complementing its dramatic function – a centrepiece for a mock knighting of Don Quixote.

The hectic, almost bewildering, pace of events, and the range of expressive contrast are extraordinary. Rapid motion is produced only partly by sheer speed: additionally there are frequent changes between duple and triple time, and concomitant changes in tempo, some in the middle of a line of text, and none of which is prepared for in the immediately preceding material; moreover, the downbeat of the closes which end sections tend to be in the new metre. The singers themselves are caught up in the pell-mell.

The call to the muses is ample, giving little hint of the fury to come. At the first mention of soldiery – 'When a soldier's the story / What tongue can want sound?' – the metre changes from duple to triple time, the tempo quickens, and the end of these lines is set to distinctive melodic and harmonic patterns, reinforced through repetition, and which can survive multiple changes of detail and context. They are in fact developed out of the first section, but of more immediate relevance is their textual association, for the soldier is the Don himself.

While most prominent motifs have their origins in the opening bars, it is the recurrence of the first cadential pattern in the second section (setting 'What tongue can want sound?') which signals, and with repetition justifies, the increasingly extreme changes of tempo and metre. Immediately after its first appearance, progress through the battle – the charge, the scramble for spoils, the mine exploding – begins and hinges around this figure's polymorphism. And crossing the boundaries of the twelve or so sections are harmonic and pitch projections which weld contrasts, and underline their impact when they occur as a projection seeks resolution. That this song is not one of Purcell's more profound pieces should not blind us to its unusual strengths.

Much the largest musical item in part one of the play is the Act V Scene II ensemble for three singers, two violins and continuo 'With This Sacred Charming Wand' (Z. 578.4), a remarkable example of musical process reflecting dramatic progress. In this respect and others it is nearer to the methods Purcell had used in *Dido and Aeneas* than any piece of stage music to date.

The rationale behind the scene is bizarre: several secondary characters conspire to ensure that Don Quixote mends his ways, and arrange a mock enchantment to make him believe he is being condemned to death by the power of sorcery. At the beginning of the scene various characters enter in disguise and the singing is given to the two 'Inchantresses' Urganda and Melissa, and to their 'leader' Montesmo, this being the disguise of Cardenio, who in the previous act had sung the celebrated 'Let the Dreadful Engines' (Z. 578.3).

There seems little doubt that the differences between the printed text of the play and Purcell's setting arose at the composer's instigation, for they are better suited to the pace of musical events, and ensure that the scene's central figure is Montesmo – especially important since the singer for the first performance was the renowned John Bowman. Without this amendment Urganda, to whom D'Urfey allocated the six lines beginning 'Nature restore', could easily have dominated the scene. Moreover, the last stretch of text – 'Appear ye fat Fiends' – is not essential to a spoken scene, but provides the necessary musical culmination (cf. D'Urfey's text below and Table 13).

MONTESMO: With this, this sacred charming wand;
           I can heaven and earth command;
           Hush all the winds that curl the angry sea,
           And make the rolling waves obey.
URGANDA: I from the clouds can conjure down the rain,
           And make it deluge once again.
MELISSA: I when I please make nature smile as gay,
           As at first she did on her creation-day:
           Groves with eternal sweets shall fragrant grow,
           And make a true Elysium here below.
CHORUS: Groves with eternal sweets shall fragrant grow,
           And make a true Elysium here below.
MELISSA: I can give beauty, make the aged young,
           And love's dear momentary rapture long.

Table 13. 'With This Sacred Charming Wand' from Don Quixote (Z. 578.4)

	Text	Scoring	Time sig.	Style	Bars	Harmonic structure
(1)	'With this sacred charming wand'	Bass (*Montesmo*) + 2 vlns	¢	Recit.	1–19	i–III–i
(2)	'I from the clouds can conjure down'	Sop. (*Urganda*)	¢	Recit.	20–30	III–VII–v
(3)	'I, when I please make nature smile'	Sop. (*Melissa*)	3/1	Air	31–70	i–III–i
	'Groves with eternal' (from solo, with five-bar ritornello to close)	All + 2 vlns		Ensemble	71–94	III–i
(4)	'I can give beauty'	Sop. (*Mel.*)	¢	Recit.	95–100	i–V of i
(5)	'Nature restore'	Sop. (*Urg.*)	3/1	Air	101–41	III
(6)	'Art all can do' and 'Why then'	All	¢	Ensemble	142–55	i
(7)	'See there a wretch'	Bass (*Mont.*)	3/1	Air	156–70	iv–i
(8)	'I've a little spirit'	Sop. (*Mel.*)	2	Air	170–85	i–III–i
(9)	'No, that fate's too high'	Sop. (*Urg.*) and Bass (*Mont.*)	6/4	Ensemble	186–202	i–v
(10)	'Let it be so'	2 Sops. (*Urg.* and *Mel.*)	2	Ensemble	203–8	V of i–i
(11)	'Appear ye fat fiends'	Bass (*Mont.*)	6/4	Air	209–33	I–V V of vi–ii–I
	'Appear ye fat fiends' (Reworking of solo)	All + 2 vlns		Ensemble	234–55	I–V V of vi–ii–I

URGANDA: Nature restore, and life, when spent, renew:
             All this by art can great Urganda do.
             Why then will mortals dare
             To urge a fate and justice so severe?
             See there a wretch, in's own opinion wise,
             Laughs at our charms, and mocks our mysteries.
MELISSA: I've a little spirit yonder,
             Where the clouds do part asunder,
             Lies basking his limbs
             In the warm sun-beams,
             Shall his soul from his body plunder.
URGANDA: Speak, shall it be so? No,
             That Fate's too high; I'll give him one more low.
MELISSA: Let it be so, etc.

The scene consists of a series of short sections, many of which are complete in themselves, yet in context imply continuation. Variations on simple musical ideas underpin the surface diversity. The opening stage direction refers to 'Dreadful sounds of music', to which Purcell responds with a sublime avoidance of the obvious. Instead of 'horrid music' in F minor, as in the prelude to the witches' scene in *Dido and Aeneas* (Z. 626.14) and the fifth act of *The Indian Queen* (Z. 630.21d and e), we have a coolly calculated opening for two violins over a descending bass (Ex. 142).

Ex. 142   *Don Quixote*, 'With This Sacred Charming Wand' (Z. 578.4): bb. 1–10

The prominence of the bass – the only really mobile part in the texture – provides the cue for a descending line to be used as the first of a number of ideas which can readily be adapted to differing contexts. It functions as a unifying motto throughout the first two recitatives, mostly in the bass (bb. 1–4, 11–15, and all of the second recitative), but also in the voice, as in bb. 11–13 where it shadows the bass, and in bb. 16–18 where it is richly ornamented to represent 'rolling'. Other melodic gestures common to both recitatives are the arpeggaic figuration when Montesmo and Urganda say they can command the elements and the rapid descent at the ends of both sections which, by stressing the lower tonic (G and D respectively), helps produce a forcefulness sufficient to mark closure, yet sudden enough to suggest continuation.

In these first two sections the highest D and F for the voice concerned become persistent focusses of harmonic reinterpretation. In the first, high F is prominent in the assertive move to the relative major. In the second it appears in a move from III to VII (bb. 20–3); while D, which until the approach to the last close had been eschewed by the first section, becomes prominent (bb. 20–1 and 27–30), culminating in a full close in D minor.

All these points are picked up in the third section, Melissa's short aria 'I when I please', which begins with material apparently new, but out of which links with the earlier sections develop. In particular, references to 'nature' and 'creation' use a line descending from the dominant towards the tonic, all closely related to an earlier pattern which referred to Montesmo's and Urganda's powers over nature (b. 8, Ex. 142). Like Montesmo's recitative, the section uses high F, harmonised as III⁶, to make an early assertive move to the relative major (cf. bb. 7–8 and 38–42).

After so much major mode, the gradual return to the tonic for 'Groves with eternal sweets shall fragrant grow' is superbly expressive. Much of its potency is because it is achieved by the voice languorously pivoting around the same high D as was used to move away from the tonic. Largely because of the concentration on D, the dominant prolongation (bb. 56–9) is sufficiently forceful to give the subsequent, quite substantial move to the relative major for 'And make a true Elysium' – which again features a prominent high F – an inevitable gravitation back to G minor.

The stylistic contrast between recitative and aria is intensified by reworking the last part of this air as a trio with violins and by the five-bar violin coda. So the return to G minor recitative for Melissa's 'I can give beauty' is a palpable return to earlier modes of operation, a connection reinforced by the III⁶ harmony in the third bar, with high F in the voice, and by the voice revolving around high D.

This new beginning sets up a gradual increase in the pace of events, reflected firstly in the brevity of the recitative itself. Urganda's ground bass air 'Nature restore' is stylistically not dissimilar to Melissa's 'I, when I please', but less ample. By giving Montesmo the words 'Art all can do', Purcell enables Urganda's last two lines to work as a discourse between all three characters. The moves to G minor and D minor during Montesmo's interjection are the most rapid harmonic moves of the piece thus far and set the scene neatly for the more urgent tone of the trio, which features the largely syllabic setting and dialogue techniques mainly associated with the verse anthems.

In keeping with the increasing speed of events, the trio begins to explore some new, distinctive harmonic progressions. Bars 146–52 include a number of strongly articulated I–iv–V progressions, the strongest pre-dominants thus far in the piece. The timing is impeccable, for the subsequent swing to C minor for the short section 'See there a wretch' both expresses the shift of dramatic interest towards Don Quixote, and expands immediately preceding events, as its three main phrases each express one component of a iv–V–i progression, ending in G minor. After this, the strongest of these pre-dominants, the rest of the scene is a comparatively stable prolongation of G minor.

The manic atmosphere engendered by this extreme range of contrasts is enormously intensified by Melissa as she launches into 'I've a little Spirit yonder', a superb depiction of malicious glee, yet sufficiently over-the-top to convey unreality.

By dividing the next lines between all three characters Purcell weakens literary structure in favour of dramatic intensity. The setting of Melissa's 'Shall it be so?' uses motivic repetition to describe a scalic descent from G to G (bb. 178–85). This is countered by leaping arpeggio lines for 'No, no'. Descent returns for Montesmo's reply 'I'll give him one more low', which ends with a strong full close in a thoroughly prepared D minor; so although there is a rhyme of local musical and dramatic function the gesture is basically expansive. To bring events to a close the short duet 'Let it be so' reworks more directly the material for 'Shall it be so?' and thus articulates a musico-dramatic rhyme ABA, corresponding to full closes in G minor, D minor and G minor respectively.

The G major solo and chorus 'Appear Ye Fat Fiends' has many characteristics of 'I've a Little Spirit' but, being free of interpolations by other characters, is inherently more stable, despite its generally rollicking nature and the bad taste of its text.[19] The participation in the chorus of all three characters plus the violins drives home the coming together of the strands which have animated this altogether extraordinary scene.

As this scene is a somewhat bizarre, exotic comedy, it might be argued that rather than being a serious shot at integrating dramatic progress and musical structure, it is a 'buffo' scene of the same genre as that of the drunken poet from *The Fairy Queen*, and that like that scene, it consists of a series of character 'snapshots', apt and musically integrated but not much concerned with personal

Ex. 143   Bonduca, Prelude to 'Sing, Sing Ye Druids' (Z. 574.13a): bb. 1–13

expression or dramatic development. But unlike that scene or, indeed, most others since *Dido and Aeneas*, its characters are real individuals, and it sees Purcell reusing for the first time that stylistic contrast, manipulation of pace and control of large-scale harmonic tension which dominated *Dido and Aeneas*.

For part two of *Don Quixote* Purcell provided just three pieces, the strophic air 'Lads and Lasses' (Z. 578.8), as neatly turned a piece of folksy art as he produced anywhere, the dialogue 'Since Times Are So Bad' (Z. 578.6) and the massive trumpet song 'Genius of England' (Z. 578.7), a piece of aggressively patriotic pomposity which succeeds through the verve, scale and conviction of its musical gestures.[20] Its methods are developed from those of earlier songs for similar forces, such as 'Thus the Gloomy World' from *The Fairy Queen* (Z. 629.43) and 'While for a Righteous Cause' from *Celebrate This Festival* (Z. 321.12).

The song is in two sections in ¢ and 3₁ time respectively: a prelude for trumpet is reworked and extended as a solo for St George (tenor) which summons up the Genius of England (soprano); the Genius sings a long triple-time solo which urges the English soldier to valour in war.

The scale of periodic units is even larger than in the most elaborate songs from *The Fairy Queen*, and is closely associated with harmonic function. The prelude and St George's solo are entirely within C major, and rework material set out in the opening bars of the prelude. For thirty-three bars the Genius too sings entirely within C, a weighting of the tonic which gives the first departure from it (bb. 60–71) particular potency. This harmonically mobile phrase is repeated three times, articulating a decisive swing towards the dominant, and this is intensified by the voice then setting off in that key for 'Who brings home the noblest scars'. It takes no less than twenty bars to reach the final close in the dominant.

Just as *King Arthur* followed *Dido and Aeneas* with a distinctive approach to musical style and musico-dramatic structure, so does each of the large scenes written in the last year of Purcell's life – those in *Bonduca* (Z. 574), *Timon of Athens* (Z. 632) and *The Indian Queen* (Z. 630). Apart from these, he was mainly concerned with instrumental music and songs. Many of the smaller of these songs are amongst Purcell's most famous, not least because they have a natural ease of expression which, unlike the elaborate recitatives, is readily appreciated by a modern audience. Amongst them must be numbered 'Man Is for the Woman Made' from *The Mock Marriage* (Z. 605.3) and 'Lucinda Is Bewitching Fair' from *Abdelazer* (Z. 570.10).

The larger songs from these late plays show a remarkable range of practice. One of the most impressive must be 'Sing, Sing Ye Druids' from *Bonduca* (Z. 574.13), which Price aptly compares to 'With Dances and Songs' from *Dioclesian* (Z. 627.13c and d),[21] though its approach to ground bass is much more sophisticated. It appears as part of a ritual scene which, more than most such, mixes speech and song to highlight the inspirational power of music.

The impressive series of numbers beginning 'Hear Us, Great Rugwith' (Z. 574.11 and 12) meets with no response. Charatach then implores the aid of 'Divine Andate' in a few lines of speech. 'A flame arises' and he commands 'Now sing, ye Druids'. For this Purcell provided a long prelude, duet and chorus in G minor which revolves around a subtle balance between repetition and change.

For the former we have the bass itself, utterly uniform in its quaver motion, while even the changes within the upper lines occur within a narrow pitch range, rarely going outside G–C (Ex. 143). The constant reworking of these basically circular ideas creates an effect which is indeed somewhat hypnotic,[22] and which is amplified in scale and intensity by the ways in which larger-scale processes operate on spans much longer than the four-bar repetitions, particularly by the ample harmonic motion through VII (b. 16), v (b. 29) and back to i (b. 38). The vocal section is an expanded variation on the prelude, taking full advantage of the latter's harmonic economy to heighten important parts of the text, as in Ex. 144, where the voices rise ecstatically out of their registral confines, continuing the quaver motion which approached the close into i to drive through to v.

The following recitative, 'Divine Andate!' (Z. 574.14) seems originally to

Ex. 144   Bonduca, 'Sing, Sing Ye Druids' (Z. 574.13b): bb. 63–70

have been intended as speech.[23] What we have is far more effective, a terse question to the goddess whether the Britons will yield or 'dye with Roman blood the field'. The setting begins in a simple declamatory style, with a line set to a scale falling a seventh from D to E♮ and is then reworked beginning on high E♭.[24] The arresting cross relation between the two registers is sorted out by the following elaborate roulade on 'Roman', which picks up both pitches and resolves them respectively to F♯ and D.

This is a superb use of music to underline dramatic irony, for although the oracle calls out 'Much will be spill'd', it will be British blood, not Roman; and all this striking musical effort will prove in vain, including the following trumpet prelude and duet 'To Arms, To Arms!' (Z. 574.15), in which two druids encourage the Britons to martial valour.

Irony is underlined on a larger scale by the stylistic contrasts between the impressively ritualistic invocations to Rugwith and Andate, and the exhortations to the Druids and other Britons. So while 'To Arms, To Arms!' is a piece of heroic bombast, it is plainly addressed to people, and 'Sing, Sing Ye Druids' captures something of the personal urgency which underlies the Druids' and Britons' pleas. The concluding piece of communal encouragement, the solo and chorus 'Britons, Strike Home' (Z. 574.16) rounds off the scene in that simple choral style which Purcell had perfected in the odes.

The one remaining vocal solo in *Bonduca* is the song from the last act 'O Lead

Me to Some Peaceful Gloom' (Z. 574.17), a fascinating piece of considered, rhetorical point-making. The opening bass, trudging up and down C–D–E♭, captures perfectly Bonduca's fatal weariness and her fanfares on the last word of 'Where the shrill trumpets never sound' is a consummate use of antithesis.

The opening ritual scene from *Bonduca*, 'Hear Us, Great Rugwith' (Z. 574.11), finely balances the repetition of musical formulae, on which the ritualistic element largely depends, with the expressive flair needed for the stage. Purcell's masterstroke lies in beginning with a tightly worked prelude for strings, whose eighteen bars turn out to be a paraphrase of the following forty for chorus and four soloists. The stark, line-driven simplicity of the opening sets up two basic motifs from which the prelude and, by extension, the choral material will be derived – the ascending fifth *a* and the stressed descending dissonance *b* (Ex. 145 (i)). The latter in particular is amenable to multifarious

Ex. 145   Bonduca, 'Hear Us, Great Rugwith' (Z. 574.11)
(i) bb. 1–4

(ii) bb. 9–13

contexts: in b. 3 it forms the basis for *c*, and both *b* and *c* are dissonant progenitors of the more consonant descending line *d* (Ex. 145 (ii)). In the chorus *a* is mainly associated with 'Hear us', and *b* and its relatives with 'Descend ye powers' – *c* appears in diminution (quavers) and *d* in its original form.

Ex. 146   Pausanias, 'Sweeter Than Roses' (Z. 585.1): bb. 27–44

Taken as a whole, *Bonduca* might seem to represent a decline in the thoroughgoing organicism which was such a feature of *Dido and Aeneas* and, more recently, of *Don Quixote*. But it is a change of kind rather than substance, for the two motivic types which dominated 'Hear Us, Great Rugwith' – especially the ascending fifth or fourth – dominate all subsequent movements, including the elaborate solo for bass and strings 'Hear, Ye Gods of Britain' and the duet 'To Arms, to Arms!' (Z. 574.12 and 15).

That this motivic economy should go hand in hand with a continuing increase in expressive scope is one of those paradoxes which defies precise analysis. An outstanding example is 'Sweeter Than Roses' from *Pausanias* (Z. 585.1), amongst the finest of all Purcell's songs.[25] It is in C minor, and the opening line has a five-bar setting whose vocal elaboration is underpinned by a simple bass which twice, with differing rhythm, states a descending scale C–B♭–A♭–G. It would have been Purcell's common practice to repeat the opening line on a different harmonic level; but instead he subjects the same text to a radical reworking in the same key. The bass again has a descending line, but it runs through a whole octave from G to G (bb. 9–14). The 'cool evening breeze' which ended the first setting here too appears in a weak close onto C minor with E♭ uppermost (though at the higher octave); but now it is extended for 'On a warm flowery shore', as the bass carries on down to G.

The most remarkable feature of this reworking is the way Purcell changes the details of text setting and emphasis: instead of the long E♭ on 'Sweeter' there is an elaborate oscillation around G, emphasising the G–A♭–G which was prominent in the continuo's preceding interlude; instead of a melisma on 'cool' there is one on 'evening'; and throughout, the same motifs might recur on different words, might be inverted or might have intervallic detail altered.

The harmonic stability of these opening bars emphasises that they achieve much of their expressive effect through economical motivic manipulation. Their cycle of events, concerned with the memory that 'Sweeter than roses ... was the dear kiss', ends with a strong V–i in C minor, and the new imagery, dealing with the poets' reaction, is juxtaposed against them by setting off firmly in E♭. This is the first clear major mode heard thus far, though it is emphatically tied into earlier events through 'trembling' being set to the same G–A♮ shivers which set 'Sweeter'. In this context the totally unprepared move to E♭ minor on 'made me freeze' is astonishing, one of Purcell's most remarkable uses of harmonic gesture.

The assertiveness with which the major mode returns in arpeggio figuration for 'then shot like fire all o'er', neatly sets up a turn to the tonic major for the song's second section and the dominance of arpeggio figuration at its opening (Ex. 146). Underlying the section's ample phrasing and harmonic structure (I–V–vi–I) is a motivic economy which is as astonishing for its inventiveness as for its terseness.

Thirds were a dominant feature of the first section, though almost always covered by elaborate figuration. This section seems to strip them to their bare essentials as it opens with a rhythmic ostinato *a*, which here and in all its repetitions includes the prominent third *x*. Then the bass has a scalic line which also outlines thirds *b* (cf. bb. 1–2), while the more mobile line *c* is based on the same outline and the motifs *y* and *z* are further elaborations.

The harmonic simplicity so characteristic of the first section is also prominent here, and the propositional restatement in V, beginning in b. 40, is neatly elided into the C major area by beginning with 'tonal' imitation. Like these two opening phrases, the rest of the piece consists either of harmonic prolongations or of circuits which clearly set a goal and then drive towards it, often with some beautifully tricky metrical twists on the way.

Another notable large song from this time is 'Thy Genius, Lo!' from *The Massacre of Paris* (Z. 604B), Purcell's second setting of this text. The two settings reveal much about Purcell's development as a song writer: the first (Z. 604A), written for Bowman in 1689, is multi-sectional, and features those heightened stylistic contrasts which can be seen in independent songs such as *Gentle Shepherds* and *Young Thirsis' Fate* (Z. 464 and 473). The second, written for 'the boy' Jeremy Bowen,[26] is a recitative in one section. Its style comes somewhere between those of the first section of 'Sweeter Than Roses' and *Tell Me, Some Pitying Angel* (Z. 196) from a couple of years earlier. It is impressive but as a stage song is curiously highbrow and was published just once, in 1697. It is perhaps significant that for *Orpheus britannicus* the earlier version was selected, and that in this and other publications it reappeared as late as the early nineteenth century.

By far Purcell's largest contribution for a straight stage play in his final year is his setting of the masque of Cupid and Bacchus for Shadwell's adaptation of Shakespeare's *Timon of Athens*, which was first performed in its Purcellian version in May or June of 1695. To characterise Bacchus and Cupid, Purcell uses techniques seen in *King Arthur* and *The Fairy Queen*, but at a much more racy pace, achieved by making individual numbers shorter and by using more transparent stylistic contrasts.[27]

The substance of this miniature drama is set up by the F major duet for two trebles and two recorders 'Hark! How the Songsters', which declares that the birds 'Sing anthems to the god of love', and by the following solo in the same key 'Love in Their Little Veins Inspires Their Cheerful Notes'. Two trebles and a bass foil the opening cheeriness with some F minor indulgences in 'But ah! How much are our delights more dear, / For only human kind love all the year'.

Bacchus gets his first look-in with a riposte from a lover of wine, 'Hence! With Your Trifling Deity' (though it is possible that Bacchus sang this part), a bass solo in B♭ with interludes on two oboes.[28] This is the longest piece since 'Hark How the Songsters' and its importance is underlined by its ending in praise of 'lusty wine' being reworked as a trio for alto, tenor and bass.

Love makes its reply in Cupid's solo 'Come All to Me', a short, lively piece in D minor for treble voice and two violins. The plea to join in 'the joys of love without its pains' has some effect, for the company responds in the same key with 'Who Can Resist' (Z. 632.15), a massive setting for four-part chorus and strings. Cupid seems victorious, but Bacchus himself now makes a plea with a superbly judged mixture of pompous grandeur and drunken repetition, 'Return Revolting Rebels' (Z. 632.16). It is in B♭ of course, and between its two statements of the first section he jousts at the trials of love by moving from duple to triple time and concentrating on minor-mode key areas. This is the nearest he gets to passionate expression, and if Cupid is to win he has to outdo him; so Cupid's solo 'The Cares of Lovers' is a recitative replete with Purcell's most up-to-date and effective rhetorical devices, in Purcell's favourite amorous key of G minor. This, like the previous minor mode, readily contrasts with B♭, the key of Bacchus' final shot, 'Love Quickly Is Pall'd'.

Bacchus' alcoholic obsessiveness cannot beat Cupid's charms; nor can he give up. So, unlike Cupid's increasingly florid contributions, the songs of Bacchus and his supporters have all been in B♭, are similarly scored for two upper instruments and one singer, and use similar techniques of question-and-answer between voice and instruments. The futility of the argument is thus brought full circle, and he and Cupid join for a duet full of concordant thirds 'Come, Let Us Agree', declaring that there are 'pleasures divine in wine and in love'. The company responds with a reworking for four-part chorus and strings.

Of the many features which make this music so suited to the stage, its strong

Ex. 147   Timon of Athens, 'Hark! How the Songsters' (Z. 632.10)

(i) bb. 1–15

(ii) bb. 18–19

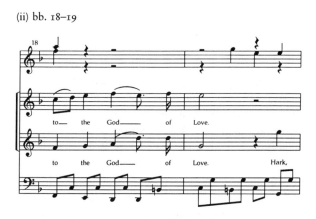

periodicity is particularly important, being crucial for direct expression and for
a racy pace which manages to incorporate extensive manipulations of scale.
Perhaps the most subtle use of these features is seen in the opening item 'Hark
How the Songsters', a free-ostinato piece which perfectly balances inventiveness
and economy. Throughout, it projects multiplications of one-bar units, set up
firstly through the ground, and secondly through the recorder repetitions (bb.
1–7 of Ex. 147 (i), for example). These multiply out into larger units which are
articulated partly by coincidence of stress patterns in all parts and partly by

modifications of the ground to produce cadential harmonies. The two main types of modification have distinct functions: a close into a prepared key is usually articulated by a pattern such as that in b. 7, with its clear V–I⁶–ii⁶–V progression; movement towards a new harmonic area, and sometimes within it, tends to be produced by extending the stepwise movement F–E in b. 1 into a longer scale, either ascending or descending (Ex. 147 (ii); see also how this figure prolongs V of D minor in bb. 24–7).

In earlier ground bass pieces using this figuration, Purcell might have created a five-bar ground made up of bb. 1, 4, 5, 6 and 7; his practice now is that as almost every bar consists of oscillations between a tonic (local or long-term) and its dominant, and any harmony can be extended just by repeating the required bar. So to open, both I and V are extended to produce an eight-bar circuit within the tonic.

One of the most important structural results of this technique is a series of statements in differing keys, articulated by linking moves such as that in Ex. 147 (ii), and by the tendency for shifts of harmonic and pitch level in the bass to be coincident with changes in text and figuration. It is largely because of this that the ending of the piece is so satisfying: for the last line of text the tonic returns along with motifs closely related to those of the opening, and Purcell brings things full circle by ending with a repeat of the opening seven bars.

Characteristically, he often overlaps repetitions of the ground with the phrasing of the upper parts. The earliest explicit example is in bb. 13–14, where the V element of the IV–V–I in F, first heard in bb. 5–8, is shortened so as to weaken the close back into I and drive on through to the move to V in bb. 18–19. Purcell picks up the possibility that the low F of the subdominant statement in b. 13 can prepare for a dissonant F on the downbeat of b. 14, to resolve the IV–V–I halfway through b. 14. Careful preparation underlies such exploration, for articulation of events on the half bar is first suggested in the second recorder's entry in b. 2 and is explicit in the vocal statements of 'Hark! how the songsters' in bb. 9–12.

The motivic economy of the upper parts is perhaps more remarkable than that of the ground. Parallel thirds are the standard representation of the unanimity of lovers; but in this piece they become part of a vertical and linear motivic saturation, and again, preparation is all. In b. 7 the $^6_4$ over B♭ functions as an adaptation of ii, and is motivated by precedent from the preceding bars. The recorders' frequent moves from C to A and F in bb. 8–12 are derived from the more drawn-out, ornamented versions in bb. 3–5, and when the semiquaver figuration enters in b. 14, it and its several derivations fill out thirds. To set 'Does from the hollow woods' Purcell has this same figure but in quavers (bb. 31–5) and for 'rebound' the motivic working does just that, with the opening figuration returning but now in the inverted rhythm ♩♪♪ (b. 36).

The chorus 'Who Can Resist?' (Z. 632.15) is a more obviously periodic structure, and an impeccable example of elaboration balanced against simplicity. It is a rondeau-based structure in D minor, and the last of the three statements of the refrain is prepared for by a prolongation of V. But by inserting instrumental interjections and by having incomplete phrases in the choir, this does not resolve to i; instead it goes to VI (b. 55) and this is treated as IV of III. Price quotes the passage in full,[29] and rightly regards it as a stroke of genius.

Considering its rapid pace of events and its sequence of short, stylistically contrasted pieces, *Timon of Athens* might justly be regarded as a resurrection of some of the techniques of *Dido and Aeneas*. The link is further supported by the copious motivic connections between pieces and by the ways in which Purcell uses certain motivic types to represent recurrent dramatic ideas, techniques well suited to the scale of the text and to its context within the play.

For his last large piece of dramatic music Purcell was faced with very different demands and essayed suitably different responses. Like *Dioclesian* and *The Fairy Queen*, *The Indian Queen* (Z. 630) is a reworking of an earlier play, with extensive cuts and emendations for periods of spectacle and music.[30] The date of composition is not known exactly, for while the fact that Henry's brother Daniel supplied music for the masque in the fifth act suggests that Henry's death interrupted composition, there is evidence that work might date back to late 1694.[31] Purcell's music seems to have survived more or less complete, but its relationship to the play is not entirely clear, and it has been suggested that the main source (BL Add. MS 31449) has some of the music in the wrong place.[32] This, plus an adaptation which seems not to have paid proper attention to the play's original integrity, make hazardous any assessment of the relationship between music and drama. We are, however, on somewhat firmer ground when looking at Purcell's approach to the musico-dramatic structure of any single scene, and this will be our main concern here.

Purcell's contribution includes one of the most famous of his small songs, 'I Attempt from Love's Sickness to Fly' (Z. 630.17h), though it is not certain where in the play either it or the inconsequential 'They Tell Us That Your Mighty Powers' (Z. 630.19) were to be sung.[33] But he was mainly concerned with four large scenes, all of which fall into the familiar dramatic opera categories. Altogether there is rather less music than Purcell provided for any of the earlier large stage works, perhaps because of limitations imposed by the recent split in the theatre world.[34] But what there is nevertheless shows a continuity of practice with even the largest of them, and some of the scenes include a meld of composite structures and potentially independent pieces which perforce involve adroit manipulations of scale.

The Prologue illustrates the extremities of the position. The six lines of text in 'Wake, Quevira' are stretched across no less than eighty-nine bars, in a

structure which combines a high level of local and long-term repetition with
strongly periodic phrasing. The four-bar introduction for continuo consists
mainly of motivic repetitions (Ex. 148), and most phrases have a harmonic

Ex. 148   The Indian Queen, 'Wake, Quevira' (Z. 630.4b): bb. 1–21

centre as singular and stable as this one, and an ending at least as strong. Such
features tend to highlight the extent to which successive phrases involve distinct
harmonic functions and types of motion. So the tonic C major is totally stable
as the vocal material unfolds across three complete statements of the bass, and
the first inflexion to the dominant goes with the next line of text, 'Our soft rest
must cease', and apparently new material, though this too is a motivic
development of the opening.

   A repeat of this last phrase's vocal line by the continuo highlights both the
harmonic proposition (V of I–I) set up in bb. 16–21 by the following repeat of
'Wake, Quevira', and the change which takes place during the vocal repeat.
In b. 33, instead of repetition by the continuo (cf. bb. 17–21) there is a new
phrase for 'And fly together with our country's peace' which ends with a much

stronger close into V. The harmonic difference between the two endings – between V of I and V as a local tonic – is highlighted by this new phrase beginning with the same bass as bb. 14–17. The dominant is reinforced by a repetition not of the previous vocal or continuo phrase (cf. bb. 17–20) but of the opening, transposed to G major.

Quevira's response to these urgings is 'Why Should Men Quarrel?' (Z. 630.4c and d), a ground bass in C minor which, like 'Wake, Quevira', features strongly periodic phrasing and subtle structural elisions designed to remove the obviousness both of structural boundaries and of large-scale repetition. The aptness of its texture depends on far more than the dotted figuration which dominates the ground and the two flute parts. The flutes, with their rapid exchanges of 𝅘𝅥𝅮. 𝅘𝅥𝅯𝅘𝅥 are the most obviously quarrelsome feature, but their lines nevertheless rework the descent E♭–D–C–B♭–A♭–G which is articulated on successive minims by the ground. The ground itself is not what it seems, for while it consists of three statements of a one-bar figure, plus a closing pattern in crotchets, the repetitions of the figure begin on the second beat of each duple-time bar and stress the downbeat of the following bar. Therefore the pitches stressed in the descent tend to be the least stable ones – D, B♭ and G – while a prickly metrical instability is underlined by the strength of the ground's ending every four bars and by the flutes refusing to agree with this pattern.

The instruments might be quarrelsome, but Quevira is not; so she deftly weaves a path through this complexity with a much more connected line featuring inversions and other reworkings of instrumental figuration, plus some scalic figuration of her own, the cadential patterns of which are often related to those heard in 'Wake, Quevira'.

Purcell shows consummate subtlety in avoiding the technical obviousness which can readily afflict a ground: the vocal entry, for example is a drawn-out reworking of the opening two bars of the ground (cf. 'Music for a While' (Z. 583.2)). The ground itself is superbly plastic, readily bending onto a range of differing harmonic levels and functions; so it is the voice which articulates the main closes in v and III (bb. 15 and 25) as well as a superb feint at VII in b. 20. The return of the vocal opening one bar after the close into E♭ is neatly overlapped so that it begins in that key, and after a reworking of the song's opening, the line which formerly approached the close into v (b. 15) is reworked to end in the tonic. The piece concludes with a reworking of the flutes' prelude.

These two large pieces have introduced the main characters of the scene, the rest of which consists of a sequence of shorter, contrasted sections setting their dialogue. The methods are similar to those of 'With This Sacred Charming Wand' (Z. 578.4), but the textures have that stronger periodicity which characterised the earlier part of the scene. One result of this is that the successive sections tend to be more strongly contrasted. The first two, for the Boy, are a piece of characteristic Purcellian recitative ('By ancient prophecies') in E♭, and a motivically taut, leaping quaver air of just six bars ('And see that world') in B♭; the third is a twelve-bar duet in G minor; the fourth is a longer, triple-time air in C minor for the Boy; the fifth is a trumpet-style duet in C, where both characters express their resolve. Throughout there are numerous motivic links which can be traced at least as far back as 'Wake, Quevira'.

The masque of Envy and Fame shows an ingenious adaptation of such composite structures to the large, set-piece methods of the masque to the sun in Act IV of *The Fairy Queen*. In *The Indian Queen* the dramatic context is much less well focussed, and the masque may even have become misplaced in the drama.[35] While its symbolic meaning is therefore open to dispute, its immediate purpose is not: Envy attempts in vain to disturb a panegyric to Zempoalla, as Fame wins out.

All this is preceded by a large C major symphony for trumpets and strings (Z. 630.5), a transposition from D of that which Purcell had composed a year or so earlier for Queen Mary's last birthday ode, *Come Ye Sons of Art* (Z. 323.1), plus a triple-time last movement. Fame then sings the short binary, trumpet-style air 'I Come to Sing Great Zempoalla's Story' (Z. 630.6) and this is repeated by the whole company as a four-part chorus with strings, oboes and trumpets, full of characteristically independent detail in the inner parts. Envy (bass) and two followers (alto and tenor) enter and sing the famous trio with violins 'What Flatt'ring Noise Is This?' (Z. 630.7).

The contrast with the earlier trumpetings is superbly judged. We shift to C minor and the violins jog along in thirds, in an agitated rhythmic ostinato, and in quasi-homophony with the continuo. The resultant bump on every downbeat is given a particularly imaginative twist in the line 'At which my snakes all hiss', where Envy's followers enter with the word 'hiss'. The ABA structure involves a textual repetition not called for by the printed text, but apt to underline the central point.

Fame responds with another short binary air in C major, this one in $\frac{6}{4}$ time, declaring 'Scorn'd Envy, here's nothing that thou canst blast'. In C minor and in triple time, Envy declares that 'I fly from the place where flattery reigns', another ABA structure not suggested by the text, and a masterstroke of musico-dramatic insight, for while it ends with a full close, it runs directly into a repetition of 'What Flatt'ring Noise Is This?', but beginning at the B section. Fame gets the last word with the longest C major air yet, which banishes the 'curst fiends of Hell' and has plenty of suitably trumpeting figures on 'triumph', while Fame's victory is given reality by a repetition of the solo and chorus with which the scene opened.[36]

As in so many such scenes, by Purcell or anyone else, it is the evil character which gets the most interesting music. The recapitulation of 'What Flatt'ring

Ex. 149   The Indian Queen: motivic connections in 'What Flatt'ring Noise Is This?' (Z. 630.7)

'Noise Is This?' is a particularly subtle case, for by picking up the B section Purcell draws attention to those personal attributes which make Envy flee – 'I hate to see fond tongues advance' – while the musical repetition brings Envy's contribution to a self-fulfilling close. This is underlined by a taut musical continuity which effects the link with surprising ease, for melodically and harmonically the end of the triple-time section is similar to the end of section A in 'What Flatt'ring Noise Is This?' (Ex. 149) and thus can act as a substitute for it.

The ritual scene in Act V is an interesting recreation of aspects of Purcell's early instrumental style. And it shows an adroit pacing of events, as it picks up the 'brisk' pace of the chorus 'All living things' to dispatch the following conventional dialogues between priest and chorus fairly quickly, and to throw the emphasis forward onto the impressive F minor processional prelude and chorus 'All Dismal Sounds' (Z. 630.21d and e).[37]

The sequence of events is to some extent a product of the printed text, but Purcell's timing is impeccable, and the chorus makes a fully convincing use of conservative sonorities within a modern stylistic context. Much of it consists of prolongations of dominant harmony, replete with deliciously spiced variations on this, and on highly unstable versions of the tonic. Indeed, the ritualistic effect depends partly on the consistency with which Purcell uses augmented triads, and other derivations of the formula whereby the fifth above either the tonic or dominant root can be replaced by the sixth. Yet these are line-driven sonorities, produced largely by imitation on the opening point, and by parts being paired in parallel thirds.

The Indian Queen is perhaps most famous for the scene in Act III, beginning with 'Ye Twice Ten Hundred Deities' (Z. 630.13) – 'the best piece of recitative in our language' according to Burney.[38] The authority of the printed text for this scene is uncertain, but it seems that Purcell chose both to set more of it to music than was intended by the play's adapter, and to omit some spoken text for the sake of a larger musical structure.[39] Zempoalla has been disturbed by dreams which seem to present bad omens, so she consults the conjurer Ismeron for an interpretation. Through a long incantation he summons up the God of Sleep, who declines to tell Zempoalla what she wants. In an attempt to console her, Ismeron then summons up Aerial Spirits who sing the duet 'Ah! How Happy Are We' (Z. 630.17a) and the large rondeau 'We, the Spirits of the Air' (Z. 630.17b–g).

Few, if any, songs by Purcell penetrate so deeply into their text as 'Ye Twice Ten Hundred Deities' (Ex. 150). Local expression acquires its strength from its

Ex. 150   *The Indian Queen*, 'Ye Twice Ten Hundred Deities' (Z. 630.13): first section

placing within a superbly purposeful musical process. Specific pitches are associated with specific harmonic areas and shifts from one area to another occur as Ismeron moves through his catalogue of spiritual beings. The 'twice ten hundred deities' are in G minor, expressed by circuits around G and B♭ (*a* in Ex. 151). The latter is emphasised by being 'enclosed' by A and C (*b*) and by the following rest. As Ismeron moves to 'Ye pow'rs that dwell with fates below' the harmonic centre shifts to B♭ (*c* and *h*), in which D is particularly stressed, just as the B♭ pitch was emphasised in G minor: even the lower D is connected to G minor only through a tortuously won return to the original G (*g* and *i*), aptly enough for 'And see what men are doom'd to do'. This climb back to G minor highlights a feature significant for the movement as a whole: motion away from the central pitch G and from G minor tends to be disjunct and return conjunct (cf. moves to G minor bb. 7–9 and to D minor bb. 10–11).

The one and a half bars of bb. 7–9 are insufficient in length and harmonic stability to balance the two preceding phrases; so the laboriously won, quasi-cadential G is in fact unstable. This drives the phrase extension (bb. 9–11), which creates a balance of length $(4 + 3 + 4\frac{1}{2})$, but a harmonic imbalance in that the G minor of b. 9 behaves as iv within a strong iv–V–i in D minor (*f*). Significantly, the same B♭ pitch is used as the departure point for the moves away from G minor, to B♭ and to D minor (*e*). It is left prominently unresolved by the tritone leaps to E and C♯ (*x*). As elements of both local and long-term structure these leaps are a superb setting of 'discord', for the non-resolution of B♭ is left hanging as the phrase reaches its D minor goal (*d* and *t*) on 'dwell'.

This close, the strongest thus far in the piece, sets up a polarity between the low D and the opening G far stronger than the mere distinction established in b. 7. The rest of the section is largely concerned with reconciling this polarity (*v*) and with resolving the B♭ of b. 10.

The next phrase begins this process by using pitch repetition to turn the D into an upbeat, intensified by the $\frac{6}{4}$ over C on the second half of the bar, and by linking the D directly to the tonic pitch G in b. 13. Thereafter the main local progression, articulated by the pitches on the downbeats, is back to E (*k*; cf. *x*) which, with the preceding G encloses F, the implied local tonic.

The whole aim of the incantation is to awaken the God of Sleep, so Ismeron's call to 'arise' includes the expressive and structural linchpin of the section. The tension between the vocal B♭ and the continuo B♮ (b. 13) captures not merely the awakening of the God but also the effort we might imagine it costs. The vocal flourish lengthens and emphasises the word, and gives the greatest tension to the middle of the bar, thus enhancing the release on the downbeat of b. 14 and the command to 'tell'.

What lifts this out of the realm of mere illustration is the multi-layered musical structure of which it is the crucial moment. Ismeron picks up the

Ex. 151 The Indian Queen, 'Ye Twice Ten Hundred Deities' (Z. 630.13): voice-leading in first section unresolved B♮ of b. 10 (e) and resolves it down to E in the register of the preceding full close (l). Moreover, the flourish is a variation on the immediately preceding cadential figure in b. 11, and this in particular intensifies the upbeat function of the II⁶ (V of V) in F and strengthens the wedging of both parts onto the C/E downbeat of b. 14 (m and k).

In another superb matching of musical timing to textual meaning, this downbeat does not resolve to the implied local tonic F until b. 16, when Ismeron finishes telling of the 'strange fate'. The leaps in the vocal part create a marked registral disjunction in bb. 14 and 15 and this is resolved at the end of the vocal phrase by the return of the bass to the same C (o), the descent of the voice to A (n) and an implied resolution of the E (j). As in the call to arise, one of the strongest dissonances of the piece occurs at a textual highlight: in this case the melodic movement during 'great Zempoalla' creates a ninth (implied $\frac{9}{3}$) which drives through to the close onto F.

Zempoalla's waiting on her 'dismal vision' is set to a process which aptly parallels that for 'and see what men are doom'd to do' in bb. 7–9; but now its aim is an unequivocal prolongation of dominant harmony, begun by a chromatic move in the bass from F to F♯ (bb. 16–17; cf. b. 8) and by turning the vocal A into an upbeat (cf. bb. 11–12). The laborious chromatic ascent fills in, and reverses the direction of, the diatonic C–A of bb. 15–16 (q; cf. bb. 7–9). The final dominant is strongly prepared by the C/E on the downbeat of b. 18 and, more particularly, by the chromatic bass (s), which encloses D with E, E♭ and C♯ (r). In the vocal part the return to C is important (q), for its functions as approaches to F and G minor are analogous to those of the two B♮s in bb. 4 and 9 (e), which were points of departure for B♭ and D minor respectively. The vocal figuration from the close into D minor (x in bb. 10–11), is reworked for the final close of the section.

The G–D polarity (v) is maintained in the remaining two sections. Ismeron's bizarre catalogue – 'By the croaking of the toad … By the crested adder's pride', etc. – is disposed across a series of statements in contrasting harmonic areas, each separated from its neighbours by a short ritornello for violins, and full of high-flown rhetorical gesture. High D plays an especially prominent role in the vocal part and is resolved strongly back to G in the final phrase of the catalogue – 'and thy neck'.

The next two lines – 'From thy sleeping mansion rise / And open thy unwilling eyes' – pick up the musical imagery and functions of the first section. In both sections a vocal line rising chromatically from D to G urges the God of Sleep to rise. This second summons has to be stronger, so the line is treated as a point of imitation and extended to cover a full octave D–D. The first nine bars prolong tonic harmony, and only as Ismeron sings 'open' does progression move out of the prolongation. The protracted chromatic wedging of the voice and continuo, with an augmented sixth resolving onto the dominant, is a superb setting of 'unwilling' and also forcefully sets up a harmonic function suitably strong to act as the springboard for the last section.

This last section is an outstanding example of Purcell's sense for expressive context. The text – 'While bubbling springs their music keep, / That use to lull thee in thy sleep' – moves away from the earlier imperatives, and Purcell's response neatly prepares for the appearance of the God of Sleep. The G–D polarity remains; but now it is resolved in a diatonic texture of scalic crotchets, descending sequential imitation, and triple time, which fills in D–G in a way entirely different from the first two sections.

Ismeron has finished, so the God of Sleep rises to the accompaniment of a beautifully somnolent symphony for two oboes and continuo. It and the God's multi-sectional air are in G minor, and while they and the later music for Aerial Spirits are fine stuff, it is Ismeron's incantation, a peerless match of musical process and expressive function, which of necessity makes the greater impact, one which seems as strong in our day as it must have been in Burney's.

Notes

1 Early years at court and home: developments to *c.* 1680

1 Most of the available evidence on Purcell's life and background can be found in Franklin B. Zimmerman, *Henry Purcell, 1659–1695. His Life and Times*, 2nd, rev. edn (Philadelphia: University of Pennsylvania Press, 1983); also in Margaret Campbell, *Henry Purcell – Glory of His Age* (London: Hutchinson, 1993).

2 Compare the differing views on parentage put forward in J. A. Westrup, *Purcell*, rev. Nigel Fortune (London: Dent, 1980) (cf. 1975 edition); Franklin B. Zimmerman, *Life and Times*; J. A. Westrup, 'Purcell's Parentage', *Music Review* 25 (1964): 100. See also the appendix to 1948 edition of A. K. Holland, *Henry Purcell: the English Musical Tradition* (London: G. Bell, 1932; Penguin, 1948; reprint edn Freeport, New York: Books for Libraries Press, 1970). For details of both men's appointments in court see Andrew Ashbee, ed., *Records of English Court Music*, 6 vols. (Aldershot: Scolar Press, 1986 cont.), vol. I.

3 Ashbee, ed., *Records*, vol. I, pp. 126 and 131.

4 For composers in ordinary see ibid., pp. 111 and 173. For Westminster Abbey see Zimmerman, *Life and Times*, pp. 70, 291–2.

5 Recent work on copyists has made it possible to provide terminal dates for some of Purcell's earliest anthems. Purcell anthems copied by William Tucker, a Gentleman of the Chapel who died on 28 February 1679, survive in part-books originating in the Chapel Royal and Westminster Abbey. See H. Watkins Shaw, 'A Cambridge Manuscript from the English Chapel Royal', *Music and Letters* 42 (1961): 263 and 'A Contemporary Source of English Music from the Purcellian Period', *Acta Musicologica* 31 (1959): 38; Eric Van Tassel, 'Purcell's *Give Sentence*', *Musical Times* 118 (1977): 381; Margaret Laurie, 'The Chapel Royal Part-books', in *Music and Bibliography, Essays in Honour of Alec Hyatt King*, ed. Oliver Neighbour (London: Clive Bingly, 1980), p. 28.

6 Margaret Laurie, 'Purcell's Extended Solo Songs', *Musical Times* 125 (1984): 19; *NPS*, vol. XXV; Ian Spink, *English Song, Dowland to Purcell* (London: Batsford, 1974), pp. 209–11.

7 For various accounts of Cooke's skills and innovations see preface to 'Matthew

Locke: Anthems and Motets', *MB*, vol. XXXVIII, edited by Peter le Huray; Robert Manning, 'Purcell's Anthems: An Analytical Study of the Music and Its Content' (Ph.D. dissertation, University of Birmingham, 1979); Westrup, *Purcell*; Rosamond McGuinness, *English Court Odes 1660–1820* (Oxford: Clarendon Press, 1971); Ian Cheverton, 'Captain Henry Cooke (*c.* 1616–1672), the Beginnings of a Reappraisal', *Soundings* 9 (1982): 74.

8 Ashbee, ed., *Records*, vol. I, p. 140.

9 Samuel Pepys, *The Complete Diary of Samuel Pepys*, ed. Robert Latham and William Matthews, 11 vols. (London: Bell, 1970), entry for 15 November 1667; Peter Dennison, 'The Church Music of Pelham Humfrey', *Proceedings of the Royal Musical Association* 97 (1971–2): 65.

10 Fitzwilliam Museum, Cambridge MS 88 is one of the three surviving large volumes of fair copies which Purcell assembled before *c.* 1690. It consists entirely of anthems by himself and other composers, and the larger part is in his hand. For a description of the contents see Nigel Fortune and Franklin B. Zimmerman, 'Purcell's Autographs', in *Henry Purcell, 1659–1695. Essays on His Music*, ed. Imogen Holst (London: Oxford University Press, 1959), p. 106.

11 Zimmerman, *Life and Times*, p. 395 n. 24.

12 See Zimmerman, *Life and Times*, pp. 41–2 and 290–1 for conjectures and evidence on his relationship with the Purcells.

13 For Locke's appointment see Ashbee, ed., *Records*, vol. I, p. 4. For an account of the background and known details of *The Siege of Rhodes* see E. J. Dent, *Foundations of English Opera* (Cambridge University Press, 1928; reprint edn, New York: Da Capo Press, 1965). For an account of the meeting see Zimmerman, *Life and Times*, p. 6. For the letter see William H. Cummings, *Purcell* (London: Sampson Low, 1881), p. 27. For a discussion of this letter and its authenticity see Zimmerman, *Life and Times*, pp. 42–3.

14 Alan Browning, 'Purcell's *Stairre Case Overture*', *Musical Times* 121 (1980): 768.

15 See Zimmerman, *Life and Times*, Appendix 3. For a contemporary record of 'severall Aires' being 'performed at ye King's dinner' see Ashbee, ed., *Records*, vol. I, p. 155.

16 Mary Chan and Jamie C. Kassler, eds., *Roger North's 'The Musical Grammarian'* *1728* (Cambridge University Press, 1990), p. 262; John Wilson, ed., *Roger North on Music* (London: Novello, 1959), pp. 299 and 350.

17 Westrup, *Purcell*, p. 26.

18 Christopher Simpson, *A Compendium of Practical Music*, 2nd edn (London: 1667; reprint edn, Oxford: Basil Blackwell, 1970), pp. 77–9. Simpson's *Compendium* exerted no small influence over Purcell's contribution to the twelfth edition of Playford's *An Introduction to the Skill of Musick* (1694) and is singled out for praise.

19 'Jacobean Consort Music', *MB*, vol. IX.

20 For examples see E. H. Meyer, *English Chamber Music*, 2nd edn, revised by the author and Diana Poulton (London: Lawrence and Wishart, 1982), pp. 254 and 259.

21 Wilson, ed., *Roger North on Music*, p. 295. See James Anthony, *French Baroque Music*, rev. edn (London: Batsford, 1978), Ch. 19, for possible links with early- and mid-seventeenth-century French practice.

22 Cf. Zimmerman, *Life and Times*, pp. 51–2.

23 Simpson, *A Compendium*, p. 78.
24 Wilson, ed., *Roger North on Music*, p. 25, n. 31; cf. p. 297.
25 Westrup, *Purcell*, pp. 245–53.
26 Thurston Dart, 'Purcell and Bull', *Musical Times* 104 (1963): 30; Zimmerman, *Life and Times*, p. 52. Note especially the Christopher Gibbons fantasia in Meyer, *English Chamber Music*, p. 335.
27 From the collection of English church music made by Tudway in 1714–20, BL Harleian 7337–42. Quoted in Eric Walter White, *A History of English Opera* (London: Faber, 1983), p. 128.
28 Chan and Kassler, eds., '*The Musical Grammarian*', p. 250; Wilson, ed., *Roger North on Music*, p. 340. A superb collection of the sort North describes has survived as Bodleian Mus.Sch.D. 212–6.
29 *MB*, vol. XXXIX, p. 8.
30 See preface to 'Matthew Locke: Chamber Music', *MB*, vols. XXXI and XXXII, ed. Michael Tilmouth.
31 Cf. Spink, *English Song*, p. 200.
32 For Westminster Abbey see Zimmerman, *Life and Times*, p. 39 and Westrup, *Purcell*, p. 24. For Chapel Royal see Shaw, 'A Cambridge Manuscript'.
33 Zimmerman, *Life and Times*, p. 29.
34 One of its most important sources is the same set of Chapel Royal part-books that contains *Lord, Who Can Tell*. In 1674 it was published in *Cantica sacra* (London) which, in addition to Locke, included music by Richard Dering, Christopher Gibbons and Benjamin Rogers.
35 Peter Dennison, 'The Stylistic Origins of the Early Church Music', in *Essays on Opera and English Music in Honour of Sir Jack Westrup*, ed. F. W. Sternfeld, Nigel Fortune and Edward Olleson (Oxford: Basil Blackwell, 1975), p. 44.
36 For a detailed analysis of this piece, including a discussion of dissonance in the quoted extract see Martin Adams, 'The Development of Henry Purcell's Musical Style' (Ph.D. dissertation, University of Southampton, 1984), pp. 11–16 and 44–52.
37 See Van Tassel, 'Purcell's *Give Sentence*', n. 7.
38 Westrup, *Purcell*, p. 207.
39 Van Tassel, 'Purcell's *Give Sentence*', n. 7; G. E. P. Arkwright, 'Purcell's Church Music', *The Musical Antiquary* 1 (1910): 63 and 234.
40 Westrup, *Purcell*, p. 215.
41 In *Reliquiae sacrorum concentum*, Nuremburg.
42 John Playford, *An Introduction to the Skill of Musick*, 12th edn (London: Henry Playford, 1694; reprint edn, with an introduction by F. B. Zimmerman, New York: Da Capo, 1972), pp. 115–16.
43 For the three madrigals see Dart, 'Purcell and Bull'. For the correction slip see Franklin B. Zimmerman, 'Purcell and Monteverdi', *Musical Times* 100 (1958): 368.
44 For a detailed account of precedents for Purcell's recitative style see Spink, *English Song*.
45 Dennison, 'The Stylistic Origins of the Early Church Music'.
46 See Dent, *Foundations of English Opera* and Curtis Price, *Henry Purcell and the London Stage* (Cambridge University Press, 1984), pp. 296–7; 'Locke: Dramatic Music', *MB*, vol. LI.

2 Years of experiment: *c.* 1680 to *c.* 1685

1 See John Downes, *Roscius Anglicanus* (London, 1708), p. 38; Price, *London Stage*, p. 30. See also Zimmerman, *Life and Times*, pp. 36 and 67–8 for speculation that this might not have been Purcell's first stage music.

2 See Murray Lefkowitz, 'Shadwell and Locke's *Psyche*: the French Connection', *Proceedings of the Royal Musical Association* 106 (1979–80): 42; Price, *London Stage*, pp. 3–11; 'Locke: Dramatic Music', *MB*, vol. LI; Dent, *Foundations of English Opera*, Ch. 6.

3 Cf. Price, *London Stage*, pp. 32–3.

4 For a more complete discussion of this term and its applications see several references in Roger Fiske, *Scotland in Music* (Cambridge University Press, 1983).

5 Margaret Laurie, 'Purcell's Stage Works' (Ph.D. dissertation, University of Cambridge, 1962).

6 For references to lost and incomplete odes see Michael Tilmouth, 'The Technique and Forms of Purcell's Sonatas', *Music and Letters* 40 (1959): 109; Franklin B. Zimmerman, *Henry Purcell, 1659–1695, An Analytical Catalogue of His Music* (London: Macmillan, 1963), p. 151; Nigel Fortune, 'A New Purcell Source', *Music Review* 25 (1964): 109.

7 For a more detailed account of the relationship between Blow and Purcell in this genre see Martin Adams, 'Purcell, Blow and the English Court Ode', in *Purcell Studies*, ed. Curtis Price (Cambridge University Press, forthcoming).

8 Westrup, *Purcell*, p. 247.

9 For a detailed discussion of the background to and techniques of these pieces see Nigel Fortune, 'The Domestic Sacred Music', in *Essays on Opera and English Music in Honour of Sir Jack Westrup*, ed. F. W. Sternfeld, Nigel Fortune and Edward Olleson (Oxford: Basil Blackwell, 1975), p. 62.

10 Cf. Fortune, 'The Domestic Sacred Music'.

11 See *MB*, vol. XXXIII and Spink, *English Song*, pp. 105–6.

12 Numerous references in Manning, 'Purcell's Anthems'.

13 Edward F. Rimbault, ed., *The Old Cheque Book of the Chapel Royal* (London: The Camden Society, 1872; reprint edn, New York: Da Capo Press, 1966), p. 17.

14 Published in facsimile (1975) by Paradine and Magdalene College, Cambridge. For a discussion of the reliability of the text, see Thurston Dart, 'Purcell's Chamber Music', *Proceedings of the Royal Musical Association* 85 (1958–9): 81.

15 It is not known who was responsible for editing the 1697 set; his brother Daniel is a likely candidate. See preface to *NPS*, vol. VII, ed. Michael Tilmouth.

16 Dart, 'Purcell's Chamber Music'; preface to *NPS*, vol. VII, ed. Michael Tilmouth.

17 Michael Tilmouth, 'A Calendar of References to Music in Newspapers Published in London and the Provinces (1660–1719)', *Royal Musical Association Research Chronicle* 1 (1961); 2 (1962); preface to *NPS*, vol. V, ed. Michael Tilmouth.

18 For some of the information about historical precedents for Purcell's sonatas I am grateful to Peter Holman and Michael Tilmouth.

19 Peter Evans, 'Seventeenth-Century Chamber Music Manuscripts at Durham', *Music and Letters* 36 (1955): 205; Meyer, *English Chamber Music*, pp. 241–6.

20 Westrup, *Purcell*, pp. 230–1; Helene Wessely-Kropik, 'Henry Purcell als Instrumentalkomponist', *Studien zur Musikwissenschaft Beihefte der Denkmäler der*

Tonkunst in Osterreich 22 (1955): 85; Tilmouth, 'The Technique and Forms of Purcell's Sonatas'; Stella Favre-Lingorow, 'Der Instrumentalstil von Purcell', *Berner Veröffentlichungen zur Musikforschung* 16 (1950); Zimmerman, *Life and Times*, pp. 97–9.

21 A. Kircher, *Musurgia universalis sive ars magna consoni et dissoni in X libros digesta, Tome I* (Rome, 1650), p. 480. For manuscripts see editorial notes in *NPS*, vol. V. For Colista see Helene Wessely-Kropik, *Lelio Colista, Ein Römischer Meister vor Corelli* (Vienna: Österreichische Akademie der Wissenschaft, 1961) and 'Henry Purcell als Instrumentalkomponist'. In the latter she states that some of Purcell's models might be found in the 1680 Bologna publication 'Scielta delle suonate a due violini, con il basso continuo per l'organo, raccolte da diversi eccelenti autori', which includes at least one sonata by Colista, albeit anonymously. Her hypothesis is strengthened by the fact that this volume was known in England at that time: BL Add. MS 31436 is a copy of it, for example (William S. Newman, *The Sonata in the Baroque Era*, 4th edn (New York: Norton, 1983), p. 138). See also Eleanor McCrickard, 'The Roman Repertory for Violin before Corelli', *Early Music* 18 (1990): 563. For problems of ascription see Peter Allsop, 'Problems of Ascription in the Roman *Sinfonia* of the Late Seventeenth Century: Colista and Lonati', *Music Review* 50 (1989): 34; also Peter Allsop, *The Italian 'Trio' Sonata from Its Origins until Corelli* (Oxford: Clarendon Press, 1992), pp. 197 and 203–7.

22 Wessely-Kropik, 'Henry Purcell als Instrumentalkomponist'; Allsop, *The Italian 'Trio' Sonata*, pp. 51 and 210. For a further discussion of influences see Michael Tilmouth and Christopher D. S. Field, 'Consort Music II: From 1660', in Ian Spink, gen. ed., *The Blackwell History of Music in Britain*, 6 vols. (Oxford: Blackwell, 1988, cont.), vol. IV: *The Seventeenth Century*.

23 Published Vienna, 1952, edited by Helene Kropik; and London, 1960, edited by Michael Tilmouth. For attribution see Allsop, 'Problems of Ascription in the Roman *Sinfonia*'.

24 For a discussion of the canzona see Allsop, *The Italian 'Trio' Sonata*, pp. 48–52; Wessely-Kropik, 'Henry Purcell als Instrumentalkomponist'. Wessely-Kropik includes a detailed inventory of movement types in Colista (and Lonati?) and Purcell. See also Tilmouth, 'The Technique and Forms of Purcell's Sonatas'.

25 Playford, *An Introduction to the Skill of Musick*, p. 125.

26 Wilson, ed., *Roger North on Music*, p. 297, cf. p. 25 n. 31; cf. also Chan and Kassler, eds., '*The Musical Grammarian*', pp. 258–9.

27 Tilmouth, 'The Technique and Forms of Purcell's Sonatas'.

28 Wessely-Kropik, 'Henry Purcell als Instrumentalkomponist', pp. 128–9.

29 Cf. Tilmouth, 'The Technique and Forms of Purcell's Sonatas', pp. 115–16.

30 BL MS RM 20.h.9 is the primary source for his *Fantasia: Three Parts on a Ground* (Z. 731) and several of the early overtures, and includes a transcription of the *Sonatas of Three Parts*.

31 Wilson, ed., *Roger North on Music*, p. 310, n. 65.

32 Robert Klakovitch, '*Scocca pur*: Genesis of an English Ground', *Journal of the Royal Musical Association* 116 (1991): 63; Zimmerman, *Analytical Catalogue*, p. 395.

33 See Tilmouth, 'The Technique and Forms of Purcell's Sonatas' for several examples.

34 Adams, 'Purcell, Blow and the English Court Ode'.

35 Martin Adams, 'Purcell's *Laudate Ceciliam*, an Essay in Stylistic Experimentation', in *Irish Musical Studies 1: Musicology in Ireland*, ed. Gerard Gillen and Harry White (Dublin: Irish Academic Press, 1990), p. 227.

36 Zimmerman, *Analytical Catalogue*, p. 150.

37 See preface to 'Matthew Locke: Anthems and Motets', *MB*, vol. XXXVIII, ed. Peter le Huray.

38 BL Add. MS 33234, for example, a source from the early 1680s compiled by Charles Morgan of Magdalen College, Oxford. It includes Italian and English music by Purcell, Blow, Cazzati, Stradella, Graziani and Carissimi, and a vast, sprawling, *Miserere* by Purcell's contemporary Henry Bowman, also notated with 'open-style' crotchets and quavers.

39 Published by Hinrichsen, 1968. See commentary by Watkins Shaw about date and purpose of this piece.

40 Cf. Laurie, 'Purcell's Extended Solo Songs', p. 20.

41 Westrup, *Purcell*, p. 244; cf. McGuinness, *English Court Odes*.

42 Chan and Kassler, eds., '*The Musical Grammarian*', p. 172.

43 Charles Burney, *A General History of Music* (London: 1776–89), edited with critical and historical notes by Frank Mercer, 2 vols. (London: Foulis, 1935), vol. II, p. 394; Westrup, *Purcell*, p. 121.

44 See Zimmerman, *Analytical Catalogue*, Appendix IV. Playford was still advertising the *Sonatas of Three Parts* in 1688 (Westrup, *Purcell*, p. 61); and in 1699, four years after Purcell's death, his widow Frances announced the sale of remaining copies (*NPS*, vol. V, p. ix).

3 Consolidation: *c.* 1685 to *c.* 1688

1 For detailed coverage see Zimmerman, *Life and Times*, pp. 137–58; Margaret Mabbett, 'Italian Musicians in Restoration England (1660–90)', *Music and Letters* 67 (1986): 237; Westrup, *Purcell*, p. 58. For an account of the relationship between music and politics in Restoration England see Zimmerman, *Life and Times*, Ch. 5. See also lists of musicians in the Catholic chapel, plus other information, in Ashbee, ed., *Records*, vol. II.

2 McGuinness, *English Court Odes*, p. 19.

3 Ashbee, ed., *Records*, vol. II, p. 3.

4 Zimmerman, *Life and Times*, pp. 136, 227–9.

5 For an account of the 1687 edition, see W. Barclay Squire, 'Purcell as Theorist', *Sammelbände der Internationalen Musick-gesellschaft* 6 (1904–5): 521; also Playford, *Playford's 'Brief Introduction to the Skill of Musick' – an Account Comprising All the Editions from 1654 to 1730* (London: Ellis, 1926).

6 Chan and Kassler, eds., '*The Musical Grammarian*', pp. 205–6; Wilson, ed., *Roger North on Music*, p. 265.

7 Adams, 'Purcell's *Laudate Ceciliam*'.

8 Spink, *English Song*, pp. 205, 221 and 227.

9 For contrasting views on *Albion and Albanius* and the reasons for its failure see Dent, *Foundations of English Opera*, pp. 165–70 and Price, *London Stage*, pp. 265–70. The Lully and Grabu were performed by the same company.

10 See Ch. 2, n. 4.

4 Public recognition: *c.* 1689 to *c.* 1691.

1 For events before and after the 'Glorious Revolution' and their effects on musical life in London see Zimmerman, *Life and Times*, pp. 151–2 and Ch. 11.

2 Ibid., pp. 161–9; Westrup, *Purcell*, pp. 62–3. See also Ch. 9 below, n. 4.

3 For cutbacks compare the several lists of Chapel Royal and other members in Ashbee, ed., *Records*, vols. I, II and V. Also John Harley, 'Music at the English Court in the Eighteenth and Nineteenth Centuries', *Music and Letters* 50 (1969): 341. For Purcell's status see Zimmerman, *Life and Times*, Ch. 12.

4 Bruce Wood and Andrew Pinnock, '"Unscarr'd by Turning Times"? The Dating of Purcell's *Dido and Aeneas*', *Early Music* 20 (1992): 373; cf. letter by Martin Adams, *Early Music* 21 (1993): 510 and Curtis Price, '*Dido and Aeneas*: Questions of Style and Evidence', *Early Music* 22 (1994): 115.

5 Richard Luckett, 'A New Source of *Venus and Adonis*', *Musical Times* 130 (1989): 76.

6 Wood and Pinnock, 'The Dating of Purcell's *Dido and Aeneas*'.

7 Dent, *Foundations of English Opera*, pp. 171–6 and 181; Curtis Price, ed., *Purcell: 'Dido and Aeneas', an Opera* (New York: Norton, 1986), pp. 4–5; Price, *London Stage*, pp. 245–6; Ellen T. Harris, *Henry Purcell's 'Dido and Aeneas'* (Oxford: Clarendon Press, 1987); Westrup, *Purcell*, pp. 113–14, 119. See also Anthony Lewis, 'Purcell and Blow's *Venus and Adonis*', *Music and Letters* 44 (1963): 266.

8 Westrup, *Purcell*, p. 119.

9 Klakovitch, '*Scocca Pur*'; Ellen Rosand, 'The Descending Tetrachord: An Emblem of Lament', *Musical Quarterly* 65 (1979): 346.

10 Cf. Price, ed., *Purcell: 'Dido and Aeneas'*, p. 5; Price, *London Stage*, p. 228; Robert Etheridge Moore, *Henry Purcell and the Restoration Theatre* (London: Heinemann, 1961; reprint edn, Westport, Conn.: Greenwood Press, 1974), pp. 42–6.

11 Price, ed., *Purcell: 'Dido and Aeneas'*, pp. 34–6; also *London Stage*, pp. 257–8.

12 *NPS*, vol. XXXI, p. 124; Thurston Dart, 'The Cibell', *Revue belge de musicologie* 6 (1952): 24; cf. Zimmerman, *Analytical Catalogue*, pp. 361 and 439.

13 Don Smithers, *The Music and History of the Baroque Trumpet before 1721* (London: Dent, 1973), pp. 201–4.

14 Ibid., numerous references, but especially Chs. 8 and 9. Cf. Peter Downey, 'What Samuel Pepys Heard on 3 February 1661: English Trumpet Style under the Later Stuart Monarchs', *Early Music* 18 (1990): 417; Bruce Wood and Andrew Pinnock, 'A Counterblast on English Trumpets', *Early Music* 19 (1991): 436; Peter Holman, 'English Trumpets – A Response', *Early Music* 19 (1991): 443. I am inclined to accept the arguments of Pinnock, Wood and Holman.

15 Cf. Smithers, *The Baroque Trumpet*, pp. 198–200 and 212–13.

16 The original draft of the preface is in BL Stowe MS 755, f.34. The published version is quoted complete in *NPS*, vol. IX. See Price, *London Stage*, pp. 264–5 for a discussion of the differences between the draft and published versions.

17 Price, *London Stage*, pp. 283–8; Dent, *Foundations of English Opera*, p. 202.

18 Cf. Michael W. Alssid, 'The Impossible Form of Art: Dryden, Purcell and *King Arthur*', *Studies in the Literary Imagination* 10 (1977): 125.

19 Dent, *Foundations of English Opera*, pp. 202–3; Price, *London Stage*, p. 288.

20 Published in the fourth book (1687) of *The Theatre of Music*.

21 See Zimmerman, *Life and Times*, pp. 183–90 for what is known about the trip. See also the list in Ashbee, ed., *Records*, vol. II, pp. 34–5.

22 Price, *London Stage*, pp. 289–97.

23 Ibid., p. 299; Alssid, 'The Impossible Form of Art'.

24 Smithers, *The Baroque Trumpet*, pp. 217–18; J. A. Westrup, 'Purcell's Music for *Timon of Athens*', in *Festschrift für Karl Gustav Fellerer*, ed. H. Huschen (Regensburg: G. Bosse, 1962), p. 573; *NPS*, vol. II.

25 Price, *London Stage*, p. 313; Smithers, *The Baroque Trumpet*, pp. 217–18.

26 Westrup, *Purcell*, p. 136.

27 Cf. Price, *London Stage*, p. 313; Moore, *Henry Purcell and the Restoration Theatre*, pp. 91–2; Spink, *English Song*, pp. 225–6.

5 'Meaning motion fans fresh our wits with wonder': c. 1692 to 1695

1 From Gerard Manley Hopkins' poem *Henry Purcell*, in *Gerard Manley Hopkins: Poems and Prose*, selected and edited by W. H. Gardner (London: Penguin, 1953).

2 Westrup, *Purcell*, pp. 220–1.

3 Ibid., p. 173.

4 For conjectures that this is actually the 'Grand Dance ... of Twenty Four Persons' see Bruce Wood and Andrew Pinnock, 'The Fairy Queen: a Fresh Look at the Issues', *Early Music* 21 (1993): 44. Also Ch. 15 below.

5 Playford, *An Introduction to the Skill of Musick*, p. 125.

6 It has recently been suggested that this scene might date back to the previous year. Wood and Pinnock, 'The Fairy Queen'.

7 Price, *London Stage*, pp. 197–8.

8 Ibid., pp. 187–8.

9 Zimmerman, *Life and Times*, p. 356.

10 For a comprehensive discussion of the controversies surrounding such playing see Wood and Pinnock, 'A Counterblast'.

11 *NPS*, vol. VIII, p. ix.

12 Zimmerman, *Life and Times*, p. 200; Price, *London Stage*, p. 19.

13 Cf. Spink, *English Song*, p. 205.

14 Cf. Price, *London Stage*, pp. 67–9.

15 Poem printed in Zimmerman, *Life and Times*, p. 299. See Henry Hall's poem, n. 23 below, for another comparison with Bassani and Corelli. See also Westrup, *Purcell*, pp. 102–3.

16 For a detailed inventory of the changes see Squire, 'Purcell as Theorist'. See also Playford, *An Introduction to the Skill of Musick*.

17 Playford, *An Introduction to the Skill of Musick*, especially pp. 131–3.

18 See Ch. 1, n. 24.

19 *NPS*, vol. XXXII, pp. 182–3; Campbell, *Henry Purcell*, p. 218.

20 See Price, *London Stage*, pp. 12–17, for a detailed account of these theatrical intrigues.

21 Zimmerman, *Life and Times*, p. 254.

22 Ibid., pp. 294–318.

23 Discussed in detail in Oliver Pickering, 'Henry Hall of Hereford's Poetical Tributes to Henry Purcell', *The Library* 16 (1994): 18.

24 Thomas Morley, *A Plain and Easy Introduction to Practical Music* (London: 1597; reprint edn, ed. R. Alec Harman, London: Dent, 1952).
25 Christopher Smart, *Ode for Musick*, 1746, *The Poetical Works of Christopher Smart*, vol. IV, ed. Karina Williamson (Oxford: Clarendon Press, 1987), p. 96. Quoted in Richard Luckett, '"Or Rather Our Musical Shakespeare": Charles Burney's Purcell', in *Music in Eighteenth-Century England – Essays in Memory of Charles Cudworth*, ed. Christopher Hogwood and Richard Luckett (Cambridge University Press, 1983), p. 59.

6 'Clog'd with somewhat of an English vein': early instrumental music, the fantasias and sonatas

1 Roger North, describing Purcell's sonatas. Wilson, ed., *Roger North on Music*, p. 310.
2 Browning, 'Purcell's Stairre Case Overture'; Fortune, 'A New Purcell Source'; R. Ford, 'Osborn Ms 515'; *NPS*, vol. XXXI, pp. xi–xv.
3 MS Drexel 5061 – see *NPS*, vol. XXXI, p. xiv.
4 For current available information on the datings and sources of these early pieces and fragments see Dart, 'Purcell's Chamber Music'; Browning, 'Purcell's Stairre Case Overture'; R. Ford, 'Osborn Ms 515'; Marylin Wailes, 'Four Short Fantasias by Henry Purcell', *The Score* 20 (1957): 59 (The title 'fantasia' is erroneous); *NPS*, vol. XXXI pp. xi–xv.
5 *NPS*, vol. XXXI, p. 117.
6 Ibid.
7 In *NPS*, vols. V and VII.
8 Cf. Tilmouth, 'The Technique and Forms of Purcell's Sonatas', pp. 109 and 114–15.
9 Ibid., pp. 115–20.
10 *NPS*, vol. VII, pp. xiv–xv.
11 Newman, *The Sonata in the Baroque Era*, pp. 134, 147 and 237. See *NPS*, vol. VII, pp. ix–x, for a comprehensive discussion of Purcell's possible intentions.

7 'Bassani's genius to Corelli joyn'd': instrumental music in the odes, the anthems and on the stage

1 From Tom Brown's poem *To His Unknown Friend, Mr Henry Purcell*, in *Harmonia sacra*, Book II (1693). See also Henry Hall's poem quoted at the end of Ch. 5 above.
2 Both sections are quoted in full in McGuinness, *English Court Odes*, pp. 95–7.
3 For a detailed discussion of these pieces and their precedents see Adams, 'Purcell, Blow and the English Court Ode'.
4 Franklin B. Zimmerman, ed., *The Gostling Manuscript* (Austin: University of Texas Press, 1977), p. 104.
5 Cf. Dart, 'The Cibell'; Zimmerman, *Analytical Catalogue*, pp. 361 and 439; *NPS*, vol. XXXI, p. 124.
6 Cf. Price, *London Stage*, p. 281.
7 Fortune and Zimmerman, 'Purcell's Autographs'.
8 *NPS*, vol. XXVI, p. 196. The thesis was first proposed by Dennis Arundell, in his 1928 edition of *King Arthur* (*PS*, vol. XXVI).

9 Ibid., p. 173.
10 In Playford, *An Introduction to the Skill of Musick*, p. 132.

8 Early mastery: sacred music to *c.* 1685

1 Arkwright, 'Purcell's Church Music', p. 63; Westrup, *Purcell*, Ch. 14 (cf. Reviser's Note, p. ix).
2 Purcell's anthems were convincingly grouped into four main categories by Peter Dennison in 'The Stylistic Origins of the Early Church Music', pp. 45, 53, 57 and 59. His classification will on the whole be followed here. A different classification, based on continental models, is attempted in Franklin B. Zimmerman, 'The Anthems of Henry Purcell', *The American Choral Review* 13 (Nos. 3 and 4, 1971).
3 Cf. Dennison, 'The Stylistic Origins of the Early Church Music', pp. 53–7.
4 There are some problems with the musical text of this anthem, but I have on the whole adopted the reading of Peter Dennison in *NPS*, vol. XIII.
5 For datings see Arkwright, 'Purcell's Church Music', pp. 240–8; Van Tassel, 'Purcell's *Give Sentence*'; Manning, 'Purcell's Anthems'; *NPS*, vol. XIII, pp. ix–x. Incomplete sources for Z. N68, have recently been discovered in Dublin.
6 A similar underlying melodic pattern is postulated in Zimmerman, 'The Anthems of Henry Purcell', pp. 43–5.
7 Westrup, *Purcell*, p. 207.
8 For differing views of some of these revisions, see Robert Manning, 'Revisions and Reworkings in Purcell's Anthems', *Soundings* 9 (1982): 29; R. Ford, 'Purcell as His Own Editor: The Funeral Sentences', *Journal of Musicological Research* 7 (1986): 47.
9 Westrup, *Purcell*, pp. 203–4.
10 *Hear My Prayer* is incomplete; yet there is no doubt that the surviving section is the opening of an anthem of this type (Fortune and Zimmerman, 'Purcell's Autographs', pp. 108–10; *NPS*, vol. XXVIII, p. 194). *O God, Thou Art My God* (Z. 35) almost certainly pre-dates October 1682, and probably was intended as a companion piece to the Service in B♭ (Z. 230) (Franklin B. Zimmerman, 'Purcell's Service Anthem *O God, Thou Art My God* and the B♭ Major Service', *Musical Quarterly* 50 (1964): 207).
11 Manning, 'Purcell's Anthems'.
12 Rimbault, ed., *The Old Cheque Book*, p. 17. Cf. Ashbee, ed., *Records*, vol. V, p. 80.
13 Zimmerman suggests (*Life and Times*, p. 124) that the original performance 'by the whole consort of voices and instruments' included hautbois, trumpets, drums and other instruments, citing as evidence an authority to pay Nicholas Staggins for the labour of copying a composition for the coronation, not only 'from the original in score the 6 parts', but also for 'drawing the said composition into forty several parts for trumpets, hautboys' (Ashbee, ed., *Records*, vol. II, p. 12). He says that this could 'scarcely apply' to any other piece performed at the coronation. However, the 'parts' could refer to any verse anthem with strings: Blow's *God Sometimes Spake in Visions* would also be a candidate.
14 In some sources this is divided into two sections, the *Benedicite, Jubilate, Cantate domino* and *Deus misereatur* being described as 'Mr Purcell's Second Service'. However, it is clear that all the B♭ canticles form a homogeneous group.

15 Westrup, *Purcell*, p. 219.
16 Anthony D. Ford, 'A Purcell Service and Its Sources', *Musical Times* 124 (1983): 121.
17 See also Fortune and Zimmerman, 'Purcell's Autographs', pp. 110–12; Zimmerman, *Life and Times*, pp. 65 and 75.
18 In Coverdale's translation, from *The Book of Common Prayer* (1662).
19 Fortune, 'The Domestic Sacred Music'.
20 Ibid., pp. 64–7.
21 Ibid., p. 69.

9 Brilliance and decline: sacred music after *c.* 1685

1 A number of continuo verse anthems are of unknown date, but stylistic evidence suggests that almost all of these are post-1685.
2 Cf. Zimmerman, *Life and Times*, p. 179.
3 Arkwright did not recognise the decline, but offers no substantive evidence. Arkwright, 'Purcell's Church Music', pp. 63–72.
4 Zimmerman, *Analytical Catalogue*, p. 5; Manning, 'Purcell's Anthems', p. 70; correspondence from Maurice Bevan, Robert Manning and Eric Van Tassel in *Musical Times* 119 (1978): 938; and 120 (1979): 1 and 114.
5 Manning, 'Purcell's Anthems', pp. 65 and 86. Cf. Arkwright, 'Purcell's Church Music', pp. 246–8.
6 Westrup, *Purcell*, p. 216.
7 It is not certain how many, if any, parts of this anthem originally included strings. No opening symphony survives, and the only source which includes strings is the 1703 edition of *Harmonia sacra*. Moreover, the Gostling manuscript does not include string parts, only a two-stave organ part. Manning, 'Purcell's Anthems', p. 78.
8 Westrup, *Purcell*, p. 81.
9 Zimmerman, *Life and Times*, pp. 238–44.
10 Tudway's account is in a collection of church music he made for the Earl of Oxford between 1715 and 1720 (BL Harl. MS 7337–42). The funeral music is discussed in some detail and Tudway's comments are reprinted in W. Barclay Squire, 'Purcell's Music for the Funeral of Mary II', *Sammelbände der internationalen Musick-gesellschaft* 4 (1902–3): 225. Also see Westrup, *Purcell*, pp. 82–3; Zimmerman, *Life and Times*, pp. 242–3; Christopher Hogwood, 'Thomas Tudway's History of Music', in *Music in Eighteenth-Century England – Essays in Memory of Charles Cudworth*, ed. Christopher Hogwood and Richard Luckett (Cambridge University Press, 1983), p. 19.
11 As in Squire, 'Purcell's Music for the Funeral of Mary II', p. 227.
12 Westrup, *Purcell*, p. 220.
13 As in Hogwood, 'Thomas Tudway's History of Music', p. 45.

10 'The energy of English words': independent songs for one or more voices

1 From Henry Playford's preface to *Orpheus britannicus* (1698). See the end of Ch. 5 above.
2 Most datings in this chapter are derived from *NPS*, vol. XXV. See Laurie, 'Purcell's Extended Solo Songs'.

3 For discussions of the authenticity of earlier attributions, see *NPS*, vol. XXV, p. viii and Spink, *English Song*, pp. 209–10.

4 *NPS*, vol. XXV, p. xii.

5 In *Choice Ayres* the second quaver of the piece is G, which has been altered to B♭ in the Purcell Society edition. A case can be made for the non-harmonic G being correct, but it does not affect the substantive properties of *b*, which are more rhythmic than melodic.

6 Spink, *English Song*, p. 213. Cf. the many examples in *The Theatre of Music*, four books 1685–7, reprinted 1983.

7 The continuo line differs in its two published sources. That adopted here maintains greater motivic concentration and brings out more strongly the differing phrasing in voice and continuo. See *NPS*, vol. XXV for both.

8 Spink, *English Song*, p. 211.

9 For this and many other observations on the larger songs I am indebted to Laurie, 'Purcell's Extended Solo Songs'.

10 Numerous examples given in Spink, *English Song*, especially pp. 58–9, 192–3, and 236–7.

11 Laurie, 'Purcell's Extended Solo Songs', p. 20.

12 Ibid., pp. 20–1.

13 Ibid., p. 20.

14 The John Playford concerned was almost certainly the publisher (1623–86). Cf. Cummings, *Purcell*, p. 46; *NPS*, vol. XXV, p. 292.

15 For commentary on time signature see *NPS*, vol. XXV, p. 292.

16 *NPS*, vol. XXV, p. 277.

17 Spink, *English Song*, p. 219.

18 In her day Katherine Philips was much admired as a poet and woman of letters. Her death from smallpox was mourned in elegies by Cowley and Sir William Temple. See Margaret Drabble, ed., *The Oxford Companion to English Literature* (Oxford University Press, 1985), p. 760.

19 *NPS*, vol. XXV, p. 288.

20 Spink, *English Song*, pp. 141–4.

21 Fortune and Zimmerman, 'Purcell's Autographs', pp. 112–15.

22 Adams, 'Purcell's *Laudate Ceciliam*'.

23 It is possible that some of these songs come from unidentified stage plays.

24 Laurie, 'Purcell's Extended Solo Songs', p. 23.

25 *NPS*, vol. XXV, p. 300.

26 Nevertheless, a number of strophic songs in the Guildhall autograph, likely to date from 1692–5, fit awkwardly in later verses, even though Purcell went to the trouble of writing them out in full. Fortune and Zimmerman, 'Purcell's Autographs'; Price, *London Stage*, pp. 166 and 183. See n. 29 below.

27 Cf. Spink, *English Song*, pp. 226–8.

28 Zimmerman has suggested that it is derived from the hamlet of that name near Hatfield Park. The same title is attached to the Allemande of the D minor suite for harpsichord (Z. 668.1), but there is no obvious relationship between the two pieces. See Zimmerman, *Analytical Catalogue*, pp. 189 and 358; *NPS*, vol. XXV, p. 302.

29 For a complete description of the manuscript, formerly known as the Gresham manuscript, and its contents, see W. Barclay Squire, 'An Unknown Autograph by Henry Purcell', *The Musical Antiquary* 3 (1911): 5; a less detailed description is in Fortune and Zimmerman, 'Purcell's Autographs', which, however, explicitly declares what Zimmerman, *Analytical Catalogue*, p. 204, implies – that the Guildhall version of *What a Sad Fate* is the earlier of the two. For comments on the revisions in the manuscript see various references in Price, *London Stage*. Dennison in *NPS*, vol. VIII, p. xi believes it to be from nearer 1695 than 1692. It was perhaps copied for Purcell's own use as a singer or for one of his pupils.

30 See Laurie, 'Purcell's Extended Solo Songs', p. 25, where both are quoted.

11 A new genre: odes to 1689

1 I use the term generically, to include welcome songs and any other panegyric of this kind.

2 For further discussion of this point and for the ode's early history see McGuinness, *English Court Odes*, pp. 1–11.

3 In Barber Institute MS 5001. See the printed catalogue of the Institute's music (ed. Iain Fenlon) for a full description and a microfiche copy of this important manuscript.

4 BL Add. MS 33287, f. 53.

5 Adams, 'Purcell, Blow and the English Court Ode'.

6 The manuscript source, BL Add. MS 33287, f. 53, says it was for 29 May. See, however, McGuinness, *English Court Odes*, p. 46.

7 See Rosamond McGuinness, 'The Ground Bass in the English Court Odes', *Music and Letters* 51 (1970): 118 and 265, pp. 119–20, for an excellent account of the relationship between the text and musical events in this piece.

8 For a fuller discussion of the development of these techniques see Adams, 'Purcell, Blow and the English Court Ode'.

9 Westrup, *Purcell*, p. 175; Adams, 'Purcell, Blow and the English Court Ode'.

10 McGuinness, *English Court Odes*, p. 16. Adams, 'Purcell, Blow and the English Court Ode'.

11 Adams, 'Purcell's *Laudate Ceciliam*'.

12 Ibid.

13 Cf. McGuinness, 'The Ground Bass in the English Court Odes', pp. 124–5.

14 Westrup, *Purcell*, p. 179, for example, where part of the choral section is quoted.

15 It has been suggested that this movement, like others in 'trumpet' style, might have had trumpets doubling at least the upper line. See Ch. 4, n. 14. Also Westrup, *Purcell*, p. 178.

12 Consolidation and maturity: odes from 1689 to 1695

1 Cf. Westrup, *Purcell*, pp. 182–3, which includes a substantial quotation from the finale.

2 For more details of Mr Maidwell see Zimmerman, *Life and Times*, pp. 414–15, ns. 3 and 4.

3 See the preface of *PS*, vol. I (1878) for an account (inaccurate in detail) of the background to this celebration.

4 Printed and manuscript sources variously have 'track' and 'tract', with the balance of evidence favouring the latter.
5 Westrup, *Purcell*, p. 184.
6 The church is a more likely candidate than Queen Mary, who is referred to as Gloriana throughout, including the final lines which Purcell seems not to have set. Cf. Zimmerman, *Life and Times*, p. 178.
7 *NPS*, vol. XI, pp. ix–x.
8 *NPS*, vol. XXVI, p. 180.
9 Westrup, *Purcell*, p. 185
10 *NPS*, vol. VIII, p. ix.
11 Ibid.
12 For the evidence of whether Purcell sang it see *NPS*, vol. VIII, p. x.
13 Westrup, *Purcell*, pp. 193–4.
14 *NPS*, vol. VIII, p. 93.
15 Playford, *An Introduction to the Skill of Musick*, p. 132.
16 Fortune, 'A New Purcell Source'.
17 Tilmouth, 'The Technique and Forms of Purcell's Sonatas', p. 109, n. 2.
18 Cf. *NPS*, vol. IV, pp. vi–viii; Olive Baldwin and Thelma Wilson, '*Who Can from Joy Refraine?* Purcell's Birthday Song for the Duke of Gloucester', *Musical Times* 122 (1981): 596.
19 Westrup, *Purcell*, p. 190.

13 Background and beginnings: dramatic music to 1689

1 These views are put forward, with varying shades of opinion, by Dent, *Foundations of English Opera*; Westrup, *Purcell*; Moore, *Henry Purcell and the Restoration Theatre*; White, *A History of English Opera*; Denis Arundell, *The Critic at the Opera* (London: Benn, 1957; reprint edn, New York: Da Capo Press, 1980); Arthur Hutchings, *Purcell* (London: British Broadcasting Corporation, 1982).
2 John Buttrey, 'Dating Purcell's *Dido and Aeneas*', *Proceedings of the Royal Musical Association* 94 (1967–8): 51; John Buttrey, 'The Evolution of English Opera between 1656 and 1695: A Reinvestigation' (Ph.D. dissertation, University of Cambridge, 1967); David Charlton, '*King Arthur*: Dramatick Opera', *Music and Letters* 64 (1983): 183; Margaret Laurie, 'Did Purcell Set *The Tempest?*' *Proceedings of the Royal Musical Association* 90 (1963–4): 43; Laurie, 'Purcell's Stage Works'; Richard Luckett, 'Exotick but Rational Entertainments: The English Dramatick Operas', in *English Drama: Forms and Development*, ed. Marie Axton and Raymond Williams (Cambridge University Press, 1977), pp. 123 and 232; Price, *London Stage*, especially pp. 3–26; Roger Savage, 'The Shakespeare-Purcell *Fairy Queen*: A Defence and Recommendation', *Early Music* 1 (1973): 201; Wood and Pinnock, '*The Fairy Queen*'; Wood and Pinnock, 'The Dating of Purcell's *Dido and Aeneas*'.
3 However, as far as *The Tempest* was concerned, at least one of these older scholars smelled a rat. See Dennis Arundell, 'Purcell and Natural Speech', *The Musical Times* 100 (1959): 323. The strongest case against Purcell's authorship of this music, except for the song 'Dear Pretty Youth' (Z. 631.10), is set out in Laurie, 'Did Purcell set *The*

Tempest?'. Nobody has succeeded in refuting Laurie's conclusions. For a stout defence of her position see Price, *London Stage*, pp. 20–1 (though Price overstates his case against Italian influence on Purcell).

4 Luckett, 'Exotick but Rational Entertainments'.

5 For a refreshingly different view, see Andrew Pinnock, 'Play into Opera: Purcell's *The Indian Queen*', *Early Music* 18 (1990): 3. For a wide-ranging critique see Alssid, 'The Impossible Form of Art'.

6 Zimmerman, *Analytical Catalogue*, pp. 282–3.

7 Cf. Price, *London Stage*, pp. 32–3.

8 See especially Price, *London Stage*, pp. 12–14.

9 Spink, *English Song*, pp. 221–3; Price, *London Stage*, pp. 155–60; cf. Olive Baldwin and Thelma Wilson, 'A Purcell Problem Solved', *The Musical Times* 122 (1981): 445.

10 Zimmerman, *Analytical Catalogue*, p. 242; Spink, *English Song*, pp. 221–3; Burney, *A General History*, vol. II, p. 393.

11 Price, *London Stage*, p. 158.

12 Ibid., p. 225.

13 See Ch. 4, n. 4.

14 For source and performance history see especially Margaret Laurie, 'Allegory, Sources, and Early Performance History', in *Purcell: 'Dido and Aeneas', an Opera*, ed. Curtis Price (New York: Norton, 1986), p. 42; NPS, vol. III; Eric Walter White, 'New Light on *Dido and Aeneas*', in *Henry Purcell, 1659–1695. Essays on his Music*, ed. Imogen Holst (London: Oxford University Press, 1959), p. 14; Buttrey, 'Dating Purcell's *Dido and Aeneas*'; Harris, '*Dido and Aeneas*'; Price, *London Stage*, pp. 225–6 and 234–45. See also Wood and Pinnock, 'The Dating of Purcell's *Dido and Aeneas*'; cf. letter by Martin Adams, *Early Music* 21 (1993): 510, and Price, '*Dido and Aeneas*: Questions of Style and Evidence'.

For reassessments of Tate's libretto see Imogen Holst, 'Purcell's Librettist, Nahum Tate', in *Henry Purcell, 1659–1695. Essays on His Music*, ed. Imogen Holst (London: Oxford University Press, 1959), p. 35; Mark Radice, 'Tate's Libretto for *Dido and Aeneas*: A Revaluation', *Bach: The Quarterly Journal of the Riemenschneider-Bach Institute* 7 (Jan. 1976): 20; Roger Savage, 'Producing *Dido and Aeneas*: An Investigation into Sixteen Problems', *Early Music* 4 (1976): 393.

15 I have here followed the example of Laurie (NPS, vol. III) in adopting the divisions into scenes and acts of the 1689 libretto, rather than Tenbury's arrangement, which almost certainly dates back to one of the adaptations. See Price, ed., *Purcell: 'Dido and Aeneas'*, p. 21; Price, *London Stage*, pp. 239–45; Harris, '*Dido and Aeneas*', pp. 69–81; Laurie, 'Allegory, Sources, and Early Performance History'. I am, however, inclined to the view that there are four scenes in *Dido*; see Roger Savage, 'Producing *Dido and Aeneas*'.

16 Harris, '*Dido and Aeneas*', p. 67.

17 See NPS, vol. III for a facsimile.

18 Cf. Price, ed., *Purcell: 'Dido and Aeneas'*, p. 25. For a discussion of '2 Women', see ibid., p. 51.

19 Ibid., pp. 34–6; also *London Stage*, pp. 257–8.

20 Cf. Moore, *Henry Purcell and the Restoration Theatre*, p. 51; Price, *London Stage*, p. 250; Price, ed., *Purcell: 'Dido and Aeneas'*, p. 26.

21 Cf. Savage, 'Producing *Dido and Aeneas*'.

22 Cf. Westrup, *Purcell*, p. 118; Dent, *Foundations of English Opera*, p. 194.

23 Westrup, *Purcell*, pp. 251–2; Price, ed., *Purcell: 'Dido and Aeneas'*, p. 29; Price, *London Stage*, p. 252; Dent, *Foundations of English Opera*, pp. 193–4.

24 Cf. Savage, 'Producing *Dido and Aeneas*'; Price, *London Stage*, pp. 251–2.

25 Westrup, *Purcell*, p. 123.

26 Ibid., p. 125.

14 'An English-man, equal with the best abroad': dramatic music from 1690 to 1691

1 John Dryden, referring to Purcell in the preface to *Amphitryon*.

2 *NPS*, vol. IX, p. ix; Price, *London Stage*, p. 263.

3 Ashbee, ed., *Records*, vol. I, p. 74.

4 In *Roscius anglicanus*, Downes says (p. 40) that it was 'perform'd on a very unlucky day, being the day the Duke of Monmouth, landed in the west: the nation being in a great consternation, it was perform'd but six times, which not answering half the charge they were at, involv'd the company very much in debt'. For an assessment of Grabu's music see Price, *London Stage*, pp. 265–70.

5 Price, *London Stage*, p. 288; also pp. 270–2 for details of the additions to the original play.

6 Moore, *Henry Purcell and the Restoration Theatre*, p. 135.

7 Luckett, 'Exotick but Rational Entertainments'; Savage, 'The Shakespeare-Purcell *Fairy Queen*'; Price, *London Stage*. But cf. Pinnock, 'Play into Opera'.

8 Dent, *Foundations of English Opera*, p. 202.

9 Cf. Price, *London Stage*, p. 273.

10 This prelude from *The Fairy Queen* is not in the main source; but its style seems authentic, and the source is reliable. *NPS*, vol. XII, p. ix.

11 Price's suggestion (*London Stage*, pp. 278–9) that in the 1693 revival Purcell replaced 'What Shall I Do?' with 'When First I Saw' (Appendix 1 in Z. 627, Zimmerman, *Analytical Catalogue*, p. 304) is plausible.

12 Price, *London Stage*, pp. 287 and 282.

13 Ibid., p. 288

14 Ibid., pp. 272–8.

15 Cf. ibid., pp. 170–1.

16 Ibid., pp. 289–97.

17 For details about revivals and sources see especially Ibid., pp. 297–8; *NPS*, vol. XXVI, pp. vii–xiv.

18 See especially Price, *London Stage*, pp. 290–5 and 318–19; Buttrey, 'The Evolution of English Opera'; Charlton, '*King Arthur*: Dramatick Opera'.

19 Dent, *Foundations of English Opera*, p. 210.

20 Alssid, 'The Impossible Form of Art'.

21 Cf. Price, *London Stage*, p. 305

22 Exactly how such tremolos were played and sung is a source of some dispute; but no sources include them in the Dance. The wavy lines are reproduced in *NPS*, vol.

XXVI, pp. 84–7 and 94–7, and in the extract from the Prelude to 'What Pow'r Art Thou?' quoted in Price, *London Stage*, p. 305. For a discussion of performance option see *NPS*, vol. XXVI, p. xxxiv.

23 Both Z. 628.18 in G minor and Z. 628.28 in A minor have been variously regarded as either the Second Act Tune or the Third Act Tune. The bibliographic evidence tends to favour the former as the candidate for this scene, but the predominance of G major and minor at the end of the second act suggests that it fits there. While A minor might seem the more natural key to follow a scene in C major, the minor dominant is plausible, especially from a composer who often used that relationship to express amorous ideas. See *NPS*, vol. XXVI, pp. viii–ix.

24 For a discussion of the instrumentation in this scene see *NPS*, vol. XXVI, p. 180.

25 Price, *London Stage*, p. 302.

26 Cf. Moore, *Henry Purcell and the Restoration Theatre*, pp. 82–4. For a discussion of this scene in terms of rhetorical gesture, see Rodney Farnsworth, '"Hither This Way": A Rhetorical-Musical Analysis of a Scene from Purcell's *King Arthur*', *Musical Quarterly* 74 (1990): 83.

27 Price, *London Stage*, p. 308.

28 Ibid., pp. 308–12.

29 Dent, *Foundations of English Opera*, p. 214. It takes, for example, much more than a neat ordering of keys to create unity, although this opinion is implicitly disputed in Charlton, '*King Arthur*: Dramatick Opera'.

30 Price, *London Stage*, p. 313; Moore, *Henry Purcell and the Restoration Theatre*, pp. 91–2; Spink, *English Song*, pp. 225–6.

15 'The pride and darling of the stage': dramatic music from 1692 to 1695

1 From *A Poem Occasioned on the Death of Mr Henry Purcell*, by 'A lover of music' (see Zimmerman, *Life and Times*, p. 296).

2 For full details see Price, *London Stage*, pp. 320–36; also *NPS*, vol. XII, pp. vii–xxiii; Laurie, 'Purcell's Stage Works'; Savage, 'The Shakespeare-Purcell *Fairy Queen*'. For a reassessment of sources and the relationship between the two productions see Wood and Pinnock, '*The Fairy Queen*'.

3 See Price, *London Stage*, especially pp. 320–9; and Savage, 'The Shakespeare-Purcell *Fairy Queen*'. See also Luckett, 'Exotick but Rational Entertainments'.

4 *NPS*, vol. XII, p. xviii.

5 Its presence is difficult to explain. See Price, *London Stage*, pp. 353–4; cf. Wood and Pinnock, '*The Fairy Queen*'.

6 *NPS*, vol. XII, p. xxi.

7 Wood and Pinnock, '*The Fairy Queen*'.

8 Purcell changed 'with one sound' to 'in one sound', almost certainly to avoid the unsuitable prominence which musical setting would give to the assonance.

9 Wood and Pinnock, '*The Fairy Queen*'.

10 Price, *London Stage*, p. 343.

11 See *PS*, vol. XX, p. xvi; Price, *London Stage*, pp. 177–81.

12 But see Wood and Pinnock, '*The Fairy Queen*'.

13 Price, *London Stage*, p. 106.

14 Westrup, *Purcell*, p. 154.

15 Price, *London Stage*, pp. 108–11.
16 Ibid., pp. 110–11.
17 Ibid., pp. 205–22.
18 Ibid., p. 207.
19 Ibid., p. 214.
20 Ibid., p. 217.
21 Ibid., p. 121.
22 Ibid.
23 Ibid., p. 122
24 Quoted in ibid.
25 Ibid., p. 82, for a penetrating analysis.
26 Ibid., pp. 60–4.
27 For the complex history of the music and text see Westrup, 'Purcell's Music for *Timon of Athens*'; Price, *London Stage*, pp. 89–96; NPS, vol. II, pp. ix–xiii.
28 Price, *London Stage*, p. 91
29 Ibid., p. 92.
30 Both Dryden and Howard have been claimed as authors. Pinnock, 'Play into Opera'; Price, *London Stage*, pp. 125–6.
31 Price, *London Stage*, pp. 126–31.
32 Pinnock, 'Play into Opera'.
33 Ibid.
34 Price, *London Stage*, pp. 16 and 17.
35 Pinnock, 'Play into Opera'.
36 The instrumental rendering of the chorus printed in PS is not found in the most reliable sources. It is possible that a dance followed, but on both source and stylistic grounds, there is no certainty that the one printed in PS (Z. 630.10) is by Purcell. (See Price, *London Stage*, pp. 134–5.)
37 Though cf. Price, *London Stage*, p. 142.
38 Burney, *A General History*, vol. II, p. 392.
39 Pinnock, 'Play into Opera'.

Select bibliography

Adams, Martin. 'Purcell, Blow and the English Court Ode'. In *Purcell Studies*. Edited by Curtis Price. Cambridge University Press, forthcoming.

'Purcell's *Laudate Ceciliam*, an Essay in Stylistic Experimentation'. In *Irish Musical Studies 1: Musicology in Ireland*, pp. 227–47. Edited by Gerard Gillen and Harry White. Dublin: Irish Academic Press, 1990.

'The Development of Henry Purcell's Musical Style'. Ph.D. dissertation, University of Southampton, 1984.

Allsop, Peter. 'Problems of Ascription in the Roman *Sinfonia* of the Late Seventeenth Century: Colista and Lonati'. *Music Review* 50 (1989): 34–44.

The Italian 'Trio' Sonata from Its Origins Until Corelli. Oxford: Clarendon Press, 1992.

Alssid, Michael W. 'The Impossible Form of Art: Dryden, Purcell and *King Arthur*'. *Studies in the Literary Imagination* 10 (1977): 125–44.

Anthony, James. *French Baroque Music*. rev. edn, London: Batsford, 1978.

Arkwright, G. E. P. 'Purcell's Church Music'. *The Musical Antiquary* 1 (1910): 63–72, 234–48.

Arundell, Dennis. 'Purcell and Natural Speech'. *The Musical Times* 100 (1959): 323–4.

The Critic at the Opera. London: Benn, 1957; reprint edn, New York: Da Capo Press, 1980.

Ashbee, Andrew. ed. *Records of English Court Music*. 9 vols. Aldershot: Scholar Press, 1986 cont.

Baldwin, Olive, and Wilson, Thelma. 'A Purcell Problem Solved'. *The Musical Times* 122 (1981): 445.

'*Who Can from Joy Refraine?* Purcell's Birthday Song for the Duke of Gloucester'. *Musical Times* 122 (1981): 596–9.

Browning, Alan. 'Purcell's *Stairre Case Overture*'. *Musical Times* 121 (1980): 768–9.

Burney, Charles. *A General History of Music*. London: 1776–89. Edited with critical and historical notes by Frank Mercer, 2 vols. London: Foulis, 1935.

Buttrey, John. 'Dating Purcell's *Dido and Aeneas*'. *Proceedings of the Royal Musical Association* 94 (1967–8): 51–62.

'The Evolution of English Opera between 1656 and 1695: a Reinvestigation'. Ph.D. dissertation, University of Cambridge, 1967.

Campbell, Margaret. *Henry Purcell – Glory of His Age*. London: Hutchinson, 1993.

Chan, Mary, and Kassler, Jamie C., eds. *Roger North's 'The Musical Grammarian' 1728*. Cambridge University Press, 1990.

Charlton, David. '*King Arthur*: Dramatick Opera'. *Music and Letters* 64 (1983): 183–92.

Cheverton, Ian. 'Captain Henry Cooke (*c.* 1616–1672), the Beginnings of a Reappraisal'. *Soundings* 9 (1982): 74–86.

Cummings, William H. *Purcell*. London: Sampson Low, 1881.

Dart, Thurston. 'Purcell and Bull'. *Musical Times* 104 (1963): 30–1.

'Purcell's Chamber Music'. *Proceedings of the Royal Musical Association* 85 (1958–9): 81–93.

'The Cibell'. *Revue belge de musicologie* 6 (1952): 24–30.

Dennison, Peter. 'The Church Music of Pelham Humfrey'. *Proceedings of the Royal Musical Association* 97 (1971–2): 65–71.

'The Stylistic Origins of the Early Church Music'. In *Essays on Opera and English Music in Honour of Sir Jack Westrup*, pp. 44–61. Edited by F. W. Sternfeld, Nigel Fortune and Edward Olleson. Oxford: Basil Blackwell, 1975.

Dent, E. J. *Foundations of English Opera*. Cambridge University Press, 1928; reprint edn, New York: Da Capo Press, 1965.

Downes, John. *Roscius anglicanus*. London, 1708; reprint edn, ed. Montague Summers, London: Fortune, 1928.

Downey, Peter. 'What Samuel Pepys Heard on 3 February 1661: English Trumpet Style under the Later Stuart Monarchs'. *Early Music* 18 (1990): 417–28.

Drabble, Margaret, ed. *The Oxford Companion to English Literature*. Oxford University Press, 1985.

Evans, Peter. 'Seventeenth-Century Chamber Music Manuscripts at Durham'. *Music and Letters* 36 (1955): 205–23.

Farnsworth, Rodney. '"Hither This Way": A Rhetorical-Musical Analysis of a Scene from Purcell's *King Arthur*'. *Musical Quarterly* 74 (1990): 83–97.

Favre-Lingorow, Stella. 'Der Instrumentalstil von Purcell'. *Berner Veröffentlichungen zur Musikforschung* 16 (1950).

Fiske, Roger. *Scotland in Music*. Cambridge University Press, 1983.

Ford, Anthony D. 'A Purcell Service and Its Sources'. *Musical Times* 124 (1983): 121–2.

Ford, R. 'Osborn Ms 515. A Guardbook of Restoration Instrumental Music'. *Fontes artis musicae* 30 (1983): 174–84.

'Purcell as His Own Editor: The Funeral Sentences'. *Journal of Musicological Research* 7 (1986): 47–67.

Fortune, Nigel. 'A New Purcell Source'. *Music Review* 25 (1964): 109–13.

'The Domestic Sacred Music'. In *Essays on Opera and English Music in Honour of Sir Jack Westrup*, pp. 62–78. Edited by F. W. Sternfeld, Nigel Fortune and Edward Olleson. Oxford: Basil Blackwell, 1975.

Fortune, Nigel, and Zimmerman, Franklin B. 'Purcell's Autographs'. In *Henry Purcell, 1659–1695. Essays on His Music*, pp. 106–21. Edited by Imogen Holst. London: Oxford University Press, 1959.

Harley, John. 'Music at the English Court in the Eighteenth and Nineteenth Centuries'. *Music and Letters* 50 (1969): 341–2.

Harris, Ellen T. *Henry Purcell's 'Dido and Aeneas'*. Oxford: Clarendon Press, 1987.

Hogwood, Christopher. 'Thomas Tudway's History of Music'. In *Music in Eighteenth-Century England – Essays in Memory of Charles Cudworth*, pp. 19–47. Edited by Christopher Hogwood and Richard Luckett. Cambridge University Press, 1983.

Holland, A. K. *Henry Purcell: the English Musical Tradition*. London: G. Bell, 1932.

Holman, Peter. 'English Trumpets – A Response'. *Early Music* 19 (1991): 443.

Holst, Imogen. 'Purcell's Librettist, Nahum Tate'. In *Henry Purcell, 1659–1695. Essays on His Music*, pp. 35–41. Edited by Imogen Holst. London: Oxford University Press, 1959.

Hopkins, Gerard Manley. *Gerard Manley Hopkins: Poems and Prose*. Selected and edited by W. H. Gardner. London: Penguin, 1953.

Husk, W. H. *An Account of the Musical Celebrations on St Cecilia's Day*. London: Bell and Daldy, 1857.

Hutchings, Arthur. *Purcell*. London: British Broadcasting Corporation, 1982.

Klakovitch, Robert. '*Scocca pur*: Genesis of an English Ground'. *Journal of the Royal Musical Association* 116 (1991): 63–77.

Laurie, Margaret. 'Allegory, Sources, and Early Performance History'. In *Purcell: 'Dido and Aeneas', an Opera*, pp. 42–59. Edited by Curtis Price. New York: Norton, 1986.

'Did Purcell Set *The Tempest*?' *Proceedings of the Royal Musical Association* 90 (1963–4): 43–57.

'Purcell's Extended Solo Songs'. *Musical Times* 125 (1984): 19–25.

'Purcell's Stage Works'. Ph.D. dissertation, University of Cambridge, 1962.

'The Chapel Royal Part-books'. In *Music and Bibliography, Essays in Honour of Alec Hyatt King*, pp. 28–50. Edited by Oliver Neighbour. London: Clive Bingly, 1980.

Lefkowitz, Murray. 'Shadwell and Locke's *Psyche*: the French Connection'. *Proceedings of the Royal Musical Association* 106 (1979–80): 42–55.

Lewis, Anthony. 'Purcell and Blow's *Venus and Adonis*'. *Music and Letters* 44 (1963): 266–9.

Luckett, Richard. 'A New Source of *Venus and Adonis*'. *Musical Times* 130 (1989): 76–80.

'Exotick but Rational Entertainments: The English Dramatick Operas'. In *English Drama: Forms and Development*, pp.123–41 and 232–4. Edited by Marie Axton and Raymond Williams. Cambridge University Press, 1977.

'"Or Rather Our Musical Shakespeare": Charles Burney's Purcell'. In *Music in Eighteenth-Century England – Essays in Memory of Charles Cudworth*, pp. 59–77. Edited by Christopher Hogwood and Richard Luckett. Cambridge University Press, 1983.

Mabbett, Margaret. 'Italian Musicians in Restoration England (1660–90)'. *Music and Letters* 67 (1986): 237–47.

McCrickard, Eleanor. 'The Roman Repertory for Violin before Corelli'. *Early Music* 18 (1990): 563–73.

McGuinness, Rosamond. *English Court Odes 1660–1820*. Oxford: Clarendon Press, 1971.

'The Ground Bass in the English Court Odes'. *Music and Letters* 51 (1970): 118–40 and 265–78.

Manning, Robert. 'Purcell's Anthems. An Analytical Study of the Music and its Content'. Ph.D. dissertation, University of Birmingham, 1979.

'Revisions and Reworkings in Purcell's Anthems'. *Soundings* 9 (1982): 29–37.

Meyer, E. H. *English Chamber Music.* 2nd edn revised by the author and Diana Poulton. London: Lawrence and Wishart, 1982.

Moore, Robert Etheridge. *Henry Purcell and the Restoration Theatre.* London: Heinemann, 1961; reprint edn, Westport, Conn.: Greenwood Press, 1974.

Morley, Thomas. *A Plain and Easy Introduction to Practical Music.* London: 1597; reprint edn, ed. R. Alec Harman, London: Dent, 1952.

Newman, William S. *The Sonata in the Baroque Era.* 4th edn New York: Norton, 1983.

Pepys, Samuel. *The Complete Diary of Samuel Pepys.* Edited by Robert Latham and William Matthews. 11 vols. London: Bell, 1970.

Pickering, Oliver. 'Henry Hall of Hereford's Poetical Tributes to Henry Purcell'. *The Library* 16 (1994): 18–29.

Pinnock, Andrew. 'Play into Opera: Purcell's *The Indian Queen*'. *Early Music* 18 (1990): 3–21.

Playford, *Playford's 'Brief Introduction to the Skill of Musick' – an Account Comprising All the Editions from 1654 to 1730.* London: Ellis, 1926.

Playford, John. *An Introduction to the Skill of Musick.* 12th edn London: Henry Playford, 1694; reprint edn, with an introduction by F. B. Zimmerman, New York: Da Capo, 1972.

Price, Curtis. '*Dido and Aeneas*: Questions of Style and Evidence'. *Early Music* 22 (1994): 115–25.

Henry Purcell and the London Stage. Cambridge University Press, 1984.

ed. *Purcell: 'Dido and Aeneas', an Opera.* New York: Norton, 1986.

Radice, Mark. 'Tate's Libretto for *Dido and Aeneas*: A Revaluation'. *Bach: The Quarterly Journal of the Riemenschneider-Bach Institute* 7 (Jan. 1976): 20–6.

Rimbault, Edward F., ed. *The Old Cheque Book of the Chapel Royal.* London: The Camden Society, 1872; reprint edn, New York: Da Capo Press, 1966.

Rosand, Ellen. 'The Descending Tetrachord: An Emblem of Lament'. *Musical Quarterly* 65 (1979): 346–59.

Savage, Roger. 'Producing *Dido and Aeneas*: An Investigation into Sixteen Problems'. *Early Music* 4 (1976): 393–406.

'The Shakespeare-Purcell *Fairy Queen*: A Defence and Recommendation'. *Early Music* 1 (1973): 201–21.

Shaw, H. Watkins. 'A Cambridge Manuscript from the English Chapel Royal'. *Music and Letters* 42 (1961): 263–7.

'A Contemporary Source of English Music from the Purcellian Period'. *Acta musicologica* 31 (1959): 38–44.

Simpson, Christopher. *A Compendium of Practical Music.* 2nd edn London: 1667; reprint edn, edited by Phillip J. Lord, Oxford: Basil Blackwell, 1970.

Smart, Christopher. *The Poetical Works of Christopher Smart.* 4 vols. Oxford: Clarendon Press, 1987.

Smithers, Don. *The Music and History of the Baroque Trumpet before 1721.* London: Dent, 1973.

Spink, Ian. *English Song, Dowland to Purcell*. London: Batsford, 1974.
gen. ed. *The Blackwell History of Music in Britain*. 6 vols. Oxford: Blackwell, 1988
cont. Vol. IV: *The Seventeenth Century*.
Squire, W. Barclay. 'An Unknown Autograph by Henry Purcell'. *The Musical Antiquary*
3 (1911): 5–17.
'Purcell as Theorist'. *Sammelbände der Internationalen Musickgesellschaft* 6
(1904–5): 521–67.
'Purcell's Music for the Funeral of Mary II'. *Sammelbände der Internationalen
Musickgesellschaft* 4 (1902–3): 225–33.
Stevens, Denis. 'Seventeenth-Century Italian Instrumental Music in the Bodleian
Library'. *Acta musicologica* 26 (1955): 67–74.
'Unique Italian Instrumental Music in the Bodleian Library'. *Collectanea historicae
musicae* 2 (1957): 401–12.
Tilmouth, Michael. 'A Calendar of References to Music in Newspapers Published in
London and the Provinces (1660–1719)'. *Royal Musical Association Research
Chronicle* 1 (1961); 2 (1962).
'The Technique and Forms of Purcell's Sonatas'. *Music and Letters* 40 (1959): 109–21.
Van Tassel, Eric. 'Purcell's *Give Sentence*'. *Musical Times* 118 (1977): 381–3.
Wailes, Marylin. 'Four Short Fantasias by Henry Purcell'. *The Score* 20 (1957): 59–65.
Wessely-Kropik, Helene. 'Henry Purcell als Instrumentalkomponist'. *Studien zur
Musikwissenschaft Beihefte der Denkmäler der Tonkunst in Osterreich* 22 (1955):
85–141.
Lelio Colista, Ein Römischer Meister von Corelli. Leben und Unwelt. Vienna:
àsterreichische Akademie der Wissenschaft, 1961.
Westrup, J. A. *Purcell*. rev. Nigel Fortune. London: Dent, 1980.
'Purcell's Music for *Timon of Athens*'. In *Festschrift für Karl Gustav Fellerer*, pp.
573–8. Edited by H. Huschen. Regensburg: G. Bosse, 1962.
'Purcell's Parentage'. *Music Review* 25 (1964): 100–3.
White, Eric Walter. *A History of English Opera*. London: Faber, 1983.
'New Light on *Dido and Aeneas*'. In *Henry Purcell, 1659–1695. Essays on His Music*,
pp. 14–34. Edited by Imogen Holst. London: Oxford University Press, 1959.
Wilson, John, ed. *Roger North on Music*. London: Novello, 1959.
Wood, Bruce, and Pinnock, Andrew. 'A Counterblast on English Trumpets'. *Early
Music* 19 (1991): 436–43.
'*The Fairy Queen*: a Fresh Look at the Issues'. *Early Music* 21 (1993): 44–62.
'"Unscarr'd by Turning Times"? The Dating of Purcell's *Dido and Aeneas*'. *Early
Music* 20 (1992): 373–90.
Zimmerman, Franklin B. *Henry Purcell, 1659–1695, An Analytical Catalogue of His
Music*. London: Macmillan, 1963.
Henry Purcell, 1659–1695. His Life and Times. 2nd, rev. edn, Philadelphia: University
of Pennsylvania Press, 1983.
'Purcell and Monteverdi'. *Musical Times* 100 (1958): 368–9.
'Purcell's Service Anthem *O God, Thou Art My God* and the B♭ Major Service'.
Musical Quarterly 50 (1964): 207–14.
'The Anthems of Henry Purcell'. *The American Choral Review* 13 (Nos. 3 and 4,
1971).
ed. *The Gostling Manuscript*. Austin: University of Texas Press, 1977.

Index of names and subjects

Index of works